FAMILY FORUM

JAY KESLER

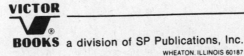

VICTOR
BOOKS ® a division of SP Publications, Inc.
WHEATON, ILLINOIS 60187

Offices also in
Whitby, Ontario, Canada
Amersham-on-the-Hill, Bucks, England

Unless otherwise indicated, Scripture quotations are taken from the *King James Version.* Other quotations are from the *New American Standard Bible* (NASB), © 1960, 1962, 1963, 1968, 1971, 1972, 1973, 1975, 1977 by the Lockman Foundation; the *Holy Bible: New International Version* (NIV), © 1978 by the New York International Bible Society and used by permission of Zondervan Bible Publishers; and *The Living Bible* (TLB), © 1971 by Tyndale House Publishers, Wheaton, Illinois. Used by permission.

Recommended Dewey Decimal Classification: 173
Suggested Subject Heading: FAMILY RELATIONS

Library of Congress Catalog Card Number: 83-51591
ISBN: 0-88207-820-8

CONTENTS

FOREWORD

For years I have been saying that if I were ever marooned on an island and could pick those people I'd most like to be with, Jay Kesler would certainly be one of them.

Like so many others, I find myself drawn to Jay for several reasons. He is a breath of fresh air in a day when this old world is choking on stale thoughts and smoggy clichés. Though a resourceful, tough-minded thinker, he is truly a caring and compassionate individual. Authentic and relevant to the core, the man never fails to press his finger into issues that matter. But he addresses them in a way that isn't stuffy, pompous, or prudish. He possesses insights on life that are nothing short of profound, yet he has not lost touch with the grit and dirt of the real world. As anyone who knows the man can testify, he takes his calling seriously . . . but in no way is he impressed with his own importance. I know of few people whose sense of humor is keener.

Jay Kesler is president of Youth for Christ/USA, a Christian organization committed to reaching out and helping this generation's youth and their families. As a hands-on ministry, YFC operates right down there in the street, on the campus, and within the homes of young people. Since Jay has been doing this sort of thing all his adult life, his concepts and convictions have been forged on the anvil of reality, not theory. I can assure you, when he speaks or writes on any subject related to today's family, his words are seasoned with wisdom gleaned from decades of involvement. I've often thought of Jay as the "E.F. Hutton of the family." When he talks, people stop and listen.

This book is no exception. Within these pages you will find the stuff of which life is made . . . and you will be glad you stopped and listened. Here are chapters that will dig beneath the veneer of superficial answers and take you to the heart of the matter. You'll nod in agreement and you may even wince in pain as he touches a tender nerve—he's good at that. The man's been known to do radical surgery with a fountain pen without

7

any anesthetic. One thing for sure, you won't yawn and fight boredom. This husband, father, grandfather, author, radio speaker, and superb communicator writes as creatively as he thinks. In today's terms, "he connects."

I commend this book to you with only one regret—that you, Jay, and I aren't able to sit down together, face to face, and talk about the things he writes about. Maybe you'd like to join us on that fantasy island encounter some day. If the three of us ever got together, I'll guarantee you one thing, we wouldn't solve all the problems or answer all the questions . . . *but we'd have the time of our lives!*

Until then . . . enjoy the book.

Charles R. Swindoll
Fullerton, California

Living in a Family

I read, as you do, the frightening statistics about the disintegration of the family in America and, indeed, across our world. I am shocked, as you are, by the sociological and spiritual implications of this breakdown. Family is God's idea. In fact, from Genesis to Malachi, from Matthew to Revelation, God consistently uses family illustrations to describe His relationship with the human race.

God is a Father, the leader of His children. He loves us with a mother's love. We are His sons and daughters, and brothers and sisters to each other. Christ is the Bridegroom; we are the bride. All these words are family words. But if a person has not experienced good family relationships, then the words make no sense at all.

We first learned this in dealing with young people in our youth guidance ministry. We would tell them, "God is your heavenly Father," but we weren't getting results. Then we began to realize that to a young person off the streets who has not had the kind of family life that we've had, family words can take on ominous meanings. Who is a father? Someone who comes home late Friday night, slaps Mom around, kicks her down the stairs, breaks an end table over your head, vomits on the bathroom floor, shouts and swears until three in the morning, and makes you so scared you can't sleep. Then we come along and say God is like that. He's the great big one, everywhere present. You can't get away from Him. He's all-powerful; He can find you wherever you are. No wonder these young people are terrified by the idea of a heavenly Father.

Think of what the world would be like if someday all family relationships disintegrated. Then people would not be able to understand God's Word, because it describes experiences that would have been turned inside out. I am deeply concerned that Christians work to maintain the family as God designed it and to heal broken relationships wherever they occur. Only with strong, loving families can we live whole lives, and only through healed, whole relationships can we understand how God relates to us in Christ.

| CHAPTER 1 |

Developing Family Relationships

The Apostle Paul says that God is the environment, the climate, in which we Christians live: "For in Him we live and move and have our being" (Acts 17:28, NIV). For a young person, the family interprets that truth. In the family all the members, but especially the children, live and move and have their being. Therefore parents are responsible to create a climate in which the things of God are *demonstrated* as well as taught verbally.

I often say that teaching, whether it takes the form of preaching or standing up and lecturing in front of someone, is like Flatland. Flatland is only two-dimensional—it involves a speaker and a hearer. But the family is like a laboratory. It's the place where these messages are put to work.

In families we don't just talk about love; we love. We don't just talk about forgiveness; we forgive. Children don't just hear about authority; they live under justice and mercy, strength and protection. Our characters and our actions create a climate that helps young people grow up healthy, secure, and open to God. In my opinion, the primary role of the family is to develop an atmosphere of godliness that is not stuffy or oppressive, sightless or indulgent, but that captures the very essence of what it means to live in our Father's world.

Christian parents have the responsibility of presenting a model that young people can love and accept. Then when the children hear that God is a heavenly Parent, they will be willing, desirous, and even eager to receive Him—His presence and His guidance—into their lives. In this chapter, we will talk about how good family relationships develop and how parents can model what God is really like.

PRIORITIES AT HOME •

At home, which relationship takes priority—the husband-wife relationship or the parent-child relationship?

I have come to the conclusion that my priority list should look something like this: God is first. Then comes my relationship with Janie, my wife; then my relationship with our children. Fourth is my relationship with friends to whom I am committed, and last comes my work responsibilities. However, I think there is a danger when we put things in a hierarchical order and flatly say, "This is the way it is written—in concrete—God first, spouse second, children third, etc." By doing that, we are ignoring the ebb and flow of life. There are times when any one of these relationships jumps to the top for a moment. At times, a job may have to take precedence over the family. Or there may be times when children and their problems jump to the forefront.

The family itself is dependent on the husband and wife, and unless that relationship is close, the children ultimately suffer. One reason we choose primacy in the husband-wife relationship is for the sake of the children and for the sake of ourselves. In fact, if you wanted to get technical about priorities, I would even insert your relationship with yourself between those with God and spouse. Unless you have your act together as a person, unless you are physically, emotionally, and spiritually healthy, you can't be a good marriage partner. But because two become one in marriage, I put those categories together, feeling that the very best therapy for self is a good marriage relationship. That is the way God intended it.

Where do the children fit in? Nearer and nearer the edge of the nest. That is, Mom and Dad always stay in the center; then as the children get to be about eighteen, Mom and Dad nudge them closer and closer to the edge of the nest, eventually pushing them gently out to make their own nests.

CREATING FAMILY LOYALTY •

Our family is always going in different directions. With all the extracurricular activities our teenagers are involved in, my husband's job, and my responsibilities, we seem to be too busy to spend time together. How can we establish family loyalty and a spirit of togetherness?

As kids grow older and develop outside interests, you're naturally going to have a different atmosphere than you had when everyone came home from school and was confined in the house until bedtime. The change is nothing to fight against. Nonetheless, I do think you can create an atmosphere that will promote family togetherness, but it will take a little effort on your part.

Let me give you an example of one couple I know. Every Thursday night was "family night" at their home. After supper they'd do enjoyable things together. One of their activities was a game they invented, called "Sock." The family divided into teams and shut off all the lights. If you caught somebody, then he'd have to give you one of his socks. And eventually one team had all the other team's socks. Neighbors would see the lights flashing on and off in the house and hear people screaming inside, and they probably wondered what in the world was going on! Even when the kids were teenagers, the family still got together at least once a week for family night.

Established traditions like this are very important. In our own family we too have established traditions. Evening meals and Sunday dinner are two of them. In fact, these traditions are so well established, that if we're not together, our kids feel offended and remind us that we've let things slip. Other traditions we try to maintain include inviting our relatives over during the holidays so the extended family can be together and planning ahead for vacations so that no one is surprised. If the family vacation is marked on the calendar before anything else, then family members can plan around it. Very often that's the greatest problem in maintaining family togetherness—people don't plan ahead.

So, if you want to establish a spirit of family togetherness, start these activities while the children are still young. Set aside family nights, establish traditions, and make sure that holidays mean something. As we establish traditions with small children, then when they get older, they tend to desire them. Trying to establish traditions with older teenagers, however, doesn't work as well.

FAMILY BRINGS UP THE REAR ●

My wife and I both work and are very involved with our local church, but we feel guilty about the way we have to limit our family activities. How can we make the most effective use of our time together as a family?

I think the long-range answer lies in taking a look at your priorities. We can't keep adding to our responsibilities without taking anything away. We start marriage without children and have full lives. Then we add children and try to stretch everything. We stretch and stretch until eventually we reach a breaking point. And that is where you seem to be.

Parents with young children need to back off and say, "What things have to be dropped during this period of time so that we can have a quality family life?" This may mean giving up some activities that are important to you, including friendships with other couples who don't have children and who run here and there asking you to join them. It's very important that you give top priority to your family. When you do this, much of the tension is relieved because you have taken a stand.

Now, at the risk of being misunderstood, let me say that the church can also be a problem. The church exists for people; people don't exist for the church. Often we forget that. The church is there to help us with our Christian lives, but our Christian lives don't really take place inside the church. There are churches and people who get the idea that this constant activity within the church is God's will. However, it is probably one of the least productive things that we do for God. When we are at church, we basically get "fueled up," prepared to go out and live the Christian life. If we're not careful, too much church activity (I'm not talking about too much God or too much Christ or too much commitment to the Lord) can rob us of family time.

We've got to make choices regarding our involvements and busyness. Then having made those choices, we've got to make more choices—like turning off the TV and doing things together that require communication. Make meals sacred times of meaningful conversation. Take time before going to bed to read to the children and talk with them. If you consistently do these kinds of things, your family, rather than outside involvements, will become central to you. But you've got to start by making some priority choices. And I believe that because God has given you children, they should be your priority.

WHEN MOM AND DAD WORK ●

My husband and I have different work schedules and as a result I feel my kids are suffering. I have a daytime job, while his lasts from 3-11 P.M. The problem is I have to take the children to the day

care center when I go to work and pick them up again when I come home because my husband refuses to take responsibility. In the meantime, they are growing up never spending time with their father. On top of that, we have to spend money on child care. Is there anything I can do or say to get him to take some of the responsibility?

Let me suggest a compromise—something that will go halfway between what you seem to have in mind and what is actually happening. You would like your husband to get up in the morning and take care of the kids until three when he leaves for work. It seems that a small problem may still exist because there is a little overlap—you work later than three o'clock.

First of all, examine exactly why you want your husband to watch the children during the day. Is your real desire to have the children know their father? Sometimes women really just want the situation evened out. But if your real desire is for the children to have contact with their father, then how about taking one day a week and naming it Dad's Day—or the children could think of it as Children's Day? Let that be the day when he does something special with the children—takes them shopping or goes to the park or to the zoo, or just plays with them in the house. This solution would lower your day care costs by twenty percent and it would also give Dad some contact with the children.

I think you are going to find it impossible to change your husband by talking to him about duty and responsibility. But he might respond positively if you present it as an opportunity to make an impact on his children and a way for his children to get to know him.

I've seen this situation many times with young families. Somehow the father has the idea that a woman ought to work twenty-four hours a day while a man need only work from dawn to sunset. The tension gradually builds between husband and wife until there's a verbal explosion or until Dad finally realizes that he can be involved with raising the children and still be a man.

Another alternative is for you to cut back your hours and spend more time at home. Usually when that is suggested, the wife says, "But I don't want to live on only one income. We have a certain lifestyle we need to maintain." This is another one of the conflicts. I suggest a compromise because I don't think either of you is going to get all you want.

OUR TV'S OUT OF CONTROL •

Our family spends so much time watching television that we never seem to know what is going on in each other's lives. My husband is as much a TV addict as the kids. I have a hard time getting his attention long enough to even discuss the matter. I don't want to antagonize anybody. What is the best way to get the TV turned off and our family life turned on?

More families struggle over the TV issue than almost anything else. And for some reason, women are more concerned about the problem than men. I don't have statistics to back this up, but it seems that males are more addicted to TV than females. It could be that women watch television all day (TV soaps, etc.) and have their fill of it by the time the family arrives home in the evening. Or it could be that evening TV attracts more male than female viewers. But whatever the case, I think the whole family needs to approach this situation.

You say your husband is as bad as the kids. If that is really true, then you have to get to the bottom of that dilemma, but at a time when you are away from the children, when your husband feels he's not being threatened. In the quiet of your bedroom or someplace where you are alone together, talk to him about developing some sort of television strategy for your home. Otherwise, the TV will run your home.

I had someone tell me a while back that their family computer had become the boss of the house. That is a serious problem. So, the two of you need to decide how many hours each evening family members are allowed to watch television, which programs are OK and which aren't, etc. It is very important then for you as parents to be examples to your children by faithfully following these guidelines.

Make sure you approach the kids about the new TV rules in the right way. If you say, "John, get up and do your schoolwork right now," and he's in the middle of watching a program, you'll come across as being antagonistic. You need to learn new phrases like, "When that program is finished, I want you to get busy with your studies," or, "I hope this is the program you want to watch, because you are not going to watch any others. If you'd like, you can start doing your homework now, so that you can watch something else later." In other words, a trade-off is much less antagonizing than an either/or mandate.

ROLE REVERSAL ●

Is it scriptural for a woman to be the breadwinner while the husband stays home with the children? Could this perhaps be the "field" referred to in Proverbs 31:16? Two years ago I postponed entering medical school in order to raise our first child, and now after the birth of our second I find myself considering the possibility of reapplying to medical school. I love mothering but I can see that God could make good use of me in the medical field. We have agreed that we don't want our children raised outside the home, so during this training period my husband would postpone his teaching career to stay in the home while the children are young. This is a big decision which could mean serious changes in our careers and in our roles as parents.

I often get up in the morning and ask my wife how she is doing on that verse in Proverbs. Did she sell any land and make any profit before I got out of bed, because I think that is an excellent idea!

Actually, the Bible gives many illustrations of strong, capable women in influential positions. Jesus and His disciples were supported by wealthy women. Lydia was a business woman. Priscilla shared a team ministry with her husband, Aquila. Deborah was the leader of all Israel in the time of the Judges. To think that the Bible-time woman was endlessly oppressed by her husband and society is to simply misunderstand the culture.

Thus in Scripture I don't see any prohibition to the woman being the chief breadwinner. But by the same token, I believe this should be a mutual decision made by two very mature people. The woman has to examine her real reasons for going to work. You say God could use you in the medical field. Frankly, I think the idea of the work force out there just panting for new people is a bit of a myth. There are more people now in most fields than are actually needed. The big question is how to find enough activity, enough jobs for all of them. Now I'm sure in your particular profession of medicine, good women doctors can be greatly used of the Lord. But more often what the woman is saying is, "Society has so used me, so worked on my psyche that I don't have any self-worth unless I am out doing something in the professions. Homemaking, being a mother, has no value whatsoever. That is something you do out of your hip pocket. I will only have value if I work in the real world."

Recognize that self-worth is imputed by God; it doesn't come by performance. So if your chief motivation for working is to fulfill your self-worth, you'd better reexamine your priorities because you won't find what you're looking for. But if your motivation is rooted in a higher calling, this could be a very fine opportunity for both you and your husband. One further aspect to consider is that your husband will have to face the emasculating position of being caught with his apron on during the daytime by his friends. Now I know that the textbooks say not to worry about this happening. But in fact, I can point to many couples where the man has begun to act very strangely because he feels that somehow he has been discounted. Our society also implants subtle messages within us that say, "A man should support his family."

The ingredients to a proper decision are maturity, forethought, prayer, and mutual consent. I think for a temporary period, while you finish your career training, this arrangement can work. I know the Lord will help you if you bring Him into the middle of it.

WHO'S LEADING WHOM? ●

My husband seems to lack confidence and assertiveness in our family, and therefore has never been the leader in our relationship. I assume the leadership role primarily because in my own childhood experience my mother always dominated our home. I don't feel comfortable in this role, but I don't see any alternative if my husband won't assume leadership. Do you have any sound advice?

It seems to me that somewhere along the line you have heard a lot of preaching about the importance of the wife being submissive to her husband. This is fine, providing it is understood within a much larger and broader context. In other words, I hear pastors preaching about how wives can teach their husbands to be stronger. Well, if they have the ability to lead them into becoming stronger, then they are still stronger than their husbands—and it probably won't change.

There are many personality types, each with their own strengths and weaknesses. Just because a husband is more withdrawn, slower to speak, or less aggressive doesn't mean he lacks strength. He may have a great deal of strength but just exercises it in a different way.

Proverbs 31 describes the ideal woman, and she is quite a woman! She gets up in the morning before her husband gets up. She buys and sells land. She orders all of the servants around. She does all kinds of productive things, and she really sounds like some sort of matriarch. This chapter in Proverbs is very interesting to me, and is so different from this female submissiveness we've had drummed into us. Of course, your husband needs to be strong and take some leadership in the family. Just don't mess up a fine family by thinking that roles have to be suddenly changed.

Find a sensible kind of balance. Find the places where you are competitive and maybe let him win in some of those areas. Don't force him to be strong in areas where he is weak and you are already strong.

TRAVELING DAD ●

I travel quite a bit in my job. Unfortunately, time with my family is very limited and it seems like the kids are growing up before I know it. Can you give me some practical suggestions on how to make our family time together a real quality time since it is so limited?

I spend a lot of time traveling—probably more than I'm really comfortable with. I've had to come to terms with this and how it relates to my own family and my own priorities. I've decided, first of all, that the old saying about quality time being more important than quantity time is true only in books. You can't have much quality without having some quantity. If people could just sit down and say, "Now, I'm going to have a quality experience," that would be something, but it doesn't happen that way. In fact, I think that even in Bible study this is a problem. The Bible, of course, consists of compressed history. We have this account followed by that account. But what the Gospel writers haven't recorded is the time it takes to walk from Jerusalem to Bethany—the down moments, so to speak. We sometimes try to live our lives as one great marvelous experience after another. It just doesn't work that way and it doesn't work in family life either.

I encourage you to work on the business of more quantity. Try to carve out more time to spend with your kids. Now, if you think the competition is stiff, think about this. Surveys indicate that the typical father spends thirty-seven seconds a day in one-to-one conversation with each of his children. Frankly, you can't pack much quality into that amount of time. Even a father who is traveling a great deal can surely do better than that, in fact much better with no trouble at all. Of course, this involves some priority choices. Many men I meet want to do it all; that is, they want to have their jobs, and those jobs involve travel. They want to have families, but they also want to have a lot of personal time. I've decided I cannot be an effective father and have a lot of personal time to devote to golf and other time-consuming activities. I've committed myself to spending quality time at home when I'm away from my job. Our family does things we can do together, even chores like yard care.

It also helps to carve out longer periods, or chunks of time—a Saturday or Sunday afternoon—that the family can look forward to. Plan ahead for these times so the family can become excited about them. For example, if you say to your son or daughter, "A week from Sunday we are going to do this," then the week before the event takes place becomes a time of anticipation. You make the flavor last. It's like taking a Lifesaver and working it down to that little fine round thing on your tongue. If you've enjoyed a sense of anticipation, it's better than simply gulping it down.

I also believe the traveling man has to use the phone. I call and talk to my family each day, because when I'm on the road it's important to keep in touch. Letter writing is another way to show you care.

Be determined: "This is a problem, but I'm not going to let it defeat me. I can carve out quality and quantity times for my family, and I can sure beat that national average of thirty-seven seconds."

HUBBY'S A GROUCH ●

My husband is under a lot of pressure at work because he constantly has to meet deadlines. Four out of five weeknights he comes home grouchy and stays that way. His moods are beginning to affect the entire family. I want to be sympathetic to his problems at work, but at the same time help him temper his moodiness. Is there a gentle way I can do that?

I think all families face this situation at one time or another, though the solution is not always the same. For example, if your husband's moodiness is of the short-term variety (about six months or so in duration), this could very well be part of the ebb and flow of life. Special business problems, personal crises, special projects are relatively short-lived but put a great deal of pressure on us. During this time it is foolish for a person to say he is happy. These people who bop along like little soap bubbles on the top of life, always pretending to be happy, are usually lying. You can't grin at everything. Sometimes you simply have to struggle a bit to accomplish a task. So, if your husband is trying to cope with short-term pressure, he needs understanding and room. Back off and let him stew in his own juice awhile. Don't lay a big guilt trip on him.

On the other hand, it's not a good idea to baby him during that period either. Let him live more or less in a normal fashion and realize that this will pass.

Actually, short-term pain can be helpful. It's similar to surgery. Though it's never pleasant to go through surgery, afterward it can be of great benefit to the patient. Maybe changing jobs and putting the family through an intentional kind of pressure will relieve your husband in the long-run.

Now, if this moodiness has lasted longer than six months, you probably ought to encourage your husband to seek some kind of counseling— either on a personal level or on a career basis. He may be in over his head or in an unsolvable job situation—in a harness that doesn't fit him. Encourage him to seek help and then stick with him through the cure even if it involves some pain for you and the rest of the family.

PLANNING AHEAD ●

How can I have a meaningful and complete family life? I am not presently married, but I'm asking because I know the importance of time spent with children. I am in the medical profession and my family time is likely to be very limited. Are there specifics I can be doing even now to insure that my priority will be with my family when that day comes?

You can't raise a family hypothetically. Lots of us would like to lay our lives out in front of us and plan slot A and tab B, but it can't be done that way. A great deal of life is lived as a response to the needs of the moment—much more than many of us would like to admit.

Nevertheless, there are things you can look at now, even before you have a family. What are your priorities in life? If family is your first priority, then you're going to build your life around your family. If career is in first place, if you're driven to be successful or recognized in your profession, then you'll probably spend an inordinate amount of time at work.

If your first priority is with your family, then you have to build your career and other plans around it. You can start right now by learning to lead a disciplined life. The undisciplined person has no time for anything. He's always a bundle of loose ends. Frankly, I love freedom, and years ago I learned that the only road to freedom is discipline. You have to work when it's time to work. I've gotten up by an alarm clock all my life. I hate alarm clocks, but if I allow myself to sleep in, then I don't have time to do what I want to do.

It's important to discipline yourself to spend time with your family. No matter how much you love them, work will usually seem more urgent unless you schedule time for them. It is also important to focus on them, and only them, when you are with them. You aren't really with the kids if your mind is trying to solve a problem at work. You hear a lot about quality time versus quantity time. I believe you have to have a certain quantity to get any quality, but by focusing your attention on your family when you are with them, you will greatly improve the quality of the time you have together.

Before you get married, find out how your future spouse feels about family time. Some wives support their husbands' activities. They don't spend their time grousing and complaining and saying, "He doesn't care about us or he'd spend more time here." A supportive wife will have children who turn out well. But a wife who is constantly complaining about her husband's priorities will telegraph to her children that they're supposed to be upset and dissatisfied with their father too.

I have many friends in the medical profession, and I will assure you that it is possible to be a doctor and a family man. If your first priority really is your family, if you discipline yourself so that you have time to spend with them, and if you marry someone who is supportive, you can be a good doctor and a good father at the same time.

CHAPTER 2

Living with Children

One of God's all-time great ideas was to propagate the human race by allowing us to have children. Obviously, He could have increased the human family in other ways, but He allows us to see our own lives in some degree lived over in our children. He allows us to participate in their growing awareness of the world and life and God Himself. This opportunity to help prepare them for happiness and making a contribution is a true privilege.

We acknowledge at the outset, however, that parenthood brings with it certain frustrations. One of these is caused by the age gap between parents and children. Part of the trick of having happy relationships with children is to be able to remember what it was like to be their age. For most of us, that was a long time ago and we find it difficult to project ourselves back that far. Yet if our memories are too hazy, or if we do not see the importance of remembering our own childhood, we may not be able to accept each age for what it is.

One of the saddest things that can happen to parent-child relationships is for parents to constantly wish that their children were a different age. "If I can just get him past the diaper stage," they say; "If I can just get him through the terrible twos; if I can just get him off to school; if I can just get him into junior high. . . ."

Parents should not say things like that. Each age has its own special joys. Let's find out what is the excitement, adventure, and discovery of each age as it comes, and let's participate in its full development. This is one of parenthood's great joys, I believe. If we approach each age realizing that God has given us the privilege not only of guiding the child through it, but also of gaining great insight into our own selves, then living with children can be a true delight.

WHY A CHANGE IN BEHAVIOR? •

Our nine-year-old's best friend moved away last month. Our son seemed to be adjusting well, but he never talked about his friend. Now he has begun to have behavior problems at school. His teacher says he is a smart boy, more than capable of finishing his schoolwork, but lately he has been bringing extra work home. I think when his friend left so did the competitive spirit that kept him going.

It's hard to tell if your son's behavior is related to his friend moving away. It may be totally unrelated. There are so many things that come into a nine-year-old's life. It is possible that he has discovered girls; it's possible that he's discovered sports and is feeling rejected.

I once had a boy tell me he really loved school. I asked him why and he said, "Well, they take you down this hall and they open the door and let you go into this room and it is just filled with all new things. Then you go down the next hall and they open the door and there is another room filled with new things." I thought, "Wouldn't it be great if life was like that for everybody?" However, about third or fourth grade many kids bog down when someone opens the door. They look in and say, "Ah, same old stuff." They become bored with everything. Bright kids especially do this because, of necessity, schools tend to aim their educational material toward the average student. As a result, they start fooling around because the doors aren't opening fast enough. It's possible that this is happening to your son. Schools try to create progressive answers to this dilemma, including advanced programs, but it is often difficult.

My mother had a phrase that I think is better than all the advice put together on this subject. She would just say, "Oh, he is going through a stage." I don't know whether she was right or not, but eventually everybody grew out of it. I like stages. I think we need to reinstill stages into parents' thinking. Adults have trouble understanding what happens in the mind of a nine-year-old. Children are constantly asked to learn and adjust to the world around them. It's tough growing up. The mind of a child is being molded and tugged at from so many different directions. As a result, there will be periods—stages—where children struggle with certain issues or circumstances. This is all part of growing and developing character.

Of course, it is possible that this situation with your son is related to his friend. If they were inseparable, that closeness probably created a certain exclusiveness about their friendship. The other kids couldn't penetrate it. Therefore, now that his friend is gone, your son may be a bit distant with others and has to learn to develop new friends. Some of the kids may be resistant because your son excluded them before.

Stay by him, give him support, love, and encouragement. Get off his back on the schoolwork and let him work through this stage.

I DON'T GET RESPECT •

How do I regain my fifteen-year-old daughter's respect? I give her weekly duties to perform around the house which she does only with much prodding. When I occasionally ask extra work of her, I return home from work to find that nothing has been done. Last week I asked her to bathe the dog because I just didn't have time to do it. She refused and I punished her. She wouldn't accept this, left for her grandmother's house, and didn't come home for two weeks. Have I failed as a parent?

Respect may be the wrong word here. I don't think you have lost your daughter's respect. You did what you felt was right, making reasonable demands of her which were not followed. She has tried to blackmail you and make you feel guilty by moving to Grandmother's house. She's punishing you a little bit. Now you are making the mistake of feeling punished.

What your daughter is doing is very typical in many households. To have a fifteen-year-old is generally to have a child who wants to do minimal labor, who does not finish the tasks he is given, who procrastinates, who whines and makes excuses about extra work, and who tells you things aren't fair. So you need to quit feeling guilty and understand that your daughter's current behavior doesn't mean she is going to grow up to be an awful person.

More importantly, you and her grandmother need to discuss what happens when she goes to Grandmother's house. It would be very good if you and Grandmother could work together to help your daughter rather than work against each other. By that I mean, if Grandmother's reaction is, "You poor dear, you are misunderstood; your mother makes you work too hard," Grandmother is trying to drive a wedge between you and your daughter. That is very dangerous and you need to confront her with that and Grandmother needs to back off. Usually Grandmother is just trying to help. She reasons, "This fifteen-year-old has run away; better that she stay at my house than go out on the street." Actually, it is best if Grandmother can remain neutral and say, "OK, you can stay here, but I'm not going to take sides between you and your mother." When your daughter comes back, simply reaffirm, "I still have demands. There are tasks you have to do here. I expect certain things of you, and I also expect cooperation from you because I'm working too." If she punishes you again, let her do it, and eventually she will learn that she doesn't get your attention that way.

KIDS FORGET THEIR MANNERS ●

Whenever I go shopping, it seems my kids forget all the manners and discipline I ever tried to teach them. It doesn't matter where we go, but the grocery store is the worst. They're always saying, "I want this," or "Mom, can I have that?" When I don't buy them what they want, they whine and make a big fuss. I don't want to make a scene in public so I usually give in just to keep them quiet. How do I handle this?

This is probably a grandfather's golden opportunity. People my age love to watch younger parents in the store and say, "Why don't they do this and why didn't they do that?" forgetting that we probably faced some of the same problems when we were that age. First of all, let's give the kids a break and realize they are small, haven't matured, and are not very well defended against the kinds of temptations put before them. Marketing is a great skill. People are paid large salaries to make packages and TV commercials attractive to children. So, when your kids beg you to buy them a toy or a box of cereal, it is probably because they have been affected by people who are a lot smarter than both of us and who are paid a great deal more.

It bothers many parents "to make a scene in public." But I would rather see a mother correct and discipline her children in public than to let poor behavior go unchecked. Besides, I think most people understand how unreasonable children can be, especially how they overreact to discipline in public to get attention.

I think that part of the solution to this problem is talking to the kids ahead of time. This is also true when you are going to someone else's home. Sit your children down and say, "Now, we are going to go to

So-and-so's house, and they have a lot of nice things. I expect you to act like big people and not touch things. I wanted to go over this with you now so we don't run into problems later." The first time they touch the antique bowl (not the seventeenth time), walk over and give them a sharp rap on the back of the hand. I'm not talking about breaking their arms, and I'm not talking about child abuse. I'm talking about getting their attention so that you can talk to them. If a child is too young to reason with, it is even more important to set up a situation like this so he understands that a painful consequence will result when he does something wrong.

Of course, the conditioning process works both ways. When your children fuss and you give in, they are conditioning you. It is like a cartoon I once saw where the little rats were running around the maze saying to each other, "I think we have the scientist conditioned. Every time we run through this little maze he gives us a cookie." This is happening in your situation, and I think you've got to start reversing that process by ignoring their fuss. Don't be so upset about what people in the store are going to think. Your children are more important. And truthfully, there is nothing quite as frustrating as observing another parent being victimized by a small child.

FOURTH-GRADE REBEL •

Our nine-year-old son is loud, energetic, and hard to control, especially since the birth of our second child two and a half years ago. We've tried to give him the extra attention he needs, but I know he feels unloved at times. He doesn't follow instructions, and we must constantly tell him what to do and then follow up to make sure he's done it. He's had trouble at school the last couple of years by not doing what he is told and not bringing home his homework. He's capable of doing well because he made A's and B's in the first and second grades. Sometimes I lose my temper with him, and I know that isn't good. We don't want things to continue this way or he may get into big trouble later on. How can we get our behavior and his back on the right track?

I'm glad you said "our" behavior, because I get the impression you are accurately describing a typical nine-year-old. This is the way they come, the way they act. If you would have described someone who always gets his work done, is always on time, follows through, keeps his dates, and always takes responsibility, you would not have described a nine-year-old, but an adult—and precious few of them, at that.

Don't carry a heavy guilt trip about the birth of your second child. You can expect some degree of sibling rivalry, but I think we often overrate its effect. Children adjust to each other, and take great pride in their little brother or sister just as parents do. So, if you are giving your nine-year-old attention and are affirming him, don't think you have done something wrong by having a second child.

Realize that an essential duty of a parent of a nine-year-old is to "nag." It is irritating, I know, and far easier to do things yourself. For example, you can pick up socks easier than you can teach a boy to pick up socks. Unfortunately, many parents conclude, "Oh, what I want is peace and quiet; therefore, I'll do it for them," and the kids grow up without having learned to do things for themselves.

Remember, too, that as you enforce rules in your home, your son is growing older, and when all of the discussion is over, you will have accomplished your goal. Children learn, they listen; even when they fail, they learn and listen. As they grow older, they gradually mature. Next year you will have a ten-year-old to work with, and the next year an eleven-year-old. Eventually, you will have a young adult who is able to follow through and respond better than a child.

The fact that your son did so well the first couple years of school is absolutely predictable. Kids are initially enthusiastic, they love the materials and eat school up. But after a while, they get a little bored. This is common. At the same time, it is important to maintain rules, enforce those rules, and stand for the right things.

ARE WE LOSING OUR SON? ●

We have a nineteen-year-old son who lives at home and attends a nearby community college. He has a lot of friends from high school and he sees some of them every day. I've told him he can have his friends come over to our house, but he only does it when we aren't home. This makes me wonder if he and his friends are doing something we wouldn't condone. He never spends time with our family, and when he is home all he does is watch TV. I feel like we are losing our son. I don't want to just sit back and watch it happen. How can we get him to open up to us?

I think you are experiencing one of the hazards of junior college. In the past, when a young man reached this age, he attended college in a distant town, or he was married, in the military, or traveling. But with the rise of the junior college, we have sons and daughters in their twenties living in our back bedrooms. This is very disconcerting because we are able to see their growing up and separating process right before our eyes.

Let's face it, one of the goals of parenting is building independence in our children. Yet when they start showing independence at this age, we struggle with what I call the problem of "deparenting"; that is, how do we let go? This can be a very painful process, but at this age it is precisely what ought to be happening. I've often thought how interesting it would be to get into the minds of parents of famous people. For instance, if you could have talked to Mrs. Churchill at the time when Winston was your son's age and working as a war correspondent in South Africa, or if you could have visited the Zebedee Fishing Company and asked Mr. and Mrs. Zebedee, "How are James and John doing?" I'm sure you would have found that those parents were just as concerned as you are.

I think one of the reasons your son may do some of the things you describe is that he has a deep fear of peer rejection. First of all, he may be afraid you will say something that would embarrass him about his friends' conduct—rock music, smoking, drugs, drinking—that you do not approve of. He likes his friends, but may not participate in their habits. In fact, he may be ashamed of his friends' habits and doesn't want you to see them. Or he may be ashamed of how he comes across in their eyes when he is around you. For instance, when he is with them at college he is a big man, grown-up, and independent. But when he is at home, where Mom and Dad have more authority, he may feel smothered and doesn't want to take the chance of his independence being overruled in front of his friends. That's probably why it's more comfortable for him when no one is around. Don't interpret the situation too seriously because it's basically the way a nineteen-year-old boy living at home reacts.

I encourage you to get to know a little more about what your son likes to do. Even if he likes to do some things that you don't like, maybe you could go the extra mile and do something together to show your interest in him.

DARLING DAUGHTER? •

Our daughter is seventeen and has been in a rebellious stage for the past three years. She won't talk to us or lift a finger around the house. When she does say something, her words are biting and sassy. We give her everything she wants and this is how she repays us. This is our middle child out of three. Our oldest wasn't like this at all.

I think you'll find it's usually true that when a young person is going through this fourteen- to seventeen-year-old period, generally associated with high school, he or she is terrifically selfish and self-centered. It's part of the definition of adolescence, their way of "getting it together," or finding themselves. I think it's even truer of today's teenagers because the future is so uncertain, and they want to get it all for themselves *now*.

If you were to really rack your memory, you'd discover that your oldest child experienced just such self-centeredness. But I find with middle children, these growing pains are amplified even further because the middle child often feels very mediocre. The youngest child is getting a lot of attention, the older one's achieving, and your middle daughter is in the middle like unsalted mashed potatoes—just kind of there. So she often acts up and tries to get attention through bizarre behavior of some kind.

You've said that you're giving this daughter everything she wants, yet this is how she repays you. Let me question that statement. We all know that no child ought to be given everything she wants, and doubtless you're not doing that either. But let me suggest that your middle daughter may not really know what she wants. What she really wants is to feel good about herself, to have a sense of independence, of achievement, accomplishment, self-worth, and you can't get that by buying a certain label on the back of your designer jeans. It's only obtainable through certain worthwhile activities. You can help by withholding certain things from her and letting her earn her own money with jobs in or outside the home. Then when she gets something, it will really fulfill what she wants— and that is a sense of self-esteem.

I'M IGNORING MY KIDS •

I have had so much on my mind lately that I find myself turning away my own children when they come to me with questions or even if they just want to play. It leaves me feeling guilty and the children feeling disappointed. I love them, but it's really hard to relate to people with so much on my mind. They are three and five, and when they come with "Why this?" and "Why that?" I just want to run. How can I gain victory over this situation?

One of our problems with children is that we think of their problems in terms of their size. If a little child has a problem, it's a smaller problem than if an adult has a problem. In reality, this is not true at all.

Children's problems are just as important to children as adults' problems are to adults. In fact, probably all the great questions of the world have been asked before the third grade. People who deal with children seriously understand this. Sometimes, as adults, we try to solve our problems in polysyllabic words, but we really haven't come any closer to the solution than some of the children's writers and workers.

I believe the specific business of dealing with your children and making time for them is a two-step process. This process will work with adults too, but since you've put it in the context of your children, let me answer it that way. First, take your preoccupations (business, finances, etc.) and give them to the Lord. As the Bible says, "Cast all your anxiety on Him because He cares for you" (1 Peter 5:7, NIV). I remember specifically one night when I was praying and working through a problem. I had been worrying and struggling night and day and was overcome by circumstances. Then my wife helped me a little by saying, "Why don't you worry for eight hours and I'll sleep, and then I'll wake up and worry for eight hours and you sleep. We can worry right around the clock if that will help." Obviously that wasn't the answer, but I remember stopping and saying, "Lord, I'm going to cast my cares on You, for You care for me. I'm going to give these things to You."

So, when one of your children comes to you with a question, the first step is to say, "Lord, help me now to give these worries to You and to believe You can handle them as I spend time with my child." The second step then is to learn to focus on the child. One of the most frustrating things in the world is to try to read the newspaper and baby-sit a small child at the same time. You've got to stop *whatever* you're doing and concentrate on that little one.

Remember, first cast your care on the Lord, and second, focus and do one thing at a time. It's amazing how rapidly your mind can learn to do this, and soon you'll find yourself applying this method in all sorts of situations.

ARE CARTOONS TOO VIOLENT? ●

Saturday morning cartoons on TV seem much more violent nowadays than when I was growing up, and I would prefer my childern not watch them. Yet Saturday morning is the only time I get to sleep in, so I really can't monitor what they watch. Am I being overly cautious?

I wish they would have had morning TV when I was a kid because I think I would have loved the Saturday cartoons. The best thing we had was "The Lone Ranger" at 6:30 in the evening. You know, "Return with us now to those thrilling days of yesteryear." And there are many people, of course, who want to do just that. They want to return to those thrilling days of yesteryear to a wonderful world with no problems. I've often thought that the thing that makes the good old days seem so good is a poor memory!

Now maybe it is true that cartoons are more violent than they used to be. But it is difficult to imagine cartoons much more violent than the old Roadrunner shows where the coyote smacks into a wall or falls off a great cliff fifteen times in the same episode. Alarmists say, "When children see that they'll go running into walls and flatten like pancakes." I think the bigger problem is when people—children and adults alike—are unable to distinguish between fantasy and reality, make-believe and real.

I think one of the things that you need to do with your children is to constantly remind them that certain things are make-believe. I debunk TV constantly. I debunk newspapers constantly. I debunk the printed page constantly. I am always reminding myself that just because someone wrote it, just because it is on TV, doesn't make it true. We try to develop a discriminating mind in our children.

So I suggest that you watch the Saturday morning cartoons. Decide which ones are OK. Give your kids a piece of paper with the program, the time, and the channel, and say, "These are the ones to watch on Saturday morning." You'll find they'll generally like this guidance, but if they disagree, reestablish that you will be the chooser. In the extreme, of course, you can always pull the plug.

IS SANTA CLAUS A THREAT? ●

Is it harmful for a child to grow up believing in Santa Claus? If we teach our little children not to believe in Santa, will they feel left out or be ridiculed by their friends? More importantly, will they doubt what we tell them about Jesus when they learn the truth about Santa Claus?

Almost everyone has a different opinion about Santa Claus, so let me give you mine. First of all, I believe that young people are helped a great deal through fun, fantasy, and make-believe. And they are quite able to distinguish between fantasy and reality. I've heard preachers get enthusiastic about Christmas, and as they do, they try to guard God from Santa Claus. Now frankly, I don't think the competition is even close. One is a nice, cuddly, little character and the other is the transcendent, all-powerful Creator of the universe. I seriously doubt if God considers Santa a big threat.

We felt that Santa Claus was a wonderful way to share gifts and love with the children without taking the credit. It is fun for both parents and children to have a part in the excitement and anticipation of Christmas. And for children, part of that excitement is fantasy and make-believe. Let's face it, if we cut out Santa for not being real, we'd have to be consistent and cut out Frosty the Snowman, Rudolph the Red-nosed Reindeer, and a host of other lovely Christmas traditions. In time, the children will grow older and it will become obvious to them that Santa doesn't exist. Yet years later they'll probably remember how special you made Christmas seem to them and carry on the Santa Claus story with their own children.

Of course, alongside the Santa Claus myth we shared the truth about the Lord Jesus and read the Christmas story every Christmas together around the tree. As we talked about the Lord Jesus, we told of the true reason Christmas is celebrated. I think our kids understood that. And, interestingly enough, they developed a somewhat crass approach to Santa Claus because they wanted to get something from him. But for the Lord they developed a real, reverent, loving attitude because Jesus meant giving and not taking. This seemed much more important to them.

I think it is a tragic thing when children are raised in very strict religious homes where parents try to establish complex thoughts and teachings which are too difficult for young minds to understand. For instance, this happened in my neighborhood. Each Christmas morning, after the gifts had been opened, all the neighborhood children gathered in the street to show their gifts to one another. But the children of one family didn't get anything. They told our children that Christmas was for Jesus and they didn't get any presents because their folks believed that Christmas shouldn't be commercialized. We felt it was too bad that these parents had lost the balance.

Christmas is one of the most wonderful times of the year, especially for children. Don't take the fun and excitement out of it, because this is one of the channels that help them become more receptive to the true meaning of Christmas.

JUNIOR'S IN A GANG ●

How could two sons turn out so differently? The older one is married, went to college, and has a good office job. The younger son has a beard, long hair, wears a leather jacket and earring, and drives a motorcycle. All his friends look just like him. He has a job working on cars. As far as I know he doesn't drink, curse, or smoke, and he says he's a Christian, but I find it hard to talk to him about the Lord. The older son was a missionary in Haiti for a while. How can we understand our younger son?

I honestly don't know why your two sons turned out so differently. Historically, people have done hundreds of studies on siblings—including those from multiple births—trying to figure out this very thing, and still no one knows why it happens. Just remember from the outset that there is nothing wrong with two children having completely different personalities. Jacob and Esau are prime examples of this.

We could speculate that your younger son has to find his place by doing something totally opposite of his older brother. You know the phrase, "The black sheep of the family." One of my dearest friends who is a deeply committed Christian wears black all the time. I'm not sure I understand just why, except that I believe he does it to identify with the downtrodden, with those who feel like your son feels. People who dress differently or who act bizarrely are usually trying to say, "If that's the kind of person they think I am, then that's the kind of person I'm going to be." They try to establish an antisocial identity. We know that people become part of motocycle gangs and other groups like this for a sense of belonging. It seems tragic to me that with all the positive peer groups in the world that a person has to seek out a group like that to feel accepted. I suppose it's a commentary on the failure of our society.

There is a need for recognition, to have an identity, to be somebody, even to be slightly threatening and fearful to other people. A man who drives down the road in a black leather jacket with an earring and a ponytail, and pulls alongside your car is a little threatening, especially if there are twenty such men together.

Fortunately, many people grow out of this lifestyle. I have met men who have told me some of the things they used to do and I just can't picture them that way. There they are in their three-piece suits, selling copiers or something, and I can't imagine that they were living totally different lifestyles just a few years before.

I think you need to love and accept your son the way he is right now, though I don't think I would try to bring his lifestyle into your home. For example, inviting the whole motorcycle gang for Thanksgiving dinner would not be a good idea because generally speaking, these people, in numbers, tend to be overpowering.

Finally, couple love for your son with prayer that he will "outgrow" this lifestyle. Most young men usually do.

FAMILY TIME TIPS ●

As we start our family, how do we make the best use of our time with our new baby? Are there any good books from the Christian perspective on child training in infancy? What activities would you recommend?

The Christian bookstore in your community is one of the greatest resource centers for men and women of all ages and needs. In the bookstore's parenting section you will find that tremendous numbers of good things have been written about every age group to help us work with our children. Someone read so many of them a while back that he said to me, "You've got to put down the book once in a while and pick up the child." And, of course, that is true. There are many authors whom I appreciate very much, but two that I think have done some very fine work on child-rearing, particularly infants, are Dr. Bruce Narramore and Dr. James Dobson. Both are committed Christians and have sound theological and psychological backgrounds. Having met both of their families, I see that what they espouse works.

Now, without trying to describe different games you can play with children, I would suggest beginning with the principle that what your children want from you more than anything else is you and your time. Several times I've sat my kids down and said, "Daddy's going to talk to some people about raising kids. What would you suggest I tell them?" Each time they suggested things that didn't require much money—just time. Take them to the park. Take them to the zoo. Play with them in the yard. Go fishing. *Do* something. Having a family means being together and doing the kinds of things that promote togetherness. Sitting in a living room and staring at each other is not too exciting for anybody. The principle of spending time with your children is a very key element in raising a successful family.

This brings me to the second point. I don't think any family can be happy or successful until the parents decide that this principle of spending time with the family is the primary occupation. When you get married, you can no longer do some of the things you did when you were single. When you have children, you can't carry on the same kind of life you had before the children came. You've got to stop and say, "We now have a child and we must start focusing our attention toward family-type things." This will mean cutting off certain activities that you have enjoyed in the past and replacing them with more family-oriented activities.

DO BAD FRIENDS RUB OFF? •

I'm concerned about the kinds of friends my children play with because they are at such an impressionable stage in their lives. Some kids in our neighborhood are extremely foul-mouthed and ill-mannered. I don't want their manners to rub off on my children. Is there a way I can subtly influence my children's choice of friends?

I always enjoy trying to picture myself in Bible times when I think about a question like this. For example, what would it have been like to raise a child in a world dominated by the Roman Empire? All sorts of wild things were going on. Soldiers were garrisoned in every town and foul language, evil games, and immoral behavior abounded. Ironically, it was in that kind of environment that the Apostle Paul wrote and Jesus chose to walk among men. In reality, the Gospel has always taken place in the hustle and bustle of the real world. It hasn't taken place in some retreat area that we have created.

As we raise children, we can assist them in certain ways. One way is to insist on certain kinds of behavior and certain kinds of language in our homes and on our property—whether it be our children or someone else's children. I've found that when children are talking in a filthy manner in our yard, it is good to say something like, "Say, we are really happy to have you in our yard and we're glad you came here to play, but in our yard and in our house we don't talk this way, and I'm asking you to quit saying those kinds of things." Of course, some kids will stand with their hands on their hips and defy you. I've had that happen a few times. Then I go a step further by saying, "Hey, you can talk any way you want to—that is between you and your mom and dad. But as long as you are on our property you will have to abide by our rules. Now, how about a glass of lemonade?"

Accept the kids, but don't condone their poor behavior or dirty language. Generally, children will respond to a combination of firmness and love, but you've got to do both at the same time. Sometimes it is good for these kids to get close to your family. Then they can begin to imitate you and the good qualities you represent, like kindness, caring, and concern for others.

It helps to realize children don't behave poorly because they're evil; they do it because they are imitating adults who should know better. Incidentally, I've found that it's not always the other children who are in the wrong. As a parent, you have to be fair. Don't take sides against your child, but sometimes you have to tell him to behave and stop taking advantage of others. Many parents don't do this. When kids sense fairness, it has a significant effect on them.

WHEN MOM AND DAD FIGHT •

Our son and his wife fight in front of their children. They say they are just playing rough, but our granddaughter tells us how frightening it is when they fight (though there is no indication that the children are being physically harmed in any way). Should we interfere by telling our son and daughter-in-law of the emotional hurt this could cause their children, or should we just let them handle it?

Physical hurt is just one way to hurt a child. Emotional hurt can be even more detrimental. In fact, if anything is important in the life of a child it is to sense that his parents are happy together and are not going to break up. When kids think their parents might split up, they feel like they are going to fall into some deep crevice, and this frightens them very much.

I would encourage you to make this serious point with your son. Do it privately without his wife, and do it in a place that is nonthreatening for him, speaking in a low, calm tone of voice. Help him understand that he might be doing something to his kids that he really doesn't want to do. Once you've made your point, back away and stay out of the situation.

Since there is no indication of physical harm, I think the problem can be resolved within the family. If it reaches the point, however, where you feel there is serious harm being done, emotional or physical, then act accordingly, calling the appropriate social service agency in your area. In the meantime, continue to pray and keep your eyes open for the sake of the grandchildren.

WHY IS MY TEEN SELFISH? ●

I've reached the end of my rope. My teenager is one of the most self-centered people I know. Why is he always thinking of himself? In fact, almost every teenager I know is just as selfish. Why is this so?

The Apostle Paul said, "When I became a man, I put childish ways behind me" (1 Cor. 13:11, NIV). This implies that there is something about youth that is childish. As adults, we forget that to be young is to be immature; to be young is to be adolescent; to be young is to be uncertain about our own self-identities. This quest to discover ourselves leads to selfishness, and it is especially strong in the teenage years.

Try to accept the fact *that* teenagers are this way; then try to understand *why* they are this way. Teens aren't selfish because they are evil or bad, but because they are unsure of themselves; they're not sure how they fit into the world. As a result, they are constantly testing and trying to prove themselves. They desperately want to feel liked and accepted by everyone.

For instance, take a beautiful high school girl who has everything that every other girl in the school would want. Yet she needs one boyfriend after another after another. You ask, "How many boys does she need to feel secure and accepted?" She always needs just one more.

Take a boy who's a star on the football team. Five thousand people stand up and cheer him when he catches the ball, but he still needs just a little more. He's got to have a certain girl "worship" him.

Teenagers are really searching for their own identities. They are obsessed with the desire to feel secure about themselves. Sometime their search makes them oblivious to the rest of us. But when they reach seventeen or eighteen, they'll begin to notice this self-centeredness in younger teenage siblings.

During adolescence, parents need to remind and encourage their teens to think of others too. But for the parents' well-being, it's a good idea to remember that this is a passing stage. As the kids mature, they will outgrow this selfishness.

SNOOPY SISTER •

My sister is always coming into my room and snooping through my things. Then she "borrows" things and never brings them back. When I ask her if she's been in my room, she lies and says no. Once I was looking for a piece of jewelry and Mom found it a couple of months later in my sister's room. My sister is eight and I'm fifteen. How can I get her to stop doing this or at least admit it when she does?

This is the kind of problem parents need to help with. It's the duty of parents to preserve the property of the various children. Mothers and dads need to "protect" kids from each other at times. That may sound a little cruel, but what I mean is that parents need to keep their kids from having serious confrontations. It is not a child's place to set up and enforce ground rules in the home. That is the parents' responsibility.

Your parents should talk to your sister and set up some rules, but there is also something you can do. Stop and think of what it was like to be eight years old. When you're eight, you look at someone who is fifteen and think that is about as old as you are ever going to get. The fifteen-year-old world is exciting, sophisticated, and full of all kinds of secrets. So, what happens is that an eight-year-old will get into a fifteen-year-old's room just to find out what happens in that grown-up world. You wear funny clothing that your little sister doesn't wear. You read things she doesn't read. So she snoops around and sees your scrapbook and pictures on the wall. She feels very big.

Rather than have her sneak in and learn things by snooping, it would be great if you would *invite* your sister into your room. Show her your clothing and tell her why you wear those things and what they're for. Tell her a little about what's going on and then she'll feel like she's a part of your life and won't have to snoop. I think it could be a real adventure for you to warn her about things and keep her from getting into trouble, without being too heavy-handed.

It's really a compliment when she wants to go into your world and look at your things. When she tries to wear your clothes and use your things, she is saying, "I want to be like my big sister." Once you understand why she does what she does, you'll no longer need to act like the resident policeman.

CHRISTIAN ROCK? ●

Should my son listen to Christian rock music? He used to listen to ungodly rock music before he was saved, but is Christian rock music any better? He says I'm old-fashioned because I don't approve.

My children call the music I like "dentist's office" music. Though I'm president of a youth organization that uses a great deal of Christian rock music in the process of evangelism, I'm obviously of another generation.

For me, this is a very troublesome subject. I've heard a lot of shrill preaching on both sides, but I've come to the conclusion that you cannot arrange little black marks on a sheet of paper in a moral or immoral fashion. As I see it, music notes are amoral. *People* are either moral or immoral. It's like having a Christian business—there's no such thing as a "Christian" business. Christians run businesses and non-Christians run businesses. So it comes down to a matter of personal taste. I do not like noise; I do not like loud, abrupt sounds; I do not like discord or distorted sounds, but there are people who like them very much. For instance, you can go to India and listen to music that is built on an entirely different kind of system, a different chromatic scale, and it sounds, to the Western ear, like cans being dumped out of a box. On the other hand, when people from India hear the New York Philharmonic, they think those sounds are very strange and overwhelming.

I do have some fairly strong opinions about the rock culture—the ethos, the whole environment that tends to lean toward sensuality, where

40

people's bodily movements and discussions center on the sensual. It seems to me that music which is regressive—music that calls out the worst in mankind—should be called into question. By the same token, many young people today have been living in the depths of that regressive decadence. To reach them, you have to start where they are, not where you wish they were, and take them where they ought to be. My own opinion is everybody ought to enjoy the Chicago Symphony. But I find that very few do. Many would rather do some sort of "moon, June, spoon, croon" guitar-type thing. So I look at the lyrics—do they exalt Christ? Is the setting the kind of place in which Christ would be comfortable? If the lyrics are honest to the Scriptures, honest to the human experience, and exalt Christ, then I don't care so much about the little black marks.

IS SPANKING WRONG? ●

I try to discipline my daughter but never seem to get results. For years I felt that spanking was wrong, but now I'm not so sure. Do you think spanking is a legitimate form of discipline? What else can parents do to discipline their children?

I do believe spanking is legitimate, but by the same token, it is one of the most difficult and demanding ways to discipline and requires more of the parent than most people might believe.

A while back, I was at a conference and a very tense young father came up to me and asked, "Do you believe in spanking?" Apparently he had heard someone speak who made belief in spanking the test of orthodoxy—"If you don't believe in spanking you are not a Christian, maybe not even American."

Well, I doubt if spanking will really solve most of the world's problems. My experience is this: When you spank it takes a great deal of self-control. First of all, you've got to get your emotions under control to where you are not lashing out in anger toward the child. It is human nature to want to hit somebody when he or she has displeased us. We act on our emotions when our adrenalin is up. If we are not careful, we end up punishing rather than disciplining. I do not believe in punishment. I believe in discipline.

Second, we've got to keep in mind the difference in physical size. A 180- or 200-pound man and a 30-pound child is an uneven match. For instance, someone could say to me, "Why don't you go out on an NFL football field and just have a little fun with those guys?" Believe me, any contact with one of those fellows would be no fun at all because of the difference in size. What they think is just a love tap would disconnect my spinal column. The same thing can be true of parents. I saw a mother in a shopping center grab a little child by one arm, raise him straight up in the air, and hit him on the rear, swinging him as she swatted. That is wrong and that is *not* spanking.

Once the parent gets himself under control, slapping the child on the back of the hand or whacking him on the bottom will usually do the job. The parent should *not* spank away until *his* emotions have been satisfied, which is often what happens. Once is generally sufficient.

Most important to recognize is that spanking is only one-half of the story—the other half is affirmation and affection. Spanking without love and affection is like one piece of a scissors without the other half.

NO TIME TO ENJOY MY KIDS ●

I have three small, active children, and just keeping up with them is all I can manage. Though I want to enjoy them and teach them things, it seems all I have time and energy for is caring for their needs. My husband works two jobs, so he doesn't have much time to spare either. Can you give me a little insight on how to be a better mother and wife and a happier, less selfish person?

You say you are selfish, but it sounds to me as though just the opposite is true. You are giving your whole life for these children, and I wish I could tell you that there is another way at this stage. Doubtless you are involved in the most demanding occupation ever invented—raising three small children. What you are probably struggling with is the difference between what you can do, which is serving the kids night and day, and your feelings of resentment over all the work that is involved. There probably isn't a mother in the world who doesn't feel overwhelmed at times.

You may wonder if you have made a mistake to have had your children so close together. You may also be a victim of what I call compressed history. This happens when you read a book by some child-rearing expert, like myself, who thinks back to the time when he was raising children and compresses all the good moments into one chapter. He shares those golden memories of reading books to his children, teaching them about

Jesus, and so on. Then you wonder, "Why can't my life be like the chapter in this book where this wonderful, always-patient Christian mother sees a Christian application in everything in the world? My goodness, isn't it wonderful that Johnny spilled the milk? Now we can learn a lesson about responsibility and forgiveness." In reality, you wipe up the milk and grab the kid, nearly pulling his arm out of the socket, and yell at him. Then you think, "Oh, I'm a failure." Believe me, the people who wrote the books on child-rearing have failed as well, but you're reading about their successes and feel intimidated by them.

Understand that you are in the most difficult period of raising children. It will get better . . . when they begin to tie their own shoes, go to the bathroom by themselves, dress themselves, stay out of the street, and simply walk around an end table instead of climbing over it. In the meantime, realize that it is natural to feel resentment toward people who consume all of your time—so don't feel guilty about it.

IS LITTLE LEAGUE BAD? ●

My son plays on a sports team in our town, but it is getting so competitive. Winning means everything to both the kids and to their parents. I'm not sure if I should let my son join the team next year. It seems like too many parents get out of control when they attend the games by yelling at the umpire, or at the kids when they make mistakes. I question if this kind of atmosphere is healthy for my son. Is this success orientation as bad as I think it is?

Our success-oriented society certainly is bad and unhealthy. Many times it can get out of hand. I think you are up against something, however, that you and your son should probably discuss together. There are some comparative values here—tension, ridicule, and being yelled at versus the rewards of being involved in sports and being accepted as a member of a team. It would seem to me that only when it becomes a problem to your son should you begin to move in and try to do something about it.

A very interesting set of dynamics takes place when a parent is sitting in the stands watching his son or daughter in athletics, because the parent is "on the line" with his child. It is a lot like what my kids face when I'm preaching. I remember one time while I was doing a commencement speech, my daughter heard the fellow behind her say, "Well, I wonder when old motor-mouth is going to quit?" When she heard that, she got defensive of her daddy.

I believe that most boys feel that the occasional tongue-lashing, the occasional disappointments, and the occasional ridicule do not outweigh the thrill of participating in athletics. Of course, the negative aspects of the game can occasionally get out of hand and be quite destructive. For instance, I decided, along with our kids, that they shouldn't be involved in informal pickup games at the town park because the neighborhood bullies pretty much ran things, making up the rules as they went, and intimidating the smaller boys and girls. There was a lot of name-calling and a lot of hurt. It destroyed my children's desire to even be involved because of the level of immaturity these bullies displayed. And yet, sadly enough, sometimes adults aren't a whole lot better.

You can be a Little League coach without a lot of experience. But coaching involves much more than winning—it involves character-building. It is a tremendous opportunity for teaching the lessons of life. If a boy gets a coach who is immature and lacks poise, one who yells and screams and manipulates his team, it can create tremendous harm. Parents need to be aware of this. Your boy will know when things are getting out of hand. He won't be able to articulate it, but he'll know when it's unpleasant. If that situation happens, don't pressure your child to stay involved in such an environment because it can be very destructive.

BROOMSTICK FIGURE ●

Our thirteen-year-old daughter is a "late bloomer." All her friends have suddenly blossomed into womanhood, leaving her and her broomstick figure behind. At the same time, her personality is changing. She isn't outgoing anymore. She avoids her previous friends and spends too much time alone in her room. She is getting on everybody's nerves and we've just about had it. How can we deal with this?

Let me suggest that you apply the great rule of parenthood—"This too will pass." There is probably more help for parents in that one phrase than in all the other things people say. Your daughter needs your patience at this very difficult time.

Let's look at what's happening from her viewpoint. She's probably finding it difficult to believe that someday she is going to turn into this woman that the other girls are becoming. She is afraid, apprehensive, and worried about the future. In her world, she only gets acceptance by being a certain kind of person. Let's face it, they choose girls to be cheerleaders on the basis of their appearance. And though you say to her, "We love you just like you are, Honey. We think you're great," that won't satisfy her because she gets hundreds of responses at school that are just the opposite.

When a young girl faces this dilemma, she can respond in different ways. She can retreat into juvenile activity—begin to play with dolls, do things she did two or three years before that used to make her happy. Or she can start reading romance novels. Why are these romance novels so popular? Through these novels, people are able to go off into a world where things are charming and nice. We all need that kind of escape occasionally.

When your daughter is moping in her room, she's in a place that is more comfortable than the hostile world outside. Eventually she will start to blossom and this moping will take care of itself, or more likely, some late-blooming boy will come along. Believe me, a late-blooming boy can solve more problems in this case than you can. Some little fellow who is feeling kind of rejected himself will notice that your daughter feels the same way too and they will get together to commiserate.

So, be patient, loving, and supportive. She'll most likely grow out of this stage soon.

THIS GAME IS NOT SO FUNNY ●

My daughter is just four years old but is constantly hiding things to get her own way. For instance, when my grandmother came for a visit, my daughter hid the cake pan she brought in hopes Grandma would stay a day longer. We thought she was merely playing games with us until one day, after visiting a friend's house, she took the girl's shoes home with her and hid them in her room. Later the friend's mother discovered my daughter wearing them. She's been playing too many of these hide-and-seek games lately and we're afraid that this habit may become a real problem.

Don't be *too* concerned. At four years of age, this child is going through a whole range of learning experiences and is intensely curious. As parents, we tend to look at our children and think they're special. But the truth is, if we back off a bit we realize that our children will go through the same growing-up problems that all children do—sexual fascination, swearing, lying, stealing, destructiveness.

A four-year-old is still quite immature as far as moral things go. Instead of becoming anxious about her growing up to be a thief, explain to her about property, how certain things belong to one person and certain things belong to another. The argument that usually works best with children is a variation of the Golden Rule which says, "How would you feel if someone took home your shoes?" This works even better if you can find something that is very dear to your daughter and say, "How would you feel if someone took your doll or your wagon?" If your daughter oversteps her bounds, be firm. Tell her she's done wrong. Make her go back and apologize. One time my mother made me take some carrots I had stolen from a neighbor's garden back to her. Mother made me walk up onto the porch, knock at the door with this little bunch of carrots, ask Mrs. Durbin's forgiveness, and then ask if I could make amends. Mrs. Durbin immediately broke into tears, hugged me, and felt sorry for me. She talked to my mother and told her the carrots were of no consequence to her, and to please forget about it. Well, that's been over forty years ago, and Mrs. Durbin still remembers that incident—and so do I. I've never stolen a carrot since!

I think of 1 Corinthians 13:11: "When I became a man, I put away childish things." Part of being a child is doing childish things.

IS OUR BOY A CHICKEN? ●

Our youngest son is afraid to try anything new. He's afraid to go to his Sunday School class and won't even try some of the rides at the fair. He misses out on many activities at his Christian school simply because he's afraid. We do a lot of things together as a family, but he will not venture out with his friends or his classmates. A couple of times we've forced him to go to school events. He's fourteen, but his older brothers and sisters are married and have families of their own. Could this be having a negative effect on him?

I don't think so. What your son really needs is some time and he'll probably come around just fine. Perhaps because he's the youngest son and he's going to a Christian school (which separates him from the rest of society), it is possible that you have inadvertently telegraphed to him the message that the world is a fearsome place and that one is liable to get hurt or corrupted out there.

I have nothing against a Christian school education. On the contrary, I think it is a wonderful thing. But unconsciously, through your words and especially your actions, you may be telling your son that the world is a pretty scary place. As an adult you know how to handle it, but as a child, your son doesn't, and so he withdraws.

It's also entirely possible that you've done everything just right. I've seen so many situations of this type. Time and patience are usually the remedy. At fourteen, a child is still quite young. In fact, aside from all of these little observations I'm making, boys have a right to want to be alone at that age. Some of the world's greatest people—inventors, writers, artists—have spent a lot of time alone. I have friends, now middle-aged, who are great achievers. I've talked to them about their adolescence, and I don't think one of them had what I would call a "normal" adolescence. Almost all of them mentioned how they didn't make it in sports and therefore they sublimated themselves into art or writing or science.

Your son may need to spend some time alone at this stage of his life. Encourage him in whatever hobbies he shows interest in. But above all, don't make a problem out of your son. This is not a problem that you have living with you—it's a boy. He is a little shy and a little reticent but, like most kids, he'll outgrow this phase.

TV FOR TOTS? ●

I let our one-year-old daughter watch educational children's programs on TV. They are secular programs but children do learn ABCs and 1, 2, 3s along with many other valuable things. The programs also contain a few distasteful things such as puppet monsters who promote being nasty. My husband is opposed to these kinds of programs and doesn't want them on at all. Should our daughter watch or not?

Unfortunately these kinds of issues tend to get cast in either/or terms. But I don't think that life works that way. Parents should monitor TV watching and teach their kids to do the same. I was in a home once where a little boy was watching television. At the end of the program he got up and turned off the set. I was pretty impressed because television programmers are smart enough to put little hooks on the end of the first program saying, "Stay tuned for the second one," and it sounded like something I would have liked to have seen. But this little guy got up and turned it right off. I commented on his action and his father told me (in the boy's presence), "This is one of the most grown-up things he has learned to do. He has learned how to turn off the television."

If your husband has such a stern view on television, he should then be willing to sacrifice his time to entertain and teach his child. It is one thing to sit in church and hear about the damage done by the media and it's another thing to spend hours with a preschooler who is hungry to learn. If there is no television or some other distraction, a child is constantly asking Mama to read him books, point to pictures, count 1, 2, 3, and line up blocks. Now this is great stuff and it's vitally important, but most mothers have a few more things to do than that, and they find that sitting the child in front of the television for a little while gives them a chance to breathe or do some washing and ironing, or some of the other things the husband wants done when he gets home, like having supper ready!

Therefore, I think you've got to come to some moderate position with your husband. Kids are able to handle fantasy. I think they understand these little monsters and don't really want to become like them. In fact, many of these monsters are really trying to teach us lessons about how to handle the nasty people in the world. One way to handle them is with humor instead of always being so grim.

HOME SOUR HOME ●

How do you handle a rebellious teenage girl? Our daughter is fourteen years old and has been brought up in a Christian home. I know most teenagers go through this stage, but it seems she is only rebellious at home. Everyone else—teachers, friends, and others—tell us she is well behaved, and they have no trouble or problems with her.

Teenagers often treat parents worse than they treat others. There was a song written many years ago that says, "Why do I hurt the one I love?" In a way, it is kind of a compliment, though it doesn't feel that way when you are the focus of venomous attacks by your daughter.

The fourteen-year-old knows that there is a certain penalty for treating teachers badly or treating friends badly—they just report you to the principal or drop you. Parents won't drop you. They understand. The problem is that parents don't always understand what is going on in the mind of a fourteen-year-old. Mom and Dad think, "My goodness, all this unearned unhappiness. We've given her everything; we've surrounded her with love and care; and yet she acts against us. What is going on?"

To be fourteen years old is quite difficult. Many people have great memories of their childhoods, but almost no one, it seems, has good memories about his adolescence because that was a time of tremendous change and uncertainty.

Recently I was in the Middle East with one of my friends who brought along a Polaroid camera. He would take a picture of a child and then give him the yet undeveloped photo. The child must have thought, "He's given me a worthless thing." But then he would look again and begin to see his own face appear. Suddenly his little face would start to light up. As the picture came into focus, his face would break out into a beautiful smile. You could just tell he was eager to run and hang it in his tent or house or show it to his mother. Similarly, fourteen-year-olds are uncertain about how their pictures are going to turn out. They sense the rejections of a cruel teenage society. And because of this fear, they keep a stiff upper lip with teachers and friends, but they let their real selves come out at home. And that's what your daughter is doing—showing her real, frightened, fourteen-year-old self. The only real cure for this is massive doses of assurance, affirmation, and trust. Demonstrate through your words and actions an attitude that says, "You may be acting a little strange right now, but we believe in you and will stick with you."

I'M BLAMED FOR EVERYTHING ●

My sister and I can't get along. We do fine with our other friends, but whenever we get together we fight and argue. Since I am thirteen and she is ten, I always get blamed for starting the trouble. How can my sister and I get along better? What should I do when I get blamed for the things she does?

You're a teenager. Being a teenager, you understand a lot more about life than your sister does because she is much younger. Therefore, you must assume more responsibility. Because you are older, you have learned more and can be more of a help.

Brother-and-sister spats are one of the oldest problems in the Bible. Remember Joseph's brothers? They got so tired of him getting everything because he was younger that they threw him in a well and sold him. Then there is the story in Luke 15:11-31 about the Prodigal Son. The oldest brother became very upset with his father because Dad seemed to treat the younger brother better than he treated him, even though the younger brother was not well behaved. So being the oldest brother or sister has what adults call "occupational hazards" connected with it. Accepting certain things, whether they are right or wrong, is part of being the oldest.

Of course, there is nothing wrong with telling your parents when you have been unjustly accused. But you don't have to scream and stamp your feet. Just calmly say, "Really, Mom, this time I didn't start it." And at least your mom will have heard your side of the story even though she has already told you to go to your room.

What your mother is really doing is honoring you by putting responsibility on you. She is saying, "You are older, therefore you ought to be able to control these things." It helps to point out what is right, but understand that all Mom is concerned about is that you quit fighting. At that particular moment, she's not looking for justice; she just wants quiet. When you are the oldest, you often end up being the target and that's just the way things are in a family.

Another thing that happens between younger brothers and sisters is that they tend to feel the need to possess people. There is competition between you for your parents' love. You both feel like the other one is getting a piece of what you ought to have. But as you get older, maturity will allow you to make room for everyone. In fact, most likely by the time you are both in college, you and your sister will be the closest of friends. It almost always works this way. In the meantime, learn to be the kind of girl and the kind of sister you know the Lord wants you to be.

CHAPTER 3

Living with Parents

I have probably spent more time talking with young people about how to live with their parents than about any other subject. Most of them have been amazed when I showed them the verse in Ephesians that says, "Provoke not your children to wrath" (6:4), though they have all heard another verse in the same chapter, "Children, obey your parents" (6:1) very often.

The Bible is very fair. It speaks to husbands about wives and to wives about husbands; it speaks to children about parents and to parents about children. But few parents, it seems, read on to the Apostle Paul's beautiful insight that it's possible for parents to exasperate their children.

It's been my prayer ever since we began preparing this book that when young people read it, they will feel we have been fair to them. Scripture is not one-sided or unfair, and family relationships should not be either.

In order to be fair, young people need to learn to give their parents the same benefit of the doubt that they ask for themselves. Parents deserve, once in a while, to be allowed to be grouchy, moody, and unfair, to make a federal case out of something minor, to overreact—the same privileges that young people hope their parents will extend to them.

Parents are human, just like young people. They too need tender, loving care and understanding. In fact, as soon as a young person is old enough to understand that his parents are being unfair, then he is old enough to understand that unfairness is part of the human condition.

Most of this book is devoted to helping parents learn to be fair to children, but in this chapter we are pleading for fairness in the other direction. Kids, give your parents a break!

THE GIFT OF TRUST ●

Why don't my parents ever trust me? They think that everything I do must have a bad motive. I want them to trust me, but I don't want to tell them every detail of my life. It's getting to the point where I don't try as hard to live up to their expectations because I know they don't trust me anyway.

———————

Trust is one of the most powerful things parents can give their children—perhaps even more powerful than love. Trusting people, especially teens and children, does more good than almost anything one can do.

But I've found over the years three big reasons why parents don't trust their kids. The first reason is that they didn't trust themselves when they were that age. They may have lived wild lives and so they think that all kids that age lead wild lives. They fear their children will be like them and so they tend to be overprotective. The second reason has to do with outside influences on parents by other people. They run into people who say, "You can't trust teenagers. If you trust them, you're nuts! Look what the kids are like today." Third, a kid's own performance may break down trust. Sometimes kids break their trust by being untrustworthy. And after they've done that a few times, parents get suspicious and begin to watch them more carefully. If you want to be trusted, you've got to be trustworthy.

Parents, let me suggest that if you're going to err, err on the side of trust rather than on the side of suspicion. A young person raised in an atmosphere of suspicion and mistrust is more apt to throw up his hands eventually and say, "Well, if that's the kind of kid they think I am, then that's the kind of kid I'm going to be." Constant distrust (even though the child may deserve it) can be very harmful.

If you're a young person having trouble earning your parents' trust, let me encourage you to begin a program of building trust. Start being trustworthy in small things. Are the lights off when they're not being used? Is the iron unplugged when you leave the house? Did you mow the lawn when you were asked? Don't become paranoid about it, but let your parents know that you are thinking responsibly about these things, because a lot of young people don't.

GREAT EXPECTATIONS •

My biggest problem is my parents. They always expect me to get the best grades possible, keep my room in perfect order, and be the ideal kid. Yet no matter what I do, they don't seem to trust me completely—especially with boys. I'm thirteen and am tired of being checked up on all the time. How can I let my parents know how I feel without being rude?

Tell your parents in a nice way just what you have told me. You seem articulate and quite capable of expressing your thoughts, and so you need to express them to your parents.

Mothers get tired of nagging their children, but nagging is the national duty of mothers. However, when nagging starts to exasperate kids, it becomes counterproductive. The Bible says that an illegitimate child doesn't have a father to chastise him or to correct him, but a real son has a father who does (Heb. 12:7-9). Perhaps this is one of the ways your folks are expressing their love for you. They are saying, "I love you and care about you so much that I want to perfect you."

Your parents have probably forgotten that they didn't get perfect by being corrected. They got where they are now by making a lot of mistakes. What they are really saying is, "I love you so much I want you to avoid all the hurts and heartaches and pain that I've had to endure. I'm going to point out your every fault so that you will be perfect, happy, and ready for the world." Yet this approach ends up tearing you down and makes you feel unhappy.

One thing you can do when you are feeling exasperated with your parents is to consider: Would you rather be underloved or overloved? Would you rather have caring parents or uncaring parents? Believe me, what you have is a whole lot better than parents who could care less.

Parents, recognize the tremendous frustration a young person feels in trying to fulfill adult expectations. A thirteen-year-old is an adolescent, not an adult. You say, "Yes, but she acts like a six-year-old." Well maybe, but when you overdo perfectionism, eventually the child will just give up. I encourage you to loosen the thumbscrews just a little bit, and be more affirming of your child's good qualities.

LIFE ISN'T FAIR •

I'm sixteen and very involved in our youth group at church. Once a month we have meetings or socials that I really enjoy. However, my dad is the only one who can drive me there. He's not a Christian and it seems like every time I want to go to a youth group meeting, Dad will come up with some job around the house that must be done before I can go to church. He always waits to tell me about these things a half hour before we are supposed to leave, and there is just no way I can get the chores done in time. I think he is doing this just to aggravate me. By the time I finally get to church I am so mad that I don't have a very good time with the kids. Is there anything I can do about this?

On the surface this sounds very unfair and you may have a good reason to feel angry. On the other hand, who said the world is fair? There are very few *fair* things in the world, and we all must learn to live with that. Have you thought of looking at this situation from your father's point of view? Maybe there is another side to the story, and maybe there isn't. But let me encourage you, regardless of the situation, that one of the most effective witnesses a person can have is obedience in the face of injustice.

The Old Testament account of Jacob and Laban illustrates this point. Laban, Jacob's father-in-law, kept making promises and then breaking them. Yet Jacob kept working for him just the same. Even though Jacob was treated unfairly, he was determined to remain fair and responsible to himself. Eventually he broke through to Laban and God rewarded him for his persistence.

The Apostle Paul gave similar advice to women in the early church who had unbelieving husbands. He told them to live consistently in the face of injustice because such a witness would break down their husbands' resistance. There are many men who secretly say to their friends, "I don't plan to become a Christian, but if I ever do become one, I want to be like my wife, because she puts up with all kinds of things from me. She must have the real thing because I don't know how she can stand it."

Perhaps you can have that kind of influence on your father, whereby he would someday say, "You know, I don't like my daughter's religion, but I'll have to say this, the way she lives it in our home, even when things are going bad, is convincing to me." It could be God is giving you this opportunity.

Now here are a couple other suggestions. One, begin to inform your dad about your schedule ahead of time. Many kids habitually do things on the spur of the moment. In the meantime, their folks have made certain plans and when the kids drop these spur-of-the-moment activities on them, which conflict with Mom's and Dad's plans, there are problems. Tell your parents well in advance when things are going to happen. You might even say, "Dad, I want to go to youth group tomorrow evening at 7 o'clock, so if you have anything that needs doing around here, maybe you could tell me now so I could get it done before my meeting." That approach will probably surprise him very much and it might even help him realize what he's been doing.

In addition to planning ahead (both informing him of your schedule and telling him you are willing to do some work if he'll just tell you what he wants done), ask the Lord to help you not to gripe or feel angry—even when a job *is* sprung on you. A good spirit will get the job done even quicker. Be an example of fairness and responsibility to your father and I think the message will eventually get through.

DAD'S NOT HIMSELF LATELY ●

I'm only ten but I'm worried about my dad. Lately he seem so somber and not like himself at all. When I try to bring back happy times he just says, "Yes, I remember that," and then I feel guilty about it. I think he feels like I love Mom more than him. But I love them both equally. Can you tell me the answer?

One of the confusing things about being ten is that often we think we cause everything that happens around us. For instance, there are a lot of kids about your age who tell me their parents have gotten divorced because of them. Somehow their folks started fighting and they think, "I must be the reason because I'm the only other person around who they would fight about." Of course, this is not true. Similarly, it is probably not you that makes your dad act differently. In fact, it may have little to do with you.

Your dad may be starting to experience what is called the "mid-life crisis." That's a term adults use to cover many of the things they don't really understand. One of the things dads get frustrated about is their jobs. They work at the same job for years yet feel like they are getting nowhere. There is no advancement, and after a while they ask themselves, "Do I want to do this the rest of my life? Here I am, forty years old; am I going to do this when I'm sixty-five?" That is a heavy load for many men. Maybe they thought they were going to be President of the United States; the president of a company. Now they see that is not going to happen, and they feel they will have to settle for less. Sometimes there are tensions over growing older. I see a lot of men sit around in their high school letter sweaters and wish they could somehow return to those "thrilling days of yesteryear." In the meantime, little "love-handles" are developing over their belts. All this adds up to self-doubt, frustration, and boredom.

So, Dad comes home from work and you walk up to him and say, "Hey, Dad, let's do such and such." He merely stares back at you and says, "Oh," and looks bored. Now you can see that it doesn't have anything to do with you; he is just working through some things. He will probably work through them quite well, but it will take a little time.

Keep pestering him. Try to get him out of his chair and interested in something. I'll bet you'll discover that once you can get him up and get him moving, he'll almost always say, "Hey, that was fun!" But getting him started is the tough thing. So regularly suggest activities to your dad. "Why don't we take a picnic? Why don't we go for a walk?" Be persistent. Once he gets used to doing things again, he will begin to realize that activity is better than just sitting in his chair.

WHEN PARENTS BREAK RULES •

I'm sixteen and my parents are always making rules they want me to obey. Yet many of these rules seem unnecessary, and in many instances my parents will not follow the rules themselves. I asked them about this once and they said, "Do as I say, not as I do." Shouldn't they keep the same rules they make?

Dealing with a problem and changing it are two different things. You can do yourself a great favor for the rest of your life if you understand we all want people to be consistent in their behavior. This is a good and desirable thing. But if you expect the world to be just and fair all the time, your life will be a series of disappointments. We live in an imperfect world where you can't always expect consistency, justice, and fairness. In fact, you yourself will find it very difficult to be fair all the time.

Yes, it would be good if your parents were consistent in what they say and what they do. On the other hand, as a sixteen-year-old, you have to acknowledge that there is a big difference between being a parent and being a teenager. Now you may say right is right and wrong is wrong; it's just as wrong when you're forty as when you're sixteen. That is true, up to a point, but many of the rules your parents give you aren't necessarily right or wrong in and of themselves. They simply help you develop the tools to deal with more mature situations such as dating, curfews, and personal habits. When you are older, you will be able to make up your own mind about these things.

Let me share an example. Early in the growing season you often see little cones or cut-off plastic bottles over the tops of tomato plants. Farmers don't cover the tomatoes to destroy them. They cover them to protect them from the elements until they are strong enough to make it on their own. Parents face a similar situation; they are trying their best to protect their children. When your parents make rules, ask yourself, "Why are my parents making these rules?" About ninety-nine percent of the time the rules are not to hurt you, but to help you. Sometimes your parents are misinformed and sometimes the things they demand seem unreasonable, but isn't it better to be overloved than underloved? Isn't it great to have somebody so concerned about you that they try to protect you too much instead of having no one who cares or is concerned about you?

Discuss this problem with your folks. Debate it if necessary, up to a point. Don't argue or fight, but say, "Mom and Dad, this is the way I feel." Express yourself; let your parents express themselves. You'll find they are really saying, "Honey, we have rules because we love you and want to help you."

HOW WILL I EVER LEARN? ●

My parents are so unfair to me. I'm in high school and they just don't seem to understand that I'm becoming an adult. It doesn't matter what I want to do, the answer is always no. And when I ask why, they say it's for my own good. How will I ever learn anything if I can't get out and experience it?

Many parents are victims, to some extent, of external information that's coming to them. Almost all the news they hear about teenagers is bad. Most parents haven't been to school lately to see the rows and rows of kids tediously doing their homework, performing well, and being responsible. Instead, they read articles in the newspapers about drugs, partying, and automobile accidents. Because of this, parents start developing a paranoia about the teenage years before their children even reach that stage. They start thinking of all the things their teenagers could get involved with, and suddenly they get scared to death. And when their kids finally do become teenagers, the parents tend to be a little overprotective.

Many parents come up to me and say, "Boy, I've got a youngster eight years old, and I don't know whether I can stand the idea of him being a teenager." To that I reply, "We've found the teenage years were the happiest years of our family life. We enjoyed them very much. It's exciting to begin to communicate with teens on an adult level and it's wonderful to become their friends as well as their parents."

Try to understand that this overprotective attitude of parents is an expression of their love. They're concerned about their children because they love them and are afraid they're going to get hurt or experience something that is irreparable. And sometimes their fears are well-founded. But here are two things you can do. First, talk with your folks and assure them of your convictions. Sit down with them and say, "Dad and Mom, I know what's going on in school; I know what the dangers are. I know there are kids involved with drugs and kids who drive while drinking. Believe me, I'm not going to get involved in that. I know where I am and I know who I am. I have autonomy and I have character." If your parents can be assured you're going out into these situations armed with convictions, they will feel more sure of you.

Second, try to prove yourself trustworthy. If you do the little things well, your parents will begin to trust you with bigger responsibilities and privileges. Many young people want to be trusted with the big things, but don't want to bother with the little stuff. And so there is a constant struggle in the household because Junior won't cooperate with the little things and the parents say, "How can I trust him with the car?" or "How can I trust him with a date when I can't even trust him to pick up his socks?" So start with the socks and work your way into the car.

YOU SEE . . . I MET THIS BOY ●

A year ago I went away to college and met a young man. We've fallen in love and plan to get married after finishing school. My parents are furious though, because I am supposed to transfer to another school to complete my education. But after meeting this

young man I want to be with him all the time. My parents resent my boyfriend and treat me poorly. I feel they don't trust me. With the summer over, I want to return to that same college, but don't know if that would be wise. Yet I want to see my boyfriend again.

This is a typical problem for young people to face with their parents. That is, you sit down with your parents and make career plans, then someone outside enters in—like a boyfriend—and suddenly there is another player in the mix. Parents feel that your priorities have all changed and the boyfriend has moved into the supreme place; he is more important now than they are. You are not following the original plan anymore. Instead you are following your heart.

You might ask yourself, "Why did I originally plan to transfer after a year?" Was it that this is a community college and it was less expensive and therefore you would have a year of less expensive college? Or was it the type of education? Were you going to get a general education at the one school, then transfer for more specialized coursework at the other? Are the career plans that you originally had being fulfilled? If not, then maybe you ought to be following the career path you first thought about. Or are you playing the dating game? In other words, if you are going to school, going to your classes, and going through the motions just to be near this boy, then probably you are wasting the time you spend at college. If this boy is indeed more important than college, then you have a decision to make.

Look at your folks' point of view too. Why do your folks interfere? Why are they involved? My guess is that your parents want you to be happy, successful, and to finish your education. These are important values to parents and I think they will be important to you as well someday.

It is always best to work out these decisions amiably with parents. To have your parents as allies is a tremendous asset. By the same token, you do have to paddle your own canoe. If you are prepared to pay the costs of your college education, prepared to be independent, then you can make more independent decisions. But you can't have your folks support you and at the same time do your own thing. I think you have got to come up with a compromise that is realistic.

MOM SAYS NO •

I'm in the seventh grade and I think I'm old enough to wear makeup and nylons. But my mom says I can't. All my friends do these things and I want to too. I think Mom's being unfair. Why doesn't she think I'm old enough?

I'm sorry, but I agree with your mother. I think many girls your age are being pushed too early into things they don't really understand, and it's causing them to miss the fun they could have had later in life if they had just waited a little longer.

I think you're a victim of advertising. If you watch television on any given evening, you'll see girls about your age who look like they're eighteen because they are wearing certain kinds of jeans and certain kinds of makeup. You think, "Boy, I want to look like that!" But the truth of the matter is, some of those girls have had some very unhappy experiences because, though they're maturing fast physically, their minds, understanding, and emotions aren't keeping up. They find themselves in over their heads in lots of ways. I'd say that your mom is probably pretty smart and she's trying to help you so you won't do something too early and thus hurt yourself.

Did you ever see a science teacher take a cocoon and cut it open? Because it hasn't been allowed to develop quite long enough, what emerges from the cocoon is half-worm and half-butterfly, and it's really quite ugly. I think this can happen to people too. When their lives are opened up too quickly, they often turn into something they shouldn't be. Sometimes this happens through things they can't help, like a girl being attacked and molested, or a child losing his parents in a terrible tragedy. Many kids have to live with those terrible experiences that may blemish them their whole lives. But in your case, your mom wants you to stay in the cocoon long enough so that when you come out you'll be a terrific butterfly.

STUCK AT HOME •

My mom has come to depend on me over the years. She was divorced when I was young and had to find a job. Because I was the oldest daughter, I had to keep house, cook, and clean for the whole family. I practically raised my youngest sister. When other kids my age were outside playing, I was inside acting like a mother.

Now I'm twenty-two, single, and still living at home. I want the freedom to live my own life and have my own friends, but my mom resents the friendships I do have. What can I do?

This kind of problem tends to gradually build up a day at a time until it eventually eats up everybody's life. I see three alternatives. One is that you continue as is. Let the resentment and hurt continue to build. Before long you will become kind of a dutiful grump. The second alternative is that you leave home and start on your own, weaning your mother of her need for you. It will be a painful process and may be fraught with great difficulties. The third alternative is to ask yourself, "What do I really want?"

Being the oldest daughter and having practically raised your youngest sister, you have probably begun to receive meaning in your life through serving others. As a result, most of the positive feedback you get comes when you've actually helped somebody. Your problem may not be that you need to get away from your mother, but simply that you're doing too much of the same thing. What you need is a vacation, some time away by yourself.

You and your mother need to talk about this. Your mother needs to make a compromise that says she needs her own life as much as you do yours. Go out and begin to make friends, as you have been doing, and have your mother see that the alternative is a very clean, real break.

I CAN'T LOVE MY DAD ●

When the Bible commanded us to love our parents, I don't think it had my dad in mind. I'm fifteen years old and just can't love him. He constantly aggravates me. I have been looking for a father figure and have fallen in love with an elder of our church. I want so much for him to be my father and for him to adopt me because, to me, he is ideal. Is it wrong for me to keep dreaming like this?

It may not be wrong, but it surely is adolescent, and a person your age with the kind of insight you seem to show ought to be able to get past this point. Your father irritates you, so you have replaced him with a more appealing father figure. Understand that this is not love in the sense of "falling in love." You are simply responding to a need in your own life—a need to be loved, accepted, and understood. Whereas your father is a disciplinarian, this person accepts you for what you are. Your father doesn't tell you that you're pretty; this man does. He may, in the guise of a father-daughter relationship, begin to hug you and hold your hand—all nice stuff. However, it may go beyond that for both of you and become very confusing. You have a response within you that is not a daughter-father response, but a male-female response, and you are beginning to feel something happening. These kinds of things can lead to deep sadness for everybody—his family, your family, and you. I think the mature thing is for you to realize you do need friends other than your own family and it is nice to have a caring uncle, even an adopted one, who understands you and to whom you can speak.

Most of all, I think you are being unfair to your father. He has to be responsible for the way you spend your money, your time, a thousand things that involve being a parent. And because of this, it seems like he's always picking on you or bugging you. But that is because he loves you. He wants you to grow up and mature in these areas. The other man doesn't have these responsibilities. You see him at his best and he sees you at your best. Get out of the dream world and back to the reality of the fact that your father loves you and probably bugs you because he wants the best for you.

I want you to try something, even though it may sound difficult. Someday soon, walk up to your dad, give him a big hug, and tell him you love him and are beginning to understand that he really does want the best for you. Then tell him in a nice way that he may be trying a little too hard, that you want to talk to him about some of the things he does which bother you. I think you'll find that your father will be much more open and receptive to what you have to say. Even if he isn't, continue to reach out to your father with love. Sooner or later, he'll grasp the significance of what you're trying to accomplish.

CHAPTER 4

Living with Grandparents and Grandchildren

Having grandchildren is one of the most fulfilling experiences of my life thus far. I believe from my memories of my own grandparents that grandparents can enrich their children's lives too. Those who have not lived near or known their grandparents are disadvantaged.

Grandparents are meant to be an asset, but a sad fact of American life is that in many families, parents and children abuse each other. Abused children tend to abuse their children, and when they are old, their children tend to abuse them. This cycle of abuse is taught and caught by observation in the family.

Fortunately, considerate and loving treatment is also taught and caught through daily family life as the different generations relate to each other. When the Bible speaks about honoring your father and mother, it's not only speaking about the sixteen-year-old boy honoring his forty-year-old father. It's also speaking about the forty-year-old father honoring his sixty-five-year-old mother. When a girl watches her mother and dad relate to their parents, then she gets an idea about how she ought to relate to her parents.

In a simpler day in our society, almost all children grew up in homes with several generations living under the same roof. This created tensions, of course—tensions that frighten modern people. Problems arise when children divide and conquer, when grandparents' indulgence interferes with the parents' plans of discipline and responsibility. But out of the crucible of those tensions, much richness can be added to life. *Fiddler on the Roof* shows how these tensions—debates and discussions and conflicts in relationships—can create enduring family traditions.

Nowadays, grandparenting is usually intermittent. As a friend of mine says of his grandchildren, "They're grand when they come and grand when they go." But it is still a very important part of the family process. With some forethought, families can still create ties that extend to more than two generations. Indeed, that is an idea for all families to seek.

GRANDPARENTS ARE SPOILERS ●

My parents and my husband's parents shower our children with gifts—sometimes very expensive ones and sometimes inappropriate gifts like B-B guns. Our kids are now beginning to expect something every time we visit the grandparents. I think they're spoiling their grandchildren, but they don't agree. This really bothers us. Can we monitor the gifts our children receive from others?

Yes. But there is no substitute for sitting down with your folks and explaining to them the kinds of things you would prefer to see your children play with, as well as the number of gifts they should receive. Be firm, but loving and gracious. Grandparents tend to play down certain problems like this because they don't want to disrupt the good times they are having with their children and grandchildren. They don't see their gift-giving as spoiling their grandchildren; they see it as an expression of their love.

So talk with them about it. I'm amazed at how few people actually talk to the person that's involved. They talk to a friend or write a letter to somebody else, but they don't talk to the one person who could really help them get to the bottom of the problem. Don't worry about offending your folks or the possibility of a broken relationship. They have lived a good many years and they've run into all kinds of problems. They'll understand what you are trying to accomplish.

Now about the problem of your kids beginning to expect a gift every time they go to their grandparents' house. Quite often the problem takes care of itself, especially if the grandparents are trying to buy their relationship with the kids by getting them expensive gifts. Before long the kids will develop an appetite for this. But one day they'll come and Grandma and Grandpa won't have anything and then they'll whine and say, "Why didn't I get something?" And Grandma and Grandpa will say, "My goodness, I thought they liked *us!* They actually like the gifts." Then they'll begin to understand that their generosity has worked against them, and they'll start to cut back on the gift-giving, not because they love the children less, but because they want the children to love them for who they are, and not for the gifts they give.

WHERE'S THE DISCIPLINE? ●

My parents don't like to see my husband and me discipline the kids, and they are beginning to interfere. After a weekend visit, it takes us a week to get the kids on the right track again and rid of all the bad manners they learned at Grandma's and Grandpa's. They really get away with a lot while they're there. How do we talk to my parents about this?

Grandparents often feel that time with their grandchildren is limited, and therefore they don't want some little discipline problem that seems trivial to them to spoil a good time. As a result, they tend to overlook some things in order to enjoy the good visit. They want to avoid tears at Grandma's and Grandpa's house. This could be part of the problem.

Another factor is what looks cute to grandparents doesn't always look cute to parents. Your children know they're not supposed to do certain things, and you've been correcting them, but now that they're in front of Grandma and Grandpa, they think they can get away with it. To go about correcting this problem, affirm your parents by telling them you are grateful they love your children and like to have them visit. But then clearly communicate your frustration. Say, "We've been trying to discipline the kids in a certain way and we need your help. We want you to feel we're doing a good job. And when we try to do a good job, we feel like you don't always approve, and that bothers us." I think your parents will understand this. But they won't know how you feel unless you explain it. And after you've explained it, they'll probably feel sorry and things will be OK.

You also need to be aware that we parents try too hard to show our parents that we can be good parents too. As a result, we tend to overdiscipline our children while at Grandma's and Grandpa's house. I know *I* did when I wanted my dad's approval. I think Grandma and Grandpa realize our overdiscipline and try to balance things by jumping on the other end of the teeter-totter. So talk with your folks and keep a sense of humor about the situation. In most cases, this is all that's necessary to arrive at a workable solution.

WE WANT GRANDCHILDREN! ●

My parents and my husband's parents are constantly talking about grandchildren. My husband and I have been married four years. We both have jobs, enjoy our work, and are attempting to establish careers. We do plan to have one child in a year or two, but meanwhile our parents are pushing us so much that we no longer enjoy our visits with them. Are we wrong to wait until I am more established in my career? After all, the child will alter our lives, not our parents' lives.

I have recently become a grandparent and I think I understand a little bit about the primal nature of grandparenting. I couldn't have predicted the rewards I've felt since becoming a grandparent. And that may be part of your parents' secret urge. On the other hand, this kind of conversation is usually more the result of "social ineptitude" than anything else. What I mean by that is your parents may say these things for a lack of something else to say, not really trying to pressure you. It's like talking about the weather, or weight. Who really cares? But people talk about these trivial things all the time. What they're really saying is, "Hey, I want to acknowledge your presence. Let's talk about something I think would be interesting to you."

Because you are career-oriented, you may also be buffeted by all the conflicting arguments about feminism. One set of voices tells you that fulfillment means staying home and raising children, while another tells you there are better ways for a woman to be rewarded. Your parents may have no idea you are struggling with all these kinds of issues. And as you are working these issues through for yourself, it is natural for you to become more sensitive to your present status as well as to your folks' remarks.

Of course, it may be that your parents really are pressuring you to have children. One of the most common reasons they do this is because their values are different than yours and come from another era. That is, very few of our parents enjoyed their youth in the same way that young people do today. Kids of a generation ago didn't have the mobility and usually they didn't have the money. About all they could do at your age was to settle down and have a family. Sailboats, weekends away, sports cars, and going to concerts seem irresponsible and flippant to people your parents' age. "My goodness, if our kids don't start having a family, when they become our age they are going to have nothing. They are going to be all alone."

Your parents may be looking at values differently than you. Realize theirs are good values, but so are yours. Simply smile and come up with a joke that you can say back to them when they ask you when you're going to have children.

WHEN GRANDMA BABY-SITS ●

How do you deal with a grandmother who won't follow through with our requests when she baby-sits. Our daughter is learning that what Mom and Dad say doesn't really have to be done because Grandma always gets her way. We are working parents so she is at Grandma's house more than she is with us. How can we teach Grandmother and our daughter that *our* authority is the final word? My husband is from a strict but happy home, and this is very discouraging to him. He feels a loss of authority. As for me, I'm caught between a rock and a hard place.

Let's look at your options. The first one is a difficult one, and that is to change baby-sitters. When family members are involved and a termination of a relationship takes place, this can be very difficult. But if you feel it has reached the stage of crisis, then you may have to do this very thing. The other option would be to have a serious talk with Grandmother—a professional talk. Don't discuss being a grandmother; discuss baby-sitting. I'm not sure what your financial arrangement is with your mother, but if you don't pay her at all, this further complicates matters. Tell your mother that you will pay her a certain amount of money each day, but as a result of this, it is her responsibility to carry out your wishes for the well-being of your daughter. Be advised that I don't give that approach a lot of hope because I don't think you can change people at her age. Most likely she will react in anger and say, "OK, why don't you get someone else if you don't appreciate me?" Or she will simply say, "I think this has reached the place where we need to renegotiate and you need to find somebody else."

Another suggestion would be to talk with your daughter about the alternatives. Tell her unless she begins to follow your rules, you are going to make a change, and she may well prefer Grandma's house to that. Your daughter needs to be told that you and your husband are expecting a certain kind of behavior because you are her parents. Young people need to be taught that life is full of ambiguities. There are differences between the way the school approaches discipline and the way you approach it at home. Insist that you intend to enforce your approach with her when she is with you, and that's the way it's going to be. At Grandma's house she may get by with certain things, but she's not going to get by with those things when she's at home. Or, if you hear that she is doing things at Grandma's that are displeasing to you or contrary to your discipline, tell her you are going to deal with her disobedience. I think children are capable of understanding that, and if they know you mean business and that you really plan to do something, then they can "shape up and fly right."

HOW TO INFLUENCE GRANDKIDS ●

I want my grandchildren to make the right decisions now that they are teens. Is there any way I can influence them to walk a more spiritual path even though I live so far away?

This concern that grandparents have for their grandchildren is universal not only for the spiritual lives of their grandchildren, but for their total well-being. Grandparents, however, must often watch from a distance and hope that the parents have learned enough to influence their children in the right way.

It is often the motivation of wanting to do something spiritual for our grandchildren that causes the greatest problems. As grandparents, we can get so concerned about our grandchildren's spiritual lives that, if we are not careful, we become little religious machines. The only things we ever say in the presence of our grandchildren are spiritual things. Now the only problem with this is that our grandkids begin to say things like, "Christianity only belongs to grandmas and grandpas. They are kind of odd because they talk about God all the time."

Don't misunderstand. There is nothing wrong with talking about God.

In fact, there is nothing more important. But grandchildren will not absorb or respect what you are saying until you first get to know them as people. Show larger interests, be loving, trusting, patient, and a good listener. Be the things that parents often have a difficult time being. Interestingly, not having this hands-on control that parents have gives you a chance to be a little more objective—to back off the situation and think a little before you have to say something. What you really want your grandchildren to say is, "My grandma is neat. She is a caring person who understands me and listens to me."

I suggest that for every time you talk about something spiritual, talk about five things that are not spiritual in nature. Having said this, let me go against my own advice. One thing you can do for your grandchildren in the spiritual realm is to subscribe to a good Christian magazine for young people like *Campus Life*. It might not be a good idea to tell them you sent it, but just have it start arriving at their house. I've found this is one of the best ways to witness to kids, even kids who aren't going to church or who aren't exposed to Christian things.

NO GOSPEL FOR GRANDMA •

I have six brothers and sisters who are all newborn Christians. But my grandmother is determined to turn us against one another. She complains we are all against her and calls each of us individually to talk about the others behind their backs. My sister wrote a beautiful letter asking her to please stop putting us down and reminding her how much we love her. Grandma denied ever receiving it. The real problem is that slowly we are beginning to quarrel among ourselves even though we know Grandma's accusations are untrue. She thinks we are lunatics because we're Christians. What more can we do for her?

Usually we hear about the grandmother who is concerned about the salvation of her grandchildren. But in our culture, which has been a secular nation for some time, we are beginning to see more and more cases where young people end up being the spiritual leaders of the older ones. This creates a great sociological and emotional problem. When someone is older they feel like they merit some sort of leadership because of their age. But then something a great deal older than Grandmother comes on the scene—the Word of God—and Grandmother becomes, in a sense, subservient to this new authority.

Grandma's problem is probably twofold. First, she's afraid of losing control. For years she has been a leader and an authority, passing along information to you. Now you have gotten new information and she is no longer the final word. Second, it is very possible that she's under conviction. The Holy Spirit may be dealing with her. As younger people, we sometimes find it difficult to believe that older people deal with many of the same problems we deal with. Therefore, Grandmother might react in the same way a friend of yours would react to the Gospel. My encouragement would be to affirm her greatly as a person. Continue to show respect to her as your grandmother. Don't try to teach her things. That will threaten her. Live the Gospel in front of her with what I call practical acts of love and concern, understanding and charity. Call her on the phone. Write to her. Send gifts. Remember her birthday. Ask her advice about things that don't relate to the Gospel.

Help her see that Christianity is not an intruder into your family, but is the normal way that things ought to be, and that it has made you more loving and concerned for her. This "winsome" Gospel will have a way of breaking through to her. At some moment, in tenderness and alone (not all of you ganging up on her), and with the Holy Spirit's guidance, share the Gospel message with her and watch her come to know Christ. It has happened many times before and it can happen with your grandmother.

CHAPTER 5

Dealing with Family Conflict

Many people live in a state of constant guilt over conflicts in their families or in their human relationships. Somewhere, someone sold the idea to many people—especially church-going people—that human beings are supposed to live without conflict. Reality couldn't be farther from this.

Life is filled with conflict and potential conflict. The real issue is not whether or not there is conflict, but how to use conflict in a productive manner for the enrichment of all concerned. The Apostle Paul wrote, "Be angry, and yet do not sin; do not let the sun go down on your anger" (Eph. 4:26, NASB).

I'm eternally grateful that the Bible does not say, "Do not be angry." Anger is a reaction, something we cannot control. It comes from our emotions. A person cannot be commanded not to have an emotion, though he can be commanded to control his actions. Actions, as the term implies, are *active,* while emotions are *reactive.* Therefore when we have conflicts, we can't help feeling certain things.

When a son does something foolish with the automobile, for example, we immediately experience fear. Fear turns to concern, and concern often leads to speaking out. Speaking out, even in anger, has its roots in fear, and that fear is rooted deeply in love. Yet the son hears distrust and lack of confidence in our words. He doesn't know that we're really saying, "I love you." He feels diminished, and he says, "You always treat me like a baby." Conflict results.

Managing conflict is one of the most important sides to human relationships. It is not the purpose of this book to deal in depth with this subject; others have done it very well. I think David Augsburger in *Caring Enough to Confront* has done the finest job on this of anyone who's ever written about it. I highly recommend this book to you as you deal with all kinds of conflict.

Conflict is normal. Yet Christians can handle conflict in a productive manner, and God can be glorified even as a result of working out our conflicts. No one would ever receive forgiveness, for instance, if no one ever had cause to offer forgiveness. We are not taking a Pollyanna approach to family life. We acknowledge that serious conflicts arise between man and woman, parent and child, grandparent and parent, but they can be handled in a way that ensures everyone's happiness and well-being. This approach to handling conflict, incidentally, is not a bad definition for love itself.

WHY ARE KIDS SO STUBBORN? •

Why are kids so stubborn? Why, when we as parents have been through it all before and know what will work and what won't, do they disregard our advice? It frustrates me to have to sit back and watch them fall flat on their faces. I know I won't always be there to instruct them, but is there anything I can do now to let them know I really do know what I'm talking about?

You can tell someone how far it is to the moon and he'll believe you, but if you put up a sign which reads WET PAINT, he'll have to go touch it to see if you're telling the truth. That's basically the story of the human condition.

Throughout history young people have had to try to prove whether or not something is true. In some ways this is the key to advancement in all of science and civilization. However, when we're the ones being challenged or whose authority is being questioned we feel threatened. We don't want to know if our ideas could possibly be improved on. After all, we know what worked for us, but does that necessarily mean it will work for our children?

I believe that as parents we first of all have to have faith in the truth. Notice the account recorded in Acts 5:29-39. The religious leaders were concerned about the rising popularity of the apostles and were making plans to stop them from teaching about Jesus. But Gamaliel, a man of the law, had some wise words of advice. He said, "If their [the apostles'] purpose or activity is of human origin, it will fail. But if it is from God, you will not be able to stop these men (vv. 38-39, NIV). Parents can benefit

72

a great deal from this Scripture. If our advice is correct and true, eventually our children will find that out.

Now, it may not be exclusively true—in other words, your child may find another way to get to the same truth. It's not uncommon for kids to come to the same conclusions as their parents, but from different directions. Even if your kids have to do some stumbling and some testing, and touch some hot stoves, they'll eventually come to the truth. Give your children the truth, but then let them discover why it works.

Many parents go out of their way to rescue their kids, and those kids grow up thinking they will always be rescued—the cavalry is always going to come over the hill and save them from every little problem. This isn't true in real life and it's very cruel to raise kids with such an idea. Kids need to learn certain things on their own, even if it means falling flat on their faces in the process. We, of course, try to keep our children away from the deep life-threatening problems, but in less severe cases, let the cause-and-effect principle operate.

STUNTED GROWTH ●

My parents, especially my mother, won't let me grow up. I'm nineteen years old and still living at home. I still have a curfew of 11 o'clock. Whenever I get home I get twenty questions from Mom about where I've been and what I've been doing. I want to move to an apartment someday, but right now I don't think I'm quite ready for that. Until then, how can I live with this?

I hear this question often, so it must be a generational problem that occurs within each family. Yet, it doesn't get solved from one generation to the next. The problem deals with the struggle for independence. The role of parenthood is to help young people stand on their own two feet. Learning how to let go of your kids is just as hard for parents to learn as it was for them to learn how to raise them.

Basically I think there is only one answer. As a nineteen-year-old you have to ask yourself the question, "Why is my mother doing this to me?" In almost every case, the answer is because she loves you. She does not want you to be hurt; she wants you to have a happy life and grow up in an adjusted manner. She probably asks you a myriad of questions because she's checking out your coping skills and trying to protect you from harm.

You have two choices. The first is to maintain your present status—live with your parents under the current tension. Every time you come home your mother will ask you twenty questions. You'll feel irritated and say, "Don't treat me like a baby," then you'll clam up and not answer her. Your mother will go to bed feeling rejected and hurt. The second choice is fairly simple. It has to do with openness and information. You open your life to your mother and tell her where you are going and what you are going to do. When you get home, you can share with her how your evening went. By giving her an inside road into your life she will begin to develop trust in you. Eventually she will get tired of hearing about your evenings because they all will begin to sound the same.

I encourage you to begin communicating with your mother. What older teens often do is say, "Mom doesn't trust me, so I am going to keep my life separate and I won't share anything with her." But you will always be her daughter and she will always be your mother. Therefore, she will always have an interest in your life. If your mother must pry, make the second choice—it will leave you much happier.

AT ODDS ON CURFEW ●

I may be an old-fashioned father, but I believe curfews are good for kids. My son is now in high school and this has become a problem for us. We agreed that he would have to be home by 10 P.M. on weeknights, but right after we set those rules, he started coming home late. I told him to never let that happen again, but it has, time after time. I've talked to him about responsibility and cooperation but he just isn't responding. Is there some other way I can get him to follow the rules?

I agree with you that it is good to have curfews and I think yours sound reasonable. One thing you might want to add to your curfew guidelines is the possibility of a phone call if your son is going to be late. Tell him, "If you're not going to make it by 10, rather than have your mom and me worry, give us a call." That would alleviate some of the tension. If your son is going to follow any of your rules, there must be some relationship between privilege and responsibility.

Somehow or another a young person has to understand the cause-and-effect relationships that should take place within a family structure. I suggest that you come up with some kind of realistic penalty for not being in by curfew. You can't say, "You didn't get in on time so I'm going to ground you for the next year." That doesn't work. I find a lot of kids caught in unrealistic situations. They say, "My dad has grounded me for six weeks." Well, no one can keep someone grounded for six weeks unless he's running a penal farm. But try something like this: "If you miss curfew tonight you will have to stay home next weekend," or "This weekend we were going to do such and such, but we're not going to do that now." In this way your son will get the idea that for every cause (i.e., missing curfew) there is a corresponding effect (i.e., temporary grounding). This element is missing in many young people's lives today. Too many parents have taken it away and don't realize that there must be a penalty for missing the mark.

MR. KNOW-IT-ALL ●

My son is suddenly a Mr. Know-it-all. I drive the car and he tells me everything I do wrong. We talk about politics and he disagrees with my views. Bring up any subject and he says, "Dad, things are different today than they used to be." I think he's turning into a regular smart aleck.

When young people enter junior high, it is often said that they enter the Sherlock Holmes stage. If you say something happened a year ago on Tuesday, they'll say, "No, it was Monday, Dad." Or you say it happened in the evening, and they'll say it was the morning; they just like to pick, pick, pick, and find the little faults just like Sherlock Holmes used to do. It's part of becoming aware of the world around them and developing some of their first opinions about things. As they get older, of course, and get ready for college they get into deeper questioning.

Teenagers deal with the world from a relatively idealistic viewpoint. They are learning everything from books; learning theories about how things *are supposed* to work. On the other hand, as a parent you've developed your opinions through experience. Your son senses that you're rigid. As a lot of kids say, "You're all mixed up and permanently set like concrete." They feel that you need breaking down. So instead of arguing with your son (which never works), try asking him these questions: "Why do you feel like this? What made you come to this opinion?" Then after he's had his say, tell him how you arrived at your own opinions. And rather than trying to make him agree with you, let him deal with the issues that caused you to think the way you think. He can then make comparisons. It's a matter of *how* you are looking at something rather than the conclusions. You'll find you'll have a lot less tension if you express your opinions to each other instead of trying to change one another.

EARLY TO BED ●

I'm thirteen years old and my parents say I should be in bed by 8:30 P.M. at the latest. I disagree. I think I should stay up at least later than my younger brother. What should I say to my parents to let them know I'm not a child anymore?

Your bedtime does sound a little early unless you are suffering from some kind of physical problem and this is a remedy your doctor has prescribed. Now you might ask yourself, "Why do my parents want me to be in bed so early?" There are probably several reasons, all based on their concern for you and for your home. First of all, most parents want their children to get enough sleep so they will be healthy and do well at school. It sounds like your parents are probably overly concerned about that. It also may be that they want a little peace and a little privacy. Getting the kids off to bed is an important time in the lives of most parents. There is a sense of relief when the children are in bed—another day has ended safely, and all is quiet. This is the only time that many mothers can find a little peace and quiet.

Now, if you have a room of your own, maybe you could go to your parents and say, "Mom and Dad, I understand that you want me to get plenty of sleep, but I think 8:30 is a little too early for bed. I mean I'm the only kid in my class who goes to bed at 8:30. I think I'll still be in good shape if I go to bed at 9:00 or 9:30. Can I go to my room at 8:30 and play or read quietly so that I don't disturb anybody?" Assure them that you just want to stay up longer so that you can have a little time to yourself. Also assure them that you'll go promptly to bed without any further hassle at the time agreed on.

You like to be alone and do things. Moms and dads need this too. It could be that your bedtime is not the real issue. Maybe it's just that Mom and Dad need to talk and have privacy. You say, "Well, I can watch television out there with them and I won't bother them." Yes, but they can't talk about certain things when you are there. I'm sure you understand that.

Another thing you might do is go to some of your friends and take a poll about when they go to bed. Don't choose the worst kids in your class, but the best. Collect some information and sit down with Mom and Dad and share what you've discovered. Of course, you should be careful about this because it may backfire on you. Maybe all the kids are going to bed at 8:15! But I think your assumption is reasonable and I think your folks will probably feel good about your suggestions. Maybe they'll offer a compromise.

LATE AGAIN •

Our twenty-one-year-old daughter stays out very late at night. When she was home from college last summer she would come in at all hours of the morning—once it was 5 A.M. On New Year's Day, she came home at 7 A.M. We've tried to talk to her about how adversely this is affecting her Christian testimony and ours, but she just won't listen. We have an eight-year-old son too, and I'm very concerned about this influence on him as he approaches his teenage years. Once he overheard us talking with our daughter about her late hours and he told us to quit picking on her. We've raised a twenty-five-year-old son and a twenty-two-year-old daughter and never before had this kind of problem.

The first issue is that of protecting your eight-year-old son from the discussions of this issue. It sounds to me like there was some anxiety on your son's part whereby he felt his sister was in some way being attacked or hurt, and so he felt he had to come to her rescue. I encourage you to have these confrontations with your daughter outside his hearing.

Most young people feel that when they reach twenty-one, according to the law and their understanding of society, they are grown-up. Any restriction put on someone who is twenty-one seems artificial and unnecessary. In our society, we start school at five, graduate from high school at eighteen, spend another four years in college, then are thrust out into the "real" world. We have an unspoken rule where, generally speaking, parents feel an obligation to see their children educated through college and to pay for as many expenses as possible. This ends up being quite a strain for the parents, and because of this stress, they feel that if they are paying the bills, they ought to be in control. To the young person, this is interpreted as blackmail.

At this point, a lot of young people will say, "I don't want their money; I won't finish college," and the parents say, "Oh, but we want you to finish college—we'll give you the money and will try our best not to put unreasonable restraints on you." I think this is the kind of tension that you are facing.

At twenty-one, it is very possible for your daughter to move out of your home. You say, "She couldn't make it financially." By the same token, not being able to pay the bills might lead her into some deeper problems, such as living with roommates you wouldn't approve of, or creating a live-in arrangement with some boy, which is very popular among kids her age. You have kind of a no-win situation. The best solution might be to talk to your daughter, not so much about her morality but about your concern for her and the types of relationships she's becoming involved in. Forget about the late hours and talk to her about the real issue.

REPORT CARD BLUES ●

My father keeps nagging and yelling at me about my grades. I'm an average student and on my report card got all C's and B's, except for one D. I've never flunked anything. I try hard, but my dad is always expecting A's.

It is interesting when I hear both sides of this particular problem. It always comes out a little differently. I'll talk to a dad and he'll explain it this way, "I try my best to communicate to my kids that my desire is for them to succeed and to reach their potential. They need good grades to get into college." And then when the young person gets his say, it goes this way, "He yells at me and is always nagging at me." Of course, yelling, to a lot of young people, is anything said to them in a negative way—anything that seems critical. When we know we are not doing our very best, then even a legitimate criticism or concern expressed by a parent sounds like nagging and yelling because it is amplified by our own sense of failure or our own sense of guilt for not doing our best.

Perhaps one thing you could do would be to talk with your school counselor. Maybe your school counselor could call your dad and mom in for a conference and explain to them what type of student you are. If your test scores and other grades show that you are working up to your potential, then your parents are going to have to accept that.

Living up to potential can be a very heavy burden. In fact, Charlie

Brown has put it best in a "Peanuts" cartoon. He says, "There is no weight like a great potential." Perhaps your father's expectations are too high. If you are doing a reasonably good job and are trying your best, getting B's and C's, then perhaps a school counselor can convince your parents that you are indeed working at the level you should be.

In the meantime, understand that if Dad is yelling and nagging, he is doing it because he loves you. If you could stop and think, "He's saying he loves me," while he's nagging at you, that will help a lot.

DAD THINKS HE'S PERFECT ●

My dad thinks he's always right. Every time someone tries to tell him something, he has an "I'm right, you're wrong" attitude. Dad won't go to the doctor because he thinks the doctor is always wrong. He even tries to tell our pastor the "right" way to run a church. This is getting hard on our family. How can we tell him that he may not always be right without hurting his feelings?

There is a prevailing attitude that fathers ought to run tight ships and be in charge of their families so everything always appears under control. So sometimes dads do things to feel like they are in charge. They say things like, "It doesn't matter whether I'm right or wrong, I'm your dad," or "I'm bigger," or "I said it, that's why." Those are, of course, weak reasons, but dads do them just the same because they are trying to live up to some standard, some ideal of what a strong father should be like.

Recognize that you cannot change other people's behavior; you can only change your own. With that in mind, I encourage you to pray for your dad, respect and love him. Don't undermine his authority or always feel, "Oh, no, there he goes again." Give him the respect due him and he may find less need to have to climb to the top of the family mountain, if he already feels he's there.

On the other hand, I think you need to approach your dad in private and say, "Dad, it just seems to me . . ." and then try to explain the situation to him from the "I" point of view, rather than the "you" point of view. For instance: "I have a problem, Dad. I tend to lose my temper because I feel like you are saying you're always right. Now you don't do that, Dad, but I feel like you do." Then back off and watch the situation begin to smooth out.

Believe me, you are not the first person who has felt this way and he's not the first dad who has acted like this. Remember too that the Holy Spirit is at work in your dad's life and is speaking to him. Pray that the Holy Spirit will get his attention to the point where he will feel relaxed enough to let you have your say as well.

STILL WAITING TO DATE ●

Though I'm eighteen, I have yet to go on my first date. My father is very protective. Every time I ask him if I can go out with a guy he says no. He thinks all boys are bad and that they will hurt me in some way. I know I could get hurt, but I have to learn to make my own decisions, and if that means making mistakes, then I am ready for that. I'm a strong Christian and play things pretty straight. I know the world is a corrupt place, but Dad can't keep me home forever. Friends have told me I should go out anyway. But he's my father and I respect him and want his permission. I know God says, "Children, obey your parents," yet I'm considered an adult. So, do I still have to obey Dad?

First, it's good to lower your anger level a little and understand that the reason your father is doing this is because he loves you. He is probably a bit overprotective and I think he's unrealistic and wrong, but he *does* love you and that is wonderful. Second, it is better to be overloved than underloved. To have someone who loves you this much, who is trying to protect you, is a very great asset.

Now, because I think it might help you, let me try to share some insights on how dads feel since I'm a father of a couple daughters myself. By listening to the radio, watching television, seeing boys on the street, and reading statistics, dads get the idea that most boys are bad. They go down to the local convenience store to get a gallon of ice cream and see a group of boys standing out front in T-shirts with cigarettes rolled up in their sleeves and looking quite threatening, and they think, "My goodness, those boys are the kind of boys my daughter goes to school with." It frightens dads to think of their daughters going out with boys like that. What's more, most dads have had some less-than-positive dating experiences when they were growing up and tend to project their own behavior onto these boys and think all boys act like they or their friends did.

What can you do? One suggestion might be to go away to a college in another city if you can afford it. Then your father might feel more

80

secure as he thinks, "My daughter is at college. She is growing up, meeting new people, involved in new activities." That is often a big help to parents. Another thing you might do is talk to your pastor and ask him to talk to your father. This tends to be more effective than having your mother talk to him, though that is the way families usually handle this situation.

I encourage you to gain your independence, and it is best if you can gain it in a peaceful manner. Eventually you have to strike out and be your own person. But do it with love—and firmly.

NO WHEELS, NO DRIVE •

My parents won't let me drive even though I passed Driver's Education and got my license. They say I can't drive until I get my own car. Right now I'm saving for college and a car is out of the question. Every time I want to go to a youth meeting at church or out with my friends, I have to ask my parents to take me, or ask someone else to drive. I think my parents are being unfair.

There is such a thing as teenage life in America without the automobile. It doesn't seem that way when you're sixteen or seventeen, but believe me, your parents have concerns that are legitimate, both for you and for the car. It sounds like they are apprehensive about you driving and want to keep you from facing it until you've reached what they consider to be the proper skill or maturity or whatever. And yet, no matter when you start driving, it's very scary to parents.

I remember our daughter got her license on the day of the first big snowstorm of the year. Hesitantly I watched her back out of the driveway and drive off to a high school basketball game. Well, it got about time for the game to end and I was getting nervous. So, I got in my car and went to the school. I sat there in the driveway a few cars away, hidden like a spy. I saw her come out. First, she took a brush and brushed all the windows of the car so she could see out. (Had I been doing this, I would have probably made a six-inch hole—just enough so I could see—and would have driven off with snow flying off the car.) Then she took off very cautiously out of the driveway. She did everything perfectly. Now my problem was how to get home before she did so she wouldn't know that I had been spying on her. So I raced home, sped into the driveway, tore up the front steps, pulled off my coat, and got into my chair. I was sitting there trying to look very relaxed (while I was panting) when she came in the door. I asked, "How did it go?" I admitted to her later what I had done! We parents can't help but feel this way. We're frightened and want our kids to be safe.

Now, you are fortunate that you have friends who are able to drive. It sounds to me that at some point your folks will give in on this, but in the meantime, don't interpret their rule as being unfair. It does feel unfair, I know, but I'm sure that someday you'll not only drive, but you'll get very tired of driving. You'll get tired of being the one picking up all the other kids for youth group.

TWO-TIMING BOYFRIEND ●

My sister is seventeen and recently got engaged to a guy who is twenty. He's a heavy drinker and can't hold a steady job. The other morning he called asking for my sister. She had already left for school so he continued to speak to my mother. He told my mother he was attracted to her, that he wanted to meet her alone. She was so upset she began to cry and hung up the phone. She told me about the conversation and I called the boy to ask about it. He denied everything and began yelling and cursing at me. He told my sister about my call to him and, of course, she believed him. She doesn't know what her boyfriend said to Mom, and we're not planning to tell her. My sister is very defensive of him and angry with Mom and me. What should we do?

I'd like to help, but this is a very complicated situation. I notice that you leave out all reference to your father so I assume that your mother is raising you girls alone. If you had a father in this situation, I would strongly urge that he confront this young man about the phone call. In either case, I feel your sister should be told. Your mother should sit down with the boy and confront him about what he said on the phone. The end result will probably be the same as it is now. That is, your sister will feel you are both picking on her, trying to keep her from getting married, and taking sides. This type of young man *is* a boy. He doubtless has the ability to state things in a way that twists your sister around his little finger.

Nevertheless, the reason you need to tell her what happened, and the reason your mother needs to confront the young man is that he will repeat his immature behavior—not necessarily with your mother, but with someone else. When this happens, your sister won't believe that either at first, and then another case will come along and she won't believe that either, because when you are in love you tend to allow yourself to be deceived. But eventually the pattern will begin to develop and hopefully before they get married, your sister will begin to see through his behavior and come to her senses. Then she will realize that you have been her friends all along.

I don't think there is any way to play this except straight. Don't try to deal with your sister if she doesn't know what actually happened. Admittedly it is very unpleasant, but your mother needs to face the situation and take the responsibility. It may hurt for a while and your sister may be alienated for a time, but when it's time to do some repair work, you will have a solid foundation on which to begin. Prepare yourselves not to seek some sort of revenge that says, "I told you so." This kind of approach is worthless and detrimental. Your sister wants to hear you, but she can't hear you through her need. And so, because she can't hear you now, you've got to wait until she can. In the meantime, start out on an honest base.

SEPARATED BY PRISON BARS •

I've only been in prison for four months, but already it has caused some serious problems at home. Besides the embarrassment my family suffers, it is very hard for them to carry on a normal home life. Are there any encouraging words I can say to my wife and daughters to make this time a little easier for them? During my imprisonment I have become a Christian.

I'm confident that the situations that led up to your going to prison were not pleasant, yet there is a sense in which you can be grateful for this experience, and your family should be encouraged by it too.

I have the privilege of working with Charles Colson in Prison Fellowship. Since my involvement, I have met many dozens of men and women in situations like yours who have found the Lord while behind bars. Almost without exception, they testify to the fact that they are grateful that they went to prison because through incarceration their old lifestyles ended. Their lives were going in one direction, then they turned around, took a new look, and are now new people able to reconstruct their lives.

From your family's viewpoint this sudden change may be somewhat confusing. That is, they may think, "Well, Dad's in prison and now has a jailhouse religion that he is using to cope. Is it really real?" It's been only four months since your imprisonment so it's going to take a little time for them to become convinced that you are a new person; it's not going to mean immediate acceptance on their part. As your letters to them convey a new kind of quality, as your concern for them becomes deeper, as you grow in Christ, you will be able to convey the nature of the transformation. This will be the greatest encouragement to them.

In the meantime, I encourage you to write to Prison Fellowship, P.O. Box 40562, Washington, D.C. 20016. Tell them about your situation so they can put your family in touch with people who can help. Some of the things your family needs you can't provide right now, and I'm sure this hurts you deeply. Yet, this is one of the main reasons that Prison Fellowship exists.

OUR SON HAS MOVED OUT •

Our nineteen-year-old son has moved out. He started doing all sorts of questionable things, and when his dad and I tried to talk to him, he'd just say, "It will never work for me to live here anymore." And so we let him go. But now I feel we should have held on a while longer. Our fourteen-year-old son is getting all mixed up because his older brother, who was his hero, is off the track. We'd like to sort through all the confusion and come out with God's truth, but our family just seems to be falling apart.

It looks to me as if you've done the right thing. The fact that your son is nineteen is important. If he were only sixteen, I'd feel differently. But a nineteen-year-old boy with a belligerent spirit is probably better off living outside the home.

Frankly, I don't think you have a lot of options. Your son's success or failure is not related to where he's living, but to what's happening inside. If you kept him in your house and he felt rebellious, what would your protection provide for him? You would have given him a place to stay, which would save him some money, but the tension level would be very high. His presence in the home, if his attitudes are negative, might harm your younger son much more than his absence will.

Now that you've let him leave the house, the law of cause and effect will begin to work in his life. He will be responsible for his own decisions;

the only person he can rebel against is himself. This will work unless you interfere and provide him with a safety net. For instance, maybe he is discovering that gasoline costs money. You used to struggle with that every time he drove the car and brought it back empty. He thought you were unfair for objecting then. Now he'll find that without gas, his car will just sit there. So to provide for his car, he will have to find a job. Then he'll find out that employers like employees to get to work on time, and if you're not there on time, someone else will soon have your job.

Your son will be learning thousands of lessons from living on his own. In fact, between now and his twenty-fifth birthday, he will probably decide that you weren't so unfair after all and that some of the things you were saying were actually true. I think you have done the right thing in letting your son go, but it is very difficult to do. Tough love is not easy, and I empathize with your situation.

CHAPTER 6

Adoption

In our modern culture, adoption is not at all uncommon. There is some trauma in all adoption—after all, it usually results from death, divorce, abandonment, or premarital sex—yet negative impact on the innocent can be lessened by thoughtful approaches.

An adopted child starts a new life without a foundation. The adoptive parent sometimes feels as if he is building the missing foundation under a house that's already been built. The process may be difficult, but it *can* be done. With care, the adopted young person's life can sit on a solid foundation as if it had started out in the finest of circumstances.

Adoption is often a fine opportunity for loving, responsible people to show their concern for victims of circumstances beyond their control. But because it is the exception rather than the norm, it requires some unusual responses at time. I offer these insights with the prayer that they will bring happiness and security into the lives of some who feel afraid, unloved, and unsure of themselves.

MIXED EMOTIONS ●

We are thinking about adopting a child, but are experiencing some very mixed feelings. We're afraid we won't love an adopted child as much as we would our own natural child. How can we deal with these feelings, and could we successfully raise a child in spite of them?

First of all, you need to spend time talking with an objective counselor, someone who knows both of you very well and can give you insight into your feelings. Then it would be a good idea to talk with parents of adopted children and see how they have dealt with this.

I think there's a lot more talk about family planning than really takes place in the world. Most children are born as kind of a surprise. I've often thought that we have this nine-month waiting period so the parents can get prepared. I suppose God could have arranged pregnancy and birth any way He wished; children could be born full-grown if that's what He wanted. But He has chosen to allow us nine months to get used to the idea.

This waiting time is especially helpful to fathers. A lot of men I've talked to feel that it takes several months or even years to get used to a child. An infant is very mother-oriented at first, and the father feels a little left out. Then as the child starts responding to him and he's able to play with the child, he grows to feel comfortable about fatherhood. Even a natural child has to grow on you, so it would be too much to expect to love an adopted child instantly and totally.

There are two ways to analyze any situation: with our minds, and with our feelings. Some people rely almost totally on impulse, and others try to do everything analytically. I think most situations require both kinds of analysis. If your mind says yes—you know that you want a child, that you can take care of one economically, and so on—then start to move ahead. But if the caution light begins flashing, it may be that your feelings are saying something to your mind that your mind can't quite accommodate. You need to look at what your feelings are saying, and until the caution light starts functioning normally, I'd move very, very slowly. But in the meantime, do seek the counsel of your pastor or some other person who knows you and loves you.

WHAT ABOUT INFERTILITY? ●

My husband and I have been trying unsuccessfully to have children. We've been through every fertility test imaginable. I've prayed about the problem and asked the Lord to remove my desire for children if that was what He wanted. Sunday mornings at church are the most difficult times. All the women my age are busy chasing after their children and I don't fit in. I try not to let anyone see

how I'm crying inside. Maybe you have some encouragement for hurting couples who can't have children.

Lynne Benke heads an organization called Stepping Stones which deals with this whole area of infertility and adoption. She tells me that ninety percent of all infertility has a physical cause. Of this ninety percent, thirty-five percent are female problems, thirty-five are male problems, and the remaining cases are a combination of factors. Fifty percent of all physical infertility problems can be cured. So Lynne's first suggestion is to seek competent medical help.

Lynne also has put together a newsletter which you can receive by writing Stepping Stones, Box 11141, Wichita, Kansas 67211, and asking for the brochure "Stepping Stones." This organization is a very serious and deeply committed Christian group that is trying to deal with the ethical and biblical ramifications of this whole subject, including the important aspects of adoption.

I have run into numerous situations where couples have had natural children after first adopting. This has to do with the psychological aspect of a person's ability to have children. This type of infertility problem is much less common and is what I would call a long shot. But nonetheless, if all other methods have been exhausted, it may pay to seek a competent counselor or other psychological help.

Often people who desperately want children adopt them for the wrong reasons. A competent organization like Stepping Stones can help you deal with the real issue of why you want children and how you can go about having children, either by adoption, or naturally. I would still encourage you, however, to seek competent medical help and maybe even some psychological help if nothing turns up on the medical side. And don't rule out the possibility that God could have a very good reason for you to remain childless at this time.

HOW WILL "OUR" KIDS REACT? ●

My husband and I would like to adopt a foster child into our home. We have two children of our own, eight and ten, but as Christians we believe we could provide a good home for one who is not so fortunate. We've discussed this and prayed about it and it appears that the Lord is leading us in this direction. But we're not sure how our own children will be affected. Is there a good way

we can prepare them for this addition to our family? How can we make this transition smooth for everyone?

I hope that you have discussed this with your children. Kids ages eight and ten, in fact even younger than this, feel much more a part of things if they are allowed to discuss the issue and be involved in the decision. This approach accomplishes several things. One, it helps children learn how the decision-making process works. Two, it helps them understand the situation they are getting into; and three, it helps them to feel a part of things.

One of the things your children need to understand is what it means to be a foster child. Many times kids get the idea that if someone is a foster child there must be something bad about him or that he's done something wrong. Your kids need to realize that foster children are usually victims of bigger people, and circumstances larger than they can control, like parent problems, death, drugs, or alcoholism. Explain to your children that this foster child is coming to live with you because he didn't have things as good as your children have had them, or that he has some problems to deal with that are much bigger than your kids have had. Sometimes he may act up and do things simply because he hasn't had the same kind of love and support that your family is used to. It is very important to discuss these things with your children beforehand so they know what to expect. By knowing what to expect, they can help the foster child in as smooth a way as possible.

I would encourage you to consider a foster child that is younger than your children. You may run into difficulties adopting a teenager because your natural children might pick up wrong behavior patterns. But if you get a younger foster child, then your kids will feel important and will usually want to pitch in and help the new child.

If your family is in it together, adopting a foster child is a very noble idea and can be something the Lord will really bless.

SPECIAL TREATMENT? ●

We have a seventeen-year-old adopted son whom we love very much. We took him to church until he was about fifteen, when he decided he didn't want to go any longer. He now drinks beer, smokes pot, and keeps bad company. I even got a part-time job so that I could help him out with gas money for his car. In

exchange for this he was to help me around the house. But he doesn't help and still expects more from us. His grandmother feels that because he is adopted he should be treated better than our other son.

Many people who adopt children carry a bit of insecurity about being adoptive parents. They say, "I know that the adopted son or daughter has needs that perhaps my own children don't have. He has had a disqualifying mark put on him, some sort of earlier problem. Therefore, I must treat him much better than my own children." They constantly overreact in trying to make up for the child's past. A young person often senses this and plays along by saying, "I've done you some great favor by letting you adopt me," and uses this attitude against the parents. Often the adopted child does this subconsciously, but nevertheless the attitude is there.

I think you have made a basic mistake in getting a job so your son can have gas money; he should earn his own. He should also do work around the house out of gratitude for his home and for the food on the table. Your natural son ought to show similar appreciation. I think you need to cut off his fried chicken, as it were, and let him begin to work if he wants some money. Help him to begin to understand the law of cause and effect, where he must give up something (his time through hard work) to get something (the reward and satisfaction of making some money). Believe me, love and respect are not won by handing life to children on a silver platter.

Disciplines within the workplace are often much firmer than those at home, and people learn life's real boundaries. In the home environment kids often learn to manipulate parents, grandparents, and other family members. Now, Grandmother feels that he needs a different kind of treatment. Different, yes, but not better. There is no doubt that many adopted children have certain insecurities and we should think about those when we are dealing with them. But sometimes by thinking about those insecurities and overreacting, we further complicate the problem. I think your son needs to accept the fact that he is adopted, understand that he is loved no more and no less than your other child, and work from there.

ADOPT MY SISTER'S BABY? ●

My husband and I have been considering adoption for the past few months. My sixteen-year-old sister is pregnant and wants to give the baby to us because she feels incapable of raising a child at her age. My husband and I have discussed this and we would love to adopt the baby, but we are worried about my sister returning to us someday and asking for her child back. What should we do?

First of all, you are thinking very clearly when you state that your sister might return someday and ask for the child. I agree. I think she will because a mother's bond for her own child is one of the strongest human emotions. This kind of situation is going to be more and more common as the Christian church begins to address critical issues like abortion. People have become casual about abortion. As a result there aren't as many children today available for adoption as in the past. Your sister is not following this tragic approach and I commend her for it. However, her decision creates other very large responsibilities—the greatest of which is that her child needs to be responsibly cared for.

In this case the best possible solution, in light of your sister's age and the apparent absence of the child's father, is probably to let the child be adopted by a Christian family through a responsible lawyer. In this way, the child can have anonymity and the possibility of his life being disrupted at a later time would be minimized. There are many wonderful Christian folks who want to adopt children and would love to give the child a Christian home. That is a situation for you to think through and pray through very carefully along with your pastor, your sister, and your parents.

Now the second issue has to do with your own desire to adopt a child. Let me encourage you to make your desires known to your pastor or to an adoption agency so that these folks can begin to work on finding a situation for you much the same as your sister's. By avoiding possible family conflicts down the road, things will be much smoother and much fairer to everyone concerned.

It is possible that your sister will not like this idea, and will decide she wants to keep the child. If so, I suggest that she accept her responsibility as mother and that you treat her as mother. Help her raise the child and provide the support and the surrogate parent-type relationships the child needs until your sister has grown into adulthood and has found a husband who is able to help raise the child in a responsible manner. The early church was filled with these kinds of situations and I believe the Lord Jesus specializes in helping people through such difficulties.

SABOTAGING HIS OWN SUCCESS •

We have a fourteen-year-old son whom we adopted when he came to the United States from Korea at age eight. We've done everything we can think of to give him a healthy self-image and a knowledge of love. This school year he has decided that no one can tell him what to do. He doesn't do any homework. He's also been caught with chewing tobacco and was suspended for three days. For a while he seemed to be getting his act together, primarily because he wanted to wrestle on the school team. But he became so upset when he was pinned in his first match that he had a chew on the way home. He's probably off the team because of that. Wrestling was his only motivation for getting his work done. He's told us that if we try to ground him he'll go back to the streets or kill himself. Why does he sabotage his own success?

Try to accept the fact that your son's behavior is typical for a kid his age. For instance, most people would find chewing tobacco either repulsive or humorous. But in fact, it's a big thing with high school kids today. I'm sure it's a passing fad.

Don't overdo the fact that this boy was on the streets in Korea until he was eight years old. Yes, this has doubtless affected him in some way, but probably much less than you think. What probably affects him most is his racial difference. There just aren't a lot of Korean kids in small towns. So because your son is different, he feels he has to prove something. He has to show his friends that Korean kids, though they are smaller in stature, are just as tough as American kids. On top of all this, he has been adopted. He didn't ask to be adopted and loved by you, so he probably feels the need to prove something to you as well. He just doesn't know how to do it.

I think, generally speaking, teachers can handle this situation better than parents. When a boy quits studying and breaks school rules, teachers are usually pretty skillful at applying the kinds of pressures he needs to get him to do his homework and be a responsible student. When Mom tries to do it, things usually backfire. Don't make more of this problem than you should. Allow him to go through this stage. Work with the school guidance counselor and his teachers to find out how you can be supportive of their efforts at school, and how they may be able to assist you in dealing with at-home problems.

NOT ACCEPTED ●

Our adopted son is having a tough time feeling accepted. His classmates have made fun of him (he's in grade school), and even his brothers and sisters don't include him in all their activities. What can we do to help our son? We adopted him as an infant.

The first and most helpful thing you can do is to stop thinking of him as adopted. If he was adopted as an infant, then he's part of your family and he doesn't remember not being a part of your family (nor do his brothers and sisters). The only way they would think of him as adopted is if you keep reminding them. Parents do the same thing when a child has had a broken bone. After a lengthy healing process, you finally let him out to play and he starts doing the things that everyone else does. But immediately you start thinking how fragile he could still be and begin to worry that he'll hurt himself again. As a result, you tend to protect him from the very things he needs—exercise and normality and being with the other kids.

Acceptance problems are growing-up problems that all children face—especially in grade school. They have hurts and they are lonely. And kids can be very cruel. This cruelty is part of human nature. If you are a Christian you understand that all have sinned and come short of the glory of God. Those who have these fanciful ideas that young people haven't sinned or don't understand sin don't know much about kids. Even Christian kids struggle.

Why won't his other sisters and brothers include your adopted son in their activities? If you take a moment to reflect on your own childhood you can probably remember your mother saying, "Won't you play with your little brother or your little sister?" All brothers and sisters feel this way at one time or another.

This child needs to be allowed to be a typical child growing up with all the hurts and pains that growing up involves. How can you help? You can help by affirming your son, by loving him, by holding him, by drying his tears, by pushing him outdoors and making him try again. You can do the things that most other good parents do, but above all, forget that he's adopted.

I LOVE HER BUT . . . ●

I have a seventeen-year-old adopted sister who, since she was twelve, has been in a lot of trouble. Though my mother tried disciplining and loving her, things kept getting worse until she was finally placed in a girls' home at age thirteen. She ran away from there time after time. Since then, she has been in jail and in several foster homes. Now that my sister is seventeen, she is to be placed in the home of the nearest relative, which happens to be me. I'm twenty-five years old, happily married with two children. I love my sister and want to help in some way, but my husband is adamantly against her living with us. What should I do if I'm asked to take her in?

The authorities who are handling the placement of your sister won't try to place her in a home where she is not welcome. In fact, I think you and your husband are a bit young to be helping someone her age. A twenty-five-year-old and a seventeen-year-old in a live-in relationship is not very easy. I think your husband is wise. This kind of relationship would probably not work unless your sister could live in an apartment next to yours. But it sounds like she needs the attention of a loving and caring parent.

Youth for Christ has been involved for many years in a program called Youth Guidance. Youth Guidance deals with troubled youth who have various kinds of problems. Not all of them have gotten in trouble with the law, but they are either truant or have family or school problems, and so forth. Many cities have a whole staff of individuals who are trained to help people like your sister. This is how the program usually works: We get a call from a judge, pastor, school counselor, teacher, or parent. Our staff member will attempt to establish contact with the troubled young person by just meeting with him and getting to know him. After establishing a rapport and building a little bit of relationship, we try to become friends. When we become friends, we attempt to help the young person rebuild his life and hopefully lead him to Christ.

I think this is the same kind of approach you can take with your sister. First, you need to be a friend to her without moralizing, without taking sides. Begin to build a relationship with her. Without that relationship, you simply can't help her. If she won't respond to your friendship, then frankly the people who work with her in the courts and the juvenile system will have to do the best they can.

| CHAPTER 7 |

Stepparents and Stepchildren

"His, hers, and ours" is not really all that humorous. In fact, blended families provide some of the most challenging realities in modern family life. Several songs say that it's better the second time around. Perhaps this is true in some situations, but it doesn't happen by chance.

Greater understanding, empathy, and care have to go into step-relationships than into natural family relationships, because, as the old phrase goes, "Blood is thicker than water." We will forgive our natural parent or our own child for things we find hard to accept from those not related to us. Pettiness, jealousy, and vindictiveness too often characterize step-relationships. Whether it's a young person who cannot accept a new stepparent or a father who simply does not understand his acquired stepchildren, the possibilities for pain, misunderstanding, injury, and long-term alienation are great.

People don't always consider the problems that may arise when they fall in love with someone who has a ready-made family. People who have come to Christ for forgiveness and have asked Him for a new start in life need to think carefully about the concerns of those who never asked to be thrust into this new situation. Blended families can work out well, but this is not automatic. According to Romans 8:28, "All things work together for good to them that love God, to them who are the called according to His purpose." Loving God means loving His children and finding ways to apply grace and understanding in difficult situations. A successful stepparent has to be utterly fair. Just as God is no respecter of persons, so there is no place in the stepparent-stepchild relationship for playing favorites or acting petty. Blended families require largeness of spirit and understanding hearts.

NO ONE'S ON MY SIDE •

My husband has two boys from a previous marriage. We have one child of our own. His boys have no respect for me. Whenever there is an argument, my husband will take the boys' side, not mine. When the boys lie, he believes them, not me. I have prayed about this, but don't seem to get any answers. I really don't know what to do.

Remarriage almost always brings additional complications into the picture. I find that many couples are aware that new difficulties will result, but they fail to go a step further by asking what those difficulties will be. With stepchildren, this is the kind of situation you run into. It just isn't as easy winning the respect of a ten-year-old whom you've recently met as it is winning the respect of a child you've known from birth. And who knows if your boys have any respect for authority of any kind, let alone respect for you?

It seems you have a two-pronged problem, and I encourage you to consider both sides. The first issue is that this is a problem between you and your husband, not between you and the boys. You need to confront your husband with this situation and discuss it. He needs to understand that there is no way you can take responsibility for these boys unless you have the privilege of their respect and his support. He is the one who can help you get that respect.

The second side is this. Very often because of our own need for acceptance and love, we long for continual assurance from others. In a situation like this we sometimes get into a tug of war over the affections of others. You may be saying to yourself—even unconsciously—"Does my husband love me as much as he loves those boys? How do I know he loves me more than he loves them? To find out, I'll have to set up some tests." If you are not careful, this kind of game-playing can consume you, whereby every little thing that happens—every yes and every no—becomes a kind of weight to throw on one or the other side of the scale. You'll try almost anything to get the other person's attention. I don't know how severe the boys' problems are. They may be very severe. But, it is possible that what you really need is not so much an answer on how to deal with these boys, but how to deal with your own sense of insecurity about how much your husband really loves you.

Frankly, I am of the opinion that the husband-wife relationship takes priority over parent-child relationships. You and your husband need to make your relationship so secure that you're working with, not against, each other.

NEW DAD FEELS BAD ●

I remarried about a year ago and am having some difficulties with my children from my first marriage. They range in age from ten to sixteen. The problem is that they tell me their new dad will never be like their old one. They just won't accept my husband or the fact that he's now their father. He feels very badly about this and has made many attempts to win them over. What can I do or say to my children to bring them around?

First of all, your children are right. Their new father will never be like the old one. Because these men are two different people, to ask the one to replace the other is unfair to everybody concerned. At ten and sixteen, children do not as easily adapt to stepparent situations as do children under ten or over nineteen.

Your children probably feel robbed, unsure about the conditions of the divorce. They don't quite know who was responsible and may feel guilty. If divorce was not involved and your former husband died, your children could be struggling with a deep sense of loss, asking why this could have happened to them. In death especially, people are lifted up to a higher level, in an almost reverent way. So if you speak negatively about your former husband in any way, casting the slightest doubt on him, your children will immediately rally to his side. Teenagers are inherently idealistic and really want to be fair about everything. In fact, this is the time of life when you've got to teach them that life is not always fair. But because of kids' inherent sense of fair play, if they sense that you are speaking unfairly about their father, they will jump to his side and be loyal to him even to the exclusion of his faults. So begin by always speaking positively of your former husband and affirming him. Your present husband may not like that, but if he wants to be accepted by your children, it is one of the only ways.

You can also help your children understand that things will never be the same. When they say, "He's never going to be like my dad," acknowledge that they are absolutely right. But by the same token, their new dad is unique in his own way. So insist on polite and courteous behavior. They should treat him nicely, not because he's their new dad or because they expect something special from him, but because he is a human being, and therefore worthy of respect. Then help your husband as he attempts to establish a relationship with them. If he is consistently courteous and thoughtful; responsible toward them in every way; not doting or indulgent, but sincerely loving; then your children will have the responsibility of making a decision. And in most cases, they'll come around, given time.

CAUGHT IN THE MIDDLE ●

My son is in the seventh grade and my husband dislikes him and outwardly shows it. He's my natural son, and my husband's stepson. I walk a tightrope between the two, trying to keep peace. We've argued a lot over what my husband calls a smart mouth or the big-baby attitude. I say this is natural for a boy his age, but my husband says he just will not put up with it. I'm afraid he's going to break my son's spirit. His grades are already falling and I'm concerned that our whole family relationship is being permanently damaged.

When people remarry, it is common to assume that the kinds of problems they had in their first marriages won't reappear in the second. This isn't necessarily so. Your present husband may see your former husband in this son and resent it. He may feel he is competing with the boy for your attention. He could actually become jealous because he wants all of your attention and not just part of it. Of course, if you mentioned this to him he would feel embarrassed, but many husbands are indeed jealous of their stepchildren. And the fact that you were formerly someone else's wife is deeply seated in this feeling of resentment. It sounds as if your husband just can't deal with it.

Add to that the fact that boys in the seventh grade can be very exasperating. You hear of the terrible twos, but I would say there is hardly an age which can be as exasperating as the junior high years. This is because the children have grown to a pretty good size physically and mentally, but emotionally they are just basket cases. Very often, they do all kinds of immature and unpredictable things.

I suggest a couple of specific courses of action. One, don't always try to balance the teeter-totter by jumping on your son's side. This will only aggravate your husband's resentful and competitive feelings. When your husband is right, you need to stand on his side. Two, talk to your son about being disrespectful. This is not something which just comes with being in the seventh grade. This comes with being an undisciplined young boy. Insist that your son treat his stepfather with respect. In addition, you need to talk frankly with your son about the reality of the new marriage situation. Finally, realize this kind of problem may never be totally solved. You can, however, work toward a peaceable understanding for all involved.

CHAPTER 8

Married Children

This one can really sneak up on you. Most parents set goals, saying, "If I can just get them out of high school," or "If I can just get them through college," or "Once they're married. . . ." We think that when our children have reached a certain stage, our parenting role will be over. But it doesn't work that way.

A while back I said to my wife, "I thought when we got them all married and the weddings were paid for, we could just kind of sit back and relax." She responded, "When does God stop being your Father?" I then realized that just as God is my Father as long as I live, so I will be my children's father as long as they live—even if they develop bald heads or have grandchildren of their own. Parenting married children is simply a new phase in the relationship.

Since this is my current stage, I will testify that it is, of all parenting experiences so far, the most rewarding for me. This is probably because more things come up with my children that match what I face in my own life. My married children and I talk about vocation, parenting, finances, politics, and other aspects of adult life. So even a parent who had trouble reaching back into childhood and identifying with small children can enjoy the delightful and challenging experience of parenting married children.

HELPING WHEN THEY'RE GROWN ●

We want to help our married children get started in life (down payment on a house, car, etc.) but we don't want to impose on them. Would we be meddling in their affairs if we asked to help?

There's a great deal of biblical precedent for parents helping children. The old patriarchs on their deathbeds often passed on blessings and inheritances to their children.

Perhaps we Americans are especially sensitive about parents helping their grown children because our forefathers came to this country pretty much on their own. In fact, many of them came to escape the European aristocratic system where inherited wealth was passed on from generation to generation. American writers not only extolled the virtues of democracy, they also talked about the virtues of self-reliance.

Self-reliance is an excellent virtue, but if it is carried to extremes, it can lead to individualism and a commitment to going on one's own. This is the opposite of family spirit. Many parents tell me that one of their greatest joys comes from helping their married children.

Of course, parents have to examine their motives. They need to ask themselves, "Is this a method of manipulation? Am I using my gifts as a way of control, a way to get my children to do what I want and to depend on me?" None of us would want to admit that we are trying to manipulate our adult children, but we all have to watch out for holdovers from their childhood. That is, the very care we gave them when they were children can cause us to want to manage their adult lives in much the same way.

If you want to help your married children, you could approach them like this: "Here's a possibility we'd like you to think about. We're able to loan you (or would like to give you) this much toward a house (or a car or whatever). We thought it might help you get started. Our parents helped us get started, and we're very grateful for the love they showed us. We'd like to pass this blessing on to you." Allow the children to talk about it and think about it themselves. Then together you can decide on the terms—if it's to be a gift or a loan, or whatever conditions you want to put on it.

The economics of today's world are such that very few young people are able to buy a house without some sort of help. And a good many of the tensions in their lives are related to this very issue. For example, both of them are working in order to save enough money for a down payment. By the time they get it together, the cost of houses has gone up, and so have interest rates. They discover that in order to maintain the payments, they will both have to continue working. This causes them a great deal of anxiety. When can they start their family? Many young couples have said to me, "By the time we're able to afford to have children, we'll be too old."

And so I believe that parents who are truly able to give without attaching strings, who are not manipulative, and who desire to help out of a heart of love and joy can be a great blessing to a young couple. Of course, in some situations, for whatever reason, the young people want to do it on their own. They resent help, perhaps seeing it as an insult to their self-reliance. In such cases it is wise for parents to hold back. They may be able to devise a way to loan the money rather than give it outright, and thus preserve their children's independence.

HARMFUL HANDOUTS? ●

How much responsibility do parents have toward their grown children? My two brothers, now in their thirties and with families of their own, are constantly appealing to my parents for financial handouts. My brothers aren't in need. Money goes toward vacations or new cars or other luxuries. When my parents object to giving these handouts, they are accused of not being good parents or good Christians. My parents are deeply hurt by this. Just how much is a Christian parent to give?

This is an individual matter and must be decided by each parent, but here is my opinion. After a parent has helped a child through adolescence and perhaps even through a college education, handouts of all types should stop. I think the kind of relationship you described can be very corruptive, resulting in deep problems. I have nothing against parents loaning money to children. I have nothing against them loaning it at low interest rates, but I think if parents *constantly* dole out money to their grown children, they are setting themselves up for a lot of hurt.

For instance, it would appear that your parents are searching for assurance that they are loved by your brothers, and feel that if they cut off the money they won't be loved. It would indeed be hard to face the truth if they did stop giving money and the kids did respond in an irresponsible manner. This fear of rejection, unfortunately, keeps feeding a potentially dangerous situation.

Your brothers are involved in a kind of emotional blackmail, and it's very ugly. I don't know how you can help your parents with this dilemma except to simply let your brothers know how you feel. Don't be spiteful toward them, but do let them know that the principle of what they are doing is wrong. Then support and encourage them to discontinue this arrangement.

One of my most respected friends in the area of finances is a millionaire several times over. He has decided that now that his children are grown he is going to give all of his money to God's work. Why? Because he does not want to corrupt his children or grandchildren. He feels that each of his children ought to be responsible for "paddling his own canoe"—not for financial reasons, but for reasons of character-building. He has already given them wonderful educations. They have had great opportunities in life—vacations and luxuries. But he really believes that his children would handle their money more wisely if they earned it themselves rather than inheriting it.

DEMANDING EQUAL TIME ●

I realize special times with families are important. But holidays and other social family times are becoming increasingly difficult because both my husband's parents and my parents live near us and get jealous when they think we're spending more time with the other set of parents. It's beginning to put a strain on our marriage because each of us is put on the spot by our respective parents. What's your advice?

Both my parents and my wife's parents live about two hours away. And so every holiday we deal with this dilemma. I've begun to associate it with Excedrin headache number 79!

I think the only way to handle this problem is to make some concrete plans. Fairness is extremely important, especially fairness about time and family traditions. Some family traditions are different than others and this can help a great deal. For instance, some families celebrate Christmas on Christmas Eve, some on Christmas morning. If both do it on Christmas morning, then you've got to come up with some alternatives as well as some compromises. It does help to sit down and simply express to both sets of parents that you're being torn by their demands. Your parents should know how you feel—that you really want to spend time with them, but they must be willing to share.

Year to year it's good to say, "Now let's see, this Christmas we'll spend the morning with this set of parents and next Christmas it's the morning with the other set of parents." You will have to keep some records in order to be fair. Believe me, your parents will probably keep track. These are tangible expressions of love and care. Now, if you do this only at holidays, then you haven't built up any equity. I think that phone calls, letters, cards, visits during other parts of the year help negate some of the pressure brought on by holidays. There's no substitute for real communication, sitting down and working these things through. Explain the situation to your parents, but above all, be fair.

MARRIED AND IN COLLEGE ●

After a year of college my daughter and her boyfriend decided they wanted to get married. We urged them to wait until they were out of school because we told her that once she got married we would no longer be financially responsible for her. But they married anyway. They are both still in school and are really struggling financially. We feel responsible to help them out, but we did draw the line before and told them we wouldn't. Should we turn back on our words and help them?

Step back from the situation and recall the real reason you told your daughter you wouldn't be financially responsible for her if she got married. This is a very common thing for us parents to say and it seems sensible. But why do we say it? Often parents use it as kind of a veiled threat—a way of controlling the young person to make sure he completes his education before getting married. However, in your case, as in most, it didn't work. Now you have cut yourselves off from the opportunity to be the kind of help you want to be.

There are some other good reasons why you might have made this statement. You may have wanted your daughter and her boyfriend to accept their own responsibility. But I think if all people who are now middle-aged and have kids this age were to look back and ask themselves, "Did we really paddle our own canoes? Did we really make it on our own?" we might have to acknowledge that we got occasional help. These kinds of gestures didn't cripple us or make us dependent; they were just nice gestures made by people who wanted to help us along the way.

Of course, it doesn't hurt to go back and talk to young people or anybody else and say, "We've reconsidered our logic. I don't know just how we came to it the first time, but we've thought about it again and have decided that we were hasty. There's no reason why we can't help, but let's help in a different way." I think one thing parents can do for young people that's very helpful is a noninterest loan; this gives the young people a real break and causes them to accept responsibility for repayment. Also, since you're the parents of the daughter, you need to think about the young man's self-esteem. That is, will this depreciate his person? Will he feel as if you're convinced he can't adequately care for her? It may be better if they go to his folks for help rather than to you. But this is something that varies from family to family. Only you truly know your family's situation.

WE'VE STOPPED BAILING •

My daughter and her husband have one child, another on the way, and are struggling financially. Her husband has gone from job to job and there have been periods when he hasn't worked at all. During their five years of marriage they have come to us for financial help and we have given them money and extended loans which have been halfheartedly paid back and then forgotten about. They are constantly overcharging on their credit cards and seem to be compulsive spenders. My husband and I have concluded that we are not helping by bailing them out every time they get into trouble. We told them we wouldn't help anymore and some hurtful words were exchanged. Did we do the right thing, or are we being too harsh? We have two sons in college and another in high school and we need to think of them too, as well as our own retirement.

I think in principle you have done the right thing. But it's sort of like when the kids were younger and made a lot of noise around the house. You allowed them to progress from normal play to an uproar until you finally had enough. Then you told them to stop and expected them to immediately go back to docile play. However, they needed time to wind down in the same way they wound up. The same problem is true with our older children if we haven't conditioned them over the years to know where zero is. That is the biggest problem people face in a world of credit— finding zero. Because we can buy almost anything we want even though we don't have the money, we learn to live in deficit; we learn to get immediate gratification rather than postponing it. Then suddenly we find ourselves in over our heads, and of course Mom and Dad are the logical people to go to for help. It sounds like you have been encouraging the spending habits of your daughter and her husband by bailing them out every time they need help. I'm not saying you and your husband are entirely at fault, but I'm sure if you think about it, you have contributed to the problem.

The method you use to solve the problem is equally as important as the decision to solve it. It sounds to me as if perhaps you have decided things more abruptly than you could have. It will help to sit down with your son-in-law and daughter and go over the numbers with them, if they're willing. Look at the deficit and then dispassionately begin to work together to get out of the hole you have mutually gotten into; begin to make some decisions that will down the road lead to a realistic view of credit and a realistic view of your own futures as well.

We need to be very careful about getting involved financially with family members or close friends because of the emotional strings that are attached. We often lay ourselves open to trouble.

SHE DIDN'T PLAY THE FIELD •

Our eighteen-year-old daughter is getting married in a couple of months. She seems to be a very mature young lady and is certain that this is the fellow she wants to spend her life with. But this is the only boy she has ever dated and we're concerned. We're afraid that someday she'll resent the fact that she never dated anyone else. Her financé is a fine young man, but we don't want her to miss out on a part of growing up. We want to be supportive of them and help them in any way we can, but we are concerned.

Your concern is natural and well-founded. What you *do* with the concern is the important thing. If you mention your concern to your daughter every day of the week you'll plant this thought in her life as a kind of time bomb that may explode later. Yes, your daughter will someday resent the fact that she did not date anyone else. At some point she will feel she has missed out on growing up. Don't think she might—she will. What she does with these feelings, however, will make the difference between a marriage that will work and a marriage that will fail. When some people have these thoughts, they immediately go out and have an affair with someone else or get out of their marriages and try to relive their youth. So, at this point, what she does and what you do are very important.

It sounds as if you've stated your case and she has said, "But, Mom, you don't know how much in love we are. We're more in love than anybody has ever been. We're special; we're different." The truth of the matter is, they are right. They *are* special. They *are* different. Every love relationship in the world is special and unique. Your daughter likes her present situation and has decided to pursue it further into marriage. And if you do oppose this marriage and create a family scene, it will blossom into a problem that may take years to correct.

Accept this marriage and begin to support your daughter and her fiancé. Pray for them. Help them in every way. Be ready to lift them up when they fail, and to encourage them. The most important thing you can do for your daughter is to encourage her to work her way through these problems when they do appear rather than to let her bail out and run from them.

It is interesting that when you analyze married people they seem to fall into two categories. One group runs into a problem and immediately pulls the switch, looking for some way out. They don't face it. The other group says, "OK, there is a problem, but we'll work our way through it and see ourselves to the other side." Your daughter's age is not nearly as important as her grasping this spirit of working through problems and seeing them to the end.

Living with Your Spouse

I don't think God ever had a better idea than marriage: creating man as male and female, allowing the two to become one, asking us to commit ourselves to another human being whom we can love and by whom we can be loved. Intrinsic to the marriage relationship is the whole dimension of our sexuality, a capacity that allows us to experience, in addition to our social relationship, a profound physical relationship that binds our spirits and lives together.

The sexual relationship can be the deepest intimacy we will ever experience, but only if it happens within marriage according to God's plan. When people try to duplicate marriage by living together without lifelong commitment, their relationship turns out to be empty and hollow. In order to have a totally intimate relationship, we must experience sex in the context that God intends. When we do, we find marriage to be life's most fulfilling and satisfying relationship. No wonder the enemy of our soul desires so much to attack us in this area—it is the very center of God's revelation of His oneness with mankind.

CHAPTER 9

Before the Wedding

We shouldn't hold it against young people that they think of their wedding as the most important thing in life, and yet anyone who has experienced much of life and marriage knows that the kind of marriage they will have after the wedding is much more important than the wedding itself. I often wish as I counsel young people planning weddings that I could see the same intensity about preparing for marriage as they have about selecting the candles and flowers and cake.

I suppose this is asking too much, because people do fall in love. I've come to the opinion over the years, in fact, that most people choose the right spouse the first time around. Something operates in human relationships to give us a sixth sense about the right person. But there can be pitfalls even in loving relationships with the right person, and some thought needs to be given to these before a person says "I do."

Bible verses about marriage are not based on arbitrary decisions. They are God's revelation to us about the way humans operate. Because it is hard for people who are unequally yoked to be compatible, God tells us not to do that. Because people who always demand their own way are not nice to live with, God tells us to submit to one another. And so on down the line. We want to help young people think about possible pitfalls before the wedding, lest after they fall into them they say, "No one ever took the time to tell me what I could expect."

Years ago when the highway through Canada to Alaska was mostly unpaved, every fall big trucks would grind their way to Anchorage, leaving great muddy holes all along the road. Then when winter frost came, these ruts would freeze however the trucks had left them. Some thoughtful truck driver made a crude cardboard and crayon sign and put it on a stick at the beginning of the highway. It said, "Choose your rut wisely. You'll be in it for the next 1,200 miles." Though marriage should not be a rut, it does last a long time. We surely must be wise in our choices.

THE RIGHT ONE •

I want to ask a girl out but I hesitate because I don't know if she is the *right* girl. Will God show me if she is the right one, and how will I know?

Everyone asks this question at one time or another. The truth is no one has ever gotten married and *known* that he or she got the right mate. Of course, *know* can be defined in many ways. Some say, "I felt so good; there were these deep feelings; I knew intuitively." Yes, we all *know* to some extent, I guess, but there is another way in which we don't know because people get married at a certain age and become different people when they are older. So I encourage you not to worry so much along these lines and, instead, follow a few suggestions.

One is, don't be afraid of the dating process. This is the means of discovering the kinds of things you want to know about a potential mate—what kind of girl she is; what kinds of values she holds; what dreams she has; how she feels about you; how she feels about your work; how she feels about following the Lord. Now there are a lot of young men who are afraid to date. They think that maybe God will do some skywriting or show them their mate by placing a halo around her head. I've known guys who really thought that way, but I've never known anyone who actually had it happen.

Though I applaud the dating process, like all other worthwhile things, it is fraught with temptations and problems, especially since we tend to look for the match made in heaven, the right girl, the perfect mate. I think we put too much emphasis on the selection process. It's like sorting through a bushel of apples looking for the one that has no blemish. We throw all the bad ones aside, find the one we think is perfect, and then take it home, only to find later that it had a hidden blemish we didn't know about. We do the same thing with people. Instead of placing too much emphasis on who our marriage partner will be, we should concentrate on godly ways to treat all potential mates. We need to know how to commit ourselves in love to this person, warts and all.

Once married, you'll find all kinds of wonderful things about your mate below the surface—good qualities you never dreamed she possessed. And yes, you will find blemishes too, but no more than you will find in yourself. And together, through commitment, you will work at solving those problems or blemishes, not finding a way to get rid of each other.

You see, in the Bible, love is not something you feel; it's something you do. Love is a responsible behavior and so if you are committed to love this woman and to be faithful to her and make your marriage work, you are on much more solid ground than if you are putting the emphasis on the selection process—did I choose the perfect girl? Let me reemphasize that you will not find a perfect wife, but let me encourage your mate, whoever she is out there, you're not perfect either. The two of you, committed together to make it work, will enter into Christian marriage— Christian because it's rooted in Christian love. So enter in with courage and God will bless you.

DIFFERENT STROKES ●

My fiancée and I are opposites. She's a reader, and I like sports. She likes traditional; I like contemporary. Will we be able to get along in marriage? We love each other very much and are both Christians.

"Opposites attract" is surely true in magnetism, but it may be a bit of a problem in marriage. In situations like this, compromises will have to be worked out. Each time there is a difference of opinion, one person will have to sublimate his or her interests to the interests of the other person, or both will have to find some common ground.

There is possibility for great enrichment in learning about another person's likes. Are both of you willing to learn and grow and find out why the other person treasures a different approach to life? If so, then your marriage can be joyfully compatible. For instance, a reader can introduce a sports fanatic to the joy of reading, and a sports fan can teach a reader to enjoy the exuberance and surprise and excitement of sports. This can broaden both lives.

But if either of you has a rigid personality, an inability to handle any kind of diversity or change, then watch out. People with rigid personalities are very difficult to work with, because what they are rigid about is relatively unimportant. That is, they can hold onto one thing with great stubbornness and then turn around and hang onto its opposite in the same way, not because of the thing itself, but because of an underlying personality problem. Rigidity is usually based on fear of the unfamiliar.

Sometimes it takes a great deal of work to help a person overcome fear. Eric Hoffer, the longshoreman philosopher, said that not to be threatened by change requires an inordinate amount of self-esteem. I believe that's true—it requires either a lot of self-esteem or a strong faith that God will take care of us, that we don't need to fear because He is the Alpha and the Omega, the beginning and the end. There are no new ideas to God; He's seen them all. God is perfectly secure, and as we are secure in Him, then we can also be secure in the midst of change.

If it is impossible for one person to adjust at all to the other one, then the spouse has to do all the adjusting. Many marriages like this work, but only because one spouse is willing to let the other person's tastes dominate. A couple thinking about getting married should establish whether their differences are simply preferences, or whether they are symptoms of deep-seated personality problems.

PREPARING TO SAY "I DO" ●

I'm getting married soon and I'd like to start now to make our marriage what it really ought to be. Where do I begin?

Like beginning anything, you've got to decide where you are right now. The short answer to your question is that you ought to make sure at the beginning that you and your mate are spiritually compatible. The Apostle Paul warned the Corinthians about being unequally yoked with an unbeliever (2 Cor. 6:14), and surely as a foundational truth, the most important compatibility that one can have is a spiritual one—to be committed together to follow Christ. Without that, all the other good things will fail. And with it, one can get by with a lot of imperfections. There's an opportunity for forgiveness, growth, and correction if one is committed to Christ at the beginning.

Beyond that, there are a number of other important things that you and your future spouse should discuss. What are your values? Where does your sense of value come from? Career? Serving others? What do you want from life? Do you want children? How many? How soon? What are your attitudes toward money and material things in general? These are just some of the subjects that need to be discussed by potential marriage partners.

Generally speaking, our instincts are usually correct about someone we're attracted to because during those times when we are initially sizing up the other person, we can at least make a basic decision as to whether or not we like him or her. A relationship has trouble developing out of the infant stages if a couple cannot even get along. But having decided already that you're going to get married soon, I would certainly encourage you to meet with a pastor or marriage counselor and let him work with you, perhaps administer some tests that would help you learn a little more about yourself and a little more about your future mate. It's far better to discover areas of incompatibility before you're married than after. At least you are prepared then for some possible disagreements.

You will save yourself a lot of misery and confusion if you spend a good deal of your engagement time learning about one another. It doesn't mean that when you discover an incompatibility the marriage should be called off. But it does mean that you have found a potential pitfall that you need to begin working on. So begin by affirming together that you want to build your marriage in Christ. And if Christ controls your marriage, you have a lot more latitude when dealing with potentially harmful situations.

READY OR NOT? ●

Everyone keeps asking us when we're going to get married. We have been dating for nearly three years and have talked seriously about marriage, but don't plan to announce it until God gives the OK. I resent these questions because I don't know when or if we'll get married. Someday I would like to be happily married, but how will I know when I'm ready?

It's tough on a young couple when people continually ask them when they're going to get married. It's not only hard on them, but it's really not polite. What we really mean to say is, "Hello. I like you two and want to show an interest in you." Asking about future marriage plans is often just a friendly way to get a conversation going, but the couple who hears it is embarrassed and uncomfortable with it. It's usually a miscommunication with no maliciousness intended, but it does have a way of forcing people into a corner.

On the other hand, people will never stop asking you this question. I think on the surface you need to come up with a kind of stock answer like, "We're dating but haven't talked about marriage yet," or "Don't talk about it out in the open here, you're wrecking my chances''—something that helps take the pressure off. It helps these people understand they are a bit out of line. And I don't think it hurts to establish with them that this particular question is not welcome. Sensitive people will hear what you're saying and, of course, the insensitive ones won't.

You say you're waiting until God gives you the OK. How will God do that? Will He light up your bedpost? Will you hear some sort of trumpet at night? I have a feeling that if you are waiting for some kind of definite sign, you may be waiting until you drop over from old age. On the other hand, you may interpret your own emotional feelings as an answer from God, and that could be a problem. What you need to do is begin to evaluate who you are and who your potential mate is. What are your aspirations in life? What are your value systems? How do you feel about the person you are dating? Do you enjoy being together? Are you both committed to God? Eventually you'll have to make a decision.

I find that many young couples today have seen so much failure in marriage that they have become frightened of making a commitment as great and long-lasting as marriage. It's like standing at the free throw line. You become so frightened that you will miss the basket, that you *do* miss. Don't get too apprehensive about it. Marriage is an involved and complex thing, but believe me, two people who love God, understand that love is a commitment, and commit themselves to each other can learn to love. And they will have a better chance than people who wait forever for the sky to light up or for something to happen that is totally subjective and emotional.

HE'S UNSAVED, I'M UNSURE •

I'm in love with a man who is not a Christian. He says he is attracted to me because I'm different. I know the Bible warns against relationships where one person is not a Christian, but I'm so in love I'm not sure I can back away.

The Bible gives some specific advice on this in 2 Corinthians 6:14. It says not to be unequally yoked with an unbeliever. We assume this yoke is a yoke of marriage, or a yoke of deep commitment in a relationship. The Bible gives this advice, not because being unequally yoked is going to upset some great eternal plan, but because it will upset your life. Why doesn't God want a Christian to marry an unbeliever? Well, marriage requires compatibility, harmony, shared relationships, and union at the deepest level. If you are a Christian, the most important thing in your life should be your spiritual welfare. But by marrying a nonbeliever you're saying that you'll relate to this person physically, financially, and socially, but the spiritual area in your life doesn't really matter. In effect, you are saying that you can have spiritual incompatibility and still be happy. You are only fooling yourself if you follow this kind of logic.

Increasingly in marriage, spiritual compatibility—the compatibility of two souls—becomes far more important than even physical oneness. So you need to take a look at this difference between you. He's attracted to you because you're different. That could be a patronizing kind of thing to say. Is he saying you're quaint or a little odd? You need to discuss that difference. Perhaps you could define that difference in relationship to a witness and begin to explain to him the substantial difference between your life and his. Your life is ruled by Jesus Christ who is the center, the priority of your life, and He is most important to you. Begin with that point so he knows he's not just getting a girl with something equivalent to a dimple. Your Christianity is something far more than that. Your Christianity is the very essence, the very fabric of your life. It would be unfair to this young man to think he's getting freckles when he's really getting Christianity. It could be that when he discovers what the true source of this difference is, he will want to be a Christian too. That would then solve your problem, wouldn't it?

FUTURE IN-LAWS ON THE OUTS •

I'm engaged to be married soon and my fiancé and I are running into a real problem with our parents. My boyfriend and I love each other, but the two sets of parents certainly don't love each other. Our parents come from totally different backgrounds and resent each other. It's causing a great deal of strain on my fiancé and me, and I'm afraid after we get married it may get worse. What can we do?

Unfortunately, it may get worse, but in a way you may not be thinking about right now. Most in-laws don't have much contact with one another after the wedding. They disappear into different sides of your life. So if they don't get along, don't push them together—don't try to mix oil and water. They probably just don't enjoy being together because they're simply not compatible.

117

Once married, you and your husband will have to be very fair and careful in how you treat them. Do not side with one set of parents against the other. To keep peace in the family, couples often unknowingly fuel the fire by agreeing with the evaluation of the complaining parents. This only reinforces the problem. You don't have to stand up for them or anything else. In the long run, it's much more effective to remain neutral when talking about your in-laws in front of your own parents.

Now we come to the reason why the situation may get worse. When you get married you bring more into the relationship than yourself; you are a reflection of your family—your parents. And unless you've made a very conscious effort to be different than they are, you will find yourself looking in the mirror and seeing your own parents right before you. You'll suddenly realize how very deeply they've affected you not just because you have the same shaped nose or chin, but because you tend to relate to your spouse and your in-laws in the same way your parents relate to each other. For instance, if you're a woman, you will tend to relate to your husband like your mother relates to your father. If you're a man, you will relate to your wife like your father relates to your mother. Even if your parents were not the kinds of people you'd like to be, you will still tend to respond to others as they do unless you make a conscious effort to do otherwise, constantly monitoring yourself to see if you are making progress.

If your two sets of parents are as incompatible as you say they are, then you and your fiancé need to get a little deeper into how you each feel about things. Maybe you aren't as compatible as you think. Sometime after the initial blush is over, you're going to find yourselves dealing with many issues which require a unified decision. For instance, how do you feel about disciplining children? Working wives? Finances? Household duties? All these potential incompatibilities will eventually come up and you'll find that they involve more than differences between in-laws.

ANOTHER RACE •

Our oldest daughter is twenty-one and is involved in a serious relationship with a boy of another race. She has come to us for advice. My husband refuses to recognize their relationship at all. He says that if there is a wedding, he will not attend. I feel we can only advise them and not try to take responsibility for their decisions. I think we should let go and let God take care of them. The situation has caused our entire family's communication to break down.

118

Some people may jump to the conclusion that your husband is a racist, but I don't think this is necessarily so. I have a black friend whose daughter is involved with a white boy, and the mother is terrified. She feels that the boy's interest in her daughter is very much tied to his desire to champion the underdog. But she fears that as the young couple grows to middle age and has children, society will not be any more tolerant than it is now. She fears that neither black nor white society will accept the grandchildren. This is not racism, but honest social concern.

But your husband's concern has motivated actions that are not wise. He is saying that if these young people get married, he will wash his hands of them. Pilate started this hand-washing business, and he's not exactly one of the Bible's heroes. A lot of people have followed him in this pious, morally superior attitude. "You can do this," they say, "but I'll wash my hands of you. I won't corrupt myself by involvement with you."

In my opinion, this is morally reprehensible. When people honestly do what they feel they should do, and then we say we won't sully ourselves by being their friend, we're not talking about friendship at all. What we're trying to do is blackmail them. We're saying, in effect, "I won't be your friend unless you think like I think or do what I do." And that's terrible.

If your husband actually does refuse to attend their wedding or have anything more to do with them, he will just drive them into a life of loneliness. The problems they would face in any interracial marriage will become even harder for them to solve. They will not have the loving, caring support of a father who is mature and knows how to help, and he will not have the companionship of his children and grandchildren.

HAUNTED BY THE PAST ●

When I was seventeen, I got pregnant by a boy who used me. I never saw him again. I decided to keep the baby, but two weeks before it was due, I delivered a stillborn baby girl. I loved the child, and my pain and sorrow were great. Now I've met a wonderful person, and we'd like to get married some day. My question is this: Should I tell him what happened? I don't want to deceive him, but I also don't want to suffer trying to explain what happened.

In some situations where one person has had a very involved past, it's often best simply to say to the person you're marrying, "Here's a general picture of my past life and the problems I had. Think of all the bad things you want to, and if you can forgive me for those, we can move ahead. If you can't handle it, then we can't. But I'm not going to spend my life answering questions about the details."

I've spent thirty years listening to people's stories, and yours is not one of the wild ones. You are a person who took a bad situation and did your best with it. You did not seek abortion, as hundreds of thousands like you have done, but you tried to do the responsible thing. In your specific situation, I think you should tell your future husband about what happened.

You'll learn a lot about him by telling him your story. If he's totally unable to handle it, then you will be fortunate in finding this out before you marry him. If his reaction is, "I'm pure, and she's dirty; I'm good, and she's bad," then he has a lot of growing up to do, and he obviously does not understand his own condition as a sinner.

Don't be turned off by his immediate response, whatever it may be. Give him time to process his feelings. Say to him, "I'm going to tell you something, and when you have thought about it and can handle it, tell me how you feel." It may take him five seconds; it may take him a couple of days. If he's truly a born-again person, he will look at your experience and say, "There, but for the grace of God, go I. I too am a sinner, and the two of us together have been forgiven by our wonderful Christ. Now we can start out our life together clean, born all over again."

| CHAPTER 10 |

After the Honeymoon

When people hear the biblical phrase about two becoming one, they ask, "Can that really be true?" Well, it can be true, but it's not easy. Becoming one flesh physically is a great deal easier than becoming one flesh emotionally, spiritually, and socially. Two never become one automatically; it takes a great deal of effort for two people to share one mind. And I believe that without Christ in the equation, they cannot do it at all.

In Christian marriage, we commit ourselves to one person, Jesus Christ. Two people can become one in Christ. But until we have adjusted our own selfishness and personal desires to fit the Lord's desires, we are only held together with baling wire. We must come to understand that our object is to submit ourselves first to the will of God and then, in mutual harmony, to become one.

I believe that conflict in marriage is not totally restricted to the individuals involved. The enemy of our soul, in his attack on the human race, has chosen to attack the marriage relationship because, if he can divide men and women from one another and bring chaos to the family, then virtually everything valuable in society will begin to break down. It's possible that twentieth-century Americans are going to demonstrate this truth to the rest of the world. But as Christians we work with all our energy against such a possibility becoming reality.

NO TIME TO TALK •

We never have time to talk! When my husband comes home I'm busy making dinner and getting the kids organized. After dinner

my husband works or plays with the kids. When the kids go to bed, I still have more work to do. Mornings are not much better—we have to rush through breakfast and then off to work. Saturdays are for shopping and Sunday is full of church activities. There just doesn't seem to be any time to discuss our progress as husband and wife and as parents. What do other people do?

This particular problem is one that almost every mother and father in the world can identify with. It has to do with the encroachment of outside influences on our lives—whether they be work responsibilities, financial cares, hobbies, or other activities. All these things creep into our lives along with a growing family and create great stress.

It seems to me that the problem of communicating falls into two categories. There are couples who have no desire to talk to each other; their marriages have grown cold, and they don't seem to like to be together anymore. If you asked them, they'd say they love each other in some dutiful sense, but they don't like each other. If you're in such a position, you need to call a Christian counselor and get started on this problem while you're still thinking about it. If you procrastinate, you'll reach the point where you don't even care—then it's all over.

The other problem of communication involves technique. "What should we do to solve this mutual problem? We're both so busy that we can't find time to be together." My first suggestion is that you sit down together and express the problem. Make being together a priority. You say your husband works or plays with the kids while you do the dishes. Maybe he ought to help you do the dishes. The two of you can talk to each other while you're standing there washing and drying dishes. It's really a great time to talk because that's a task that doesn't take a lot of thought. Perhaps you might get up in the morning before the kids get up. For some of us that's the only way we can have any time together. Go down to the kitchen, drink some coffee together, read the Bible and pray with each other, and talk before the day starts. As you start your day with the Lord, the rest of the day will begin to mean more. Maybe it would also help to "make an appointment" to be together—say Saturday at lunch. You say, "I can't afford it." Well, lunch is a lot cheaper than a marriage counselor, believe me.

WORLDS APART? •

I can't get my wife's attention. I know she loves me, and she's a splendid mother and housekeeper. But when it comes to intelligent companionship, we're in different worlds. We never have truly meaningful and creative discussions. I wish she would spend some time learning about my business or thinking about creative new aproaches to our livelihood, but she doesn't. When I really need a confidante, her only response is that business is boring. I just don't know how to get through to her.

If you took a poll of all the men in the country, I think you'd find a lot of them with your frustration. And if you took a poll of the women, you'd find that most of them wish their husbands would show more tenderness. Actually, the two complaints are very much the same—they boil down to *lack of appreciation.* Both men and women want to be noticed, to be cared about, but men feel that their wives don't appreciate their work, and women feel that their husbands don't appreciate their persons.

A man who is very work-oriented finds that his work and his personality are intertwined; to ignore one is to ignore the other. If he's not appreciated, he can easily feel like a dray horse in a harness. People let him do the work and bring in the money, but they don't really appreciate his effort. Many women don't seem to understand that if they want their husbands to show them tenderness, they should appreciate what he does.

By the same token, if you want your wife to appreciate what you do, you need to notice and value her work, to show interest in her life. A woman once told me, "You know, my husband has destroyed me. He thinks all the things I do all day long are unimportant, and he acts as if they ought to be handled by somebody else. He has important things to do, and he can't be bothered with my activities. But these things are the sum and total of my life." So one very important way of getting your wife to appreciate you is to begin showing interest in her life.

Some homemakers mistakenly think that because they can run a vacuum cleaner without an education, there is no need for them to develop their minds. But an education has to do with enriching all of life, not just providing a means to an income. I would suggest that the two of you develop intellectual interests together that are not tied to either your work or hers. For instance, you could begin to read books together. Janie and I have found this very helpful. We read novels together and talk about them. This creates a world of our own that is not tied to function.

It is not tied to my function in Youth for Christ, and it is not tied to her function in the home. It's a gateway to life in general, and it helps both of us to stay intellectually alive. Developing a mutual interest like this might help you and your wife. But the first thing both of you need to do is to learn to appreciate each other.

I NEED A LITTLE ATTENTION •

My wife is so wrapped up in taking care of our two-year-old son that I feel left out in the cold. By evening she is worn out. We can't even sit and talk for a while because she is constantly jumping up to check on the baby. I'm not really jealous because I love our child as much as she does. All I'm looking for is just a little more attention.

I think a good place to start would be to tell her just that. Most men don't like to admit they feel competition with a baby, especially if that baby is their own. On the other hand, most of us grown men do feel this way once in a while. Striving for attention works both ways, incidentally, because a two-year-old child is capable of feeling competition from you as well. He or she has Mom all day long, but when you come home at the end of the day, the child senses you are encroaching on his territory. So he begins to develop ways of getting Mom's attention, like starting to cry or getting into things—anything—to get her undivided attention. You ask, "Where in the world does he learn to do that? Did someone teach him?" No, it's just the way children are. If Mom responds to all these demands, she is encouraging this poor behavior as well as jeopardizing your relationship with her.

Tell your wife how you feel, then sit down together and figure out how to be smarter than a two-year-old. Now, of course, you are not trying to do him in or cause him to feel neglected. He's your son and you love him deeply. But figure out the difference between the noises he makes when he is really in trouble and those he makes when he just wants to dominate his mother's time. What's the difference between the kinds of behavior he shows when he *needs* attention and the kind that is just an attention-getting device? What might also help is that when your son starts making these attention-getting noises, *you* get up and go to him. Get down on the floor and play games with him; read to him; take him for a walk. Spend time every day when just the two of you can be together. In fact, I've suggested to men who struggle with this problem that they sleep on the outside of the bed so instead of their wives getting up constantly, they get up once in a while. Then the child begins to develop a bonding between both mother *and* father.

DO YOU STILL LOVE ME? ●

I'm in a touchy situation with my wife. Almost every day she asks me if I love her. Of course I do—I married her, didn't I? But she doesn't think I really mean it. She seems insecure about my feelings for her. I try to reassure her, but it is getting more difficult to be patient. How can I help her feel secure about my love?

It is very interesting to me how universal this question is. In the Broadway musical, *Fiddler on the Roof,* the husband asks this same question. Strangely enough, it is often the woman asking this, but in this case he asks, "Do you love me?" She says, "Of course, I love you. I darn your socks, I milk your cow, I've had your children, I share your bed—of course, I love you. What are you talking about?" Yet he is a romantic. He wants poetry and candlelight. He needs this constant assurance. I have come to the conclusion that in most cases people who are opposites get married. The man will be practical, the kind of fellow who gives his wife snow tires for Christmas or a new egg-washer for the farm. The woman is a romantic who wants poetry and flowers every evening after supper. Or the roles can be reversed where the woman is the practical one and the man is the romantic. But in either case, they have a different love language. One person's love is based on performance while the other person looks for "impractical" things like flowers or a surprise evening out.

It sounds to me like you may be the practical type and your wife's the romantic. I would suggest you try to get on top of the situation. Take some initiative and think of what you did when you courted her. Too often we believe that once we are married there is no reason to court each other anymore. This lack of courting is one of the key reasons many marriages become dull and dry. So think back to your courting days. Did you send her flowers? Did you write her poetry? Did you whisper sweet nothings in her ear? Whatever you did then must have worked because she married you. So I suggest you start doing those things again. Start thinking of those things even though you think she might take them for granted.

Begin to make lists of things you can do and develop some sense of surprise in your relationship. Ask yourself, "What can I do today that will make her feel loved?" Clip a poem out of the newspaper and put in on her pillow. Send her some candy; buy her some flowers; tell her she's beautiful—take the initiative. I think you will find that it will help if you learn to speak the same language.

A CHILDLESS MARRIAGE ●

For years my husband and I have been trying to have a child, but without success. We have prayed and fasted and waited. Surely God is interested in our happiness, but of late we have not been experiencing much of that peace and happiness we are supposed to have as Christians. I can't understand it. Physically there is nothing wrong with us. How can we cope with a childless marriage?

Let me suggest that you aim your spiritual energy in just a little different direction, and that is to pray and fast as you wait on the Lord for *His* will, not for your will. You can express to the Lord your desire to have children and tell Him all your reasons why, but also be willing to listen to Him—be willing to take no for an answer, even though you don't understand why. Let Him know you trust Him and that you're willing to obey Him—even if He leads you to adopt a child.

I think you will find that when you have yielded yourself to the Lord's will and lowered your anxiety level, you may well find that He will answer your prayer in the way that you originally intended. That is, you might find yourself having your own child. But should He not, then be willing to have His will, which might be to be free of children so that you can give yourselves in Christian service in some unusual way that you don't now understand.

Yield to God's will and trust Him totally.

HE WANTS KIDS, I DON'T ●

I enjoy my work, feel very fulfilled in it, and have no immediate desire to have children. My husband, on the other hand, wants lots of kids, and is really starting to put pressure on me. How should I as a wife respond?

Obviously, the two of you have to work out some sort of a solution. This is a difficult problem that does not lend itself to compromise. You can't have half a child.

It would be wise to think back on any premarital discussions you and your husband had regarding a family. What were your values then? Did you both agree on having children? Did you discuss how many children you wanted and when you'd begin your family? Have your thoughts and feelings changed since then? If so, why?

Often couples begin marriage with a euphoric sense of expectancy. They picture themselves at a certain economic level "x" many years down the pike. They dream of owning their own home, achieving a certain place in their careers, and starting families. However, circumstances of life often interfere with these initial dreams and plans, and though a couple may have fully expected to be at point C, they find themselves only at point B financially and career-wise. When that happens—when the goals of marriage aren't being met as first intended—the couple needs to decide whether they are going to proceed as planned, only with a different time schedule, or alter their goals.

Much of the decision depends on the values each person has. In your case, you seem to place a higher value on career than family. Is this the same value you had before marriage? If you and your husband have never had a serious discussion regarding your goals in marriage or your values, now is an excellent time to begin. Discuss your husband's reasons for wanting children and your reasons for not wanting children. If you both agree that you do want to start a family eventually, make definite plans on when and how many. If there is disagreement on future family plans, perhaps you should seek the help of an outside counselor to discover why each of you feels the way you do, and work toward a livable solution.

The worst thing you can do is have a child merely to please your husband. If you don't want that child, he'll sense your rejection of him. There's nothing wrong, in my opinion, with working as a mother. I think there are ways to work out this situation in a very fine manner. But I think if it's not worked out in your mind and in your soul, then it's very unfair to have a child.

NOT DOING HIS FAIR SHARE •

My husband and I agreed that since I was going back to work, he would begin to help around the house. This arrangement worked fine for a while. He helped with the cleaning, the cooking, and even the shopping. But the uniqueness of his new role has worn off and he has stopped lending a hand unless I nag him. I don't know whether I should stop asking him and do everything myself, or continue prodding him, thus becoming a nagging wife.

You and your husband need to reestablish the arrangement you initially worked out. Your husband needs to be reminded that he is backing out of your original agreement. Of course, he'll say he's tired, but you might remind him that you are too. Many times men have the misnomer that women are supposed to do the housework. They are supposed to be tired all the time. They are supposed to work after the husband gets home. A couple comes home together from work, he sits down and reads the paper and she gets supper, cleans up, does a little ironing, and so on. This is simply unfair. Simply put, your husband isn't picking up his end. I doubt if there is anything short of confrontation that will help you with this.

To keep nagging is a weak approach because this puts you in a position of begging. Sit down with your husband and simply give him the facts. Intellectually speaking, he will acknowledge them to be true. But how will you get him to make the kind of commitment he needs to make? It may be that you will have to establish specific divisions of labor or, if you have done this, alter the tasks you each are supposed to do. I think there are some tasks that men can do equally as well as women and there are some tasks that women can do much better than men, and vice versa. The division of labor in any home is one of the more important things to domestic fairness, to a sense of partnership and oneness in relationship.

Every family arrangement does not have to be the same, but each one should be perceived to be fair by the participants. They have to have an arrangement that works for them. My wife, for instance, loathes my being involved in "her" kitchen. It's her turf, and I seem to be a problem there. By the same token, I don't expect her to mow the lawn, wash windows, clean out gutters, etc. I would be embarrassed to have the neighbors see her crawling around on a ladder. And so we try to divide these things rather equally within our home, and you too need to agree on household chores. Then each of you needs to be committed enough to stick with the agreement.

WHO'S MANAGING THE HOME? •

I'm a working wife with an active two-year-old, an excellent day-care sitter, and a job I genuinely enjoy. My husband works forty-plus hours a week at a job he likes. When I come home at night I feed our boy, start supper, and clean up a bit. When my husband comes home he watches TV, reads the paper, and enjoys the meal. About 8 o'clock he is ready to go to bed since he gets up at 3 A.M. I put our son to bed and still have tons of housework to do. The problem is that my husband wants me to go to bed when he does, and when I don't he gets angry with me. Yet, he's the one who complains if the house isn't cleaned or if he doesn't have clean clothes to wear. He has promised to help with the chores, but he just won't lend a hand. He says he works hard all day. I've tried going to bed at 8 o'clock and then getting up and doing the work later, but when I do I never feel rested and have almost no time to myself.

Your dilemma is quite typical of the modern family. Because of economic conditions and partially because of the standard of life we want to maintain, more than fifty percent of all mothers in America are working. As a result, an increasing number of husbands and wives are changing their traditional family roles. More and more wives are joining the work force, and more and more husbands are being asked to assume more responsibility at home. Suddenly there are three jobs to do—one of them managing the home—and only two people to do them. Naturally, this creates new kinds of personal and sociological problems for the family.

I know that many Christians think the solution to this problem is simple. A woman ought to quit work, stay home, and reassume her conventional role. But before we adopt that position, let's do a little math. Take a look at modern situations—the average home in America costs about $85,000. When a young couple gets married today, it often takes three or four years to be able to scrape up enough money for a modest down payment. Even with some help from their parents, they are straddled with a hefty mortgage and an exorbitant interest rate—a situation which forces the husband to earn enough to pay not only the mortgage but all the rest of the household expenses. The math just won't work, so couples are both working, not just because they want to, or because the wife is a feminist, but because they have to. They are trapped.

There is no easy answer to this problem, but I think the best thing to do is to work on a solution together. I don't know whether you have done this or not; most husbands and wives don't. Tell your husband exactly what you have told me. Ask, "Honey, how would you solve this situation?" Most couples who have a real stress in their relationship haven't really sat down and looked at the whole issue. They pick at each other over specific issues—the ironing isn't done, the clothes aren't clean, dinner's late, sexual intimacy is missing—but they miss the big picture.

So, the two of you need to make some decisions. And the first decision is to divide the labor. Once you've determined who is going to do what, you'll have conquered the most difficult part of the problem.

WHY DO WE ARGUE SO MUCH? ●

My husband and I argue a lot but we never solve anything. We say we're sorry and vow to never do it again, but we always do. Sometimes I think we get so caught up in the argument itself that we forget about the real problem. Can we learn to argue in a way that will solve something?

You have already made some fine observations. The rule is that you aren't getting to the bottom of the issues and resolving them; you are just wearing each other out and then deciding, "Hey, this is silly. Our love for each other is more important than this issue anyway. Let's just forget about it and move on." However, whatever it was that prompted the argument in the first place had some validity or else it wouldn't have become an argument. Because you didn't solve the real issue behind the argument, it just resurfaces. It is like pushing a beach ball down in the pool. You push it down in one place and it will come up someplace else.

One of the most helpful things I have ever seen on this subject is a book written by David Augsburger called *Caring Enough to Confront.* He presents five possible steps to solving disagreements.

The first one is "I win, you lose." I think most argumentative people like that one, though I can't say as much for passive types. Another is "You win, I quit." We've all done that at one time or other. A third one is called "Doormat." One person decides, "Well, walk on me; step on me; peace at all costs—I don't care about the substance of this issue, but at least we will have peace in our home." The trouble with this is that the home can sometimes be led by the most willful, tyrannical person and truth gets trodden underfoot. The fourth possibility is "I'll meet you halfway," which is surely superior to any of the other three. However, even "I'll meet you halfway" can have weaknesses because sometimes one person is altogether right and the other is altogether wrong. Meeting halfway can be too great a compromise and too far from the truth. The fifth and most biblically sound way to deal with conflict is "Caring enough to confront." And by this, Augsburger is suggesting we confront in love, which means we accept responsible behavior.

It sounds to me like the two of you are pretty strong-willed people and have not been able to distinguish in your own minds between discussion and argument. It's possible to disagree on an issue and discuss it with each other if you are both willing to seek truth. What we really want is not for one person to win or be right or be on top. What we really want is truth. And in most cases, truth lies somewhere between the viewpoints of two people. I think you are on the right track, but it will help most if, rather than argue, you discuss some issues in-depth and with some content.

JEALOUS SPOUSE ●

Whenever another woman talks with my husband I get jealous. My husband says I don't trust him. It's not that, but he is a normal, attractive man and I know what kinds of temptations he must face every day at the office. When he doesn't explain where he has been and why, I get upset. I know he's never been unfaithful to me and I also know he loves me, but I don't seem to be able to stop these feelings of jealousy. How does a woman cope with jealousy?

There are really only two basic reasons for this type of jealousy. Either your husband is doing something that is causing you to be jealous, or you are conjuring in your mind all kinds of circumstances that have no valid premise. Now strangely enough, the response to either situation is about the same. Let's begin with the first one. If your husband is unfaithful or is flirting, your display of jealousy is probably the worst strategy you can take. This only causes the situation to get worse because your husband will become defensive and deny everything. A better approach would be to talk with your husband over a candlelight dinner and tell him how much you love him. Gracefully explain the problem. Don't pin the blame on him. You will get much better results if you explain to your husband that you are struggling with these feelings and you would appreciate his help in dealing with them. In most cases, the husband feels a little embarrassed and tries to rectify the situation. If your husband doesn't and things get worse, professional help may be the only answer.

Now let's take the second situation—that your husband gives you no real reason for jealousy. The first thing you need to do is adjust your opinion of what is a normal, attractive man. Frankly, I think the kind of man you're thinking of is pictured in TV soap operas, but doesn't exist in real life. Contrary to what TV often tells us, most men do not stand around waiting to act like an animal every time a woman walks by. Yes, it is true that men can become more quickly aroused than women, especially over things like physical appearances. But give men some credit. They do possess some self-control. Most men are not unfaithful to their wives. They do not act out their fantasies. So, the idea that your husband is kind of a helpless blob of responses is not true. He's a human being with a will, and if he knows the Lord, he has the Holy Spirit on his side as well.

Perhaps the reason you are jealous is that you have a low opinion of yourself. You don't feel attractive or that you can compete, and therefore you are frightened that the other women your husband meets are much better than you. The more you can work on building up your self-esteem, the less frightened you will become. I think if you attack the issue at this point, you will find it a great deal more helpful than trying to straighten out your husband.

HARD TO ACCEPT CRITICISM •

My wife and I both find it difficult to accept criticism. At times I tend to be very domineering, which may be part of the problem. We both love each other and are willing to change. What is the next step?

Being willing to change is, of course, the major part of the battle in accepting criticism. Yet, I think the business of confrontation and criticism is overrated in our society. The theory that we ought to always confront each other with what we don't like works so nicely in textbooks, but in real life, few people can take criticism very well. In fact, when we are criticized we throw up a smoke screen, a sort of defense mechanism, that makes the real problem difficult to get at.

One of my best friends used to say, "Most people are sugar horses, not whip horses." In other words, most people are helped by affirmation and encouragement more than they are by criticism. For example, in a marriage the idea of remaking each other through criticism into an ideal spouse probably isn't very effective. I would put my emphasis instead on the goal of accepting each other for what you are. Allow your partner to do his or her own changing rather than feeling you have to help him change.

In fact, I think the idea of Christian commitment being a behavior modification technique is also misunderstood. As I study the life of the Apostle Paul, I see that he was very much the same person psychologically, emotionally, and personality-wise after his conversion as he was before his conversion. Paul was a hard-driving, rather rigid, accomplishment-oriented person before *and after* he was saved. So far as our personalities are concerned, we really don't change much simply because we get married or become Christians. What can change, however, are our attitudes toward others and our desire to reach out to them.

You have admitted that you tend to be domineering and that might be part of the problem. To see that trait in yourself and to feel the compunction to confess it is a great beginning. We as men often feel it is our duty to dominate, to be in charge. We even believe certain Bible verses give us that right. Let me encourage you, since you both want to change and are willing to change, to submit yourselves to an external authority, that is, to a counselor where the two of you can work through this situation. Erase the image of what you want each other to be. Submit yourselves together to the image of what Christ wants each of you to be through the help of a counselor, and I think you can both make some real progress.

WHY ALL THE FUSS? ●

My husband and I are always fussing with each other. I feel like I'm living with my younger brother again. I've been told that the first year of marriage is the easiest, and if that's so, the rest may be unbearable. Is there any way we can stop treating each other like siblings? In some ways I feel more like his mother than his wife.

I don't know who has been telling you the first year of marriage is the easiest, but I think I would have to disagree. Scripture says that when we get married, two become one. That is very hard to do mathematically, let alone socially, spiritually, physically, and psychologically. For two people to blend their lives into unity and oneness obviously takes a while. What your friends probably mean when they say the first year is the easiest, is that initially you are living in the bliss of love. I think when it gets right down to the nitty-gritty, when you get back into the world of work and busy schedules, adjustments become pretty traumatic. So if your first year has been tough, don't assume that the rest of your life will be all downhill. You don't know what tomorrow is going to be like. I would suggest it will probably get easier, not more difficult. That is the way it usually works.

I find many men marry and secretly desire a mothering kind of wife. The first thing they do when they get up in the morning is say, "Where are my socks?" And from then on, a woman is supposed to find everything for him, iron everything for him, and, in short, be his valet. This puts terrific pressure on the woman. But, ironically, most women like that pressure. In fact, our culture has really encouraged women to be caretakers of their husbands.

Many women carry mothering to extremes, however, and they try to perfect their husbands. This has to be one of the greatest sources of marital conflict—trying to perfect one another. Now that you have had a year of marriage, begin to accept your husband as he is. Decide that you will love him as he is, and love each other as you are. Then each of you, before God, will take on the task of straightening out your own imperfections. If you look at your husband's imperfections like some sort of little project you need to take on, you will find a lot of tension in your marriage. That is what older sisters do to younger brothers. They try to mother them. I think you need to back off, take a new look at what has happened, and begin integrating your two personalities into one. This means accepting the other person, not remaking him into someone like yourself.

WHEN PERSONALITIES COLLIDE ●

Before I was married I had my own apartment and car. I was used to doing things for myself. But now that I'm married, my husband considers things like my car his responsibility. That's fine except when a small problem develops, he is usually too busy to fix it. So I keep driving until the problem gets serious and costs us a great deal of money to repair. If I were single I would take it in

134

at the first sign of a problem. I think that it is cheaper in the long run, but my husband doesn't see it that way. He says he can fix the problem himself, but he never finds the time to do it. Am I being a spendthrift when I want to take the car to the service station? My husband says that I am.

I don't pretend to be an expert on money matters, but because this is such a typical kind of marital problem I want to talk briefly about it. Recently, I counseled a couple who was soon to be married. Frankly, since both of them were doctors, there wasn't much I could teach them about anatomy or the physical side of sex. But then they asked, "What kinds of problems can we expect in our first year of marriage? What sorts of things will be struggles?" I said, "Probably the greatest struggle is the fact that you are going to hear something in the marriage ceremony about two becoming one." The reason I said this was because these two people were both very independent, career-oriented individuals. They had found their own way in life and were accustomed to doing things a certain way. It was going to be much more difficult for these two independent people to become one than it would be for two people who hadn't lived such independent lives.

That is the kind of problem you face. You have been in an apartment; you have kept your own car; you have some specific ideas about how things should be done. Your husband also has his ideas about the way things should be, and these two well-formed opinions have been forged together in marriage and are causing some sparks. In your case, it may just take some extra time for your strong, independent personalities to learn to work together. Perhaps a clear division of responsibilities would help. You do the cooking your way, for instance, and he trims the lawn his way. A lot of couples don't like that. They feel this is too male-female and they both want to be involved. If you can't divide the labor, then let me make some other suggestions.

First of all, acknowledge where your husband is coming from. He probably is wary of your taking your car to be serviced because he knows how many mechanics prey on single women and their car problems. On the other hand, your husband may not be as concerned about the money aspect of getting your car repaired as he is about proving his own mechanical competency. His masculinity is tied to his ability to cope with a mechanized world and so he wants to prove his competence in that way. Keep records for a few months on each car. Keep your car your way, let him keep his his way, and afterward compare the costs of the repairs.

Maybe you'll have some objective data on which you can make decisions in the future.

UPSET OVER SURPRISE GUEST ●

My husband's sister is single, and about four times a year she comes to visit us. She always plans her visits with my husband and they never consult me. After all, I'm the one who has to cook special meals, clean, and plan the weekend. The least my husband could do is ask me if it's OK, especially since he never remembers to check our calendar for conflicts. Am I being unrealistic or unfair to my husband and sister-in-law?

It sounds like you are being realistic and that your husband and sister-in-law are being a bit unfair. But let's try to understand why situations such as this occur.

Your husband's sister is special to him. She is family. You don't have to make any sort of special preparations for a sister—after all, she would not expect anything special. He may come from an informal home—the kind that always makes room for another guest or sets an extra place at the table in case someone drops by. Everyone hangs loose, so to speak, and adjusts easily to any situation. There are many homes like that. Usually when people from that kind of background read the story of Mary and Martha in the Bible, they like the idea of waiting on Jesus and dropping everything to care for His needs.

But there are other people who never quite come to terms with that story because they have the kind of personality that fusses, worries, and struggles. They say, "Yeah, that's just fine that she stops and waits on Jesus, but then who cooks the meal, and who dusts around here?" Once I was teaching the Bible story about the friends who lowered the man down through the roof for Jesus to heal. After the story some fellow piped up and asked, "Well, who fixed the roof?"

Apparently you don't like the informal approach to life. Probably the best way to handle this situation is head-on. Say to your husband, "I just need to be told. I'm the kind of person who doesn't like surprises. I like to be warned." In the meantime, perhaps you could even say to your sister-in-law, "You know, you probably can sense when you come here that I'm a little tense and not what I want to be. It is because your brother forgets to tell me you're coming. How about you and me having a little conspiracy together? When he invites you, call to tell me that he has invited you and I'll be happy to adjust. I love you, but I just have trouble being my best when he springs this on me." Maybe that will help.

THE STING OF SARCASM •

When my husband and I were first married he promised never to hurt me by word or deed. Lately, however, his tongue has become increasingly sharp. I know some of the things he says about me are in jest, but they hurt. How can I help him understand that his sarcasm is really getting to me? What can I do about my own attitude toward this?

Sarcasm often contains a veiled message. Many truths are said in jest but the person saying them can be unconscious of the fact. I think the first thing you should do is tell your husband what he is doing. Share your feelings and help him realize that his sarcasm depreciates you. If he is the type that truly doesn't understand what he is doing, he might say, "Why, Honey, I didn't know I was doing that. I'm sorry." And that's usually the end of it.

On the other hand, if he says, "Well, yes, there is a problem; this is how I feel," you can start getting into the meat of the matter. Find out what bothers your husband. You could offer, "If these things are true and they are so irritating, help me solve them." That takes a lot of humility, I know. Very few of us like to ask help from someone else, but I think this attitude is within the spirit of what Christ teaches us in the Word. Be willing to say, "Honey, I don't think I can overcome this by myself. I need your support, your encouragement. If it involves some sort of counseling, then help me."

Often a spouse will complain about things in terms that are much too general. For example, "My wife doesn't keep house." Well, that's probably not true at all. What the man is trying to say is that she doesn't vacuum the floor or she doesn't like to dust or the dishes don't get quite clean. My point is that if your husband doesn't like something you're doing he needs to stop veiling his complaints in sarcasm and speak to you in love about *exactly* what is bothering him. Then you can start solving these problems.

In many cases, a spouse's sarcasms are simply statements about general discontent and may not even be related to his mate. They may be related to the frustrations of daily life that he is struggling with. You end up being the scapegoat—the visible object of his discontent. In these situations, pets and children *and wives* take an awful lot of abuse.

I think the first step in your situation is to confront your husband and find out if he is willing to work on his sarcasm. He may not even know he's doing this.

HE FORGETS MY BIRTHDAY •

Too often my husband forgets my birthday and our anniversary. These occasions are important to me and should be to him too, but it doesn't seem to bother him when he forgets. This is very depressing for me. I hate to have to remind him about these special days, because then it isn't a genuine show of his affection.

We all yearn for recognition and affirmation. But if we have to fish for it, it doesn't feel good when we get it. You want people to recognize your special days and accomplishments spontaneously. Something that might help would be a monthly calendar that lists all the important dates, not just yours. You want yours noticed, but you also put his on there and the children's and his mother's and father's and your mother's and father's. Put the calendar on the front of the refrigerator and then say, "Hey, this month we have your mother's birthday coming up and our son's birthday, and, incidentally, my birthday." By including your birthday or anniversary in the mix of monthly events you will be saved the embarrassment of having to remind your husband of these special times. I'm sure your husband isn't intentionally ignoring your birthday and anniversary. He probably is quite content with his family and loves you very much.

On the other hand, your husband's family background may be totally different from yours. As a boy growing up, your husband's family may not have put much emphasis on birthdays, holidays, or other special occasions. By the same token, you may have been treated like a princess on your birthday and therefore have become accustomed to royal attention. Let's face it, some people just don't get into family traditions as much as others. So, while you are trying to help your husband become more sensitive to these things (and he should be), you may need to be sensitive to his perspective and background and lower your expectations a little.

When he does remember something, affirm him. Make it worthwhile for him to remember. If he does manage to bring you something on your birthday, make that a memorable time for him as well, so that he will think, "Boy, it pays off. She's a lot nicer when I do that." So in a manner of speaking, condition him to behave the way you want him to.

ANSWER TO A SHAKY MARRIAGE ●

My sister is planning to leave her husband. They've gone to their pastor and to marriage counselors, but nothing seems to help. This is her second marriage and she feels like a loser. My husband and I had the same problem a few years ago, then he turned to Christ and eventually won me to Christ too. I've told my sister how Christ has helped my marriage and how He can help her marriage too. She tells me there is no peace in her life. How can I communicate to her what it means to have Christ as the head of a marriage?

The story of your marriage has a Cinderella ending where everything turns out and everyone lives happily ever after—and that is terrific. I think that we could surely pray and hope that your sister's marriage will turn out the same way. Yet I think it may be wishful thinking when we analyze the situation. In your case, your husband had a real desire to serve Christ and was patiently willing to wait for you. He obeyed Christ and then prayed for you. Then you accepted Christ as your Saviour and committed your life to Him. So the two of you aimed at this one goal of pleasing the Lord and were brought together in your marriage.

Now take your sister's situation. There is no indication that either your sister or her husband has this same interest in pleasing God. Apparently they have a different set of values. I don't really know, but perhaps your sister's highest value is to be happy or to find fulfillment in her life, whatever that might mean to her. She may be chasing some kind of rainbow. She may think that happiness comes from success or money or having a beautiful home in the suburbs. This is a false value system. Her husband may have some other values we don't know about. His greatest desire may be sexual pleasure, for instance. So when people have divergent and selfish values, there is no way to assure that they will come to mutual happiness.

If both husband and wife are committed to Christ, then their highest priority is to please Christ. This goal brings fidelity and commitment to a marriage and these things are the glue which holds people together. I think the best thing you have going for you is the success of your own marriage—the fact that you eventually came to the end of yourselves and sought Christ. Your example is working right now in the lives of your sister and her husband. They watch your marriage and see why it works. They probably *know* what the right path is, but are at this point unwilling to walk it.

In the meantime, encourage them to work things out even though they are in a painful situation. Help keep the process alive by being supportive but not judgmental or "preachy." Pray that the Holy Spirit will get through to them because it is only God, through the power of the Holy Spirit, who can change hearts—not you.

——————— | CHAPTER 11 | ———————

Sex and Romance in Marriage

Sex was God's idea. Man may have perverted it and twisted it into something ugly, but God Himself has given us our sexuality with a beauty and intimacy available in no other human experience.

The Bible is straightforward and practical about sex, and many good books have been written on this subject by Christians. In fact, a recent survey by *Redbook* magazine indicates that evangelical Christian women enjoy the best sexual relationships of any women in America. This came as a surprise to the editors, I'm sure, but it did not surprise Christians. We know that sex and romance are God's idea, and when they are carried out within the confines and guidelines of Christian commitment, they reach their full fruition.

Yet misunderstandings about sex probably constitute the single greatest difficulty in marriage relationships, even for Christians. If you asked all the men in America what they most want in their sexual life, they would say more sexual activity and more intimacy. If you asked women the same question, they would say more intimacy and more romance. Both desire intimacy, but if men ask only for sex and women ask only for romance, neither may find the closeness they both want.

I often pray that women would understand men's cry for physical, sexual expression as well as they understand the psychological and emotional side of intimacy. I also pray that men would understand the importance of the psychological and emotional side as well as they understand the physical. Sex and romance truly go together, and one without the other is incomplete. Men and women are incomplete without each other, and they can find completeness only by discovering the oneness and wholeness God can give us in the marriage relationship.

STUCK IN A RUT •

Our marriage has fallen into a rut and we have forgotten the ABCs of courting. How can we again demonstrate love to each other, especially if we don't feel it strongly anymore?

I think there is a general misunderstanding about the difference between love and romance. Love is responsible behavior, the respect one person has for the personhood of another. In the Bible, love is something you do, not something you feel. Love is behavior; it is being considerate, thoughtful, unselfish. It involves the kinds of attitudes and actions listed in 1 Corinthians 13. You don't necessarily have to *feel* love in order to behave in a loving way.

Romance is also loving in the sense that it involves responsible behavior. Romance is the relationship that a man and a woman have toward each other that has to do with their sexuality, their mating procedure. After marriage many people forget about this romance or courtship which is the very thing that attracted them to each other in the first place. For instance, if you ask couples, "Why did you get married?" they'll usually say, "We wanted to spend time together." Then, after they get married, they don't spend much time together.

I suggest you start spending time together, romancing each other, and as you do, you may rediscover the reasons why you wanted to get married. Romance or courtship is made exciting by the little surprises, the discoveries, the unpredictability of it. But after we get married we often become too practical and we buy each other new furniture or something like that. One of the best ways you can romance each other is by spending time together in private, not with other people. Take the time to light some candles; send gifts and notes, poetry, flowers—these are the gestures of romance. Within your style, I'm suggesting you restore the very things you did when you were courting, and you'll find that it will bring the sizzle back into your marriage.

AN "F" IN ROMANCE •

My husband is a loser when it comes to romance. I told him last week I loved him and he said, "Well, if you say so." He's sort of plain and boring in almost everything. Should I forget about being romantic and act like him? I don't want to, but I feel hurt when

I'm in a romantic mood and he's not. I've hinted that I want him to be nicer when it comes to saying "mushy" things, but he doesn't feel it's important.

It is obvious the two of you have different personalities. Different people express love in different ways. One partner will always be more expressive than the other. This is found in varying degrees in every marriage. But if in response to "I love you," your mate says, "Well, if you say so," then there is probably some sort of problem.

Most often this kind of person falls into the "feelings-behavior model." They say, "Well, I happen to feel bad, and so I will be honest about my feelings." The problem is that someone has given them the wrong definition of honesty. What they really mean to say is, "I'm glad you love me and I love you. But right now I don't feel very loving." Interestingly enough, this same person goes to work, walks in the door full of smiles, says hello to everyone, and looks very happy. Why? Because he knows that his coworkers are not interested in his problems and they are not about to say, "Oh, Honey, what's wrong with you?" In a sense, he's forced to be nice because he knows that at work no one pays attention to you if you are a grump. But at home it is different. If you feel sick or you're kind of grumpy, you get quite a lot of attention.

God does not command us to have emotions—feelings are reactions. He does command us to have actions. Though you can't control your husband's behavior, you can continue to show love and concern by your behavior. Don't respond to him in revenge, saying, "Well, he treats me this way, so I'll do the same thing to him." Then the two of you will never express love. Try to do two things. Continue to do what you are doing— that is, being loving and responsive to him. But also try to get behind what he is saying. What he may be saying is, "She says she loves me but she's not showing it in a way that I understand." I find in many marriages, the woman wants to express verbal romantic love, but the man feels that his sexual life is unfulfilled. And so, she is saying words and he is saying, "But I need your love expressed in another way."

THE NEED FOR A NIGHT OUT •

My husband and I had our first child almost seven months ago and since that time the two of us have not spent one evening alone without the baby. Before our daughter came along we would go

143

out to a movie or to dinner at least once a week, but now that she is sharing our lives, we feel guilty about leaving her with a baby-sitter. I know it's a tremendous responsibility to care for her, but we need our time alone together too. Is this a normal feeling for new parents?

This reminds me of churches which invite people forward every Sunday to make a commitment. Over a period of time the most sincere people and those with the most sensitive consciences respond over and over again, and those who really need it just sit there and let the others respond. My son used to respond every Sunday to the invitation in Sunday School and we'd have to sit in the parking lot and wait for him because his little heart was so tender in wanting to serve Jesus.

In the same way, you want to be as good a mother as you possibly can. Perhaps you're also a victim of what I would call guilt-inducing messages that talk about crumbling families caused by parents' irresponsibility. Therefore, you are trying to correct the entire problem with one little seven-month-old person. Now if your seven-month-old baby could speak, maybe she'd tell you she wouldn't mind some variety. Maybe the child would like to see a baby-sitter or somebody else. Simply said, I think you are overreacting to a very great need in our culture—that is, the need for good parents and good solid families. But you have rightly put your finger on the fact that you also need some time for yourselves.

Many couples tell us that they can't afford baby-sitters. To those couples I say there are ways of solving that budget-breaker. One solution is to find other young married couples in your church and trade baby-sitting. This provides two things. First, it provides free baby-sitting and second, it puts your child in the hands of caring and responsible people like yourselves. It also gives you a chance to reciprocate by caring for their child. If you can't arrange that, find a trustworthy baby-sitter to care for your child. I think the idea of setting aside one night a week that is "your" night is a very good one. Being together and looking at each other across a table, preferably with a candle in the middle of it, is a very important thing for you, for the baby, and for your future family. You can be a much more resourceful and caring mother if you are fresh than if you are physically and emotionally tired.

KISS IN FRONT OF THE KIDS? •

I feel very uncomfortable when my husband kisses me in front of the children. I don't mind a good-bye kiss in the morning, but at other times I just don't feel he should do that. My parents never kissed each other when we were in the same room. Am I being too prudish?

Most couples get their ideas of how to relate to one another by watching their parents. For instance, after every meal in my home, my father, would get up from his place, walk around the table, kiss my mother, and thank her for the meal. I thought that was the way all men did it. So when I got married, I did the same thing. Later I found out it wasn't what everybody did, but it got me some good brownie points nonetheless!

I've discovered that people raised in homes that don't show affection have a great deal of difficulty expressing affection themselves. Sometimes this is because they feel that these expressions between a man and wife are sexually oriented in some way, and therefore should be done in private. Thus, they rob their children of something that is really very important.

I believe children need to be raised in an atmosphere where they are totally confident that Mom and Dad love one another and are not going to separate. Kids need to know that there is a solid bond between Mom and Dad, and that almost every problem can be overcome by that parental love, by that sense of security. How can children know that parents are deeply committed? I think one of the few ways they can really know is to *hear* their parents express themselves to each other and to *see* their parents show expressions of affection and love to each other. I encourage you to overcome your own sense of hesitancy and, for your children's sake, begin to express yourself and to show affection to your husband in front of them. It will not only help them relate to their spouses when they get married, but it will also give them a sense of assurance and confidence right now. As you read the New Testament, you will find that God encourages husbands and wives to share affection with each other. It is not dirty or something to be hidden. God not only approves of such affection, but smiles on it. In fact, it was His idea in the beginning.

TOO MANY INHIBITIONS •

My wife is afraid to take her clothes off in front of me. I think she sees all the beautiful models on TV and feels she doesn't compare. She's afraid I won't be impressed with her after I look at them. She comes from a fairly conservative background, but I don't think I've done anything to encourage this.

People have different approaches to modesty. For some people, modesty is based on insecurity and fear. For others, it is based on a sense of propriety or a conviction about what is right and wrong. If a person has been raised all her life with the idea that the body and sexuality are somehow inherently wrong, then the body becomes something to cover up and be embarrassed about.

This can be a deeply ingrained attitude that must be approached with much care. The great doctor and humanitarian, Albert Schweitzer, talked about the sanctity of the soul. I believe there is also a sanctity of the body. One should not attempt to break down those barriers without taking a great deal of care.

I've counseled many couples who disagree about various kinds of intimacy, and it's my opinion that if the less inhibited person tries to break down the other person's barriers by force—be it psychological or physical intimidation—it does almost irreparable harm. It's a form of assault, a rape of the other person's sensitivities. If your wife is protective of her body, a slow and gentle approach over a long period of time will be better than sitting down saying, "I think you ought to take your clothes off." Tell her she is beautiful. Affirm her. Tell her you love her. Turn off the overhead lights and light candles in your bedroom; take showers together (it gives you something to do besides staring at her). And consider the possibility that certain areas ought to remain private, not that they are taboo or ugly or sinful, but in the name of respect for the other's personhood.

The quest of this age is intimacy. Intimacy takes place not only in the physical and sexual areas of life, but also in the intellectual and emotional areas. In our deeply impersonal society, it can be difficult for people to share with one another. People are desperately afraid of exposure of or allowing other people to gain an advantage over them. But according to Scripture, "Perfect love casts out fear" (1 John 4:18). As we learn to love one another, we become less fearful of one another. We learn to share the deepest secrets of our souls. We are even able to expose to each other the imperfections of our physical bodies.

In long-term marriage, the goal is to develop intimacy between two human beings, for the two to become one, to overcome their fears and to share their innermost selves with each other at every level. But this can't be done in a day or a week or a month. I've counseled many young people who want to begin sexually at a point it may take them twenty years to reach.

One of the beauties of the marriage relationship is that in it we learn to know each other. Most happy middle-aged couples, though they realize that young lovers have a physical advantage over them, still wouldn't trade the intimacy, self-disclosure, and security that they have achieved over the years. So don't be in too big a hurry. Intimacy needs time to develop and love is sweeter as the years go by.

AFRAID TO MAKE LOVE ●

My wife and I just had our second child, and we are afraid to make love. We can't afford any more children now, but we don't want to do anything permanent in terms of birth control in case things change in time. Are our fears natural, or are we being overly cautious?

I have talked to many couples on this issue, and I can assure you that your anxiety is both common and natural. I think this is the time to go to your doctor and have him prescribe a form of birth control that is effective and comfortable for you, one that is not permanent. We hear a lot about vasectomy and other forms of sterilization, but they are not the only ways to enjoy a sexual relationship without fear of pregnancy. With caution and care, regard for one another, and a joint commitment to responsible marriage and parenthood, you can find other ways to avoid pregnancy. Even if pregnancy should occur (and not even sterilization is 100 percent effective), careful, caring, responsible people find ways to handle it.

Problems arise, of course, when people are careless or insensitive. Sometimes a man will, in the heat of passion, lose his good judgment for a moment and insist on some kind of satisfaction that ultimately is irresponsible. But if the two of you discuss this and decide together to exercise caution, it's highly unlikely that pregnancy will occur. Your doctor can help you find the method of birth control that will meet your needs.

MARRIED BUT AVAILABLE? ●

I'm married but still struggle with the feeling that I would like to date other men. It doesn't happen too often, but when it does I don't know how to deal with it. Is there something wrong with me? Could there be something I'm doing that makes me respond to other men? I know it's selfish of me to have these feelings, but when they come I don't know how to handle them.

Let me commend you for your honesty. The best way to deal with your feelings is to be honest about them and acknowledge them. When we don't face the real issue, then it becomes very difficult to find the solution. For example, we often deal with God dishonestly. In our prayers we say something like, "Dear God, I don't want to do this. I need Your help because I keep doing it." Probably a more honest prayer is, "Lord, I *do* want to do this, but I feel it is wrong and You wouldn't want me to do this. Help me to get in line with what You want me to do." Being honest with God and with yourself is the first step.

You asked if there could be something you're doing that makes you respond to other men. Usually, it comes from some deep insecurity within that says you must constantly prove who you are. You need to be reaffirmed. In my opinion most infidelity is based on this need. I have dealt with hundreds of couples in my life, and I can't think of one time when the problem was wholly sexual. Usually, people wonder if they're beautiful or attractive, the kind of people others would want. They question their self-worth. They have offered themselves to their mates and their mates have said yes and have married them. But then they go on through life saying, "I wonder if that affirmation was really true?" To find out, they stray outside their marriages to see if others will affirm them as well. How many more times will it take before they are satisfied? Always one more.

I believe these problems are basically spiritual. For instance, when a person understands that he or she is loved by God, totally accepted by God, and can do nothing to make God love him more or less, he can relax in his inner person. He no longer needs constant affirmation from others, saying, "You're OK, you're OK, you're OK."

So, struggle with this not so much on the level of your desires for men, but on the level of your relationship with God and the sense of security that you should have within yourself. When you become secure with yourself, then you won't feel you have to be a flirt, always looking for attention. Stay out of situations of compromise; don't lead men on with flirting. Begin to attack the problem at its root, which is personal security and self-worth.

Praise from others is temporary and very often shallow. Praise and affirmation from God is rich, deep, and lasting. And best of all, it's guaranteed. You've already got it.

GREENER PASTURES ●

My husband is constantly looking at other women. This really bothers me. He says he loves me and I know he has never cheated or messed around, but if he were really satisfied with me, would he still be so willing to look at others? He always says, "I look but don't touch." I guess he thinks that makes it OK, but is it? I even canceled our cable TV because he was watching topless dancer shows.

When you say, "I canceled the cable TV" rather than "we," it sounds as though you have set yourself up as protector. If you become territorial and frightened, jealous and threatened, you will not be in a very good position to struggle and fight for the things you believe in and love.

This kind of tendency on your husband's part is a natural part of being a man. The sexual trigger for males is in the eyes—what he sees and what he thinks he sees. This is what turns men on physically toward women. This is simply the way God made us. But if a man is a Christian, he should understand that his appetites and desires must be in submission to Jesus Christ—not only the appetite for sex, but the appetite for food, power, or whatever.

It is much better that you both have been able to talk about it openly than for him to be sneaking around looking at women in private. Those who sneak around tend to fall into some very deep problems. But talking about it tends to keep men away from these deeper problems. The two of you might find it very helpful to enter into serious counseling where you can talk about this on a deeper level.

Living with Others

Man is a social being, but that does not mean that social relationships come easily. Our contacts with other people can provide great and satis-fying happiness. They can also bring great pain and hurt.

Learning to live with others is part of loving God. No person can truly know God through a vertical relationship alone. In fact, as the Apostle John argues, "If a man says, 'I love God,' and hates his brother, he is a liar: for he that loves not his brother whom he has seen, how can he love God whom he has not seen?" (1 John 4:20)

In other words, love for God and love for other people are tied together. In a sense, our relationship with others are a mid-term exam testing the validity of our claim to love God. John argues that if we love the Father, we will love His Son. It follows that if we love His Son, we will love the people whom He has redeemed.

| CHAPTER 12 |

Friendships

Our world is much larger than our immediate family, and we cannot pretend to be islands unaffected by everyone else. We affect those outside our families and they affect us in return. Our relationships with those beyond our families can affect us both positively and negatively. Sometimes outside influences bring joy to our lives; sometimes they are heavy weights to bear. But healthy friendships and the ability to interact with those outside the family, on the one hand, and the ability to develop our characters without undue influence from peer pressure, on the other, can all be important values in our lives.

God made us to be social beings. The enemy of our souls, of course, wants to break down all social relationships and turn them into chaos. God wants the love we have in our immediate families to expand to the entire human family. In fact, the family is a model for the way all people should relate. It is important to think about how we relate to others, because our relationships can have an influence far greater than we might imagine.

GETTING TO KNOW YOU ●

How do you strike up a friendship with someone you don't know? There are so many people I'd really like to get to know, but I just don't know what to say to them and I'm afraid that they won't want to know me.

Your first step is to stop worrying that people won't want to be your friend. They will. People who start out with that feeling have difficulty ever developing friendships, because they've already decided that others aren't interested. It's like the man who comes to do the door and says, "You wouldn't want to buy any books, would you?" And you say, "You're right, I wouldn't," because the salesman has already put the idea in your mind. So when you say, "I'm afraid they won't like me," you're really saying, "I think I'm not worth knowing."

Developing friendships requires a positive and realistic outlook. About ninety-five percent of the people you'll meet during your lifetime are lonely and in need of a friend. And the majority of them would be glad to be your friend. It's much easier to build friendships by starting with that premise than by starting with the belief that no one wants you as a friend, or that some people are so self-contained they don't need friends. Actually, some of the people who appear most self-contained are the people who are the most lonely. You've heard the phrase, "It's lonely at the top"—that's true among many famous people. They're lonely because most people assume that everyone else must be the famous person's friend. Therefore, nobody really talks to the person, leaving him to go through life without any true, long-lasting friendships. So if you want friends, be a friend.

Friendship is a two-way street—a relationship which requires giving as well as receiving. Often, high school kids will say they want a friend. But what they really want is to be associated with the most popular person in the high school so they can become popular too. They don't really care about this person; they don't care to know him or her. All they want is to be seen with him and hang around with him.

You'll find it's much easier (and more beneficial) to pick people who are lonely, who perhaps don't have as many friends. Get to know them, introduce yourself. Then, as you learn to develop friendships with the people who are not being fawned over by everybody else, you will acquire some skills that will help you make friends for the rest of your life.

HUSBAND NEEDS FRIENDS •

I worry about my husand. He doesn't have any close friends. It's true his schedule is busy right now with a full-time job plus evening school, but at times he seems lonely for some good male

**companionship. I realize I can't push him into becoming friends
with the husbands of my friends, but what else can I do? He says
to me, "You are my best friend." But that in itself may get tiring
and boring after a while.**

I feel strongly that you should let your husband come to this conclusion
by himself. You're right in not trying to push him into specific friendships.
Still, I agree with you that he needs at least a few close friends of the same
sex.

What you might do is gently get him interested in joining a men's
fellowship group in your church. Often the strength of these groups is
in getting men of different spiritual and emotional maturities to sit down
with each other and complement one another's strengths and weaknesses.

Dr. Ted Engstrom, one of my spiritual mentors, told me once that
every man needs both a Timothy and a Barnabas. That is, he needs a
friend whom he can affect in a positive way—like Timothy—and he also
needs someone like Barnabas, whom he can walk with, talk with, and
share his innermost thoughts and feelings with. There are many Timo-
thies and Barnabases in good men's fellowship groups.

I've been a part of many such groups. Right now, I meet with a group
of guys every Saturday morning just to goof off for an hour and a half.
We call it "Wasting Time Together," and we drink coffee, eat Danish
pastries, and talk. Sometimes we end up praying or reading the Bible, but
we don't start with an agenda. I think this is important. So when the
meeting is over, what we've said to one another is, "You guys are worth
spending ninety minutes with, even though we didn't have anything
specific planned." It's a definite friendship-builder.

In similar groups I've found that often a certain kind of man—usually
shy, quiet, even somewhat inhibited in relationships—will come to the
group for up to six months before he really starts to share in the conversation. Then one day he says, "Here's something I'm concerned about." He
finds that the group accepts and understands him, and soon a whole new
vista opens. He becomes one of the strong ones who then begins to help
others.

Maybe your husband has similar characteristics. I would encourage
you to gently, patiently get him into a good men's fellowship.

HE'S IRRATIONAL, I'M IRATE •

My best friend, whom I've known for fifteen years, just moved across the country. She wants me to visit her this spring and I would like to go, but my husband refuses. I know we can afford the air fare, but he says I'm an adult now and I should put away childish things like girlfriends. Is he being irrational? Surely he could take care of the children for one week!

I agree with you. Husbands need to acknowledge the fact that taking care of the children and being homemakers are tremendously demanding jobs. And like anyone else, homemakers need and deserve vacations.

That doesn't always mean taking a vacation with the family either. Often, when that happens, a homemaker carries all of her work responsibilities with her. A short vacation by herself is a reasonable request. Even Mary, the Lord's mother, went off alone to visit her cousin Elizabeth, and she was pregnant at the time. They talked and encouraged one another, and out of that time came one of the warmest passages in the New Testament (Luke 1:39-56).

It seems to me that your husband is being a little unreasonable. Similar situations, in which the husband reacts with jealousy to letting the wife have any life of her own, are rooted in insecurity and childishness. If you've observed children, you know how exclusive their relationships are. One little girl will approach another and say, "I want you to be my friend, but I want you to be only *my* friend. You can't play with So-and-so if you play with me." Children use each other as possessions sometimes.

This kind of thing seems cute when we see it on the school playground, but when it happens in a marriage relationship it is far more tragic than funny. I suggest you hang in there and debate this problem with your husband.

FRIENDS RATE OVER DAD •

My daughter is ashamed to be seen with me when she's around her friends. She is in high school and active in sports. I would like to see some of her games, but she doesn't want me to attend. I'm trying hard to show an interest in the things she's doing, but she isn't helping matters.

You can be sure that the problem isn't you. All kids your daughter's age fear jeopardizing their friendships.

In fact, one of the most difficult things a teenager faces is to be standing among friends when his mother and father walks up. Your child is thinking, "O Lord, help me! Keep my mom and dad from making fools of themselves. Keep them from saying anything dumb. Help them not to treat me like a baby. Don't let them ask stupid questions."

Teens are desperately afraid they will lose the friendships they've worked so hard to cultivate. So when your daughter tries to keep you away, it's not because she's ashamed of you. She's just playing it safe.

I always put these kinds of situations in a category I call "normals." There are certain constants you can count on, especially with kids. Normal character changes always happen during the teenage years. A preacher's son will begin to swear to prove he's really a man. A girl who has been dedicated to the youth group will start dressing in a cheap manner. And all kids will do out-of-character things to be accepted by their peers.

Don't blame yourself. Instead, just continue to love your daughter, and give her a little space. In a few years, she'll want you at her games.

MAKING FRIENDSHIPS LAST ●

How can we get to know people beyond a superficial level and develop deeper friendships? Several times we have invited couples from our church over for a meal. But they never invite us over to their place. Maybe they don't like us, but we always seem to have a good time when we get together. We just don't know how to get to know these people on a deeper level.

Keep trying.

The Bible stresses the gift of hospitality, and I consider it a Christian responsibility to invite people over for meals and fellowship even though they don't always reciprocate.

One thing you might try is to invite different combinations of people. My wife and I have found that it is much more difficult to have one couple over than to have two couples. The selection of couples, though, is an art; you need to find people whom you think have something to share with each other. But when the chemistry is right, you have the satisfaction of being used by God to draw people together into friendships.

As far as people not inviting you to their homes is concerned, I think you have a couple of things to think about. First, it's possible that you mildly intimidate the people who come to your house. I've seen this happen before, even to my wife and me. Sometimes people see your home and say to themselves, "Oh, this house is so well kept, and everything is in its place in such a clean and attractive way; I would be embarrassed to have them come to our home."

The second possibility is that people simply are too busy. One family told me once that they had considered putting a revolving door on their house. And some families seldom have time for meals together with their own members, let alone meals with people from outside. It's sad but a reality.

Still, the first conclusion many of us draw when our invitations are not reciprocated is, "Maybe they don't like us." I've concluded over the years that this is a response that comes more from our insecurities than from reality. I doubt that many of us can generate enough energy from our own lives to be truly disliked. So I wouldn't worry about that.

The important thing to remember is that the Bible asks us to be hospitable. Hospitality is a commitment to the Lord, and I would urge you to exercise the gift.

LETTING HIM DOWN GENTLY ●

I've become very good friends with a boy who is thirteen years old. I am nineteen. He's a nice kid, and we have fun together at some of the church activities. But lately he has started to look at me as more than a friend, and I don't think this is right considering our age difference. I don't want to encourage this, but I do want to remain his friend. I've heard about students thinking they are in love with their teachers and I wonder if maybe this is that kind of situation. How can I handle it?

I think you need to be aware, first of all, that letting your friend down can be a traumatic experience for him. Yet it's obvious that you need to do something.

The best thing is to let him down slowly and gently. Begin to season your conversations with statements that help him to understand that the path he's heading down is a dead-end street. Even as you ease him toward this realization, be prepared to hear a thud. It will, in a sense, shatter his dreams, and he'll feel a strong sense of loss. But there is no way to avoid that; the only thing you can do is help ease the impact.

Another thing you can do is to keep him from feeling embarrassed about his crush. Make sure he knows that the matter is just between the two of you. You may need to sit him down in a quiet place where the whole matter can be talked out. Don't be surprised if there are some tears. Assure him of your continued friendship and, above all, let him be assured that his friends need not know what has happened.

You're dealing with what appears to be an innocent case of puppy love. But, as they say, puppy love is real to the puppy. Keep this in mind. Also, for your sake, I think it's important for you to realize that there's nothing dirty or unnatural about the situation. In a way, it's sort of a beautiful thing. I think that most of us get our first opportunity to deal with our feelings during a phase of puppy love. You can make it a very positive experience for your young friend.

NO FRIENDS IS NO FUN •

I'm fourteen and I don't have any real friends. When I ask to be a part of some project, the kids say, "We'd like to let you, but . . ." and then they make up some kind of excuse. I have a high IQ, and I'm not ugly or overweight. I go to a Christian school but maybe some kids think I'm more sinful than they are because I like rock music, dancing, and boys, and they don't. How can I be their friend? Am I too young to like boys?

Though I risk sounding a little harsh, I'd encourage you to look for another group of friends. What often happens with girls your age is that you'll choose a group of very popular kids, such as cheerleaders, with whom to be friends. You will say to yourself, "I've got to be in that group." But what you really want is to be accepted into that group and then in turn exclude others from joining.

If you look around, you will find many girls who are in your present situation. Why not call some of them together to form a new group of friends? Having been hurt as you have, you can really feel a camaraderie with girls who can't seem to "fit in" either. Your new group could actually set an example for others by not excluding people who feel that they don't belong with anyone.

Regarding this business about liking rock music, dancing, and boys, I think it may be more of a problem with you than it is with your class-mates. It sounds to me like you've talked about these things with others, maybe even argued about them. It's possible that you're really beginning to ask yourself whether or not some of these things are right for you. If you're trying to defend yourself, it's a sure sign that you're not as secure about these things as you originally may have thought.

Concerning your question—"Am I too young to like boys?"—no, you are just about the right age, and your feelings are perfectly normal. Don't fool yourself, though. What you may like most is being accepted and cared for by boys. It's great to have someone say to you, "Hey, I think you're special. I think you're pretty, and you're the kind of person I want to be with." All of us like such affection. It affirms our self-worth.

HOLED UP AT HOME ●

My sister-in-law dropped out of college in her senior year and went back to live with her parents. Five years ago, she stopped driving her car and hasn't gone more than two blocks from her home since. Her parents have confronted her about this, and she says she is a better individual by staying home. She is a very intelligent woman and works diligently around the house. But she just isn't interested in getting out. I can't believe this is a healthy situation for her. Doesn't she need social interaction? My husband tried to talk to her about this; she got very upset and ran from the room. Would you suggest something as drastic as bodily taking her for help?

That would be the least attractive alternative. I am encouraged that you want to help your sister-in-law, but we can never force people to seek help. The old saying applies: "You can lead a horse to water but you can't make him drink." Taking your sister-in-law bodily to a counselor will not work.

I think there are some things you can do, though. First, you need to examine your own unwillingness to let her be different. Let's face it, many people have chosen lives that parallel your sister-in-law's situation. Such individuals choose lives of quietness and reclusion. Sometimes they take care of people who are invalids. I've found that many times they aren't unhappy, nor are they repressed in any way. They simply prefer a qui-eter, less action-oriented lifestyle.

On your part, it takes a lot of maturity to allow others to live differently than you do. Our natural inclination is to make everyone we know align their lifestyles with our own. I call this having a "cookie-cutter" attitude—trying to cut people out in the same shape. Some of us even do it in the name of the Gospel, making cookie-cutter Christians. This attitude conveys a kind of immaturity on our part whereby we can't stand diversity.

On the other hand, you know your sister-in-law well, and you seem convinced that she needs social interaction. In that case, you and your husband need to provide that interaction. But love her, don't criticize her lifestyle. Try to take her places where she feels comfortable. If she feels uneasy around people, take her to the park for a picnic. Let her feel loved and secure. But give her love in the form of actual acts of love rather than by advice and criticism.

CAN YOU BE TOO NICE? •

People are forever taking advantage of me. My husband says I'm *too* nice, but I do like to listen to people and reach out. However, I have my limits. Friends call and keep me on the phone for hours. I hint in more ways than one to end the conversation. In fact, I even tried lying once and said someone was at my door. My husband and I had some surprise visitors one day who stayed for five hours. I wasn't feeling well and must have said at least seven times that I really needed some rest, but they just sat there and didn't pick up the hint. I know God doesn't want me to lie or make excuses to get rid of people and I really don't want to hurt anybody's feelings, but what can I do?

I would say that you need to learn how to be more direct with people. If I were to draw a picture of you, it would look like a cartoon in the *New Yorker* magazine where the person is drawn with fuzzy edges instead of clear lines. Everyone is pulling at you, and you are losing your edges, your shape.

Practically speaking, when you need to get off of the phone, don't hint. Say, "Maude, I need to hang up because I have some other things I need to do." Or when people come unannounced to the house, say, "We have another commitment in half an hour, and we're going to have to excuse ourselves." If the commitment is to get in your car and drive around the

161

block, it's still a commitment that you have to make to yourself. In your particular case, you have a commitment to get some rest. It's not deceptive to admit that.

You've got to learn such directness. Otherwise, you will cease to exist, being nibbled to death as if by minnows.

HOW TO BE YOUR OWN PERSON ●

When my friends tell dirty jokes, I laugh along with them because I don't want my friends to think I don't approve. Later, I feel wrong for laughing because I know that God doesn't want me to do that. How can I get my friends to stop telling those jokes? And how can I keep from laughing when the jokes are told?

We can't change other people's behavior; we can only change our own. In most situations it helps to accept that fact. I doubt if you can persuade your friends to stop telling these bad jokes. Strangely enough, the problem you are facing isn't unique to young people. In fact, if you were to talk to your dad or your pastor or even your teachers at school, you would find they face the same kind of problem. There are also people around them who say things they don't agree with, and they often don't know how to handle it either. It might be helpful to ask them how they handle it. In fact, your dad would be interested to know how you feel about this, and together you might be able to come up with some ideas.

Let me suggest what I would do. First of all, I don't feel that I am obligated to laugh. In fact, I have sort of a little twist in me that says I don't have to be a chameleon, turning color to match whatever I sit down on. I like to decide my own response. I've concluded that the ultimate freedom in life is the ability to choose one's own response. That is, you can be with people who are laughing but you don't have to laugh. You can be with people who are crying but you don't have to cry. I'm not talking about just being obstinate. I'm just saying that I don't like to absorb my environment. I like to be the actor rather than the reactor. I think the strongest medicine you can give people who say things that you don't agree with is to be silent. Eventually, they will catch on that, for some reason, you are not going along, and if they want you to go along, they will have to do something else.

What constitutes a dirty joke? There are various categories. The worst kind fall into the categories of degrading people, God, or holy things.

162

Jokes that degrade people ethnically, racially, or sexually are ugly and destructive. Jokes against God are blasphemous and very dangerous. Jokes that make fun of holy and sacred things as well as things that history has proven valuable are also wrong. And then there is a whole category of coarse things. They are not evil as such, but have to do with manners. People who are civilized and have good manners don't talk certain ways. So let me encourage you to change your behavior; don't laugh just to be accepted. Your friends will catch on and quit talking that way to you. If they don't, you may want to reevaluate the friendships you seek.

WHAT TO DO ABOUT BULLIES ●

It seems there is always someone on my street or in school who wants to pick a fight with me just to aggravate me. Almost every morning the big kids push me down or pick on me. I can't keep running and can't seem to make friends with them. I want to fight them, but there are just too many and I'm not big enough. I'm sick of getting beaten up. Would it be right to fight them?

Virtually every boy in the world has felt this way except maybe the few bullies who cause the problem. In fact, most dads struggle in trying to give their sons advice along this line. I remember going through deep agony with my son, trying to figure out how to advise him about the bullies who enjoyed picking on him. I wanted to tell him to hit the other kid. But stop and think about that a little bit. If we do that, then we are giving in to the worst in mankind. What are we going to do when we grow up? If we have a little problem with someone on the street, do we jump out of the car, break his car window, and smack him in the face? Do we get a shotgun out and blow the neighbor's TV antenna off his roof? What do we do? I think we have to come to the Lord and seek His help. He tells us to do some rather specific things when we are picked on, including: "Turn the other cheek," "Walk the second mile," and "Love your enemies." That sounds very weak, and to many Jesus probably looked weak. They plucked His beard and hit Him in the face and waited for Him to strike back. But Scripture says, "When they hurled their insults at Him, He did not retaliate; when He suffered, He made no threats. Instead, He entrusted Himself to Him who judges justly" (1 Peter 2:23, NIV).

You have isolated much of the problem when you say the bullies pick on you just to aggravate you. But if they can't aggravate you, then their purpose is thwarted. I encourage you to attempt as best you can to withdraw—back away and let these bullies struggle among themselves. Of course, some people will tell you to fight back. People who say that haven't lived in a neighborhood where people have knives and guns. No one wins in that kind of confrontation, and, believe me, these kinds of things happen in the best of neighborhoods.

Many times, smaller kids join together and pick on someone even smaller. That is why a lot of kids join gangs. Another reason kids join gangs is because it's the only way to get the bullies off their backs. That's unworthy. You don't need to swear and start talking dirty and do daring, stupid things that make you look brave but that will destroy you. Joining a group like this won't solve anything.

An alternative is to seek the Lord's help and seek the help of those adults who are in charge. Some people say that's squealing, but I say somebody is going to have to start getting civilized. I think you need to talk to your parents or school officials, and they need to confront the parents of those bullies.

LOSING FRIENDS? •

I'm twelve years old and having trouble with my friends. One friend tells me she can't play and then goes to play with someone else. I don't know why she does this. Sometimes, other girls call me a brat or a jerk. I don't know why they do this either, because I really don't even know them.

Young people often say and do things without thinking about the effects their actions and words may have on others. If you were to ask them why they call you names or why they do some of the things they do, they probably wouldn't be able to give you a well-thought-out reason. Until they mature a little, they'll continue to act this way. There is a verse in 1 Corinthians 13 that encourages us to always think the best of others (v. 7). Let's apply this to your situation. When you talk to your girlfriend to ask her if she can play with you, she asks her mother and her mother says, "No, I don't think you ought to right now." So, your friend tells you she can't play. Then, later, you see her out in the street playing with someone else. You say, "I thought you couldn't play!"

What has probably happened is that at first her mother told her she couldn't play because she had some homework or some chores to do around the house, but then she finished these duties; another friend called and asked her to play; and her mother said it was OK. Or, maybe her mother is the type who isn't consistent. Sometimes she says yes, and sometimes, no. Perhaps the girl was persistent and finally her mother gave in. Your friend is probably not thinking of rejecting you at all. She is glad to be allowed to go out and play, but when you see her playing and confront her about it, she doesn't like being threatened. So she calls you names, which then reinforces your idea that she is rejecting you. We learn from this example that the best way to keep a good friend is to assume that she doesn't really want to hurt you. And most of the time you will be right.

This leads us to another reason why your friends might treat you badly. Young people, as they are still immature, tend to think of friendship and love in a possessive way, as if they own somebody. That is why some little boys like to have a clubhouse. The first thing they do is set up rules to keep other people out. They say, "All the guys who are going to be in this club are going to have red hair," or, "They are all going to be part of our team," or whatever. Immaturity is always exclusive. Immaturity can't stand other people or diversity. In fact, lots of times when kids are very young, they say, "How about you being my friend and not anybody else's friend?" When we grow older and more mature, we realize that to love somebody or be someone's friend is not to possess that person. So don't do the same thing they do. The worst thing you can do is say, "Hey, I'll find a friend and then we'll be exclusive and we'll put the others on the outside and make them feel bad just like they made us feel." That would be doing the opposite of what Jesus said. He said we should return good for evil, not evil for evil.

OUT IN THE COLD •

I want to spend more time with friends but it seems that most of them have started dating. Now they spend so much time with their boyfriends that they don't have time for me. I don't feel right asking them to take time away from their boyfriends just to be with me, so I spend time by myself. Am I just feeling sorry for myself or is there some other way I can spend time with my friends?

When I was a kid, we had a song, "Wedding Bells Are Breaking Up That Old Gang of Mine." This is happening to you, only they are not wedding bells, but going-steady rings, sweaters, etc. That is the way things happen as you grow older, and it is difficult not to feel sorry for yourself. While your warm little group of friends was together, you were happy because you felt part of that group. But what you might not have known was that there were hundreds of kids who weren't in a clique like yours. Those kids were desperately lonely. Every high school and college has a large number of kids who long to feel part of a group. They would do almost anything to feel like they belong. But those who are already in a comfortable group don't notice them. It is only when we are rejected and left out that we might begin to notice the outsiders. What is happening to you is a normal phenomenon that was bound to happen. Had you met a boy first, you wouldn't be thinking a lot about your girlfriends who would be having your problem. That is the way it works.

I think there is an overriding spiritual lesson in all of this. The lesson is that life is full of rejected, lonely people who desperately need friends. I often tell high school kids, "If you want a friend, be a friend." From the strength you have received from having been a part of a group, I encourage you to start trying to locate these lonely kids around school rather than sitting around moping and thinking about yourself. Tomorrow, when you go to school, take a piece of paper and start writing down names of all the kids you see whom you think are on the outside. In reality, about ninety-five percent of the people you'll meet in your lifetime are lonely and in need of a friend—the majority of whom would gladly be *your* friend. Therefore, you've got to go about the business of rebuilding friendships on the basis of understanding how others feel. When you grasp the concept that almost everyone you meet would love another friend, you will have learned one of the most important lessons of life—you will begin reaching out to others.

By the same token, don't discount the value of time alone. There will be a time in your life when you will beg to have some time to yourself. So do some of the "alone" things now while you have the opportunity.

I have a hunch that the deeper fear you may be facing is that no young man will want or find you. Many girls have been concerned about this, and almost all of those who wanted a boyfriend found one. So don't let that throw you into panic. Pray about it; commit it to God; then forget about it and be a people-helper. I believe God will reward you in your spirit for it.

BREAKING INTO CLIQUES •

Our church youth group has a problem with cliques. I try to make friends with those in the clique, but they act as if I'm not even there. They speak, but it sure seems forced. I love the Lord and enjoy having fellowship with other Christians, but it is hard to have fellowship when there seems to be a brick wall between me and the clique. Deep down it hurts me and is giving me an inferiority complex. Why don't they accept me?

There is no good reason why they don't accept you except that people who are weak tend to gain strength by clustering together in groups and excluding others. This is what many people do in life, and in actuality, though the kids in the clique often appear to be the stronger, more popular kids, they often demonstrate their adolescent weakness by being so exclusive. This doesn't help you, of course, because you don't want to be rejected.

Many kids caught in your situation create a second clique. They find other outsiders and form their own exclusive groups. This is not the way to deal with your situation. One of my most penetrating observations came from the poet, Carl Sandburg, who said the most obscene word in the English language is *exclusive*. I tend to agree with him. In fact, I think it may be the most anti-Christian word there is. Jesus was against exclusiveness. He was a friend of drunks, politicians, and tax collectors. Jesus went to the downtrodden and offered Himself to them. In fact, many people wonder why America has been blessed of God. They think it is because of democracy. I doubt if that's true. I think America has been blessed of God because of the phrase at the bottom of the Statue of Liberty: "Give me your poor, your tired, your huddled masses. . . ." As people accept the poor and the excluded, they are doing a Christlike thing. Develop the desire to include people. Find another excluded person and include him. And then the two of you find another excluded person and include that person. Before long, you will have a group. But always keep reminding each other that to be Christlike means keeping the group open. Always be the person who opens the group, who unclasps your hand to invite the other kid in. Be a Christlike example.

I think it might also be good for you to express to your youth leader how you feel. One of the greatest tasks of youth leaders is to break down these cliques. Your youth leader may be able to help you by giving you some insight as to what you do. You may come on too strong; you may be one of those people who badgers folks and just can't understand why they don't want to hear you all the time. Your youth director can help you with this. But let me encourage you, if you want friends, first be a friend.

THE OPPOSITE SEX •

I'm in high school and every time I try to make friends with a girl she thinks I'm trying to go out with her. If that doesn't happen, and we begin a friendship, my friends and hers think we're dating and put pressure on us. I'll admit that sometimes when I do get to know a girl I would like to date her, but that's not my main objective. How does a person develop a quality relationship with the opposite sex?

For starters, don't lead girls on. Don't give them the feeling that you think they're special and that you want them as special friends. Many young people try to find a steady boyfriend or girlfriend simply to fulfill their need of being accepted. Once they have been accepted by this person, they drop him or her and go on to someone else. A lot of guys play this game. It's like putting notches on the belt of a gunslinger. You get one girl to like you, then you move on to the next, then on to the next, and soon you have a trail of broken relationships behind you.

One of the keys to having successful friendships is showing interest in more than just one girl. Try to be a friend to everyone—guys and girls alike. Be a friendly person, and then people won't mistake your motives. If you're somewhat of a sullen person, who has only one friend at a time, the kids in school will likely misunderstand when you start showing interest in someone. They will think you want this girl as a girlfriend.

On the other hand, some guys will ask the same question you've asked in order to protect themselves. In other words, they're afraid of rejection. A guy may try to be friends with a girl and when he feels like she's going to reject him, he'll say, "Oh well, I didn't want a girlfriend after all. I don't need a girlfriend." But deep in his heart he really is aching to have a special friend—a girlfriend, but he's afraid that no girl would really like him. Therefore he protects himself with this game of "I'm going to be everybody's friend." If this is true of you, then you need to admit that. It isn't some terrible character flaw; it's just part of being a normal guy growing up. No one in the world likes to be rejected. In fact, there's probably nothing quite as painful as offering your love and then not having the other person return it. Love is a two-way street, and there's no guarantee that it will run both ways at the same time.

─────────── CHAPTER 13 ───────────

Communication

Almost every bit of advice we get about family or marriage or human relationships boils down to *communication.* And yet communication in itself solves nothing. Communication can be good or bad, ugly or kind, loving or irresponsible, clear or unclear. We do not want just communication—we want honest, straightforward, loving, accepting communication in our homes.

We hope that by our loving relationships we can create a climate that encourages open communication. We want an atmosphere of total acceptance, one that says, "Not only am I sharing with you my real self, not only have I let down my guard, but I am willing to be understanding of you and to let you put down your guard too. There is no danger of any hurt here."

"Perfect love," wrote the Apostle John, "casts out fear" (1 John 4:18).

STRAIGHT TALK ●

How do I get a straight answer from my parents? Whenever I question my dad about a responsibility or a discipline he's given me, he answers, "Because I said so," or, "You're too young to know." I'm in high school and I feel I can handle a little more than that.

─────────────

Let me point out some of the reasons why this happens. First of all, and most likely, when your dad was a boy, he was probably treated this way by his dad. This is what his dad said and did, so this is the only way he knows how to act toward you.

Second, it is quite possible that your father is influenced by the people around him—coworkers, school board officials, even church members who tell him that he's got to "win his medals" each day by being a master sergeant with his family; a real father is in charge! He needs a tatoo on his forearm that says, "I'm boss here." I don't know where this idea of the macho-type father came from, but too many fathers feel they need to conform to this image. Unfortunately, you've become the victim of that image and it's very tough on you.

A third reason you may be having trouble getting straight answers from your parents, especially your dad, is that they don't hear the "why" question as being really what it is you're saying. You ask, "Why?" because you honestly want to know. But most of the time, when your dad hears you ask "Why?" he thinks you're being a smart aleck. "Why?" means you're questioning his authority. So, begin by letting him know you plan to comply with his wishes. Agree and start doing what he tells you to do. Then *after* you've done what he's told you, come back to him and say, "You know, I'm going along with this and I'm doing it. I have no problem with your authority. You're my dad and you're in charge, and I'm not trying to shoot you down in any way. But, why do I have to do this? Let's talk about it a little for my own benefit. I'd really like to know." And you'll find that once he knows you don't plan to violate his authority, he'll probably be much more ready to answer you.

Of course, the embarrassing part may be that your dad really doesn't know why he does some of these things. Many times dads say a certain thing because it's the thing dads are expected to say. Sometimes, we say no because we're trying to protect ourselves; we don't really know what the answer is. Later on, when we have a little less tense situation, we can work our way through it and say, "Well, I really don't know why I asked you to do that. Maybe we ought to change things." But it is hard on your father if your questions seem like an attack on his authority.

A BATTLE OF WORDS ●

Why does every conversation with my teenagers turn into a battle? It seems that every time we speak to each other we end up arguing. I know none of us wants to fight, but we always end up that way. Can you give us some pointers on how to communicate without yelling and disagreeing?

Some of this conflict is related to temperament. There are certain families who have decided that they're going to live at a certain decibel level, and they do. In fact, I'm very confident that families make this choice consciously. You decide if you want a loud home or a quiet home. And I'm told that depending on your heritage or background, you are more or less programmed this way. For instance, Mediterranean people do more shouting and gesturing than do Eskimos.

But I think some of it may also be an excuse. With parents and teenagers especially, one of the key reasons we end up in arguments is because each of us has a position on which we're just not going to back off. Years ago, someone gave me some real help by pointing out the difference between *demanding* respect and *commanding* respect. If one demands respect, he tries to come down on someone, insisting on his own way simply because he holds the upper hand. To command respect, however, means that you've won the right to be heard. Another person has observed the wisdom and quality of your life and has developed a respect for your opinions. So, due to your fairness and the way you relate to others, you command respect because of the kind of person you are. I think a parent needs to work very hard at commanding respect as opposed to demanding it. But when two people each want their own way, then one person has to submit. And what usually happens is that the parent says, "Because I'm buying your food, you're going to have to start agreeing with me or I'm going to start taking away some privileges." It's really a method of blackmail. This then leads to shouting matches and heated arguments because each party insists on winning the battle. Don't get into win-lose situations because it's not worth the price to win the argument and lose the respect of your child.

It might be helpful for parents to remember a basic rule: *Let the other person finish speaking before you start.* Then ask a clarifying question, such as: "Am I understanding you correctly?" "Is this what you've said?" This slows down the whole process and focuses on the real issue. It also goes a long way toward preventing any misunderstandings. Some people have wondered why Jesus stooped down and wrote in the sand when the religious leaders were going to stone the woman taken in adultery. Many feel that what He did was a very dynamic thing. He slowed down the whole process. He got everybody's attention. While He was quietly writing in the sand, the others were composing themselves a little bit and preparing for His response. Apply this rule to your relationship with your teenagers and watch the results manifest themselves.

COMMUNICATION BREAKDOWN ●

What are some of the "communication killers" in a family? Sometimes, my kids will go through a stage where they just won't talk to me at all. The more I ask, the more silent they become. I'm sure it must be something I say or something I do, but I'm simply not aware of it. Can you help me avoid these situations?

"Communication killers"—that sounds like the title for a good book! I tend to categorize this topic under "King-of-the-hill." Young people will not play king-of-the-hill with an adult—not their parents anyway. By that, I mean they will not get into a no-win situation where Dad is always standing on top and pushing them off the cliff. Dad's older; he's more experienced. Kids won't argue with that. When Dad gets the idea he's always right, children know they can't win. Kids just quit talking when they lose every time. If kids are ridiculed and invariably overruled, communication will die. If they're not allowed to finish their sentences, this will kill communication too.

I was recently with a family where there were teenagers and, naturally, I tried to get the kids involved in the conversation. We've always done that in our home. We didn't let the kids monopolize the conversation, but we did allow them to be seen as people, and so we'd ask, "How do you feel about that?" "What do you think?" I tried that with these kids, and their mother would not let them finish one sentence. They would start to mumble something, and rather than let them deal with it, the mother cut in, possibly afraid her children would embarrass her or might say the wrong thing or sound dumb. Unfortunately, that's the precise message children heard that evening: *Mom thinks I'm dumb. She doesn't think I can finish a sentence so she's doing it for me. I'll just be quiet because she doesn't have confidence in me.* Now the mother wasn't actually saying that, but that's what she was telegraphing to her children loud and clear. A dogmatic parent, who's always right, will grind communication to a halt in no time.

Then there's the kind of parent who has to correct each mistake his child makes. Like an accountant, the parent has to make sure all the little dots are perfectly in place. I'm sure you've been with a couple where the husband or wife says, "Last Tuesday, we went to see So-and-so," and the spouse immediately stops the conversation and says, "Honey, it wasn't Tuesday; it was Monday." You don't care whether it was Monday *or* Tuesday—it's irrelevant; it's trivial; it doesn't matter. Parents who are mistake-correctors kill communication.

If you want to start a conversation with young people, ask the question, "How do you feel about this?" or "What is your opinion about this?" You'll find that the doors of communication will begin to swing open once again. Young people enjoy talking about their opinions, their feelings, their thoughts.

BITTER WORDS BRING GUILT •

The guilt of not treating my parents right has haunted me as long as I can remember. I've never hit my mother or father or anything like that, but all too often my mouth gets the better of me, and I say things I later regret. I've prayed about the problem, but my human nature obviously has a loud voice. I dearly love both my parents, but I just don't know how to control my tongue. My parents have told me that God is going to repay me for my wrong. I'm confused and frustrated.

Let me make a suggestion. Nowadays the world is saying, "Get in touch with your feelings." Well, there's nothing wrong with getting in touch with your feelings. But if you *act* out your feelings, I think you may be stepping outside your Christian responsibility.

I'll explain. Your parents say something, and that makes you angry. Now, you can't control anger. It's an emotional reaction which sneaks up on you and swells up inside before you even know what has hit you.

You can, however, control your actions. The Bible says, "Be angry, and yet do not sin" (Eph. 4:26, NASB). Well, what does that mean? There is an interval (I call it the "response" interval) between the time that you experience anger and the moment you respond to it. You actually have a moment to choose between snapping back at your parents or quickly saying, "Lord Jesus, help me to get this under control." If you snap back, you'll continue to hurt yourself and your parents. But by habitually acknowledging the Lord at the precise moment of your anger, you're much more likely to answer back responsibly and in love.

We surely know that it is a right thing to respect and honor our parents. Yet sometimes the tongue gets in the way of our good intentions. It's an ancient problem; the Bible describes the tongue as unruly, evil, full of deadly poison. And we are instructed that if a person can bridle his tongue, he can control his whole being.

The first step to gaining such control lies at the moment of your anger.

Season your response by obediently acknowledging God, and then respond in love.

NO SHARING, NO CARING ●

I've been married a year, and in that time I've cried more than the last five years put together. At first, I thought it was part of adjusting to my marriage, but now I'm afraid it's much more than that. You see, when something is bothering or disturbing me, I want to share it with my husband. I think sharing burdens, no matter how trivial, should help people get to better know each other. But when I do this, I get a brush-off or sarcastic remark when what I really need is love and understanding or just a listening ear. This kind of reaction makes me think I would be better off keeping silent. It hurts not being able to share things with my spouse.

Have you expressed how you feel about this to your husband? I think you need to do that first. Then try to open him up a little. Ask him questions about his feelings. Try to dig a little bit into his dreams and aspirations. If he's really willing to work at solving this communication problem, you can solve it together.

Unfortunately, many men don't want to share their intimate feelings and dreams. They say, "You ought to be able to handle those private things yourself. I handle mine, and you should handle yours. Then we'll talk only about the more important things." I had a friend tell me once, "My husband reduces all of my problems to trivialities. When I share something I feel is important, he says, 'Get the plumber to do that' or 'Call the carpenter.' " She added, "The truth is that my life is tied up in these things, and he crosses out the meaning of my life by thinking everything I do is trivial."

That seems to be the nature of your problem. And it's a very common problem. Many couples go through their entire married life without ever being able to solve it. If your husband is someone who just doesn't want to share in things he calls "trivialities," then I suggest you begin to develop a relationship with a neighbor or perhaps a woman from your church. Find a best friend who is willing to listen to your daily problems, no matter how small they seem.

Even if your husband won't listen or talk about smaller things, I don't think your marriage has to suffer. A best friend can sometimes fill communication gaps.

HIS LIPS ARE SEALED ●

How do I get my husband to talk to me? I've read many books on communication in marriage; I'm trying to be open and interested in what he does and the things he likes to do. For instance, when we get home from work in the evening, I like to ask him about his work during that day. I'm sincere in wanting to know about it, but he says he'd rather not talk about it, that he leaves his work at the office. How can I get him to open up and share with me?

Rather than saying, "How did work go today?" you might try saying simply, "Tell me about your day." Or start talking about yourself or your relationship with each other. Talk about the future, about your children, about the house you want to build someday. Maybe you want to own a cottage by the lake or make a big contribution to the church. Your husband's profession might be a sensitive subject—especially at the end of the day. Get him talking about other things first.

I think there's a great difference between a husband not wanting to talk about work and a husband simply not wanting to talk to his wife. A lot of men feel a need for escape from their jobs when they come home in the evening. They're tense, tired, and what they look for is an entirely opposite environment. To even think about the office brings back the tension. It's more work to rehash the day's activities.

Now, maybe it would be good for your husband to talk about work some evenings. But don't start with that subject. Gently pull him away from it; then, if it seems he might be willing to reflect on his day, ease him into it that way.

Not every husband can be turned into a sparkling conversationalist. But the surest way to get him to talk is to find out what *he* wants to talk about. If you can discover those areas, he will start opening up more.

SILENT TREATMENT ●

I have a problem with my father. He's a good man and father, but when I want to discuss anything important he doesn't want to talk. When I was younger his attitude toward things I mentioned

to him was almost mocking. For example, he'd say, "Don't be silly, it's not that important," or "Can't you figure it out for yourself?" Now that I'm older (I'm twenty-five), I still want to share concerns with him, but it's as though he wishes I wouldn't try to talk to him about anything heavier than the weather. This gets very frustrating. There are things I would like to share with him and ask him, but I just get no response. Is there anything I can do to help him open up?

––––––––––––––––––

After twenty-five years you may not want to hear this, but here it is: keep trying. In working with children, we sometimes say, "Wait for that teachable moment." In your father's case, I would say, "Wait for that golden moment." Now, I can't tell you when such a moment of communication will take place, but I can tell you that it will be a wonderful experience when it comes.

I had a young man tell me once that his father, a policeman, had been severely injured on the job. The accident happened when the young man was only three years old. For years after that, he always tried to talk to his father about the crippling accident, but the father never would say more than a few words. Finally, when the young man was a senior in college, he brought the subject up one Sunday afternoon while he and his dad were watching a football game on television. Suddenly, his father opened up about the accident, and the son told me he learned more about his father in that hour than he had learned in the previous ten years.

So keep looking for the right moment. It's more likely to come along if you spend time with your dad. What does he like to do? Good conversations come out of shared activities like fishing, driving the car, walking, or working on a project together. As you spend time with each other, he will gradually begin to see you as more of a man than a boy, and then he will open up. I've found that certain fathers will not share intimate things with their children, simply because they still see them *as children.* Through your own maturity, you can change that.

Also, there are topics of conversation that a parent just never wants to talk about. You need to be sensitive about those topics. In the area of spiritual maturity, for instance, a father may feel that there are problems he himself has not worked through, and rather than reveal that he is confused, he will simply not talk about them. The subject of death is such a topic. I've found that people who are spiritual and emotional giants in other areas simply cannot find the courage to discuss death. Leave such conversations alone.

176

TALKING TO A STONE ●

I just started leading a senior high school Sunday School class and have two questions. First, how does one communicate with a bunch of stones? And second, do you have any suggestions on Christian books for teens?

You've taken a very noble step. Teaching high school kids is more difficult than it was even ten years ago. This is because today's kids relate differently to formal instruction.

Teaching isn't dialogical like it was in the '60s and early '70s. Students back then were used to a question-and-answer type format, even in Sunday School. There were "rap" groups, where kids would sit in a circle and fire questions at the group leader. The leader would guide the often lively discussions, and that's how the learning process took place.

But kids aren't into that kind of thing anymore. So when you expect feedback, you're going to be disappointed when the kids sit there like "stones." They're afraid of rejection; their self-images are bashed and damaged. It makes you want to wave your hand in front of their faces to see if they're really awake.

The most effective philosophy for today's teens is the one that says, "Don't be discouraged because you're not getting any feedback." Just lay out your ideas as interestingly as you can and hope the kids will get involved even if they do it without emotional fervor. When you go home from church each Sunday, commit your class to the Lord. Know that the Holy Spirit is working and that the good words and concepts you've shared have not been said in vain. They have been lodged and stored somewhere, however sterile the place, where sometime in the future they will bear fruit from the soil of your kids' lives.

Curriculum is important, and I suggest that you write to many evangelical publishers to obtain samples of their materials. Understand, you're not looking for the "best" materials as such; rather, you want to find the ones that best fit your particular group of kids.

I also recommend a visit to your local Christian bookstores. Talk personally with the clerks, and ask them to point you in the right direction. Then take time to read through as many youth sources as you feel is necessary. I highly recommend our own Campus Life books. We have a whole line of them, some of which speak to the problems you've shared here—how to minister to stone-like people, etc.

QUEASY OVER GOD'S LOVE •

How can I tell my teenage boys how much God loves them without making them feel uncomfortable and embarrassing them? They try to act strong and brave on the outside, but I know that they need the security of God's love on the inside. I would like to remind them daily of His love, but I know they would just say, "Mom, I know that." How can I communicate this concept without making them feel awkward?

The best way you can communicate God's love is to truly love your kids. "For anyone who does not love his brother, whom he has seen, cannot love God, whom he has not seen" (1 John 4:20, NIV). Turning the concept around, how will your children know God loves them unless it's by really experiencing their parents' love?

Don't overly worry about whether or not your kids understand that God loves them. If you've shared this biblical truth with them, they will only grow to understand it through the love they receive from you. Your love will provide the receivers, the sensors as it were, through which your boys will eventually come to appreciate the Lord's love. Then, when they are old enough to appreciate higher concepts, they will realize God's love through an understanding of the redemption story, through God's patience with the children of Israel, and through God's forgiveness through Jesus.

Now, by showing your kids that you really love them, I don't necessarily mean hugging and kissing them all the time. In fact, when boys get to be seven or eight years old, they usually don't like that "smother" love. Instead, sit down with them and get to know them. Ask them questions that relate to their interests. And when it's time to be firm, show them a firmness that is rooted in love.

As a parent, you don't constantly have to say, "God loves you," to get the point across. By actually demonstrating God's love on a daily basis, your boys will pick up the message stronger than you ever imagined.

UNSPOKEN COMMUNICATION •

My teen says a lot of things to me without opening her mouth—by a glance, a shuffle, or hanging around the kitchen. How do I learn to detect the feelings she is trying to communicate, and how should I respond to them?

Unspoken communications are very important. They are usually signals that mean, "I want you to notice me," "I want help," and so on. It is important to respond to your teen in privacy. That is, if she seems to be moping, don't comment on it in front of others. If you do, she will try to save face by saying, "Oh, nothing's wrong." She may even come back with some unfortunate retort that sours the whole situation.

Instead, pick up on her cues and then at a later moment say, "Laura, I was noticing that you seemed troubled at breakfast. Can I help you in any way?" I think parents have to respond, show interest, and then back off. To try to force the young person to reveal what's on her mind is meddling. Sometimes the young person has only enough courage for the preliminary grunt or shuffle. If you probe, she then becomes fearful, backs off, and talks about something else.

Sometimes young people will bring up a relatively unimportant topic to see how you will react. If you seem willing to handle it, then they may say, "Well, that's not really what I wanted to talk about. Here's the real issue." Or sometimes if you don't jump in and start talking, they have a chance to gather their courage and say what's on their minds. Often when I'm counseling young people, a moment of silence comes after we've begun to talk. I try to let it percolate. Sometimes I've sat for a full minute or two with nothing going on. Sometimes they've walked across the room, looked out the window, and then come back and said, "OK, let me tell you."

I don't think parents can gain their teens' confidence unless they spend a quantity of time together. It's good to go shopping with kids or take them out for hamburgers so they have a chance to open up about what's on their minds. Kids have trouble doing this when their parents are staring at them, waiting for them to talk. It's easier for them if something else is going on, like walking from store to store, driving in the car, fishing, working around the house, mowing the lawn, painting a bedroom, or fixing a bicycle. We in the Youth for Christ ministry try to create these moments through stress camping. It creates a situation that speeds up the communication process and allows young people to get their problems out and talk about them. Parents who are willing to be available without being pushy will have many such teachable moments with their children.

CHAPTER 14

Responsibility

The Scriptures teach us that "whosoever will save his life shall lose it; but whosoever shall lose his life for My [Jesus'] sake and the Gospel's, the same shall save it" (Mark 8:35). The Christian message is the only message in the world that encourages us to get our minds off ourselves and begin to live for other people.

A great many people find this advice naive and foolish. Modern writers teach us to look out for "Number One," to learn how to get ahead through intimidation. In fact, some go so far as to say that parents have no real responsibility for their children, and that children have no responsibility to their parents, but each is an independent being who is responsible only to and for himself or herself.

Such rampant selfishness is bringing great heartache and pain into the world. Not only is it impractical at the social level—look at all the relational breakdowns in homes, governments, businesses, international relations, and so on—but it is even untrue within our own selves. A person all wrapped up in himself is a very small package.

The Christian message turns selfishness inside out. If we live for ourselves, we are condemned to live for ourselves forevermore. But as we are responsible to God and one another, as we live for God and one another, then we begin to experience great personal happiness. Christian maturity is the ability to think about others in all our relationships. For a mature Christian, it's not enough to say, "How will this affect me? Will this make me happy?" One has to say, "How will it affect God and His creation? How will it affect the other person? What is the fair and just and loving thing to do in this situation?" In spite of what the world says, we are our brothers' keepers.

OVERCOMING PROCRASTINATION •

I have a problem with procrastination. I'm always telling people I will get something done or be somewhere at a certain time, but usually I don't come through. Then I make up excuses for myself. I know I must learn to discipline myself, but I don't know how. As a Christian, I know my actions speak loudly. In my case I guess it's my lack of action that speaks loudly. How does one overcome this? What responsibility do I have to present the right image of Christianity to those who don't know Christ?

You're not alone. I've struggled with this problem, and almost everyone I know has had to deal with it at one time in his life. Mention "procrastination" in any group of people, and you hear lots of oohs and ahs.

When I was in college I finally realized I had to adopt some kind of systematic method that would help me beat procrastination. Out of those years came a belief that I simply couldn't have any true freedom from procrastination without exercising discipline. My course of discipline includes the following:

• I have to be in bed by a certain hour. Otherwise, my morning is shot the next day.

• Every day I make up a "to do" list, on which I list that day's activities. I live by a rule that says, "Do difficult things first." That way I get the most taxing problems out of the way while my energy level is high, and I can coast for the rest of the day. Also, I do one thing at a time, and when each task is finished I cross it off the list.

• I'm learning how to say no. I used to feel guilty every time I told people that I just couldn't find the time to do something for them. It took a long time to learn that it is much more noble to say no than to say yes without following through on your promise.

Discipline and freedom go hand-in-hand. Probably the best recent book on the subject of cultivating discipline in your life is Richard Foster's *Celebration of Discipline*. I recommend that you get a copy. Don't put it off!

LOOKING AFTER KID SISTER •

Though I no longer live at home, do I still have a responsibility to my little sister, who is just starting high school? I'm worried

she might make friends with the wrong crowd. My parents aren't churchgoers so she doesn't have much spiritual guidance now that I'm no longer at home. My other sister and I both made it through the high school years without becoming involved with the wrong crowd, so my parents must be doing the right things. But since I'm a Christian and they aren't, do I have a responsibility to her?

Yes, I think you're responsible for the spiritual and emotional growth of your sister—but as a *sister,* not as a *parent.* To move in on your parents in any way would be a great mistake; it would harm your parents *and* your sister.

As a sister there is much you can do to model a Christian lifestyle. You can listen to your sister, counsel her, pray for her, and take her to social activities where there are sharp Christian kids her age.

I think your concerns about her falling in with the wrong crowd in school have some substance. Public high schools are a lot different than they used to be, and I believe it's a lot harder to be a student today. There are more temptations, more bad influences.

Just the same, it sounds as if maybe you're not giving your parents enough credit. You said yourself that they raised you and your other sister right, and that you both managed to stay out of the wrong crowd in high school. So your parents seem to have provided a home environment that is stable enough to nurture good thought processes and common sense. Coupled with that, your Christian influence has a very good chance of rubbing off on your younger sister.

But, again, don't assume a role that extends beyond sisterly love and concern. Be careful not to create an impression that your parents have failed because they aren't churchgoers. And temper any religious advice you give with love for your family members.

MIXING FAITH AND POLITICS? ●

Why don't Christians like to get involved in politics? Over the years I've been reprimanded, publicly ridiculed, and classified as a social activist because of my attempts to help Christians understand the importance of knowing about a political candidate before they vote for him or her. I am told, "Oh, what's the difference?" or "I never discuss politics." How can we combat the political blindness of Christians?

I think you're on the right track in trying to educate Christians about candidates and issues. But too often, politically minded people wind up trying to influence rather than educate. Instead of telling people, "Examine the candidates and make up your mind," the injunction often is, "If you don't agree with my candidate and me, you haven't properly examined the candidates." Or even worse: "Take my advice or your voting lies outside of the Gospel." The tendency is to wrap our political preferences in the cloth of the Gospel, and this is not right. Human beings and human organizations are all sinful; thus, it's actually idolatrous to make the Gospel of Christ synonymous with a human endeavor such as politics.

Also, in voting for political candidates, there are many variables for Christians that should be worked out in each person's mind and heart. Consider, for instance, the matter of voting Christians into public office. I know wise Christians and ignorant Christians. If I see that an ignorant Christian is running against a non-Christian who is a wise and moral person, it's up to me to decide who should be elected. I may choose the non-Christian while another brother (or sister) feels strongly that only the Christian should represent him. We both wind up thanking God for the democratic process.

The Bible doesn't tell how to vote in a democracy. What it does say is to pray for those in power and believe that God is ultimately in control. If you can remind people that these truths apply, then I'm all for you. But in regard to particular political candidates, educate, don't influence.

SIMPLICITY NOT SO SIMPLE ●

My wife and I have decided to live more simply. After visiting the poor and oppressed of Asia, we have become more conscious of excessive luxuries in the United States. Unfortunately our twelve-year-old daughter is having trouble adjusting to our new budgeting. Her friends get all they want whether they need it or not, and she feels that we must not love her as much as their parents love them. This is certainly not true. How can we help her understand our love for her as well as our concern for others around the world?

You need to sit down with your daughter and really communicate why you feel the way you do. Perhaps you feel that the Lord allowed you to see the poverty in Asia firsthand so that you would be sensitized to your own lifestyle. Share this with your daughter.

Also, make her feel a part of your decision to streamline your lifestyle. A decision like this should be a family matter. For instance, you may want to ask her what she would like to do to be a better steward of her money. Draw her into the situation.

One way you can do this is to go to the library or a bookstore and pick up a few illustrated books that discuss world poverty. Recently, I came across a book called *The Emerging Order,* by Jeremy Rifkin. The author believes that evangelical Christians hold the key to dealing with world poverty because the Gospel message asks people to live for someone other than themselves. We can serve as models for other people. You can share information like this with your daughter and then ask her, "If Christians don't set an example, who will?"

Let me remind you to empathize with your daughter too. It's difficult for a twelve-year-old to understand why the kids next door just got new ice skates and she didn't. Furthermore, it sounds as though only you and your wife went to Asia, so there's no way your daughter could possibly have had the same life-changing experience. It's something you and your wife are going to have to communicate to her. Spend some time talking about it, and let your solutions be family solutions.

DO WE NEED PARENTAL OK? •

I am twenty years old. My fiancé and I are both Christians (as are my folks) and have a desire to serve the Lord. But my mother doesn't want us together. My father has a positive attitude about our relationship, yet says he will not consent to our getting married because of the position it puts him in with my mother. He told us that if we want to get married, we'll have to do it on our own. I have been praying for the Lord's leading, but am wondering if we can get married without the official consent of my father. And what should I do if my mother totally disagrees?

First, I don't believe there is anything this side of your relationship with God that is more important than your relationship with your parents. A marriage needs the blessing of both parents. You need to ask why your mother is opposed to your marriage. Is she simply trying to control you, or does she have good reasons that you're not willing to admit? And you need to ask yourself, "Am I willing to wait a year to allow God time to intervene in this situation?"

Most of the time parents have their children's best interests at heart. We need to listen to them because they've lived longer, and we should naturally respect their judgment. On the other hand, if you're experiencing a dilemma that just won't be resolved no matter how much you trust the good intentions of your parents, you have to realize that it is your life and you have certain decisions you have to make too. Perhaps you've communicated every angle of the problem to your mother and yet you still don't see eye to eye. In this case, it may be necessary to go against her wishes.

But the best possible action you can take at this point is no action at all. Wait. Leave it in God's hands for a year, pray about it, and then make your decision.

CONDONE OR CONDEMN? ●

One of my closest friends just became engaged to a man who isn't a Christian. I've told her how I feel about the relationship and she's concerned too, but she won't call off the wedding. Should I support her now, or should I still try to change her mind? Have I done all I can, and should I now enter joyfully into the celebration and pray for the best?

I would let your friend know one more time exactly where you stand. Then reassure her of your continuing friendship even though you feel she's making a big mistake in marrying a non-Christian. If your friend goes ahead with the marriage, and it breaks up because of the unequal yoke, she will know that she can turn to you because you didn't reject her. That will mean a lot.

I've never been able to take the opposite stand in matters such as this—that of totally rejecting a person when you see he or she is stepping out of God's will. You could make yourself feel righteous and pious by telling your friend, "I refuse to be in your wedding. I can't give you my blessing." But that would only serve to give you a false feeling that you've washed your hands of the problem. You might feel clean, but what would you have accomplished? I believe it's more important to let yourself be known as a true friend whose love is unconditional.

I also believe that you can go only so far in trying to change a person's mind. Christians cannot baby-sit the human race. You can warn your friend about the potential danger she's approaching, but you can't stop her if she's determined to take that step. All you can do is to be there redemptively if and when she realizes her mistake.

GOSSIP OR THE GOSPEL? ●

Where do you draw the line between gossip and true sharing of needs? A woman called me to pray for a mutual friend's physical problem. She even wanted me to ask our church to pray for this friend. But she told me not to tell anyone why we were praying for her, lest this friend be too sensitive about it. The physical problem described was of such a serious nature that I feel the friend needs the support and help of those around her. But I'm struggling with what to do with this information that I was told in confidence. Do I go against the woman's wishes and tell people why we are praying for this friend? I feel that asking the church to pray without telling people why would be too vague and would really start them wondering what the problem was.

My shortest answer is that you shouldn't share anything with the church if you've been asked to keep the woman's problem confidential. Don't even mention her name. Simply tell the congregation, "I have a friend who has a need; would you all pray for her, please?" That's not very specific, but it may be all you can do.

Sharing confidential matters is a problem in many churches. When prayer requests are offered, it almost sounds like a gossip session; "Did you hear about So-and-so?" Then people get hurt because everyone knows what their problems are.

But by the same token, I think Christians should be mature enough to be vulnerable at times. If we really expect specific prayers to be said on our behalf, then we have to get used to revealing the depths of our souls. A lot of people won't do that. Then, when no one comes to visit, they complain that their church doesn't care. Church people don't have psychic powers that automatically tune in on everyone's illnesses, and they don't always know when someone is really hurting. This is another reason why I feel that every church member should belong to a small group. It's easier to be vulnerable with ten or twelve close friends than it is with four or five hundred people.

THE BAD BORROWER •

My sister loves to borrow things, but she always forgets to bring them back. She's borrowed cooking utensils, records, and even my sewing machine. When I ask her about these items she says, "Oh, I forgot, I'll try to remember to bring them back next time." I almost have to take back things forcibly. We could stop loaning things, but she would just borrow them from someone else. Is there some way my husband and I can subtly break her of this habit and help her become more considerate?

I doubt if anything subtle will get her attention. Be direct with her or she may put your comments on hold too.

I would suggest that before you loan things to your sister, put time limits on each item. Say, "Yes, you can borrow the sewing machine, but I need it back two weeks from today." Then, when you know she's coming to your house, call her ahead of time and say, "Hey, Sis, I just thought I'd call to remind you to bring the sewing machine." Be the monitor at both ends of the transaction. That's how libraries stay in business!

There will always be people who borrow things. And you can let it be a constant irritation to you, or you can actually turn it into a kind of ministry. Use the time you spend loaning things as a point of informal contact with your friends. Years ago, my father found that a number of friends were asking to borrow tools from him. So he went out and bought a complete second set of tools strictly for loaning out. He called them "borrowing tools." His investment, he always felt, paid high dividends because he got to know and serve lots of friends this way. He never held it against people that they were borrowers. I guess he felt that some people simply cannot afford certain things, so they borrow.

Your sister evidently is a borrower. You love her and want to avoid hurting her. So I wouldn't take any action that could jeopardize your relationship. Just be firm about the things you loan, and give her limits on how long she can keep them.

TIME TO STEP BACK? •

My husband and I let our daughter and her two children move in with us after her divorce. Since then, she has remarried and now

they all live with us because her new husband just can't make enough to support them. The children are five and eight and get into all sorts of mischief. When we suggest that our daughter doesn't discipline them enough, she gets mad at us. We recently told her it is *her* responsibility to raise and support her own family and this caused more hard feelings. My husband and I are in our sixties and we're too old to be raising young children again. We'd like to ask them to leave but hesitate because we are really the only positive influence in our grandchildren's lives.

You're in a difficult situation, and you need to weigh your own inconveniences with the positive impact you're having on your grandchildren. You can ask your daughter to leave or you can view the situation as a mission. Suppose God had called you and your husband to a foreign mission field. Chances are your basic inconveniences would be magnified a hundred times. But you would stick it out when you saw that villagers were coming to Jesus and growing in the Christian faith. True service to the Lord almost always involves inconveniences; realizing this is the first step to eliminating tension as you seek to serve God in your present circumstances.

What makes your situation perhaps even more difficult is that your grandchildren are really your daughter's responsibility. Though you want to see them brought up right, you have to be careful about inserting yourself into the role of parents. Still, you can continue to be an influence for good in their lives by gently encouraging them in the ways of the Lord and by modeling a mature Christian lifestyle. I suggest that if you want your daughter to leave, move her slowly. Don't do anything out of spite or resentment. Consider this your mission for the Lord and make the most out of these impressionable years with your grandchildren.

CHAPTER 15

Dating

Dating is a topic that consumes the minds of young people in the Western world. A mouse living under a bed in any camp dormitory could testify that as teenagers go to sleep at night, ninety percent of them are talking about love, dating, and courtship.

There's really very little in the Bible on the subject. There is a great deal about human relationships, male-female relationships, and responsible marriage, but not much to help with the courtship practices that have developed in modern society. In the biblical culture, of course, parents arranged marriages. Family stability was guaranteed by marriage contracts which often included a bride-price and a dowry.

Today, by contrast, young people are thrust into a sex-saturated society with all sorts of physical and peer-induced temptations. Add to this the increased mobility brought about by the automobile. Young people a few miles from home are virtually anonymous; they do not have to worry about what the neighbors will think. Much dating is done with little adult supervision.

There is no way to avoid our society's influence. We cannot isolate ourselves and live in cloisters and communes. We cannot build walls around our young people. No matter how hard we try to shield them, they will be exposed to our culture's mores and folkways through television, books, magazines, radio, school, and a whole array of other sources. They will be well aware that their parents' ideology is not the only one around.

And yet there's nothing inherently wrong, just because it's different from courtship in Bible times, with the dating process. In fact, there's a great deal that's right about it. But as a modern invention, it bypasses many of the safeguards that other cultures have set up for young people.

It is very important for young people to have built into them an internal set of guides and commitments, promises and helps, that will enable them to walk successfully through this mine field. Parents can help equip them for this exciting but dangerous time.

DATING GUIDELINES ●

What dating guidelines can we give to our teenagers? How do we help them through the "dating game"? Our ideas about dating seem miles apart from theirs.

My ideas may seem wild, because I'm at least as old as the parents of most teenagers. But let me make some suggestions.

First, to date alone with a boy in a car, a girl ought to be at least a junior in high school. Younger kids can date in groups of two or three couples, but I think parents are very wise to delay single dates in cars. I also think it's good for young people not to date more than one grade up. If this is one of your rules, you won't have problems with premature car dates.

Second, insist on meeting the boy before he takes your daughter out. Don't allow him to blow the horn or meet her on the porch. Have him come in, sit down, and talk for a while. It's good for him, for you, and for your daughter.

If your child is the boy, encourage him to meet the girl's parents, tell them where they are going, what time he thinks the event will be over, and what time they can expect their daughter home. I impressed this on my son—on one of his early dates, he called the girl's parents when they arrived at their destination, and he called again when the event was over. I think he was a little extreme, but he impressed the parents greatly.

Third, make the kids promise that they will not mix alcohol with dating and driving. Look the young man in the eye and ask him to promise that. A promise to a parent can hold kids more strongly than a lot of teaching; most kids want to keep their word. Since their lives are at stake, you can't afford to tolerate any exceptions to the no-alcohol rule.

Fourth, ask them to call you if they have to be later than expected. You don't need to spend your evening worrying that they may be stranded on a country road or smashed against a semi.

Fifth, make a rule that they don't sit in the car when they get home. They should come into the house. If they are slow to do this, there's nothing like a flashing porch light to get the message across. On the other side of that, be sure to give them privacy when they come in. They need someplace to talk alone rather than to be stared at by parents. Still, the thought that a parent might walk into a room at any time has an interesting effect on young people.

Let me suggest three books that I think are very good: *I Loved a Girl,* by Walter Trobisch; *Letters to Karen* and *Letters to Philip,* by Charlie Shedd; and *A Love Story,* by Tim Stafford. These are excellent books for parents as well as for teenagers.

WHAT TO DO ON A DATE ●

What kinds of things can a Christian couple do on a date? There are hardly any movies we want to see. We've gone to some concerts and done some roller skating. What else is there to do? I'm at a loss to find things that interest my date and are suitable for two Christian young people.

This question reminds me of a friend of mine who was sitting at the breakfast table with his little boy, who did not want to eat his oatmeal. My friend said, "A lot of little Indian children would love to have what you are eating," and his little boy responded, "Name two." It's easy to say there are lots of things for a Christian couple to do on a date—until you try to get down to specifics. But let me offer three suggestions.

First, I think it's possible that you're spending too much time together. I hate to say that to a young man in love, but eventually boredom results when a couple spends almost all their waking hours together. It's not a realistic way to prepare for marriage—married people have jobs and housework to do. And it puts an obligation on you to be constantly thinking of ways to fill those long hours together.

Second, get involved in group activities. Your church youth group probably has activities that you could join. Community groups also sponsor planned events. If you join them, you won't have to do all the planning yourself.

Third, think about what the two of you can do for others. It makes sense for two Christian young people to think about service as well as entertainment. Many couples find meaning in taking responsibility together. For instance, could you volunteer to help the junior high schoolers in your church? They can take up a lot of time, and they're a lot of fun too.

I'm sorry I haven't been able to suggest any fascinating new places to go, but I think if you spend less time alone together, join more group activities, and look for ways to serve, you will find that you have more than enough to keep you busy.

TOO YOUNG TO DATE? ●

My daughter is fourteen, but she thinks she's a lot older. Her boyfriend is eighteen, and my daughter says she loves him and wants to go out with him all the time. Isn't she much too young to be getting serious? We've tried to limit the time she spends with him, but I'm afraid she's sneaking out with him.

You have a justifiable concern. My guess is that your daughter is in some way telegraphing to the boys that she is older than fourteen, either by her clothing, her makeup, or by her friends. As you know, even if she looks eighteen, she still has only fourteen years of experience, and she may not know how to handle all the situations that can arise with older friends. Therefore, you need to protect her from herself.

One way to protect her is to draw certain guidelines, such as not allowing them to go out together in his car. We set a rule that our kids couldn't date anyone more than one grade ahead of them, but since your daughter already is dating this boy, to introduce this rule now would cause more problems than it would solve. Their friendship may be perfectly legitimate; young kids can fall in love like this. He can be responsible, and so can your daughter. But I think it would be good for you to sit down with him and explain your concern to see how he responds.

Say, "Doug, you're eighteen, and it's quite unusual for someone your age to be interested in a girl of fourteen; after all, she's still very young. Now, I'm not saying you have bad things on your mind. I'm just saying that she's very young, and I'm sure you can understand my concern for her." If this young man has any maturity at all, he will understand what you are saying. But if he responds in a negative way—if he argues with you, sulks, or threatens to see her in secret—then you have a pretty clear sign that this is not a relationship that will help your daughter. In that case, you could even seek the protection of the law, because he is of age and she is not. On the other hand, if they will keep some rules like staying around where you can keep your eye on things, I think you'll be better off allowing them to see each other. Let's face it—if you do restrict her severely, she will probably feel challenged to meet him during the day when you can't be watching her.

GETTING SERIOUS SCARES ME •

My daughter, who is fifteen, likes a boy in our church who is also fifteen. The boy seems serious about her, and that scares me. I want to be a firm, loving parent, and I've had several mother-daughter talks with her about the problems of being serious at her age. She is a lovely Christian girl and wants to go to a Bible college when she is out of school. I just pray that she will continue that determination. I want to do what I can for her, and yet not be too hard on her.

Is a daughter—especially your own—*ever* old enough to get serious with a boy? Actually, fifteen is just about the right time. You can be grateful that the boy is only fifteen—it would be a lot harder for you if he were eighteen. You can also be grateful that he's in your church, because that means that you and his parents probably share a similar set of values. His parents can be real allies of yours if they try to keep some control over him while you're doing the same for your daughter.

You say you want to be firm and loving. I'm amazed at how often people think a firm, loving parent is someone who says no all the time. Your daughter's falling in love is the most natural, normal, beautiful thing in the world. In fact, it's refreshing to see how wholeheartedly teenagers love; they have not yet experienced the hurts that may make them too cautious later on. And relax—a fifteen-year-old is more interested in affirmation than in marriage. Your daughter needs somebody to tell her, "You're a special person. You're pretty. You're thoughtful"—which is no doubt exactly what this boy is doing.

Now, I can tell you to affirm her and love her and show your affection for her, which you certainly should do, but don't expect to have the influence over her that you had a few years ago. Any fifteen-year-old in the world will throw over all her parents' affirmation for affirmation by some kid who is living out of a Clearasil bottle. And this is normal. Pray for your daughter, encourage her, set up some guidelines, give her realistic hours that match those of her friends in the neighborhood. Be realistic and loving and caring about it, and know that God will protect her and your love will guard her as she grows up.

BRINGING CHRIST ALONG ●

I'm interested in knowing more about keeping Christ at the center of dating relationships. I want to be able to know a man for who he is, and not out of mere physical attraction.

Few people find it easy to move down the intensity scale. That is, a person who has been involved in an intense physical relationship finds a platonic relationship less satisfying. You will have tensions as you try to do this.

Be careful, though, of an attitude many people develop when they become Christians. They hear about the three kinds of love in the Bible, *agape, philia,* and *eros,* and they decide, "Now I'm going to turn my back totally on the physical. All my loving is going to be *agape* loving." John had to deal with people like that in New Testament times. They were trying to flee the physical life in order to get to the spiritual. These people were called Gnostics, and their teachings were considered heretical.

In reality, physical love (*eros*) and brotherly love (*philia*) are just as much part of human experience as *agape* love. When we become Christians, of course, we have to learn to practice *agape* love, but we are still physical beings. So don't try, in the name of Christ, to swing the pendulum clear away from the physical. After all, God thought up the idea of creating beings with bodies. You aren't in the process of becoming Joan of Arc. You are in the process of becoming yourself, a good Christian woman.

One practical step you can take is to pray: first, about whom you should date, and then just before you go out on a date. A Christian couple is wise to pray in the car before they leave the curb. Not, "Lord, we know we are going to have all these temptations . . ." but, "Put Your hand on our relationship and make this a good evening." Some couples who are moving from a worldly relationship into a Christian relationship have told me that they take a Bible along and put it in the frontseat between the two of them. Then before they get involved in a physical relationship in the car, they have to lift up the Bible and move it out from between them. They have to pause to do that, and that makes them think about what they are doing.

You can also help yourself by dating in groups and being around other people. And then, watch your own behavior. Some girls contribute to the problem; as soon as they are alone with a boy, they clam up and quit talking. It's as if they are saying, "Now the physical side begins, and we will start communicating by Braille." That invites problems. Besides, you need to talk to your date about interests and concerns and compatibilities if you want to get to know him totally.

Changing the style of your relationships will not be easy, but if you face the problems head-on, you will find that a lot of men also are looking for whole-person relationships.

WITNESSING TO A DATE ●

There is a girl at school I would like to date. But I'm concerned about her salvation. I don't know if she's a Christian, but I have to assume she isn't. How do I explain the plan of salvation to her in relation to asking her out for a date?

Sometimes you can't do two things at once. It's hard to play a violin and bat a baseball at the same time, for instance. You have to do one or the other. It's a rather heavy thing to ask a girl for a date. And it's even heavier to deal with her salvation.

You have to decide what your motives are. If you are primarily concerned about her salvation, then you are thinking of her well-being. You are not thinking about how much you would like to date her, or about the honor points you are collecting by being a soul-winner. That kind of witnessing doesn't work anyway; the other person immediately knows you have ulterior motives. The only acceptable motive for witnessing is so that the other person might come to receive the grace of God shed abroad in Jesus Christ. Your interest in witnessing to her, then, has to be selfless.

Your interest in dating her, though, is primarily for your own benefit. Of course, you might be doing her a great favor by letting her meet you, but you probably want to date her because you'd like to get to know her better. There's nothing wrong with that, but it is not selfless.

Now if you try to mix your selfless concern with your self-oriented concern, you come across as if you were saying, "I want to have her cleaned up so she is worthy of me, so she meets one of my requirements. I want to turn her into a Christian for my benefit." Suddenly your witnessing is nothing more than manipulation.

You are going to have to separate your two concerns. I would suggest you try developing a friendship with her first of all. Don't have an ulterior motive; don't even think about dating her. Simply love her and care for

195

her and tell her about the wonderful thing that has happened to you—that you have come to know Christ, that He has changed your life, and that you would like her to be happy also. Then you may find, after you have built a solid relationship with her, that asking for a date is no problem at all.

COLD FEET ●

I'm lonely and want very much to date Christian girls, but I'm shy and nervous when it comes to meeting girls. I don't know the first thing about dating.

You are part of a very large group of young men. In fact, probably ninety percent of all adolescent boys feel very inadequate in this area, though some try to overcome it by overcompensating and becoming outgoing and boisterous. The advice I'm going to give you may sound a little cruel at first, but I think it is realistic: Play in your own league.

I meet many fine young men who can't get their eyes off the pompom girls or cheerleaders. They say, "If I can't date one of those, I won't date anybody." The truth is, they may never date anybody if they don't get over that idea. There are a limited number of cheerleader types, and they seem to be metered out to the athletes and class presidents.

I think this emphasis on physical beauty is foolish. Beauty really is only skin deep. Many people, even though they don't attract you physically at first, turn out to have real beauty when you get to know them. In twenty-five years, if you go to your high-school class reunion, you'll be surprised to see that many of the sought-after, beautiful girls now look quite ordinary, while some of the girls you didn't even notice in high school will have become beautiful middle-aged women. I know this is hard to ask you to believe now, and that's the cruel part of my advice. You're just going to have to accept that you shouldn't always aspire to something you cannot attain.

Now, to get started dating—find a close friend or a youth director who will fix you up with somebody. Have this friend put you in touch with a girl who is also a little bit shy, who feels as nervous about meeting boys as you do about meeting girls. Get together, and get to know someone whose skills are about the same as yours. You can discover each other. You may do it in a fumbling, halting way, but she will enjoy being with you anyway. You'll get practice in talking to a girl, and before long you'll begin to feel almost comfortable. This is the way boys have met girls from the beginning of time, and it will work for you as well.

WHEN DATING GOES TOO FAR •

Our son has been dating a girl about six months. They are welcome at our home, but lately they have been spending their time at her house. Normally that would be fine, but her parents both work and are away much of the time. To me, it seems dangerous for those two kids to be there alone.

I think you're right. It is dangerous, and your concern is valid. But just putting pressure on them probably won't solve the problem. Let's face it—if kids want to get involved sexually, there probably isn't any way to stop them. They will find a place; if not at an empty house, then somewhere else.

I think the way to approach this is to sit down with your son and begin to talk about sexuality. For one thing, it might be very revealing to him to know you understand sexual response and sexual temptation. Usually kids don't believe they came into the world that way. Everybody else did, but not them. It can open their eyes for you to say, "I dated your mother and other girls, and I had certain responses; I know what it's like to be in a situation where there is restraint, and I know what it's like to be where there's no restraint. Therefore, because I love you and don't want you to get a bad start in life and in marriage, your mother and I want to help you with this. We've asked you to come to our home, and you've come here, and that was fine. Now you've started to spend all your time at your girlfriend's house. Is this because we're not giving you enough freedom and privacy here?"

Keep in mind that kids do need privacy—not too much, but just enough. They need enough so they can talk to each other and say intimate things and even steal a kiss without feeling smothered by the family. It doesn't seem quite right to carry on a dating relationship in the company of half a dozen kids, two parents, and a dog. If that's what you offer, you can be sure they'll go somewhere else. So it will be good for you and your son to have a talk to find out if there's any way you can make your own home more attractive to him and his girlfriend.

If the two of them continue to use the girl's home, you need to have a talk with her parents. It may well be that her parents are happily working at their offices, thinking that their daughter is under your good supervision, when in reality the kids are working both ends against the middle. That's not a new idea; it's been done for ages. Simply say, "We're afraid that you might resent our son for being in your home when you're not there. Are you aware of this?" Chances are, they're not. They may be more than willing to join you in looking for solutions. But discussing your own understanding of sexuality with your son and his girlfriend will help more than just putting your foot down, because they will always be able to find a place that's not under your foot to get together.

SON WON'T DATE •

Our son goes to a Christian school, and his teachers say he is very mature for his age. He studies hard, gets good grades, and wants to earn a scholarship for college. But he doesn't get involved in many social activities at church or school. Shouldn't he be dating by now? He just turned sixteen and has really never been on a date. Have we sheltered him too much?

I don't think so. There are a lot of sixteen-year-old boys who haven't dated. In fact, for years I've done sessions at camps on how to ask a girl for a date. It sounds very basic, but this is one of the most crowded sessions. It's a lot bigger than the sessions on understanding sexuality. It's a strange world in which you can drive a several-hundred-pound car at sixteen, but you can't muster up the courage to ask a one-hundred-pound girl for a date. But for many boys, that's the way it is.

I don't think you should be concerned. His teachers say he's mature for his age. Often when a boy is timid and has some reservations about his social capabilities, he'll try to excel in something else. It's good that he has goals, because working for good grades and a scholarship will take him further than a date every week. The typical letter I get from parents says, "My boy wants four or five dates a week, but he won't do his schoolwork and I'm wondering if he'll make it into college." You have the kind of son they want.

We hear a lot of talk about homosexuality these days, and a great many parents say to me, "I'd like to talk with you about my son. He's not dating." They talk and talk, and eventually it comes out that down deep they fear he may be a latent homosexual. If he'd only get interested in girls, they'd be relieved of this worry. Believe me, very few boys who are shy and slow to begin dating are struggling with a problem of homosexuality. Instead, they are struggling with the age-old problem of insecurity. They are afraid their social skills are not yet up to the challenge of dating.

DEFENSIVE ABOUT DATING •

Our twenty-two-year-old daughter doesn't like to date. She is quite attractive, and she is normally outgoing and friendly—except when we talk about men her age. Suddenly she becomes defensive and doesn't want to talk. Recently she was asked to a dinner where she was to receive a scholarship and was invited to bring a guest along. When we asked her about her date, she curtly informed us that he was her escort, not her date. Why is she like this?

People who win scholarships at age twenty-two are probably heading for graduate school or some other form of specialized advanced training. It sounds to me as if your daughter is an organized, systematic kind of person. She's undoubtedly disciplined; she knows what she wants and looks at everything analytically. She's a precise person; probably the *date-escort* issue has to do with definitions. A date has a future; a date is someone with whom you might be heading toward something. An escort is someone who goes to just one event with you. Your daughter wants you to understand that this particular person is an escort, not a date. She is planning her future, and she wants you to know that she has goals and directions and is therefore not interested in this person—or anyone else for the moment—as a date.

She may feel that you are pressuring her to be conventional. By conventional, I mean to meet the right man, get married, settle down, and raise a family. But this may not be the thing for her. In fact, increasingly we're going to see men and women who decide not to adopt the marriage model. This won't be because they are strange or deviant, but because in our culture, with its demands and opportunities, some people are going to choose other options. So try your best to take the pressure off her, even if it's no more than your furrowed brow. She can sense that you want her to date and get married, and she doesn't want to do it right now. She's becoming defensive in order to defend herself against you.

MOM'S ON MY NERVES •

I'm twenty-one, and my mom is always pestering me about my dating life. She wants to know if I've found the right man yet. In truth I don't date much, but when I tell Mom this she goes into a lecture about her daughter becoming an old maid. She seems to think I'm in college to get an "Mrs." degree instead of an education. Someday this may be important to me, but it isn't right now. How can I get this across to my mother? She is really getting on my nerves.

Most girls in your situation repeat themselves over and over again. This does not always get through to Mother, however. You have a better chance of communicating with her if you understand why she thinks the way she does. No doubt what she really wants is for you to be happy. Now, to most mothers, what does it mean to be happy? Generally speaking, a happy woman in her generation was one who married early and fulfilled the conventional wife-mother role for the rest of her life. In today's world, women tend to marry later; they may choose unconventional as well as conventional marriage styles, and many marriages are temporary. Your mother may, on the one hand, think you will not be happy unless you follow the pattern she followed. On the other hand, perhaps she is afraid that you will fall for all features of today's style, including those that are obviously un-Christian.

You need to help her understand that your values are not just like hers, but neither are they exactly opposite. As a Christian, you agree with her that marriage should be permanent. But as a woman of your own generation, you also have career goals. Perhaps you will wait awhile and then marry someone with whom you can have a successful two-career marriage. Or perhaps you will not need to marry in order to be happy. In any case, marriage is no guarantee of happiness; thousands of mismated couples would testify to that.

Once your mother understands your point of view, she still may not agree with you. It would be helpful if she knew women who were happy and single, or who were happy in spite of marrying later, but her circle is probably composed of conventionally married women like herself. She may never see things your way; you will need a great deal of patience with and love for her. It will help if you understand, "Her goal is not to nag me or push me into early marriage or make me unhappy; she wants to make me happy by putting me into her own mold." If you are understanding and gentle, your mother may do quite a bit of growing through this process. She needs to understand that to be single is not to be unhappy.

PUSHY PARENTS ●

One of our neighbors has a daughter who is good friends with our teenage son. Both the girl and her parents are anxious that she be popular and have dates every weekend. While our son is fond of this young lady, he has many friends that he likes to spend time with. We are glad to see that he has not committed himself to one person at such an early age, but how can we handle this aggressive young lady and her ambitious parents? We don't want to offend them, and we'd like to remain friends.

The overriding rule in this kind of situation is for the parents to maintain their objectivity. No doubt your son's dilemma troubles you, just as their daughter's popularity is a high priority to your neighbors. But it is very important for you to keep adequate distance from your children's concerns. Try to treat this with polite good humor—"the kids are having this little problem"—and try to let them straighten it out themselves. Frankly, that's the way it has to happen anyway. Relate to the young lady as if you're totally unaware of the situation; be a friend to her because you like her and because she's your neighbor, not because your son has been dating her.

You'll need to help your son deal with this as a Christian, in a polite and gentlemanly manner. Sometimes a boy caught in this kind of trap will react abruptly. He will decide he has to do something, so he'll dump his whole load of resentment on her, all at once. That hurts the girl, and it hurts her parents, and it creates problems for you. On the other hand, sometimes a boy will be so afraid of confrontation that he will string the girl along indefinitely. She will quite naturally assume their relationship is much deeper than he thinks it is, and great pain is sure to follow.

So talk to your son about strategy. He should be nice to the girl, but at some point he has to sit down with her and say, "Now, I really enjoy this relationship, and I'd like to keep on seeing you. But I have lots of other friends too, and I want to spend time with them as well. I'm not ready to limit myself to dating one person, but I'd like very much to be your friend." She will not want to hear that. It will hurt her, and there will be tears, but it's all part of growing up. You will make it much easier on both kids if you can achieve your goal of maintaining a warm relationship with the girl's family. Then it won't seem to them like a bitter divorce where families take sides and the pleasant atmosphere of the neighborhood is lost.

CONSTANT CRUSH ●

I seem to fall in love with almost every boy I date. Each time a new boy comes along I just know he's the one. But after we date a month or two, I decide he's not so great after all. I don't know whether I fall in love too easily or if I'm not satisfied with a boy after I've got him. My mother says a lot of girls are like this at my age (nineteen), but I'm beginning to think something's wrong with me. Should I be concerned about this?

Yes, but not overly. Your mother is right—a lot of girls are like this. But by age nineteen, this stage should be coming to an end. Maybe it will as you begin to understand what's happening.

You are calling your attachments "love." Really, they are not love so much as your response to legitimate personal needs. Deep in your heart you have some natural concerns—am I lovable? Am I attractive? Will boys like me? And so a boy becomes a goal; you want to get him to like you. When he does, you feel good. But then after a while, doubt begins to enter in again. You say, "OK, he liked me, but I wonder if I'm really all right. I may not be really attractive. I'll have to see if this other boy will like me." So you become attracted to him and you "catch" him, but when your relationship settles down, the process repeats itself.

Your frequent changes, then, are fed not by love, but by your own legitimate needs to be loved and accepted. This is a normal adolescent behavior pattern, and you will outgrow it. While it lasts, though, it is important for you to understand what is going on so you do not get too deeply involved, emotionally or physically, with any of your boyfriends. You do not want to do things you will regret later, just to satisfy your need for affirmation and acceptance. Real love is not based on an inner need for acceptance so much as on a wish to commit yourself to and be responsible for another person. You haven't really been in love yet. Next time you think you are, give yourself time before deciding. Real love lasts.

202

IS BEAUTY SKIN DEEP? •

I've been dating a girl for several months and really enjoy her company. I'm beginning to wonder if God is leading us into marriage. We are both Christians, have good communication, and get along well together. But I constantly compare her with other girls I know. Though she is quite attractive, I find other girls are even prettier, and then I wonder if I really love her. I feel guilty over the comparisons I'm making. How important is physical appeal to a marriage?

They say that beauty is only skin deep, but unfortunately that is all most of us can see. We are first attracted by people's physical characteristics, and then we learn about their other fine qualities as we get to know them. Though physical attractiveness is an important factor to marriage, it is not nearly as important as some others.

When I was a young man, an older man talked with me about his wife. I had never met a man who loved his wife as much as he did, so I was eager to listen. "She's not the prettiest girl in the world," he said. "I've met other girls who are smarter too. But she's not just a face; not just a body; not just a mind; not just a sense of humor. She's a composite, a total human being. I'm in love with that total person. I'll never meet anyone else just like her." That attitude shows maturity.

But it sounds to me as if your girlfriend's attractiveness may be only a surface problem for you. The real problem is that you're not yet ready for a commitment to her. You are still in the searching stage, looking from one person to another and trying to establish what's important to you. Until this searching stage is over, don't jump into something you're not ready for.

DATING AROUND •

My eighteen-year-old daughter has been dating her first boyfriend since she was fifteen. He's a nice boy, but I feel she should date other boys as well. I've told this to both of them, but to no avail. My daughter is now away at college. Her boyfriend still lives in our town. They call each other every week and have vowed not to date anyone else. Is there anything I can do besides praying for them?

That's kind of like saying, "After I've dropped the atomic bomb, what else can I do to destroy this place?" I believe in prayer. We Christians tend to neglect it. We do far too much meddling, talking, manipulating, and finagling, and far too little praying. So let me encourage you to continue to pray with care and concern. Don't stop at giving God advice; listen to Him and read His Word, attempting to get His heart and spirit on the things you are facing. Really, prayer is the Christian's most powerful weapon, and we need always to be aware of this.

But if you want your daughter to have friendships with other young men, take heart. Statistically, this relationship hardly has a chance. Very few relationships last when one goes to college and the other stays home. Your daughter will grow socially and intellectually. Her world view will expand. When she comes home to visit him, it will be as if he had spent the time in a cocoon. He will not have kept up with her. Very likely she will then make other friends, and someday this boy at home will receive a "Dear John" letter. So you need to pray for him and support him, because if this happens he will be deeply hurt.

Now, if this doesn't happen, consider the possibility that their relationship is God's will. The Lord may have brought them together in the first place. So you can do far more by giving them support and affirmation and understanding than to insist that it is the national duty of every girl to date several men before making her choice. Let me encourage you to put this in the hands of the Lord.

I DON'T LIKE HER BOYFRIEND •

Our nineteen-year-old daughter is becoming serious about a boy who would certainly not be our first choice for her. He believes in God and prayer, but he's of a different church background and we feel this is going to create problems. We're trying to be patient and understanding and most of all to love her. We've committed the situation to the Lord, and we're trusting Him. Perhaps time is all she needs. Can you give us some guidelines?

You give yourself some pretty good counsel. Patience, understanding, love, trusting the Lord, and allowing time to work—what more can I tell you?

You mention that their difference in church backgrounds could create problems. With whom? It doesn't sound like it's much of a problem for them. It could be a problem for you, though, and you could make it into a problem for them. The important thing to keep in mind is that your daughter is nineteen years old. We parents remember when our children were little babies, and we want to manipulate their lives toward goals that we have preset for them. One of our toughest tasks is understanding that they eventually grow up, and we have to help them develop independence. Part of independence, in Western society, is choosing one's own marriage partner.

Your way of responding to the situation is fine. Love her, support her, draw her young man close to you. Let him learn something about your family. Let your faith and values rub off on him. Trust that this bringing together of two families can be beautiful. Cross-pollination can bring out strengths on both sides. You are doing what you ought to do. You are worried, but you are committing it to the Lord and giving these young people time to grow up. That's beautiful.

DUMPED FOR ANOTHER •

I dated a man for over four years, and we had talked about marriage. Then one day I received a letter from him saying our relationship was over. Soon afterward, he married another woman. How could he move to another relationship and be so happy when he has caused me so much pain and heartache? I know the Bible says everything happens for good, but I can't see any good in this.

The Bible doesn't say everything happens for good; it says that "all things *work together* for good to them that love God, to them who are the called according to His purpose" (Rom. 8:28, italics mine). Whether or not an event "works together for good" has to do with one's response to it.

Something that cannot be considered good has happened to you. You've been hurt. If you do not obey God, you will become belligerent and bitter. You will feel rejected, worthless, and discounted. You may jump at the first opportunity that comes along to marry someone else. Or you may write to your old boyfriend and try to break up his marriage. If you do these things, your situation will not turn out for good; God will not be honored and glorified.

But the situation can work together for good if you accept the fact that God loves you, that as your heavenly Father, He cares for you even more than you care for yourself. He can take something that was intended for evil and turn it to good in your life. Perhaps He will build patience into your life, or wisdom in forming relationships, or the ability to communicate in greater depth. As a result of this experience, you can be a better person than you would have been if it had never happened.

You are feeling this hurt very deeply right now; women often react to such experiences with their whole persons. For men, relationships with the opposite sex may be much less involved. They are often like bumblebees going from flower to flower. Your former boyfriend, in his maleness, may not know how deeply his actions have affected you. He may feel he has done a very responsible thing, when in fact he has broken your heart. But however he interprets the situation, it is now reality, and you will have to accept it. Commit it to the Lord as an experience that you don't understand, even though you do understand that God loves you and cares for you. Put yourself in His will and say, "OK, Lord. I'm willing now to see what the future holds. I'll be obedient to You." If you do that, this experience will work out for good.

DATING OLDER MEN •

A friend of mine is nineteen years old and dating a man who is twenty-seven. He still lives at home with his family and is overly pampered by his mother, who is dead-set against this relationship (his father seems to take a backseat in the whole matter). For instance, she won't let him come to the phone if he's having his evening cup of coffee. When my friend calls, his mother acts as if she doesn't know who she is. Last summer his mom put so much pressure on him that for a while he stopped dating my friend and went with another girl. He says he did it to keep Mom happy. Now my friend's parents are telling her to forget this relationship because things will never change. Is it normal for a man his age to be so fearful of his mother?

I think your friend's parents are right that things aren't likely to change. Devotion to parents is one thing, but this is quite another. The man's mother is apparently a strong-willed woman who has her husband under her control, and now she intends to get her son under her thumb too. This young man may leave home and get married, but he will still live under his mother's domination. This is a pattern she has set and he has agreed to, and it will continue.

206

Your friend needs to decide just how much interference and control she can take. Then she needs to tell the young man what her limits are, and see if he is willing to make a clean enough break to satisfy her. If he will not, their life together will be miserable. There will be hostility and competition between the two women, and you can be sure the man will side with his mother.

The best thing you can do for your friend is help her not to panic. A bird in the hand is not always worth two in the bush. If she marries this man, things won't change for the better. More likely they'll get much worse, and the heartache she has already faced will intensify beyond itself. Now is the time to face into the situation. Perhaps you can help her meet young men her own age.

CHAPTER 16

In-laws

A whole array of nervous and cruel jokes surround the subject of in-laws, and yet the in-law relationship provides great opportunities and possibilities. Ideally both families are enriched by close contact with each other. The added traditions, understandings, experiences, and relationships can strengthen both sides.

An outstanding biblical example of a good in-law relationship is that between Moses and his father-in-law, Jethro. Moses was raised in a fragmented family. His real mother was not available to him during his adolescence, and even in his younger years he was raised as the son of Pharaoh's daughter. With conflicting information coming at him on every hand, he was confused and ambivalent about God's will and the part he was to play in bringing it about. But God led him into the wilderness where he became Jethro's son-in-law. Jethro acted as a father to him. He advised him and helped him throughout his long career as leader of the children of Israel.

I would like to be that kind of in-law, and I would like to believe I'm humble enough to receive that kind of help from my own in-laws. One of my dreams is once again, this time in heaven, to sit with my father-in-law and talk with him. I'd like to share with him my appreciation for the many things I learned from his example and advice. The word *in-law* should not immediately throw up a red flag and cause us to run in fear. It should stand for a welcome and anticipated addition to the enrichment of our family life.

INTERFERING IN-LAWS •

Sometimes I feel that my in-laws are interfering with our family business and affairs. My wife doesn't always support me as head of the household when her parents' views conflict with mine. Is there anything in the Bible about dealing with in-laws?

Though the Bible contains no explicit instructions regarding in-laws, Genesis 2:24 does give an implicit message about in-law relationships: "Therefore shall a man leave his father and his mother, and shall cleave unto his wife." It appears that this new couple needs to be independent of their parents, to begin to develop their own lives. To the degree that parents on either side interfere with that process, there will be conflict and problems.

But let me encourage you not to make too much of your in-law problems. Sometimes a man in your situation will start doing arbitrary things that don't make a lot of sense, just to see if his wife will be loyal to him or to her parents. Or he will do everything exactly opposite to what her parents want, even if what they want makes sense, just to assert his own authority. You probably cannot change your wife's behavior, but you can control *your* attitude, which may in turn affect *her* behavior. Try to evaluate her parents' ideas on their own merit, committing yourself not so much to your answer or to theirs but to the sensible answer, whatever it may be.

If you and your in-laws attend the same church, your pastor may be able to help you both put things in perspective. He may be able to help her parents to back off and you to see some practical way to relate to them.

MEDDLING IS UNSETTLING •

My mother-in-law writes frequently, about every couple of weeks. But every letter begins with some comment about how we haven't written her and how nice it would be to hear from us. She lives far from us, and we seldom have time to write letters, but we do call her every couple of weeks. That doesn't stop her complaining. On top of that, she still chides my husband as if he were a little boy about why he didn't do this or that. He gets upset when these letters arrive, and I get irritated. Is there anything we can do?

You can be grateful that she lives far away. We hear a lot of jokes about the Jewish mother; I think we could tell a few about the evangelical mother too. This kind of mother feels a great sense of responsibility for her family. She thinks she must be like a mother hen, getting them all under her wings and controlling them. This comes from her legitimate interest in others and her willingness to take care of them, as well as from the sense of youthfulness she gets when she feels in control. Ask yourself what your mother-in-law needs most—information? Attention? Control? My guess is that she's asking to be needed, to have a central place in your lives from which to give advice.

I would suggest that you begin to write her rather than phone. It may take more time initially, but you'll spend less time worrying about her response. Some people don't count phone calls. The phone's too easy—it doesn't take any time or thought. Only letters matter to them. Write to her, and ask questions in your letters. What would she do about this? How does she feel about that? What is her opinion on such-and-such? If what she really wants is to offer help, this will give her a chance. You may run into problems if you don't take her advice, but at your distance she probably will never find out.

Try to understand that mothers-in-law who act this way are not trying to be a pain in the neck, even though they sometimes are. They are doing it because they've spent their lives training their children to live a certain way, and now their opinions no longer seem necessary. So in order to help your mother-in-law feel that you respect her opinions and want her to participate and be informed, write her tedious letters. A lot of people don't like letters full of detail, but she will. Fill pages with the kinds of things you think are unimportant. You'll find this is very helpful to her. She'll begin to feel like she has a part in your life. In fact, next thing you know, she'll be coming to visit.

HE WANTS IT HIS WAY ●

I love my father-in-law, but I wish he'd mind his own business. Whenever I mention plans to do some work around the house or yard, he tells me how it should be done. I usually know how to do it, since I have worked in construction, but my way is never up to his standards. I figure it's my house, my money, and my time, so it's up to me to decide how to do the work. Is there a gentle way to tell him I'd rather do it my way?

Often older men feel they have the right to tell younger men what to do. And often it is wise for younger men to defer. On the other hand, in-laws would be well advised to back off and allow the younger people to do things their own way, letting them learn from their own mistakes.

One way of handling this situation would be to ask your wife to tell her mother how you feel, and then to let her mother, who has handled this man for a good many years, take care of him on this issue. The confrontation scene will probably go something like this: Some night when your in-laws are lying in bed, talking, and everything is going swell, she'll say, "You know, I've been thinking about you and Son-in-Law, and it appears that he does things quite well. Not as well as you do, of course, but it would probably be helpful if you would let him make his own mistakes. You know, these young fellows are ignorant, and he'll have to touch the stove to see if it's hot, but I think it would be good to let him do it, because I don't want him resenting you. You know, you really are a great guy."

You ask if there's a gentle way for you to tell him to leave you alone. That depends a lot on him. Some people have to be hit over the head before they can hear anything. One way to do it, if you don't want to go through the circuitous wife to mother-in-law route, is to say, "Dad, I have a problem. I always feel inferior and intimidated by you." He'll say, "Oh, you shouldn't," and then he'll tell you he doesn't do what he really does. But your reminder may make him more conscious of his behavior, and he may begin to back off. That's how the textbooks say it ought to be done, and it probably is a good way, but not many people are able to pull it off. If this is any comfort, you have about the most typical relationship that a son-in-law can have with his father-in-law.

FEELING LEFT OUT •

My parents don't pay any attention to my husband. They address all their conversation to me and totally ignore him. They invite me to visit them and don't ask him to come along. I think they are being very rude, and I don't understand what they have against him. The worst part is that I don't think they know they are doing this.

The obvious solution is for you to be as honest with them as you have been with me. If they truly do not know they are doing this, they will be helped by your telling them. They may be appalled when they realize it, and they may be quite willing to change.

In your discussion, though, you may run into some problems. They may deny excluding your husband. Then you will have to give specific illustrations of what you mean—"You invited me to dinner Sunday but you didn't invite him," or "You spent Thursday night with us and never directed one comment to him." It is possible that your parents will try to gloss over what you are telling them, to pretend they don't understand or that it isn't important. If this happens, you need to probe to find the reason.

I can only suggest some possibilities. Sometimes parents don't want their daughter to get married and move away from home, and even though she has been married for some time, they still don't like to acknowledge the fact. Sometimes parents think their son-in-law took their daughter away from them, that he is "competition." Sometimes they don't want to be in-laws. Their daughter's husband looks so big and mature that they think, "I don't want to be called Mother by somebody that old. I don't want to be called Dad by someone who looks like one of my buddies." Your parents may be struggling with one of those problems. Give them a chance to respond, and in most cases they will do very well without a lot of advice.

COMPLAINT DEPARTMENT ●

My mother-in-law has suddenly begun to dislike me. She is eighty-four years old and lives a couple of hours from us. She has told me not to visit her anymore, and yet my husband doesn't want to make the drive alone. She even told me not to write anymore. When my husband calls her, she always greets him with the complaint that he hasn't phoned often enough. Thus their conversation is ruined before it even gets started. My husband and I have prayed about this and feel a responsibility for her. Is there anything we could have done wrong to have started this behavior in her?

Try to realize that people in their eighties often change. They may return to childish ways. Your mother-in-law's exclusiveness resembles a child's love. She apparently thinks you are competing with her for her son.

The worst thing for you and your husband to do is to let her manipulate you into feeling guilty, as if you have done something wrong. Of course you haven't always done your best—no one ever does. I haven't done my best with my children, my marriage, or my job; but I have tried to pace myself so I can live life in a sane manner, to do a good job, and to trust grace to make up the difference. We have to do that in all parts of life.

I would suggest that you pray for her, love her, and accompany your husband. You don't need to spend a lot of time with her if that causes problems; you can go someplace and have a cup of coffee while he visits her. Drop in for a few minutes, though, and if she treats you badly, return good for evil. You may have to excuse some of her behavior, just as you would an adolescent's. She is old, and she too is going through a stage.

Living with Yourself

"Love your neighbor as yourself" has always been an important part of Christian thinking. Only recently, however, are we beginning to understand that if a person does not love himself, his neighbor is in real trouble.

Many problems we have with one another result from our unhealthy feelings about ourselves. We often send these feelings out in the form of hostile messages to those with whom we live and work. Therefore, in order to get along with other people, it is very important that we have a positive self-image, know who we are, and feel secure before God.

First of all, we must know that we are created in the image of God. Without this understanding, everything else we do for ourselves is only cosmetic. Education, exercise, good looks, polished manners, money— all these things are of little value to the person who does not have his foundation in God. Such a person is only an empty shell. But life is full for a person who knows who he is in God's eyes.

"Know thyself" is still an important admonition. When we live fragmented lives, when our inner selves do not match our outer selves, we have deep, deep problems. Perhaps this is why the Apostle James said, "A double-minded man is unstable in all his ways" (James 1:8). Learning to know oneself and to accept oneself, to live a healthy interior life, is essential to proper Christian involvement in the larger world.

CHAPTER 17

Self-image and Depression

Most of what's said today about self-image is cosmetic in nature. It attacks the problem of low self-image from the outside in. We hear suggestions that we need to get more education, get a better job, dress for success, improve our conversational skills, go on a diet, and so on. These can all be good things, but they are good only when one is also attacking the self-image problem at its roots.

The real root of a positive self-image is understanding who I am and why I am here. This can be answered only from a God's-eye perspective. Every human being on the face of the earth is a creation of God. He or she was God's idea. Only when we see ourselves as creations of the holy God, only when we realize that criticism of self is criticism of the Creator, do we understand who we are. Only when we've finally understood that God thinks we're valuable, so valuable that He gave His Son to die on the cross for our sins, do we begin to develop a positive self-image.

Depression is a serious problem nowadays, and it is often tied to the same questions that affect our self-image—who am I? Why am I here? We either fulfill our goals and find that our achievement is empty and unsatisfying, or we do not fulfill them and feel like failures. But at some point in life, we find that we cannot "live by bread alone" (Matt. 4:4). We learn that living for ourselves, our goals, and even our families will not fulfill our deepest human needs. Only as God fills our needs and as we find our relationship with Him can we find victory over depression.

There is such a thing as clinical depression; it is a disease that has to do with one's biochemistry. I'm not talking about that. In fact, a person who is suffering from clinical depression surely needs to seek medical help and get his or her physiology straightened out. But a person who is

217

functioning physically well has to approach self-image and depression at its very foundation—a proper understanding of one's relationship with God. Any identity that defines the self separate from the Creator—be it national, racial, educational, athletic, work-related, or even religious—will eventually be weighed in the balance and found wanting, leaving the person empty and depressed.

HE THINKS HE'S STUPID •

My son is eleven years old and has a very low picture of himself. He feels he's stupid. He does have a learning handicap but isn't in any special classes at school. The other kids tease him about this sometimes. I've tried to encourage him to do the best he can, but he feels he has failed even before he starts. When he was younger he lived with his father who slapped him around and told him he was dumb.

You use a phrase that intrigues me—you say your son has "a very low picture of himself." That's an accurate way to talk about self-esteem. All of us have a picture of ourselves in our minds, and we tend to live up to that picture. Jesus looked at Peter, a hot-tempered, fast-talking, vacillating person, and said, "You are a rock" (Matt 16:18—*Peter* means "rock"). He gave Peter a vision of himself as someone who was solid and firm and stable, though Peter was anything but that at the time. Then Peter spent the rest of his life trying to live up to the picture the Lord gave him of himself.

Your task is to give your son a new picture of himself. Unfortunately, eleven-year-olds are about as cruel as anyone can be with the possible exception of six-year-olds. Elementary school kids can be almost cannibalistic. To a boy your son's age, being a victim of playground taunts is very difficult. So he will need a great deal of understanding, affirmation, love, and encouragement from you.

In addition to helping him directly, get him in an environment where he can begin to rebuild his picture. Talk to his school teachers and Sunday School teacher to find out what they have observed about his interests and strengths. Find something he enjoys doing, something he is good at, and begin to build on that. Discover his growing edge, and help him move out from there. I would also encourage you to try to get him into a children's group at your church. Talk to the leaders about his need to rebuild his picture of himself. Let them know what his special interests are. Every step your son takes toward improving his picture of himself will make him a happier, more confident boy.

CAN'T STOP SINNING •

I became a Christian a few months ago, but I'm still plagued by overwhelming feelings of worthlessness. Sometimes I feel that suicide is my only way out. I've been under the care of a psychiatrist for fifteen years, but I'm getting worse instead of better. I feel hopeless. I pray, but I commit the same sins I did before I was saved. I confess these sins, but I seem helpless to stop committing them.

If you've been seeing a psychiatrist for fifteen years, you have obviously struggled through some very deep waters; and you've done very well, because you've hung in there for a long time. On the other hand, now that you have become a Christian, you may need a psychiatrist who is also a Christian and can understand your newfound faith. If your present psychiatrist does not fit these characteristics, let me encourage you to speak to your pastor and get his counsel about your situation. He could probably help you find someone who could counsel you more effectively. Your first doctor has helped you a great deal, but sometimes an additional opinion or another approach can help also.

When you have such deep feelings, especially about suicide, you need someone near you whom you can trust, to whom you can talk. Such a person can keep you from doing something that you would be very sorry about later, something that would hurt your friends and that you ordinarily would not want to do. Your pastor may be able to help you here. He may even have the key to some of your guilt feelings. The sins that plague you, he may tell you, are not as important as you think they are. You may be a victim of perfectionism; your standard of what a Christian ought to be may be false. If you feel you must be a hundred-percenter, then every time you make a mistake you take one percent away. Personally, I look at it the other way. I'm a zero, and every time I have a success I add one. But a hundred-percenter is destined to feelings of defeat and failure. Let's face it—success is not just getting up; it is getting up every time you fall. God knows we are dust, and He is very compassionate about our failures. We shouldn't be harder on ourselves than He is.

A CONFIDENT PARENT? •

My husband is always criticizing himself for the way he handles our family. Whenever anything happens, he blames himself. I think he really does a fine job of heading up our family. But when I tell him that, it doesn't register. Are there any guidelines for developing confidence as a parent?

I'm not sure about guidelines—the human condition doesn't always lend itself to ABCs. But I can tell you some things that tend to help.

Your husband is probably fishing for admiration. He's not necessarily feeling that he's all that bad; perhaps he wants reassurance that he's actually quite good. I got a big insight on this from a young lady who told me what happened once when she was feeling insecure. Her friends started saying to her, "You're just fishing for a compliment. Wake up, straighten up, quit fishing." But her boyfriend was different. He affirmed her. He said, "I know you want a compliment, and I want to compliment you. I think you're just wonderful." And she said to me, "Isn't it wonderful that he knows what I need and gives it to me rather than telling me I don't really need it?"

I've been helped by that story, because I tend to get impatient with people like that. I want to say, "Cut it out—you know you do well, so quit fishing." But when people need affirmation, they need affirmation. Your husband apparently needs to be affirmed, so affirm him.

Now the guidelines for developing confidence as a parent: First, commit your marriage and your family to God. Realize that you're all going to make mistakes; you're all going to need grace and forgiveness. Ask God, through His Holy Spirit, to give you guidance.

Second, understand that God will not ask you to do something you can't do. Parenting can't be all that complicated. People do it worldwide, from the simplest tribal villagers to those in the most complex situations. Frankly, whenever I land at O'Hare Airport in Chicago and see all those lights down there, I am amazed to think of how many of them represent houses where people are functioning quite well. So understand that God has not asked us to pole-vault twelve feet; he has given us something that we can do.

Third, trust your instincts. They are based on a lifetime of experience, and if you truly love God and your family and your children, then your instincts are almost always going to be correct. Be confident that even if what you're doing is not perfect, at least your motive is good and you're seeking the best for the other person.

Finally, remember that there are two of you. Neither one of you should try to do the whole job by yourself. Confer about your family concerns. Discuss them with each other. Together you have more strength than either one of you has alone.

NO ONE LOVES ME ●

I have a friend at school who has a terrible self-image. How can I convince him that he is worth something? He is from a broken home and his family has low morals and values. He just became a Christian and knows God loves him, but he can't believe others could like him or find anything attractive about him.

You are already helping him by being his friend, encouraging him, and listening to him. But be aware that many boys use this particular ploy to get close to a girl. He may figure that you have maternal instincts, and besides, you're a Christian, so probably you would bring home any bedraggled puppy you found on the street in order to mother it. Some boys are pretty smart. They know if they tell you all their troubles, they can get close to you. So you have to figure out for yourself how much of this is his line and how much is real (he himself may not even know).

Let's for a moment remove romance from this and look at how to be a listening, caring Christian friend. Affirm the good that you see in him. Encourage him to achieve and accomplish things; ultimately one's sense of self-worth comes from having done something worthwhile. Encourage him to achieve his goals, finish things, and not to give up. The youth pastor and other young people should be able to help you give him this kind of affirmation and encouragement. Whatever you do, don't give him sympathy and overindulgence. That would just lead him further into the kind of weakness he seems to have developed already.

You mentioned that he knows God loves him. That's not just a little churchy thing we say—"Well, he knows God loves him and therefore his soul is saved." God's love is the only answer to low self-esteem. That is, a person's self-esteem can be strong only when he understands this relationship with his Maker. Say to this young man, "You are a *unique* creation of God. He loves you so much that He sent His Son to die on the cross for your sins. He values you so much that He gave Himself for you. If you criticize yourself, you are ultimately criticizing your Maker and your Redeemer. You are worthwhile, not because of your achievements or appearance, but because you were created and saved by God." Work on getting this message through to him, because it will help him more than any cosmetic approach you could give.

NO ROOM FOR APOLOGY ●

My husband had an affair several years ago. At the time, he was in a very public job situation, and the whole community found out. He has never told me he is sorry, and that really hurts. I'm not going to ask him to apologize—I feel this should come from his heart. Meanwhile, I'm getting deeper into depression, and no one has even noticed. Am I wrong for wanting an apology? I can't seem to forget what he did.

———————

You say, "I'm getting deeper into depression, and no one has even noticed." In other words, "No one sees that I'm the hurt party, and no one gives me any sympathy. I'm even getting depressed and no one cares. My attention-getting device isn't getting me anywhere." Get off that tack immediately and start in another direction—confront your husband and simply share with him, as you have with me, your feelings about his not having apologized to you.

Apologizing does not necessarily prove sincerity, and not apologizing does not necessarily show bad faith. Some people will immediately ask forgiveness just to get the other person off their backs. It's possible that your husband is at the other end of the spectrum—he may feel so distraught by the situation that asking for forgiveness looks cheap to him. He may want to prove his remorse by actions rather than by words.

Once you have told him how you feel, I think he owes you something. Insist that the two of you enter into long-term professional counseling that will enable you to get to the bottom of your problems. He needs to discover why he let himself get into this situation, and you both need to learn how to improve your marriage so you don't have to face the same situation again in the future.

No amount of counseling, of course, will change the past. Your husband's infidelity will always be a fact. But one of the most beautiful things about being a Christian is this—we can find forgiveness from God for our sins; therefore, in appreciation for the forgiveness God gives us through His Son, we can offer forgiveness to other people. Your kind of situation would be very hard to solve for people who don't know the Lord. Time doesn't necessarily heal all wounds, but Christ can, for both you and your husband.

LONELY FAR FROM HOME ●

When my husband and I got married eight months ago, we moved far away from family and friends. I never imagined how lonely and depressing this could be. My husband's medical work keeps him away most of the time, and I don't know anyone I can really talk to. I write many letters to my old friends, but they don't usually write back. I've always wanted to be a social worker, but even my interest in school is diminishing. When I was growing up I had to cope with close loved ones dying and my parents' divorce, and I guess maybe I have become too sensitive. I know others go through rough times and are strengthened. How can I be strengthened through times like these?

Other people may have been strengthened by hard times, but a lot of people remember their experiences in much more glowing terms than they would have used when they were actually going through them. Many of these people felt very defeated at the time, so don't put yourself up against what you imagine their standard was.

I am concerned about your depression. A few years ago I would have talked with you about your spiritual well-being and the benefits of counseling. These are still important things to consider, but I'm now convinced that much depression is physically based. The first step in dealing with depression is to go to a medical doctor. Tell him, "I've felt depressed for several months. I've had problems—losing friends, broken home, moving—but I think this depression has lasted too long. I should have snapped back by now. I'm wondering if it may be physiologically based." Don't accept no for an answer until after he has done some tests. If he's not equipped to do them, go to someone who is.

Whether or not your depression has physical roots, now that you are in this new community you are facing some deep disappointments. You married a man because you wanted to be with him, and now he is away most of the time. You are in a new community, your old friends don't write, and you don't know where to find new ones. Let me suggest that the church is the best place to find friends—not the Sunday morning service, but small-group settings. You need to go to Sunday School, small-group meetings, evening service, prayer meetings, wherever you can get to know people whom you would only shake hands with on Sunday morning. As you make friends you will find they will begin to fill the empty space left by your old friends, and I think they will help you through this period of mourning.

FOLLOW THE LEADER ●

My best friend (she and I are both fifteen) is always comparing herself to me—her grades, her weight, her clothes, her singing ability, and lots of other things. When she doesn't do well, she gets down on herself. I love her, and it wouldn't bother me if I didn't do as well as she did all the time. I want to help her feel good about herself. How can I do it?

Certain people are always going to feel more comfortable as followers than as leaders. Some of the disciples were like that. When Jesus left the scene, most of the disciples began to follow Peter and John. Your friend is probably of this personality type.

Now don't do what I sense you may want to do—don't fail for her sake. If you could just fail, you think, she'd feel better. This seldom works; few people want to be patronized. They would rather be beaten than have you let them win. Continue to do your best, but point out her good qualities and affirm her in the things she does. Point out things she does well that you aren't as good at. She may respond, "Well, OK, I know I can do that, but I want to do these things that you do." She is so used to her own strengths that she doesn't value them like she values yours. Keep affirming her; you may help her see her own good side.

The secret, I think, is to love her, accept her for who she is, and understand that she may always need someone like you. It's important for you to be her friend.

HIDDEN TALENTS ●

We love our teenage son very much and are concerned about his self-image. He's a fine young man, but he really isn't good at any one thing. He sometimes feels he can't do anything right. How do we go about affirming him? Should we dig deeper to uncover his hidden talents or strengths?

Help your teenager discover his strengths and talents, but don't try to fit these into a *specific* career or job description. At this age it's probably too early to try to discover what he is going to do in life. Most teenagers are somewhere between running a pizza stand and becoming a medical missionary; this broad spectrum of interests is part of the problem. Nevertheless, this is a good time to *begin* exploring different career options. Just remember, there are about 40,000 specific, trainable kinds of work in America today. It's tough to ask kids to choose *one* at this stage of life!

Let me also encourage you not to tie performance to self-worth. There's no question that people who perform well in something tend to have greater self-esteem. A kid who is a great figure skater probably has a more positive self-image than one who pitches pennies. But self-worth that is tied to performance is very fragile because—what happens if the person can no longer perform? If the figure skater should lose a foot, then his self-worth would be utterly destroyed. So his self-worth should not be tied to his performance but to who he is as a person. If you have confidence in yourself as a person, you can handle almost any setback. But if your confidence rests in your performance, you're setting yourself up for a big fall.

Your son needs affirmation—"You're a good son; we love you; we trust you; we have confidence in you." How do you affirm your son and build his self-esteem? First of all, trust him. A person who is trusted believes he is trustworthy. He has value. Second, respect his property. Give him the privilege and responsibility to have things, to own things. Third, respect his opinion. If a young person is sitting at the table and says some inane thing, don't call him a dummy. Instead, ask him to explain. Tell him you didn't catch what he was trying to say. You might find that he really has a good opinion on something, that it has validity from his point of view. Now it may not have any validity from your point of view, but *you* don't have to live every day in the local high school. Fourth, respect his privacy. Let him have some time when he is able to be alone to think and meditate on things. These four principles edify the person rather than focus on performance.

Many kids have the idea that if they can't do something such as quarterback the football team or play a band instrument or understand computers, they don't have any worth. It's our responsibility as parents to show them they do have worth—because they are the unique creations of a holy God.

CHAPTER 18

Morals and Ethics

The Christian life does not take place in a vacuum. All ethical and moral questions arise out of human experience, and life is filled with small and large questions and dilemmas. For a person who does not take his faith seriously, it's simply a matter of survival and avoiding personal hurt. For the serious Christian, however, there is a plumb line, an expected standard—the example of Jesus Christ.

We have not been left alone to figure out the answers to our questions. God Himself came to the earth in the person of Jesus to give us an example of how we should behave. His is a unique example, different from society in general. Jesus created a counterculture, one that is demanding, satisfying, and absolute. Even so, in our fallen world we are always facing situations that perplex us and force us to struggle.

PARENTING IS TOUGH TODAY ●

It's tough being a parent in today's world. There are many things I don't want my kids to do that I find myself doing, like watching certain television programs. How do I maintain values and convictions so I can be a good parent in this modern age of temptation?

I'm sure you've heard the phrase, "What you do speaks so loudly I can't hear what you say." We must be examples to our children. The Apostle Paul made a statement recorded in 1 Corinthians 6:12 and again in 10:23 to this effect. He said, "Everything is permissible—but not everything is beneficial" (NIV). In other words, some good things are not always proper at all times. This is especially true for parents. There are certain things that adults can handle that children can't. That's part of maturity and adulthood. But parents shouldn't use this fact as an excuse.

For instance, more and more families have cable television in their homes, and many of the movies are very questionable. Parents don't want their children exposed to these movies, but should adults be exposed to them? For instance, you're watching an ordinary TV program and on comes a scene in which there is an implied adulterous relationship and the beginning of a love-making scene. If the family is in the room, it embarrasses you as parents because your children ask questions: "Mommy, what are they doing?" And if you have older children, there's silence in the room. The kids don't even blink. These are the moments they really watch for. As parents we don't know how to react to these situations, so we become embarrassed. We turn off the TV or leave the room. But when the kids aren't in the room and such a scene comes on, as adults we vicariously enjoy it. Now, what is the sin in that scene? Is the sin the physical adultery or is it something deeper? Obviously, God is opposed to adultery because of what it does to the social climate, to society—how it destroys families, relationships, and people. But the real issue is whether we as Christians should enjoy things that are sinful simply because we are adults and can "handle it." I say no. In fact, the reasons we don't want our children to watch these things are probably less legitimate than the reasons adults shouldn't be watching them.

We're getting used to things in our society that we have no business getting used to. And I believe the Christian home is going to have to draw some lines. There are things available in one's living room right now on television that would have caused your grandparents to literally discuss the end of the world. It would be that appalling to them. But to cut some of these questionable things out of our lives is a very tough thing for parents. It requires a firm decision and a lot of sacrifice. But maybe we should start moving in this direction if we want our children to grow up with the same Christian values we hold.

WHOSE VALUES? ●

My children, and most of their friends, seem to be developing completely different value structures from my husband's and mine. In fact, now they're questioning the values we've taught them. How should we respond to this? And how can we minimize the powerful effect these friends have on our kids?

The effect that peers have on our children is immediate and strong. But parents are not helpless. Our young people will tend, in the long run, to pick up our deep and abiding and lasting values.

In the meantime, however, they will be influenced by their peers' attitudes toward things like drugs, rock music, and sexuality. These things can have serious consequences, such as addiction and pregnancy, and I'm not saying that parents shouldn't take them seriously. What I am saying is that you shouldn't write yourselves off. Don't feel that your lives and your opinions are having no effect at all on the kids. Over the long haul, you will probably have a greater effect on your kids than their peers do. When they are in their late twenties and early thirties, they will begin to revert to the training you gave them. This should bring you a little comfort, even though the experiences they are having right now may be very difficult.

It's important not to get too uptight. I'm always amazed at how many parents of younger teenagers ask me this kind of question. It seems as if the greatest fear is expressed by people whose kids are just ready to enter junior high. Don't be like the basketball player who is so tense at the free-throw line that he shoots right over the backboard. If parents get their spring would up too tight when the kids are young, and as a result tighten the thumbscrews when the kids enter junior high, they may have real problems.

It's normal for children to question. In fact, they should question the status quo, why we do the things we do. The most important thing in their development is not the fact that they question. It is not even the answers we give them. It is the stance we take while giving the answers.

Sometimes when a young person questions something his parents believe very deeply, the parents overreact. They go into a tizzy and say, "How could you possibly say that? You mean you actually believe those things?" When that happens, the kid is in a control position. "I've got my parents on the run," he thinks. "All I have to do is say something like this and they just have a committee meeting!"

I've found it's much better to be relaxed, to say, "That's interesting." If you're relaxed, you can tell your son or daughter how you think and why. You can show him or her the logic behind what you do. Remember that the Christian message is not arbitrary. Given to us from the mind of God, it is based on truth and experience. It will win over error every time—we have to have faith in that. If we present the Christian message in an atmosphere of confidence in the faith, our kids will eventually see that we have access to the truth, which means access to God Himself.

SHOCKING DISCOVERY •

I was shocked to find a magazine of questionable character while I was straightening up my sixteen-year-old son's room. He doesn't know I saw it, and I don't know where he would have gotten it. Should I say something to him about this? Should I be concerned?

Yes, you should be concerned, but perhaps the pictures of nude women are not your greatest worry. Your son, along with the rest of us, lives in a sex-saturated society. Of course he is affected by this. But the fact that he left his magazine in his room where you could find it indicates that there's probably a great distance between the way he views sexuality and nudity, and the way you view it. He could easily have hidden it where you would never have found it, but he probably didn't think it was that shocking a thing.

You have to realize that young people in today's world see the human body and nudity differently than we do. Sadly, sometimes they are so jaded by a constant barrage of sexually stimulating material that they tune it all out and become insensitive to normal sexuality. You also have to realize that men and women see these things differently. It is normal for males to be interested in visual images; it is normal for sixteen-year-old boys to be curious about female bodies. You don't want to turn your son away from sexuality, but you do want him to keep sex in context. It is not right to see other people as objects or to look for sexual gratification without responsibility, and sex magazines never look at women as persons or at sexual relationships as permanent commitments. That's where they could be harming your son, and that's what you need to talk to him about.

PUTTING VALUES TO THE TEST •

I transferred from a Christian college to a secular college and am now questioning some of the values I was taught. The Christian college taught me to view things from a narrow perspective, while the secular college gives a broader point of view. Is there any way I can test my values without losing my faith?

I'm persuaded that questions are very good things. In fact, even doubt has its value. Questions and doubt are raw material that you feed into a machine called the human mind. When the machine is done processing them, it brings out tried ideas that you can use in your life. Doubt, then, is the fuel of the mind.

There is a big difference between indoctrination and education. Indoctrination is a close-minded approach that tries to avoid problems and simply states its position over and over again. If you repeat the lie often enough and loudly enough, people will begin to believe it. Hitler's regime was big on indoctrination. Education is much broader. It faces questions squarely, deals with them, and tries to come up with adequate, workable, satisfying answers.

Education is based on faith. Faith believes that God is in control, that He made the world, that He can handle any problem we might raise. Faith says, "Bring on all comers. Let's put them in the arena and wrestle with them. I'm not afraid, because I know God will come out on top." Indoctrination, by contrast, is based on fear—and fear often won't wrestle. It says, "Oh, no, I don't dare bring that up, because God might lose." Fearful people don't have faith. They are always trying to protect God. But it seems to me that if I'm big enough to protect God, He's in real trouble. Instead, God protects me.

I believe that God and truth are synonyms. God's truth and man's truth are parallel; the only difference is that there is far more of God's truth. I would encourage you to move out of a child's view of faith with great confidence, knowing that there will be no devastating surprises. God can handle all the questions you come up with.

THEY DON'T WANT OUR ADVICE ●

We have two teenagers and neither has come to us for any advice concerning morals or daily living patterns. Our daughter takes her problems to the Christian Education director at church, with whom she has built a strong relationship. Our son gets counsel from his Campus Life director. We get along well with our children, but I guess the problem is that we are jealous of these workers. Are they really competent to help in these matters?

You need not be jealous: your children know who their parents are and they are patterning themselves after you. Youth for Christ spent a lot of time and money on research and we learned that in a typical home situation, by the time kids reach their mid-twenties they are almost carbon copies of their parents. That is, they have the same value structure, believe the same things, vote the same way, and attend the same kind of church. In fact, they may be more firmly committed to their parents' views than even their parents are.

However, your kids are in a testing period right now. They are trying to find out, "Does my parents' advice really work?" They already know what you think; that's why they're not coming to you. So they go to someone else to find out if your opinions match. If they do, your children will think, "What wise parents I have." If they don't, they may try something you would have advised against. If it turns out that your way was better, the kids will think, "They were right. That's how I'll do it next time."

At Youth for Christ, we try to help our staff understand this dynamic. Their role is to be interpreters: to interpret adults to youth and youth to adults. They have to be mature enough not to enjoy the adulation of youth so much that they build a wedge between parents and children. We think that's a bad thing to do to a family.

But let me assure you—you *have* passed your values on. You have passed them on through a thousand little things you have said, through all sorts of examples, through experiences in your home. Some people worry that they have never put their philosophy into words. They need not be concerned. They have communicated it through their daily walk with God.

Ten years from now, your kids will have kids of their own, and they'll be raising their children like you raised yours. It's a little scary to think about, but that's the way it is.

WHEN CHILDREN LIE ●

My ten-year-old daughter has a problem with lying. It's gotten to the point where she does it almost spontaneously. Is this some sort of rebellion. Have we overlooked some simple method to keep her from telling lies?

The fact that she is ten years old may partly explain her behavior. I'd worry a lot more about it if she were twenty. As Scripture says, "When

I was a child, I spake as a child" (1 Cor 13:11)—and for many children, that includes some lying.

On the other hand, you want to guide her toward the kind of behavior that will be expected of her when she's grown-up. It will help if you ask yourself, "Why do children lie?" Often it's because they don't like life as it is. They want to change reality by creating a fantasy situation. Some children lie because they think adults couldn't possibly be interested in their real lives. Mom or Dad asks, "How did it go at school today?" and what's the kid supposed to say?—"Well, we played, and then we put our heads on our desks and rested, and then we drank milk, and then we did finger painting." Once when I asked my son that question, he answered, "The bus broke down." I said, "Oh, really?" and he continued, "Yeah, and the bus driver had each of us pick up a piece of the bus and carry it to the service station, and the man at the station put it back together, and then we came home." For several days he insisted that this story was true, until I finally figured out what he was really saying: "If I told you what really happened, you'd stop listening before I finished."

When kids realize that we are really interested in their lives, that we really care about their concerns, then they are usually much more willing to share reality than to try to create a new reality. If parents really listen to their child, the child feels that what he is saying must be important because Mom and Dad are not trying to read the paper, or looking some other direction, or changing the subject, or acting hurried. But a child who can't get our attention any other way often tries to manufacture a new life.

DESCENT INTO SIN? ●

We suspect our daughter is living an immoral life. She graduated from high school last year, got a job, and moved into her own apartment. In the past she has gotten too involved with some of her boyfriends. Her present boyfriend is at her apartment almost every day, even into the late evening. She calls me a couple of times a week to talk, and I've asked her quite frankly what goes on between them. She says that they aren't doing anything wrong and that she is saving her purity until she gets married. I wish I could believe her, but her past record causes me to distrust her. What can we do to keep our daughter from sinking further and further into sin?

When our children reach the legal age of independence, it is impossible for us to control their lives. Actually, we haven't completely controlled them ever since they stopped being portable, and once children are away from home several hours a day, our control over them weakens considerably. As you no doubt realize, nothing you can do will absolutely prevent your daughter from living whatever kind of life she chooses.

Your daughter needs to be loved, affirmed, encouraged, and accepted as a person. I am sure you are doing these things for her; but for many girls her age, the affection of one adolescent young man can be of greater importance than all the affirmation her family can provide. This is just a fact of life.

However, let me suggest that you change your thinking in one area. You talk about your daughter's descent into sin. This has a theological twist to it that makes me suspect you misunderstand sin to some degree. It sounds like you think of sin as something impersonal that, if committed, will cause God to condemn a person. Actually, sin is a way of living that hurts people. A better way to look at this is to say, "What can we do to keep our daughter from being deeply hurt or scarring herself so that she can't recover?" This puts the emphasis on your daughter's well-being rather than on getting rid of something external called sin.

You see, as long as you are concerned about the theological implications of your daughter's conduct, you are unable to help her. But when you become concerned for your daughter rather than for her sinfulness, you begin to work toward a solution. If your observations are correct, she probably is living away from God. That means she needs your understanding, love, and help. Through you she may come to understand that true loving and caring come from God through committed relationships.

ONE THING LEADS TO ANOTHER ●

Do you believe that it is wrong for an unmarried couple to hold hands, kiss, and embrace? I don't believe it is, but my parents do. They say one thing leads to another, and such behavior could be a stumbling block to young Christians. I know the Bible says to honor your parents, so here is my idea. Though I don't agree with them, I will obey them because I am living at home. But when I'm on my own, I will be able to be more intimate with my boyfriend. Wouldn't this be honoring them?

I'm happy that you take seriously the idea of honoring your parents. You want to honor them because God said to, and that is a terrific attitude. However, I think your parents are right when they say one thing leads to another. People always get more involved sexually, and not less. You start by holding hands, and then you kiss, and then you neck and pet. It does not move in the other direction: you don't start by kissing and then move on to holding hands. Your parents are concerned because they understand how sexuality works.

The same Bible that says "Honor your parents" also says "Flee fornication" (1 Cor. 6:18 and 2 Tim. 2:22). Most kids don't use the word *fornication* every day, and so they may not know that it means sexual relations between unmarried people. People can rationalize and say, "That means we shouldn't be involved in intercourse." But sexual intimacy is a total package; you can't separate one piece from the rest. And sexuality is extremely powerful. It's like nuclear energy: it can be a great gift of God or an incredibly destructive force. So I would encourage you to use all caution with your expressions of intimacy. When you are young and eager, whether you live at home or in an apartment of your own, listen to your parents—they have had more experience with intimacy than you've had.

IS SECULAR MUSIC SINFUL? ●

My friend condemns anyone who plays popular music, even if it is slow, quiet, and melodic. He says if a Christian didn't write the score, then it must be sinful. He can't be right, can he?

It is impossible to find in the life of Jesus Christ a sacred-secular distinction. Everything Jesus touched was sacred, because this is His Father's world. I believe that the world and all that is in it belongs to God; this is what Scripture teaches. It is more helpful to divide good music from bad music than sacred from secular.

Some music, of course, is specifically religious. There is some very bad religious music being played today. It has trite lyrics which are untrue biblically and experientially. There is also some very bad secular music, with lyrics that tear down all that is positive. It is cynical and filled with despair. I don't think it is good for a Christian to listen to bad music, whether it's religious or secular.

234

As for the music itself, it is impossible to arrange little black marks on a staff or to beat a drum in an immoral manner. What makes music moral or immoral is the context in which it happens. I take the time to watch a good many rock concerts; I try to be aware of what's going on. I see an atmosphere in certain rock environments that I feel is totally negative. It is ugly and sensual and not at all uplifting. The atmosphere is the problem, not the music itself.

People like your friend are usually reacting to their own backgrounds. Either they have heard some preaching that has set a standard they are trying to maintain or they are reacting to their former lifestyle. A recovered alcoholic is not neutral about liquor, and a person who has spent a good deal of time in a negative rock environment may not be neutral about secular music. It reminds him of his background and frightens him. Your friend needs balance. Maybe if you love him and are patient with him, you can help him achieve it.

CHEATING FOR LOVE ●

I'm a sophomore in high school and I have a problem with cheating. All my life I've wanted my parents and friends to like me. I'm rather overweight and constantly feel pressured to get good grades so people will love me, so I cheat. I know God forgives me, but I still have guilt feelings. Should I tell my teachers what I've done? I'm almost afraid to go to school because I don't want to risk cheating.

You're halfway out of the woods because you already understand that one of your big problems is self-acceptance. Somehow, you feel as if you're not worth much because you are overweight. You think the only way people will accept you is if you excel in something. Grades look like a way to do it, so if you have to cheat to get them, you will do so.

What you're doing is wrong and you know it. It makes you feel bad. In fact, even when you get a good grade after you've cheated, it's not yours. Let me encourage you first of all to confess this to the Lord and ask His forgiveness. Then I think it would be a good idea to go to the teachers involved and tell them. That could be dangerous; the teachers could take away your grades. But many teachers understand that they are teaching more than just math or English. They know that teaching has to do with life itself. My guess is that most of your teachers will say,

"All right, I'll let you start out with a blank slate and earn your grade for the end of the year. Just don't cheat from here on."

Then, I think you need to begin two projects. First, start doing your homework faithfully. It really takes less energy than cheating, because you don't have to be sneaky and you don't have to deal with guilt. Second, begin to realize that you are a creation of God. He loves you for what you are. And believe me, He loves girls who are a little wider and broader as well as the tall, thin ones. God has a place for you. If you know that the Lord loves you, then you have a good head start on solving your problem.

BREAKING BAD LANGUAGE ●

I'm ten years old and I'm having a problem with bad language. What can I do?

You've already taken the first step—understanding that using some language is bad and wanting to get help. A lot of people never come to that stage. Bad language doesn't please your parents, it doesn't please God, and it doesn't make people respect you and take you seriously. And so you want to stop using it.

Have you asked yourself why you use bad language? Usually boys and girls your age swear because they want to be accepted by other kids. Swearing makes you feel big. It lets the other kids know you're not a sissy. In fact, strangely enough, some of the best kids have the most trouble with bad language—preachers' kids are often the worst swearers in school. Now I don't want to pick on preachers' kids; I have a few of those myself! But if they swear, it's because they get so tired of everybody accusing them of being good. They don't want people to think that they don't know what's going on or that they are stupid or naive. Saying those things makes them feel as smart and tough as anybody else.

The Apostle Paul spoke about something like this. He said, "When I became a man, I put away childish things" (1 Cor. 13:11). I think that as you get older and more mature, you will find you won't need to prove you're big by doing silly things. When you get big enough to have good judgment and you no longer need "crutches" to say "I'm big," then you won't feel the need to use bad language any longer.

SWEARING IN GOD'S NAME •

My brother-in-law swears constantly when he visits, cursing in the name of Christ. I'm afraid this could have a damaging effect on our two-year-old son. Should I ignore the situation, or should I speak out and defend the name of my Lord?

Very few people who swear know what they are saying. When they say "Jesus Christ" as a swear word, they are not making some connection and saying, "Now let's see, Jesus Christ came into the world as the Son of God and died on the cross for people's sin and rose again for their justification, and now I'm going to condemn Him and call Him a bad name." All they are doing is making sounds that, for them, add emphasis to what they are saying. Someone has said, "Swearing is the effort of a feeble mind to speak with authority." Though I surely am opposed to swearing, I don't think we Christians should be so thin-skinned as to read meanings into it that aren't there.

Whatever you do, don't yell back at your brother-in-law and say, "Quit your swearing; you can't say that in front of our son; you are corrupting our home." But do say to him, "Say, could we talk a little bit?" Get his attention over a cup of coffee or a piece of pie or out walking in the yard, and say, "I have a problem. First of all, as you probably know, I'm a Christian. You may think I'm just being irritating or religious, but the truth is that it's a very meaningful thing to me. And since I'm a Christian, Jesus Christ is very important to me. Now, when you use His name like you do, this offends me, because Christ is my Saviour and my friend. Now, if someone came into our house and talked badly about you, I'd defend you. I'd say, 'You can't talk that way about my brother-in-law.' So on that basis, I'd like to ask you not to talk that way about Christ. Second, I'm trying to raise my little son as well as I can. This world is full of all kinds of problems, and I want him to grow up to be as good a boy as he can be. I believe that Jesus is the one Person who may really make his life meaningful, and I don't want anything to take away from the awe and reverence he should feel for Christ's name. You may not believe the same way I do, but I know you love my son. I'd appreciate it if, when you're in our house, you'd clean up your act." I think this gentle, reasonable approach will work.

AN EYE FOR WOMEN ●

I'm single, a dedicated Christian, and a man with a great appreciation for beautiful women. Some say God made fall colors and beautiful women both to charm the eye; others say that every look is wrong. Is there a wholesome way for a man to look at a beautiful woman?

There surely must be, or God wouldn't have given us eyesight! Read the Old Testament books of Ruth and Esther. Both these women must have been very beautiful, and there's no indication that Ahasuerus and Boaz shouldn't have looked at them. On the other hand, Paul's challenge to Timothy is also relevant to your question. Paul tells Timothy to treat his young female coworkers as sisters (1 Tim. 5:2).

I think Paul meant that these women should be seen in context. That is, your sister is never an object. She is a person, the daughter of your parents, a human being with feelings and abilities. A man looks at his sister and sees a person, not a no-deposit, no-return object to use for himself. Lust is what happens when we look at people out of context, devour them with our imaginations, and act selfishly and irresponsibly toward them.

As for a wholesome way for a man to look at a woman, I would suggest this. Thank God that He made each woman beautiful in her own way. Pray for each woman you admire, that she will be able to avoid superficiality and externals and narcissism. Pray that she will be able to find happiness in the right context, that she will find the right husband who will love her, and that she will have children who will adore her. In short, see her as a person.

As soon as we find ourselves taking a woman into that warm, moist little corner of our heart and beginning to devour her there in privacy, we know we have overstepped the bounds. The Holy Spirit will always reprimand us when we do that. Then back off immediately and say, "Lord, forgive me. Help me to see her as You intended."

IS IT GOD'S WILL TO KILL? ●

Is it right to kill someone in war? Is this going against God's will? My fiancé recently joined the Air Force and has been struggling with this issue. He's just not sure he could go into battle and intentionally kill another man.

Equally committed and deeply sincere Christians disagree on this issue. InterVarsity Press publishes a book called *War: Four Christian Views* which you might find very useful. You will learn from the book that each view comes from a different stream of the Christian church, and that each stream has made great contributions to church history, to the evangelization of the world, and to Christian thought. God has not blessed one to the exclusion of the others, and I cannot run anybody out of the Christian faith based on a sincerely held belief on any side of this issue. You and your fiancé need to come to your own conclusion on this.

If your fiancé concludes that he cannot be a Christian and fight in a war, he should be aware that throughout American history our government has made provisions for loyal citizens whose consciences do not permit them to fight. He needs to express his convictions to his chaplain or his commanding officer, and then fill out the proper forms to request a transfer into some branch of service that is not going to kill people. For instance, he might join the medical corps. Nobody accuses medical corpsmen of being cowards: it takes tremendous courage to run through fire to carry the wounded back to the lines. It's conscience, not fear, that directs some men to these branches of the armed services.

It will help your fiancé to stay in close touch with a sympathetic chaplain, because he will probably get plenty of testing and harassment just as soon as he expresses his views. The people he has to talk to may be very understanding, or they may be difficult to deal with. But this should not surprise him; matters of conscience are rarely easy.

THE EXCESS OF SUCCESS •

Several motivational programs about business growth or improving family relationships are being advertised around the country. These interest me, but I'm wondering if it would be biblically wrong to get involved with them. On the surface their concepts seem helpful, but many of them seem to have yoga, humanism, and other religions at their origins.

There is such a broad range of these programs that they surely cannot all be painted with one brush. In one category are those programs with their origins in yoga and other forms of Eastern meditation. When programs have a religious overtone, I think Christians ought to stay away from them. They are simply the evangelistic arm of certain Eastern religions.

However, there are other programs, some of them advertised in Christian magazines, that do not have a background in other religions. In those cases, one ought to ask what the motivation of the program is. Is the purpose to make money or to become a success in business? I personally question these goals, because I think Jesus was a countercultural leader who preached the kingdom of heaven rather than the kingdom of this world. In New Testament Christianity, spiritual values are placed above material values.

The Apostle Paul said that his motivation came from knowing he would one day stand before the Judgment Seat of Christ. "For we must all appear before the Judgment Seat of Christ," he wrote, "that every one may receive the things done in his body, according to that he hath done, whether it be good or bad" (2 Cor. 5:10). That got to Paul, and it gets to me too. There's a little rhyme that says, "Only one life, 'twill soon be past; only what's done for Christ will last." We have to ask ourselves, "Is what I'm doing really part of God's eternal kingdom?"

So when you study Jesus' and Paul's motivations, and compare them with the motivations that some people put forth—how to get rich, for example—you have to say, "Am I on some kind of sidetrack? Is someone just adding Bible verses and Christian phrases to old-fashioned materialism?" You know that materialism will leave your soul dry and empty. So you have to decide what your primary motivations are, and then stay away from any programs that would get you off the "kingdom track."

CHAPTER 19

Thoughts, Attitudes, and Emotions

Our interior life is important because the voice that talks to us from within is the voice that tells us who we are. No matter what we say to others, no matter how people think of us, if inside ourselves we are in turmoil, the inner voice is saying wrong things to us. If our inner being has not been submitted to the Saviour, then our exterior life begins to come apart.

In *The Portrait of Dorian Gray,* the main character's interior life begins to show in his portrait. As the portrait shows the hatred and avarice, envy and lust in his inner life, these traits begin to appear on his face as well. A wise man once said that we all deserve the face we have after forty. This surely points up the importance of having our thoughts, attitudes, and emotions in submission to the Lord.

We need to be aware of how our feelings affect our actions and how our actions affect our feelings. Generally speaking, people attack this exactly opposite of the way it should be attacked. That is, they wait to feel a certain way before they act. But the Bible teaches us that if we first act responsibly, then our attitudes, emotions, and feelings will follow.

It is a biblical truth that feelings follow actions, not the reverse; therefore God does not command us to feel but to act. Love, in the Bible, is not something we feel but something we do. And as we do loving acts for one another, we begin to feel loving also. Understanding that feelings follow actions opens up a whole array of opportunities to change ourselves. Happiness becomes a choice, not an accident—a choice to act responsibly and thus have our emotions, attitudes, and feelings under control.

The Bible further states that as a person "thinketh in his heart, so is he" (Prov. 23:7). Thinking is an action; thinking is controllable. And how we think determines what we are. Good theology leads to good living. Bad theology can lead us into a swamp of pitfalls that are sometimes worse than having no religious life at all. That is why it's important to be part of a congregation, to have a pastor who is trained in the Word of God, and to be surrounded by Christian friends who can test our ideas.

We must develop a consistent Christian world view, one based on the consistent revelation of God as shown in His written Word and in Jesus Christ. To know Him is supreme. That is why the Apostle Paul wrote "Let this mind be in you, which was also in Christ Jesus" (Phil. 2:5). Our thoughts, emotions, attitudes, and feelings all begin with right thinking about the nature of the world, life, and human relationships as revealed in the Word of God.

ROLLER-COASTER EMOTIONS ●

What causes sudden changes in my teen's behavior? Why is he so joyful and pleasant one moment and so sullen and low the next?

It's frightening when an exuberant, excitable, curious twelve-year-old suddenly turns into a self-centered, pensive, moody thirteen-year-old. All parents struggle with this problem, and yet in some ways it's the most easily explained adolescent behavior pattern. It has a physiological base: young people at this stage are in-between. They are not children and they are not adults. Just look at a picture of junior-high kids in a classroom. Some of the girls look like mature women; others look like children. Some of the boys are shaving and look very masculine; others are skinny little people with acne. Adolescents don't know who they are, or why they are different from their friends. They often experience a great deal of insecurity, hesitancy, and fear. They tire easily and usually take on more than they can handle.

To worry about this unduly is to bring unnecessary problems on yourself. You can't be constantly picking at a young person, saying, "Honey, why are you acting this way?" This simply makes the situation worse. In fact, by the time you get him to answer, his mood has probably changed anyway.

Teens need solitude. They need to work through some of these things themselves. They will talk back or act sullen or disrespectful sometimes, but trying to work through every teenage breach of etiquette is to make mountains out of molehills. I think it's far better to let some of it pass, unless the behavior is prolonged.

For instance, if a young person is spending day after day in her room, has no energy, isn't doing her homework, is losing her appetite, has the stereo plugged into her ear, and never does anything but watch test patterns on TV, then you might begin to think there's a real problem. It may be a drug problem; you need to explore and find out what's going on. But all kids will exhibit some of these behavior patterns in one way or another at some time during their growing-up period. The key is not to get alarmed over a single incident. Think back to your own adolescence, to the times you just wanted to sit and think and stare into space; to the time you spent in fantasy, wishing things would be different, not knowing quite how to face the adult world.

When you ask, "What are you doing?" and they say, "Nothing," that is probably exactly what they are doing. They are just spending time collecting their thoughts and putting them together. It helps if they can talk to their friends about their concerns. In fact, I think there's far too much pressure on kids to stay off the phone. Their long conversations are part of growing up and they're probably quite helpful.

The teen years are a time of trying to find independence, yet fearing to leave the security of childhood. Kids have to do this on their own; we parents can't help them. If we try, we will only prolong their childhood and interfere with the maturation process.

OVERCOMING OVEREATING •

I've been praying for strength to overcome an overeating problem. I've made promises to God about not overindulging, but I fail miserably. I've been involved with a weight-loss program and have even had psychiatric treatment, but none of this has helped. I know God can give me the strength to overcome this, but I'm not sure what more I can do.

You surely won't have any problem finding someone who wants to help you with this. There are dozens and dozens of books and diet plans and special foods you can buy to try to solve a weight problem. Concern with weight has become a fad, and the Christian church has jumped on the bandwagon. It's much easier to think about losing pounds than to fulfill the real demands Jesus makes on His disciples: to love one's neighbor as oneself; to care for the lost, the downtrodden, the disenfranchised, and the poor; to raise our children in the fear and admonition of the Lord. Actually, God probably isn't quite as concerned about the arrangement of muscles and flesh as we are.

It is possible that you are the kind of person whose body type is heavier than average. If so, find ways to be a blessing, heavy body and all. D.L. Moody did. He was a round man who accomplished great things for the Lord. If I had my choice of being skinny and being like some people or being fat and being like D.L. Moody, I would rather be D.L. Moody any day. What I am trying to say is that it's important that we not get caught up in this whole business of externals. There are much greater things to think about. We need to keep our weight within certain healthful limits, and some people within those limits will be pudgier than others. I would certainly encourage you to continue attacking this business of overeating, just as you would attack any other problem in your life. But don't relate every problem you face to your weight. You are a valuable person, whatever your size.

TRIGGER-HAPPY TEMPER ●

I'm having trouble trying to live a Christian life and set an example for my family. I have a quick temper with my children, who are ten, seven, and four. Whenever they disobey or do things that upset me, I flare up and start yelling at them. Sometimes I even throw things around the room. I'm trying to bring my children up in the church and teach them how to live their lives for the Lord, but what kind of example am I giving them when I act like this? I feel like a hypocrite. Sometimes I even feel like giving up because I feel unworthy of God's love. What can I do to control myself?

You know what kind of example you're giving. You're teaching your children to act like you do when they get frustrated. Later in life you'll find that they will also lose their tempers, yell a lot, and throw things around. How can you stop giving this kind of example?

I doubt if your temper is your real problem. Temper is a combination of characteristics including strength of character and determination. Yours may be headed in the wrong direction, but it also may be the very thing that allows you to make it through difficult circumstances. It sounds to me as if you may be a single mother, so you need strength and determination even more than most mothers.

What you need to deal with is not your temper, but frustration. What is the root of your frustration? Three young children can certainly provoke frustration, but most mothers can keep it within bounds. When a mother starts losing control, she needs to begin to search for what is really going on. I would strongly encourage you to seek professional counsel from a pastor, Christian counselor, or someone else who could help you understand your deep feelings.

It is possible that your frustration is based on resentment. Maybe you've been left alone to raise these three children; or if you are married, maybe your husband is not cooperating as he should. Perhaps you feel as if the family has taken away your freedom, and every day with them reminds you of how trapped you are. Maybe you have fears that you will not be able to raise them properly. These are the kinds of things you need to deal with. You need to get behind your actions and find out why the children trigger your fuse.

The Lord surely understands your situation. You don't clean up your life and then come to the Lord and say, "Now, Lord, I'm no longer yelling and throwing things, and I'm not going to do these bad things ever again. Now I'm all set, and I can be Your child." No, you come to Christ and ask Him to help you. The Lord *will* help you if you bring your troubles to Him.

HANDLING SEXUAL DESIRES ●

I am no longer married and I miss the intimacy of a relationship. I am finding it difficult to handle my emotions when I feel the need to satisfy my sexual desires. I pray about this, but prayer does not seem to help. Is there any Scripture that can help me?

Sexual desire is strong and normal, and I doubt if any verse of Scripture will take it away. Instead, you need to find worthwhile activity to get involved in. You need to channel your energies into other areas of life and trust that God will provide for your needs, either by sending you another mate or by giving you fulfillment some other way.

Prayer and resolutions do not seem to help much in controlling sexual desires. Suppose I told you it was OK to think about whatever you wanted, with one exception: you absolutely must not, under any circumstances, think about pink elephants. Obviously, if I told you that, you'd be able to think of nothing but pink elephants. The same thing happens if you say, "Please take away my sexual desires," or "I'm not going to have sexual desires." Eventually sex is all you can talk and think about.

A better approach is found in Philippians 4:8. The Apostle Paul wrote, "Whatsoever things are true, whatsoever things are honest, whatsoever things are just, whatsoever things are pure, whatsoever things are lovely, whatsoever things are of good report; if there be any virtue, and if there be any praise, think on these things." This advice is practically, psychologically, and spiritually sound. Paul is saying, "Put your mind on positive things. Focus yourself on positive activities." When you do this, you will have a healthy sense of accomplishment. You will also have less time and energy for the thoughts that are troubling you.

SHAKING GUILT •

A high school student drowned at a church youth camp while I was in charge. I wasn't near the lake when it happened, but I still feel responsible for the accident. I've asked God to clear my heart of this guilt, but I keep thinking there must have been something I could have done to have prevented this tragedy. I've talked with the boy's parents, and they don't lay any guilt on me. I must be doing this to myself. How can I forget about this and shake the guilt?

It's possible that you're doing this to yourself, and it's also possible that the enemy of your soul is attacking you at this point. The devil does not give up when we become Christians. Though we're on our way to heaven, he would like to make us ineffective while we're on earth. Few people are less effective than those who are filled with guilt, living through the rear-view mirror, and thinking about the past. That is why the Apostle Paul wrote, "Forgetting those things which are behind, and reaching forth unto those things which are before, I press toward the mark for the prize of the high calling of God in Christ Jesus" (Phil. 3:13-14).

Think about that for a minute. The Apostle Paul could have had constant voices in the night reminding him of the evil things he once did. He heard Stephen cry out as he was stoned to death. He breathed out "threatenings and slaughter against the disciples of the Lord" (Acts 9:1), and may have been responsible for the death of some Christians. But he was forgiven, and he put it all behind him.

246

A lot of people in the helping professions—Christian youth work, counseling, the pastorate—inadvertently forget *who* the Saviour is. They get a messianic complex and think they have to win every situation they meet for God. If they don't succeed, they feel they have failed God. It's as if God and His Holy Spirit have nothing left to do when they're around. When such people fail or face problems, they suddenly feel great guilt because they haven't been able to control the circumstances. Sometimes a youth sponsor will think, "I'm supposed to be in control of these people's lives. I have to arrange effective programs; I have to cause things to be preached that will change their lives." Such an approach becomes very man-centered. Then, when something awful happens, this kind of person will blame himself because he was the one in charge.

Let me encourage you to turn your ministry over to the Lord. After all, God and His Holy Spirit are at work in all these circumstances. I don't mean that you should be irresponsible. Of course you ought to do everything that you can. If you did some things wrong in connection with waterfront safety, next time do them differently. But turn this tragedy over to the Lord and let Him be the Saviour. If He's the Saviour, he has some responsibility for this situation. You don't have to carry it all by yourself.

PARENT PUT-DOWN ●

I'm seventeen and a senior in high school. My parents were divorced when I was nine and I have lived with my father since I started high school. I love my father and desperately want to feel his acceptance and love, but it really hurts me when he puts me down in front of my friends. He may think he's being funny or cool, but sometimes I hurt so much I just want to cry. I don't think I should, though, because it's an unmanly thing to do. Maybe I'm being too emotional. What do you think?

I don't know how emotional you are, but all people ought to have the capacity to be hurt and to know when they are being hurt. How can they feel other people's hurts unless they have felt hurt themselves? Second Corinthians 1:4 says we can help others the way God helps us. So your own sensitivity is preparing you to help some other young man down the road who is in the same situation you're facing.

Let me suggest three things. First, when your father puts you down, usually one of several things is happening. He may, as you suggest, be playing "king of the hill" with you. If so, that is unfortunate. Or he may be trying to communicate with you. You aren't getting the message, so he gives it in front of your friends in hopes that they will join in with him and try to bring you around.

The second thing I want to suggest is that you not make a battle of it. You're seventeen; why not just lie low until you're about nineteen? By then you will be out of your father's home and on your own. Chances are you won't be able to change your father, but you can be the kind of person you want to be with or without his affirmation.

Third, begin to build your own life. Take these negative experiences and determine that you are not going to repeat them in your own children's lives. Begin to develop friendships and relationships for the future. Then you will be able to say, "I'm the beginning of a brand new family and a brand new life, and things are going to be different this time around."

ASHAMED OF MOM ●

My problem is with my mother. She looks so sloppy that I'm embarrassed to have my friends over. She wears faded housedresses almost all the time and never fixes up her hair or takes care of her appearance. I know she could look nice if she just spent a little time on herself. She used to get her hair done every now and then, but lately she just doesn't seem to care about how she looks. I feel terrible being embarrassed about my mother because I love her, but how can I get her to take an interest in her appearance?

I would like to challenge your statement, "My problem is with my mother." I think more likely your problem is with your attitude toward your mother, and you probably won't be able to help her until you change it. You say you are embarrassed about her. Few of your friends will really respect you if you don't respect your parents, because it is obvious to everyone how much they have done for us. Start with your own attitude, then. Be grateful toward your mother for what she has done for you rather than critically looking on the outside. Her hair and her dress are not really basic to her human characteristics.

Usually a person's personal appearance, as well as the appearance of his home and car, reflects his own self-respect. That is, people who lose respect for themselves eventually begin to look sloppy and unkempt. So the answer to your problem is not to talk directly to your mother about her appearance, but to help her feel better about herself. Some way or another she doesn't feel loved; she doesn't feel important anymore. She feels as if she has been used, turned into a public utility instead of a person. The way to help her get her self-respect back is to begin to show love to her. Hug her and kiss her and tell her you love her. Affirm her for the things she does well. Then, gradually, beginning inside and working outward, she will begin to look different. It may take a long time—she did not begin feeling bad about herself overnight, and she won't feel good overnight either. But have patience; it's the only way to solve this problem.

DISCOURAGED DAD ●

I'm a discouraged father. My family isn't really where I'd like them to be. All my efforts to do something about this situation fall on deaf ears. Now I find myself developing a bad attitude toward my own family. How can I keep a positive attitude toward them and keep my emotions from getting the best of me?

Our heavenly Father could ask this question. His human family must certainly be discouraging to Him on a daily basis and for much the same reason. God has given people His image, and in that image He has included the right of His children to choose their own courses of action. Therefore, if the objective observer were to look at the human race, he would probably say that God the Father has surely failed because His family is killing each other, hating each other, and living for their own selfish desires. There are very few who really desire to love and serve Him, and a great many of those who claim to love Him are actually using and manipulating Him for their own ends.

The point I am trying to make is that a family is not something you can manage like a business. As part of the American system, we get the idea we can fix everything—computers, automobiles, people. But we cannot fix people; people have to willfully fix themselves by personal interaction with God. Some of the very finest parents in history have had wayward children through no fault of their own.

Yet what *can* we do when our families aren't where we'd like them to be? We can certainly use the strongest of all tools for motivating people to change their behavior, and that too is our example. Christ lived by example. He didn't beat us or force us or yell at us to follow in His steps. Instead, He pointed the way, then got down to the business of loving and caring for others—even if they didn't return His love or care.

I've sometimes said that one of the reasons Americans have trouble understanding the Bible is that they are citizens of a cattle country rather than a sheep country. Cattle are driven; sheep are led. We want to be cattlemen and drive our families instead of shepherding them. A shepherd walks ahead, finding the snakes and other dangers, then leads his sheep down the safe paths. Sheep do at times go astray, but they can be gently led back in the right direction. Like sheep, if your children choose to follow, the rewards will be great.

| SECTION 5 |

Living without a Spouse

The traditional family of employed father, unemployed mother, two children, and a dog is fast becoming a thing of the past. Nowadays, a third of all children will spend at least part of their growing-up years in a one-parent family, and more and more young adults are choosing to marry later or not at all. If because of divorce, death, or choice you are living without a spouse, you are certainly not alone.

But in spite of the fact that many American families do not include two adults, American society often still operates on the Noah's Ark principle—come in pairs or not at all. This can cause problems for single adults in many areas. Happily, the church is becoming much more aware of single people. In many cases, however, it still has a long way to go. If you do not feel out of place at church services, you may still feel awkward at social gatherings. You may be tired of seeing only other singles, yet couples may not include you in their activities. If you have children, you may wish to acquaint them with other adults. And, face it—you may be lonely.

Nevertheless, being single is neither a curse nor a disease. Single people have several outstanding role models in Scripture. Jesus and the Apostle Paul were both single, and Jesus' mother Mary probably spent much of her life as a widow. Jesus recommended the single life for some people and Paul even called it a gift. As with most circumstances in our life, being single is neither bad nor good in itself. It all depends on what we do with it.

CHAPTER 20

Single but Not Alone

Singleness is not a disease or a social malady. A single person should not be pitied or looked down on; he or she is not someone who is left out of the human experience.

Many people choose to be single, and rightly so. They choose a single life for economic reasons, to pursue a vocation, to be free to develop their own sense of personhood or to accomplish some goal that would be harder to achieve with a spouse and children. Singleness is not something to be overcome, like tuberculosis; it is a conscious way of living. In fact, the Apostle Paul encouraged Christians of his age to consider choosing singleness because of the external dangers the church was facing at that time.

Of course there are those who desire to be married and cannot find the right person. Our desire is to help these singles understand that there can be happiness and fulfillment in the single life. It is far better to be single than to be tied forever in a marriage that should never have taken place. Neither marriage nor singleness is, in itself, ideal. Either state can be within the will of God. What is important is to be in Christ, whether single or married. This is the beginning of happiness and fulfillment in life.

THE SINGLE STIGMA ●

I recently joined a Christian singles group, and I'm noticing that the general attitude is negative. These men and women seem to be saying, "Woe is me—I'm single." It seems as though a lot of the people are just looking for potential mates rather than trying

to build strong Christian friendships. The turnover is great, and quite a few are discouraged because the numbers have been steadily decreasing. Is there any way we can turn this attitude around?

The only way you can begin to turn it around is by confronting it just as you have here. I think it would be good to express your feelings to the group and see if others feel as you do. I would guess that many do.

One problem with singles groups is that singles face very real problems, especially in the church. These problems are not imaginary, and the negative attitude you see may be based on a true understanding of the situation. It used to be that when men or women got to a certain age, they were either "young marrieds" or "old maids." Only recently have churches begun to develop curricular materials for singles. Besides, many people in the church, even though they may not articulate it, have not come to terms with the fact that singleness can be desirable and normal. They deal with singleness as an exception to the rule, which may not be accurate. I've been told that by 1990 there will be more unmarried thirty-year-old males than ever before in our history.

I find that in singles groups you have three types of people: those who are seeking mates, those who don't want mates, and those who are willing to go either way depending on the conditions. So if you have people in your group who have decided they want to be single mixed in with people who are earnestly looking for mates, there is bound to be tension. But you have to acknowledge the situation before you can begin to work on the tension.

All three types of singles would benefit from learning to develop human relationships that are not sexually oriented. In fact, it would be a good idea for the singles group in your church to study how to develop deep, meaningful, caring relationships with people of the same *and* opposite sex. Maybe if you articulate these thoughts to your singles group, you'll begin to see changes.

LONELY HOLIDAYS ●

I'm single and my family lives far away. I have a feeling I will be spending this Thanksgiving by myself. I won't be able to visit my family, and no one from my church has invited me home for the day. Do you have any suggestions on how to get through the holiday without wallowing in self-pity?

You don't have to wait by the telephone when you find yourself in this situation—you can become active in planning your holidays. You need both a long-range and a short-range strategy. As a long-range strategy, start developing friendships with families in the church immediately. By Christmas or Easter or whenever you face the same problem again, they will stop and say, "Hey, I wonder what So-and-so is doing today?" I say this to students who come to our church. Many of them attend a nearby Christian college, and they drop in and out of church. That is the worst thing they can do. Students ought to get involved with several families in the church. Then they will have a surrogate family, a church home to care for them.

But you don't have to wait for Christmas or Easter to have a good holiday. Perhaps this Thanksgiving you can organize a dinner for the out-of-towners. Put together a potluck with the young men and women of the church. Or you can go and serve dinner at the local rescue mission. I venture to say that if you do this, it will be the most memorable Thanksgiving you have ever had. Another thing you might do is to find some old gentleman or lady in the church, some grandpa or grandma who isn't cared for. Invite one or two of them for dinner. Start saving now, and take them out to a nice restaurant.

Any of these activities will be rewarding, because you'll be thinking of someone besides yourself and your family. For goodness sake, don't waste the day for yourself and others by wallowing in self-pity.

BACK HOME AGAIN ●

I'm twenty-five years old and I recently moved back home with my parents after my divorce. Now some of my friends are asking me when I plan to move out. I want to wait until I've paid off all my debts so I can start fresh. It's not easy to live at home after living on my own, but I do my best to get along. Am I wrong to want to wait and adjust to being single again before looking for an apartment?

Your best answer when your friends ask, "When do you plan to move out?" is simply, "When I'm ready." You can explain your reasons if you wish, but you don't owe them an explanation. You are guilty of nothing. You are simply living at home because that's your best choice.

Sometimes people who get divorced begin to feel a sense of powerlessness. They think they have failed, feel a lack of self-worth, and suddenly believe everybody else has a right to run their lives. This isn't true. All of us fail sometimes, but that doesn't give us license to back away and say, "Now someone else can take over my life." So don't let your friends push you around.

I think your idea is sound, assuming you get along well with your parents. Often there is more trauma with divorce than the person realizes at first. Almost forty percent of marriages end in divorce, and four out of five divorced persons remarry within five years. Unfortunately, over forty percent of these end up divorcing the second time. I think one reason is that they decide to remarry in a moment of stress. They feel weak, vulnerable, and lonely. They don't allow themselves time to heal. I would strongly encourage you to follow your plan. Your parents can give you more than financial support. They can give you companionship and protection from people who might try to manipulate you.

GLAD TO BE A VIRGIN •

My mother scolds me because I'm still a virgin at twenty-six. I gave up dating to devote my life to Christ, but Mother keeps pressuring me to date. She compares me to my five sisters, who are all married and have children. Right now, I don't need marriage, sex, or kids. How do I explain this to my mother without hurting her?

It sounds like you may be still living with your mother, so I think your first step should be to move out and begin to live independently. This would help you get a little distance from her. And if moving out doesn't do it, moving away may be necessary. Whatever it takes, you need to establish your own autonomy.

You may find that your mother will continue to pressure you, even after you've established your independence and told her exactly what you have told me. Then you need to analyze why she is insisting that you change your behavior. To your mother, *happy* means to be married and to have children. She obviously values children—she's had six of them. Maybe she feels defensive about having so many. If so, she may feel threatened when you do the opposite of what she did. She may see you as a living rebuke to her value system. If she can get you to do what she did—to get married and have children—then you are affirming her way of life. On the other hand, she may simply want you to be happy, and she probably doesn't understand this devotion to Christ that you feel the Lord has called you to.

So the only thing you can do is to assert yourself. This may bring you some pain or some tongue-clucking. You may feel that your mother and sisters are always talking about you. In their eyes, you have become an "old maid," and you may have to put up with their comments. Wear a knowing smile—after all, you know some things that they don't know. You know it is possible for a woman to be fulfilled, to be a whole person, without being married. It may take some time for your mother to accept your way of life, but eventually she will probably come around.

SINGLE FOR LIFE? ●

I really want to get married but so far haven't found the right person. Do you think that God has a purpose in my being single?

It is very possible that He does. In some of the Apostle Paul's letters to the early church he actually encouraged many believers not to get married because of the extreme difficulties of the times. In those days it was very dangerous to be a Christian, and Paul felt that marriage could be an added burden to the early believer's mobility and safety.

Instead of thinking about the *purpose* of being single, think about the *process.* Many people spend their lives preparing for some future event. They say, "If I could just get over this hump," or, "When this finally takes place, life is really going to start being great." They live in the future and never really enjoy where they are today. I found that it helps to look at life as a process rather than a series of goals or humps to get over, like marriage or the perfect job. It is far more beneficial to think about the good you can accomplish today. Enjoy the process of doing what you can today, allowing the process of becoming whatever God wants you to be in the future to be a blessing in your life.

You may not want to be single, but the process of singleness has some very attractive qualities. One has more mobility, usually more money, more adventure, and more freedom to experience things that you probably won't experience once you are married. An adjusted single person can become an adjusted married person; a maladjusted single person will not become an adjusted married person—it just doesn't happen. It takes two whole people to make a whole marriage. I encourage you to spend your energy making singleness a good experience rather than something to overcome or to get out of.

God may certainly have a specific purpose for you in being single— teaching you how to build relationships, how to develop confidence with other people, and so on. But this preparation should still be looked on as a process. Don't look ahead to see where this preparation is leading. Look instead at the process and the goals you are accomplishing for today. This day-by-day process can give a depth to your character that you can take into a marriage relationship if you choose to be married. Many people who enter marriage have never really developed an in-depth relationship with anyone before, and their marriage partners are the first people they try to do this with. Sometimes marriages suffer because one partner's aptitude for developing relationships is so narrow that he or she has trouble developing a relationship with a spouse. Enjoy being single— many people do for a lifetime.

CHAPTER 21

Single Parents and Widows

A spouse's death—no one ever asks for it, nor can anyone ever be prepared for it. To be a single parent as a widow or widower is uniquely challenging. While a widowed person does not have the sense of guilt that is often associated with divorce, he or she does have an enormous sense of loss.

A widowed person is often less independent than a divorced person. Many divorced people anticipate the breakup and prepare themselves emotionally and financially for it. Widowed people, on the other hand, are almost always surprised, disappointed, confused, and unwilling. It's not as if they left something they didn't like in order to try to find something they do like. They have been forced to give up a happy relationship and now must try to go it alone. Often they must overcome loyalties to the former mate before they can try to forge new friendships or even before they can begin to change their style of living. These are touching and difficult experiences.

Their children, of course, have many of the same problems, and the kids have to deal with them with much less maturity. They wonder how God can let such a thing happen; they wonder why they aren't allowed to have both parents watch them in a school play or ball game. They feel cheated in life, and they've barely begun. And their newly single parent must deal with their problems as well as his or her own.

The cries of the widowed single parent are often left unaddressed by the church. They are only a small proportion of the congregation, and few churches have enough of them to form a group. Perhaps this is for the best—it's not healthy for them to spend all their time with other singles. And yet married people are often insensitive to their needs, and this presents them with an additional set of problems.

Widowed parents must understand that they have a special place in the heart of God. The New Testament gives special instructions for the care of widows and modern widows fall into the same category of God's concern. We must remind ourselves and them of this truth and offer them special love and understanding.

FATHER YES, HUBBY NO ●

I am widowed and feel my kids are being deprived by growing up without a father. How do I go about finding a good role model for my sons? I'm really not interested in remarriage at the present time, but would like my children to become acquainted with a father-type figure.

Divorced women have this same problem. This is where a strong involvement with your local church becomes especially important. Your sons need to be exposed to Sunday School teachers, pastors, youth pastors, and other people in the church who can serve as good role models and with whom the boys can build solid relationships that don't compromise you in any way. Christian youth organizations like Youth for Christ, Young Life, or Campus Crusade for Christ also have these kinds of role models. Encourage your boys to be a part of them. If the boys are younger, programs like the Boy Scouts, AWANA, or Pioneer Ministries can be quite good too.

Often, widowed women can look to the men who were their husbands' friends to serve as father figures. Of course, I have no knowledge of the friends your husband had, but usually a man chooses his friends because he respects them. There are qualities in his friends that he likes, and therefore these qualities might well be the ones that he would like transferred to his own sons. Men who came to your husband's funeral, men who try to help you, those who befriended your husband during his illness or you after his accident—whatever the situation was—these men can often be very good resources. You can say to your sons, "This is a man your dad really liked. Dad liked to fish with him, or Dad liked to spend time with him because Dad respected him."

Understand that having no father does not necessarily cripple a boy. In fact, too many boys have fathers who aren't the kinds of role models they need. This is all too common, and the effect on these boys can be even more detrimental than not having a father.

IT'S ALL UP TO ME •

How does a single parent handle discipline? It gets so difficult when there is no one to consult and every decision rests squarely on me.

I've found that people with difficulties in their lives, whether divorce or a handicap or single-parenthood, often approach problems by saying, "How does a handicapped person handle this?" or "How does a divorced person handle this?" or "How does a single parent handle this?" It's much better to say, "How does a person handle this?" "How does a parent handle this?"

I believe it's a mistake for a single parent to think "single-parently," to approach every problem through the grid, "I am a single parent." True, you are single, but that doesn't affect many things you face with your children. The problems caused by divorce or the death of a spouse do not lead to different methods of discipline. A single parent should discipline just like a married parent does. You must be consistent, fair, forgiving; you must discipline according to what's happened, not according to your feelings; you must be willing to listen; you must be careful not to make mountains out of molehills. In short, everything that's true of married parents is also true of you, and it's a great mistake to start thinking of yourself as needing different disciplinary methods because you are single.

Of course you face differences in some areas of child-raising. If you are a woman raising a teenage boy, you cannot do everything for him, and you would not want to keep him at home and turn him into a mama's boy. You need to help him find some men who can be role models for him—Sunday School teachers, youth leaders, teachers, scout masters, employers, uncles, pastors, people from whom he can learn the meaning of manhood. But in spite of the obvious lacks for which you will have to compensate, it's a mistake to think that now, because you are single, everything will be different. Nutrition for a child raised by a single parent is just like nutrition for a child raised by two parents. Corn flakes are corn flakes, junk food is junk food, and discipline is discipline.

REENTERING THE JOB MARKET •

Recently my husband died, and soon I will be forced to go out and find work. I'm scared. It's been so long since I've worked that I don't even know if I'm qualified to do anything. Where do I start?

Your fear is surely justified. Stepping out in any new pursuit is often threatening, and being scared is nothing to be ashamed of. Many women are in your situation, and most of them are less than confident.

One good way to begin is to think back to where you left off. What were you doing before you were married? If you liked what you were doing, it might be a good place for you to put your toe in the water. Go to your public library and look for new books for women who are reentering the job market. A classic book on job-finding is *What Color Is Your Parachute?* by Richard Bolles—buy a copy and do some of the exercises in it. If there are professional journals in your field of interest, read a few copies. Take a look at *Working Woman* magazine.

Many community colleges or public libraries offer workshops for women who are thinking about going back to work. The cost is usually moderate, and through class sessions or talking with an individual counselor, you may discover that you have more usable skills than you thought. Or perhaps you will see both what you would like to do and how to go about getting the necessary preparation. One word of warning, however: Don't spend large sums of money for private counselors or employment agencies. In looking for work, what you pay is not necessarily what you get. The best advice is usually free or inexpensive.

Once you have an idea of what direction you might want to go, tell everybody—friends, relatives, your minister, the friendly librarian, the woman who always walks her dog when you're sweeping your front steps—that you're looking for a job. Talk to people who already do your kind of work. The more contacts you have, the better. It will bolster your faith in yourself and in the human race when you see how eager people are to help. There's truth in the adage, "It's not what you know, but who you know that counts."

During the time immediately following the death of a spouse, many adjustments are necessary. This may be a good time to pick up new skills or brush up on those you have not used for a long time. This is not only good preparation for work, it is also a great help in dealing with grief. You will learn that you are not alone, that many others are in the same situation. You will make new friends and begin to develop a new life, perhaps one that will be very fulfilling for you. I've talked to many people two or three years after this experience who have found that their new life, in terms of independence, strengths, autonomy, and accomplishment, is more satisfying than the life they had before the adjustments were necessary.

The worst thing you can do is to let fear keep you from going out and trying your skills in the marketplace. One way to boost your courage is to think, "I may not be the best-prepared person in town, but I'm surely not the worst. There are many who have far fewer skills than I do. I must be somewhere in the middle. Therefore, there must be a place for me." If you have confidence, you will find a place to start. Begin to answer ads, talk to people, and get the "lay of the land" so that you know where you are. Solid information, preparation, and human contacts all help dispel blind fear.

CAN I MARRY AGAIN? ●

I am a widow, and it is one of the worst experiences I have ever gone through. My husband and I had thirty-three years together in Christian marriage, and now I'm in my fifties. Is it wrong for me to ask God if I might marry again? I dream that my husband says he wants me to marry someone who will love me and care for me. Is this my own idea, or could it really be God's will?

It sounds like a good idea to me, and it could very well be in God's will. There is certainly no prohibition in Scripture against it. In fact, in the Bible you will find story after story of people remarrying, both men and women.

I think your husband, if he could speak to you from the other side, very likely would be the first to encourage you to remarry. I'm sure he would say, "Go ahead, if you find a compatible person who is going to be a real help to you." I wouldn't be surprised if there is a man somewhere who is thinking, "I'd like to find a fine woman I could share my life with. I'm lonely." Scripture says, "It is not good that the man should be alone" (Gen. 2:18). Well, it probably isn't any better when you are fifty than when you are twenty-two, is it?

Remember, though, that you and your husband lived together for thirty-three years. That's a long time—more than half your life. It may take you awhile before you feel really comfortable about looking for a new mate. But when you are ready, I would certainly encourage you to do so. I would remind you that the place you look will have a lot to do with the kind of person you find. To find someone whose values and ideals are like yours, look within the church—the various fellowships your church provides or the Sunday School classes. I feel that the Lord can lead you best within His church to someone who will understand and meet your needs.

THE NEED TO BE NEEDED •

I'm fifty-three years old, widowed, and have a grown family. For years since my husband died, I have felt unimportant and like no one needs me. I don't fit in with my married friends, and my church has little to offer those in my situation. I've received much criticism because I'm not looking for another husband. Frankly, I like my independence. But I wish people would be more sensitive to a widow's need to be needed.

It's interesting to think about this need to be needed. I'm convinced that it is a basic human need, like our need for food and water. My mother showed a strong need to be needed. Every day of her married life started with my father saying something like, "Where are my socks?" From that moment on, Mother served him and us children. Her whole life was tied up in serving others; I think she must have been a saint. People like my mother who willingly serve others are responding to a need to be needed. They get their sense of purpose and meaning from serving. When the opportunities for service are taken away—a husband dies, the children grow up—the most important part of their lives is gone. They may try to find meaning by traveling with women's groups or joining a bowling league, but they won't succeed because they are conditioned to find meaning in giving, doing, and serving.

I think you will find your greatest fulfillment in the helping professions. You need to find some way to help others, whether as a volunteer at the hospital or by doing church volunteer work or helping at the old folks' home. You're going to find that your life will not be full until you are serving again, until you feel needed. We live in a world of "get," and it's not incidental that we have more spiritual emptiness than ever before. Many people in this world of "get" sense, deep in their souls, that something is missing. Meaning won't come from getting, but from giving, serving, and following the Lord's example.

WHEN LONELINESS LINGERS •

When my husband died, my son persuaded me to move a thousand miles to be with him. I did so because I couldn't bear the thought of living alone. But instead of living *with* him, I live in half a duplex and he lives in the other half. Though he is next door, I still

live alone. The only thing that keeps me company is the radio. I keep it tuned on a Christian station all day long. How do I get over this loneliness I have felt since my husband died?

I can't take your pain away. It's a normal and natural part of the grieving process. In a sense, it is even a great tribute to your relationship with your husband. You lived with him for many years, you loved him dearly, and now he is gone and you feel alone. This is much better than the kinds of relationships where people can't stand each other and can't wait until the other one is gone.

Now your pain is intensified because you have moved across the country and away from your friends. You have traded one set of problems for another. You wanted to be close to your son, and that is good; but your lifetime friends are a thousand miles away. I would encourage you to write to them or keep in touch with them by telephone. I sense also that you are disappointed in your present arrangement. You thought you would be living with your son, but he is busy with his own life and you are just as lonely as before. You don't sound angry with him for that; you no doubt understand that he also has needs to meet. But that does not take away your loneliness.

Several things may help. First, time will help to heal your longing and grieving for your husband, though those feelings will never totally disappear. Then, you know that the Lord has promised that you will see your husband again. You will have an eternity together. We Christians should think often about that promised reunion. But you also have a life to live here. You dare not just sit in your room with your radio. It is important for you to take courage and get out and do things.

The first step will be the hard one. You need to begin to look for a church with a program for people your age. Try out the various programs, just like you'd try on clothes, until you find a group you enjoy. I guarantee that you will find others in that group who are looking for a friend just like you. It will take courage to get out and do this, but as you go back for the second or third time, it will get easier. You will begin to develop friendships and your life will begin to take on meaning again. This will not take away your pain, but it will keep you from being submerged by it. Think of it as a gesture of love toward your husband. He would want you to do this.

LONELY AND IN LOVE? ●

I'm a Christian and so is my mother. At least she always acted like one until she met this man. Now she is slipping away from God and our church. The man she is seeing is starting to spend nights at our house. I've talked to her about it, but Mom acts as though she couldn't care less. I don't know why she is doing this; she always seemed like a strong person. My father died a few years ago—maybe she is lonely. But I do know that what she is doing isn't right. I want to help her, but I don't know how.

What will help her the most is for you to love her, support her, pray for her, and spend time with her. The worst thing you can do is nag and preach at her. She already knows what she's doing is wrong. She already feels guilty, and because of that, she will react to any preaching with hostility.

It is important to keep in mind that widows and divorced people are vulnerable—open to attack, defenseless, feeling they cannot help themselves—because they are lonely. Your mother is probably so intensely lonely that she doesn't know what to do about it. All her friends have husbands, and when she hangs around them she feels like a fifth wheel. Some of them may even feel threatened by a single woman like your mother. When she joins a church group and starts talking to some man, his wife may say to him on the way home, "Why were you talking to So-and-so?" Widows quickly sense such coldness and rejection.

Some widows are afraid. They ask themselves, "Am I going to live this way the rest of my life? Am I always going to be single? Am I unattractive?" Some put themselves on a bargain-basement level because they feel, "One in the hand is worth two in the bush. If this person is interested in me, then at least I've got him." They may settle for very little, even though they are attractive and have a lot to offer. With a little more patience, they might find the right man.

All these things are true, but you can't tell them to your mother. It would be just like telling a high school girl that a boy who is showing interest in her is not good for her. Your mother is struggling with something more persuasive than logic—she is losing her self-esteem. She needs deep, personal Christian help. This can come from the Holy Spirit, from her pastor, or from friends. A lot of it has to come from within herself. But one thing she probably doesn't need is a sense of further rejection.

As you pray for her, sometimes you tend to think, "I'm not really doing anything. I should be scaring this man away; I should be helping Mother directly." Your intentions are good, but your ideas won't work. They will only intensify the problem. Know this—the Holy Spirit is always faithful. He is constantly at work in your mother's heart. I believe that as He works in her heart and as you show her the love and acceptance and affirmation she needs, she will begin to seek a solution to her loneliness in the proper manner.

WHEN MOM STARTS DATING ●

My dad died a couple of years ago and since that time my mom has been trying to keep the family together. She's been doing a great job and I've tried to give her all the support and help I can. Recently she started dating again and, for some reason, I resent her for that. It's hard to accept the fact that your mother is out on a date. There is no reason that she shouldn't date, but it bothers me. I feel like it's not fair to my dad. I want Mom to be happy and live a full life, but how do I overcome these negative feelings toward her dating?

It is very natural to feel the way you do. Everyone in your situation has similar feelings, and you shouldn't feel guilty about having them. Of course you recognize your mother needs companionship now more than ever, but this doesn't change the way you feel. Still, a few ideas may help you line up your heart with your head.

First, realize that no one can replace your father. That is a unique relationship that no one else can have with you. But your mother is not dating in order to replace your father. She is looking for someone to enter her life as a companion and husband and lover. It is possible that since your mother chose one man you liked, she may choose another that you also like, though not in the same way. On the other hand, it's also possible that you won't like him all that much. It may be hard for you to feel close to her new companion. But this is not really in your area of responsibility. Your responsibility is to be a Christian gentleman, to respect your mother's choices, and to respect the men she dates.

Ask yourself what your father would say about this situation. Suppose he were able to sit down on a stump with you and talk about it. Wouldn't he say, "Son, your mother needs someone to take care of her. She's given so much to you kids. She's supported you and taken care of you. But someday you will fall in love with some girl and take off, and she will be left alone. I think we ought to be happy that she has found someone to help her"? Thinking this way may help you get the larger picture.

Realize that your feelings of resentment are basically territorial. Someone is coming onto your turf. You feel like you ought to protect your mother, your home, your territory. See your feelings for what they are, but then back off and let your good sense control your actions. Commit this to the Lord. Make it a matter of prayer; the Lord can really help you with this.

CHAPTER 22

Divorce and Separation

Hardly a family in the country is untouched in any way by divorce. A generation ago people tended to talk about divorce in the abstract because it was not so widespread. Now none of us can deal with divorce in theory only because people very close to us are experiencing it with all its attendant disjuncture, fragmentation, hurt, and—we hope—healing.

I've had pastors tell me that they don't have problems with divorce in their church. By talking to these men and listening to what they're saying from the pulpit, I discover the reason. Their comments project a kind of spirit that effectively screens people with divorce problems out of their lives. Their message is loud and clear: "You're not welcome in this church; you are a social leper."

None of us—especially those who have been divorced—wish to say that divorce is a good thing, or that it can be done without pain or tremendous personal or social disorder. But to deny its existence or to treat divorced people as if they were inferior and unworthy to be in the church of Jesus Christ is to miss the entire point of redemption. We are against divorce. Most divorced people are against divorce. Surely God's Word speaks against divorce. But divorce, nonetheless, is a fact. We cannot wish it away by Pollyanna thinking, nor can we make the problem any less real by putting divorced people out of our minds.

We must deal with divorce as a reality, and with divorced people as fellow human beings who are loved by God and into whose lives God wants to bring forgiveness and reparation. God wants to take away the pain and alienation that sin brings to all of us. There is a new place of beginning for divorced people, as for all of us, in the grace of God.

LASTING IMPRESSIONS •

My wife and I are separated, and I'll admit I treated her unfairly while we were together. But recently I met Christ and my life has changed. I want to repair my marriage, but she says she's heard all that before and won't give me another chance. She doesn't realize that this time, with Jesus Christ in my life, I truly am a different person. She calls it the old religious experience excuse. How do I convince her that this is for real?

First, you have to find out whether she wants you to convince her. Many times in marriage breakups, the "innocent" partners have been looking for a way out too. Once they have their proof that the spouse is no good, they can go about life letting the spouse take the blame for the problems in the marriage. In some of these situations it's virtually impossible to convince the other person of anything because the other person doesn't want to be convinced.

But let's assume that that's not true in your case. Let's suppose your wife would like a reconciliation, but she just can't make herself believe you're real because you've been a phony so many times. You've lied so much, you've broken her trust so many times—why should this conversion be any different?

There is no simple solution to your problem. You will have to prove yourself to her by consistent, stable, loving, caring, responsible behavior over a period of time. Hopefully, you will not lose her to someone else during this time of trying to reestablish yourself in her eyes. Assuming this does not happen, you will need to approach her as if you were courting her for the first time.

People become involved with one another because of the delights of courtship—courteousness, thoughtfulness, pursuit, caring. This courtship makes them say, "We'd love to do this all the time. Let's get married and make our relationship permanent." So they get married, and usually they quit courting. But marriage does not have to be the end of courtship. Remember what you did when you first dated her and try those same things. Try to do even better than you did before. Trust that she'll begin to be won by this behavior.

It's not surprising that, to her, your conversion looks like jailhouse religion. Lots of men repent in jail—the judges, the police, everyone has heard this a thousand times. Your experience sounds to her like a conversion of convenience, and so you'll need to convince her that it is real. You can't force her to believe you. You'll just have to continually try, trusting that the water dropping on the stone will eventually make a lasting impression.

A SECOND CHANCE? ●

When I was twenty I got married. About a year ago the marriage fell apart and my wife asked for a divorce. I was deeply hurt by this and went through a time of depression. Then a colleague shared the love of Jesus with me and I became a Christian. I've now met a lovely Christian girl in my church. We have much in common and are seeking the Lord's will as to whether He wants us to marry. In the light of my past and my newfound faith in Jesus, is God giving me a second chance?

Quite possibly He is, but let me encourage you to have a long conversation with your pastor before you move ahead. Get into the Scriptures and learn how God feels about this subject. Let your pastor help you isolate those things that caused your first marriage to fail.

Sometimes we assume that because you became a Christian, the other person must have been at fault. It is wonderful to be a Christian and to have God's forgiveness, and you surely have that. But you must still deal with the root causes of your problems in your first marriage. You can't slice bread so thin that there aren't two sides. Most marriages fail because of two people. You need to think about that.

Divorce and remarriage is not an easy subject. Though a great deal of sincere, careful, biblical scholarship has centered around the topic, Christians do not always agree about how to interpret the biblical teachings. It is easy to come up with a legalistic answer about what is right, but if divorce happens to you or to someone you know well, you end up adjusting your answer to fit the circumstances.

So I don't want to give you a flat-out yes or no about remarriage, because I don't think that's the way it works. The most important thing is that your life amount to something, that you be a contributor in God's plan, that your life from this time on be redeemed and reclaimed. The victories the devil achieved through getting you to fail the first time should not happen the second time. I'm sure that your pastor will want to help you move responsibly into this next phase of your life so that you don't make another mistake. You need to seek God's will for your life with your pastor's help and with careful prayer.

271

TIRED OF "RELIGION" ●

I am a Christian but my wife is not. A year ago she left me and the three children. The note I found said she was tired of "all that religious junk." I've asked her to come back, but she objects to church attendance, Christian education for the children, and prayer at the dinner table. How much should I compromise to avoid a divorce? If compromise is not possible, is it biblically sound to obtain a divorce?

I'm going to skirt the issue of divorce because I think that is something you need to discuss with your pastor. A great deal more information than you have given me needs to enter into such a decision. But let me attempt to respond to your questions about "religious junk." That is a very offensive phrase to you, I am sure. But remember that there is a big distinction between religion and Christianity. A lot of people confuse the two. They mix up lifestyle—prohibitions and legalism—with the core truths of the Christian faith. Christianity teaches that God created the world and sent His Son to redeem the world. It offers hope and a reason for living. But many people add a lot of baggage to these central truths, baggage that can be repulsive to people they live with. It's like playing crack-the-whip at the skating rink. You are converted to Christ, and you make a quick about-face. The person who is hanging onto you can get whiplash from this. Your wife may be in that situation.

Your desires—church attendance, Christian education for the children, prayer at the dinner table—sound sensible and it would seem that any reasonable woman ought to go along with them. But what do you mean by those things? Do you mean attending church five or six times a week? (I know people who do that.) By Christian education, do you mean pulling your kids out of a good public school to put them in some ad hoc outfit that is more interested in indoctrination than in education? Are your prayers really sermons in disguise? You need to take a look at how your new lifestyle affects your wife. If your brand of Christianity is totally boring or repulsing her, then perhaps you do need to do some things that you are now calling compromise, but that may instead be a return to the essence of the Christian faith and away from certain extremes. I encourage you to talk with your pastor or another counselor who can work with both of you until you find a solution for this problem.

272

INCOMPATIBLY YOURS •

Ten years ago I remarried after a divorce. I'm not sure why we got married, because we don't love each other. We have thought about separation and possibly divorce. The only reason we stay together is for the sake of our two children. We both love the Lord, but we just can't seem to get along with each other. We are so incompatible.

Very often in life we tend to paint ourselves into a corner. Perhaps someone else can show us the door that we can't see ourselves. In a loving way, let me challenge you on two levels. Number one, you say you do not love each other. Number two, you say you love the Lord.

In our culture, we have confused the meaning of love. Love has meant a feeling; it has been made into an emotion. But love in the Bible is something you do, not something you feel. It is a verb. There are feelings associated with love, but sometimes the feeling is pain. For instance, Jesus loved the world. You might have asked Him, when He hung on the cross, "How does love feel?" In the Bible, love is associated with obedience and fidelity more often than with feeling.

Sometimes when people tell me they love the Lord, I get the idea that they want to roll their eyes back in their heads and read poetry. I would call that sentimentality, not love. Love is obedience. Love is fidelity. Love is commitment. Happiness, if it comes, is a result of obedience. Unfortunately, in our world today we have elevated happiness and pleasure to the highest level. We have said, "If I'm not happy, I'd better go out and do something to get happy." I think that approach is backward. It is anti-Christian, and it will not work.

I believe that the words *duty* and *responsibility, obedience* and *fidelity,* are more descriptive of love than are *happiness* and *pleasure.* In the front of my Bible is a little saying, "I slept and dreamt that life was joy; I awoke and found that life was duty. I did my duty, and God gave me joy."

You say you don't love each other. All you are saying is that you don't have feelings for each other. You think that if you had feelings, you would act differently. But it doesn't work that way. If you begin to act responsibly toward the other person, if you begin to serve the other person in the biblical sense, the feelings will follow. Feelings always follow responsible actions, but if you wait for actions to follow feelings, the feelings never come. Let me encourage you to think about that before you think about divorce. Keep in mind that you have already done that once.

DISAPPEARING ACT •

A couple in our church suddenly stopped attending. We discovered they were getting a divorce. They haven't come to church for the past few months, but I'm not sure many people have noticed. As concerned friends, is there anything we can do to help them? Or should we stay out of their business?

You point out a terrific need in our society and in our churches. You mention that this couple hasn't been to church for several months, but that almost no one in the church is aware of it. That's quite a long time not to be missed, especially if the church people are supposed to be their close friends. Their situation surely illustrates the isolation that is so prevalent nowadays. So many people just have superficial relationships.

First of all, you need to inform your pastor. He has an excuse to call them up and say, "We've missed you lately," or, "Is there any way I can help you?" If they open the door to him, he could suggest other people in the church who might be able to help. But in a situation like theirs, I doubt if there is much that you or anyone else in the church can do, because there is so much distance between you and them.

It's hard to overvalue fellowship in our culture where people often live far from their families and friends. If you had a regular relationship with this couple in a prayer- or Bible-study group, for example, so that you knew them, you would have something that I call *equity*. That is, you would have something invested in the relationship that would allow you to sit down with them and say, "We are your friends and you are ours. You've proved it in a thousand ways over the last several years. Now we understand you are having a problem. We've had problems ourselves. There's no need to be embarrassed about this, but we would like to help. We don't want to meddle or interfere, but we are available as your friends."

That's a pretty intimate and straight-on speech. You can't say that to a stranger. It's hard enough to say to a close friend. So while you probably can't do much for this particular couple, take this experience as a lesson. Don't let a similar thing happen to anyone else in your church. Begin to develop relationships with others. If you wait to talk to them until they are having serious problems, they will want to ask, "Why didn't you help us earlier, when we really needed you?"

TRAUMA HITS HOME ●

My best friend came to me with the news that her parents got a divorce. She is a Christian and goes to church with her mother every Sunday. She is also a member of our youth group. But right after the divorce my friend started taking drugs. Her mom doesn't know anything about it, but I do. I would like to help her see that she doesn't need drugs. But what can I say to her?

I have met this kind of problem thousands of times since I have been in youth work. It helps to realize from the outset that drugs are a symptom of a deeper problem. They are not themselves the problem. People take drugs because they can't adequately cope with life as it has been handed to them. Your friend is facing a deep sense of loss. She feels lonely, frustrated, and maybe even guilty. I find that many teenagers feel they must have caused the divorce by something they did. So in dealing with your friend, remember that you are dealing with emptiness, loneliness, and frustration, not with drugs.

So how do you approach her? Probably not with advice or condemnation or preaching. Instead, offer friendship and loyal support. Those are the things that help people with her kind of problems. Picture her parents holding hands and your friend sitting on those joined hands. Then picture her parents' hands being torn apart. What happens to your friend? Before she hits bottom, she is in a terrible, agonizing position.

If you can move in and gently put your arms under her, you can help her see that she can survive. Lots of people have lived through their parents' divorce. It is an ugly thing, but it is a reality. She must deal with it, and she will come through. Affirm her strength, and move in with prayer and concern.

CHILDREN AND DIVORCE ●

My friend's wife ran off with another man. The pastor tried to talk with her, but she insisted it was God's will that she leave her husband. What I really can't understand is that she left behind her two little children. How will it affect those innocent children when they realize someday that their mother didn't want them?

It's obviously not God's will that she leave her husband and children for another man. People who want to be disobedient will rationalize any way they can to justify what they want to do: they are entitled to happiness, they have been mistreated, they need a new start—they will say all sorts of things.

At first it's hard to talk to people like that. Often the best path is to try to keep the separation from becoming permanent, to leave a door open for them to come back, to give them time so that as the Holy Spirit speaks to them and they come to their senses, they are able to repent and begin to repair the damages. Sometimes it's impossible to do this because the runaway spouse has slammed the door shut behind her. She has gone to the divorce court; she has married her new lover. But even in this case, she may not have permanently put her children out of her life. We need to be sure that our horror at her action does not isolate the children even further.

As we observe the situation, we wonder, "Can't she see what she is doing?" The answer, I suppose, is that she can't. "Doesn't she know she is hurting her children?" Yes, she may, but she rationalizes that this hurt is better than the former situation, whatever it was. We realize the hurt and rejection these children face, however, and it is up to us to try to build structures around them of love and concern and care. If their mother never returns to them, someday they will realize they were not wanted. We need to be sure they understand that it was not their fault. They did not do anything to cause her to reject them; they were not inferior; they were not bad, and they should not have to feel guilty for their mother's bad decision.

It's safe to say that no young person with this kind of problem grows up unscarred. They all face more than their share of insecurities, and unless loving people reassure them and help them to heal, their own behavior will be affected. In the best of cases, with love from other close relatives, support from their pastor and friends, and affirmation and encouragement from other people they meet, they may mature and have relatively little damage in spite of this experience. Most such children, however, are affected permanently for the worst. That is why God hates divorce (Mal. 2:16). It is not some arbitrary decision on His part, interfering with people's desire to be happy and to escape pain. Our actions do affect others and ourselves, not just in a surface way, but permanently.

CUSTODY CAPERS •

Since our son and daughter-in-law got divorced, it has become increasingly difficult to see our grandchildren. Our son gets to visit his children on weekends, but their mother doesn't want us to see them. We don't want to do things behind her back, but we would like to spend some time with our grandchildren. Don't we have a right to see them?

You surely have a right and the law provides for it in most states. Your daughter-in-law probably cannot legally keep you away from them and you need to see them. It's good for them and it's good for you.

But before you rush in and grab your grandchildren, think about your daughter-in-law for a moment. It's easy, in a divorce situation, to build up a head of steam and take sides. Very few people have the objectivity to overcome their own blood relationship. But as Christian people, we need to try especially hard to be fair. First Corinthians 13 gives us an interesting set of definitions of love. "If you love someone you will always believe in him, always expect the best of him" (v. 7, TLB). For a minute, think the best of your daughter-in-law.

In many cases, when parents divorce, the parent who doesn't have custody of the children tries to make up for all those missed days and experiences in one great, overwhelming splash. He takes them to Disneyland and buys them cotton candy and asks them what they would like to eat and wear and do. The children go through a couple of days of "me, me, me" and then they are returned to the parent who has to take care of them seven days a week. Grandparents can do this just as well as—if not better than—fathers. The full-time parent then has a week or two to try to get the kids back into shape. It's not easy, so whenever you plan to be with your grandchildren, think about what you could be doing to their mother if you're not careful.

Whenever you have the children, help their mother. Speak well of her. It's never useful for a hurt parent or grandparent to tear down the other parent. Children are helped most when you support and build up both their parents. If your daughter-in-law senses that you are a help rather than a hindrance, she will feel better about you seeing the children.

A HOUSE DIVIDED ●

I'm divorced, and every other weekend my ex-husband takes the children to his place. When we worked out this arrangement we agreed that, for the good of the children, I wouldn't try to alienate them from him and he would avoid blaming me for all our problems. This started out all right, but lately whenever the children come home from a weekend with him they are rebellious toward me. It seems they have gotten everything they asked for and very much resent the routine of our home. I find myself becoming defensive and critical. I know this isn't good for the children, but I'm at a loss as to how to handle this.

It sounds to me as if your ex-husband is keeping the bargain that you made. He is probably not tearing you down. Instead, he is missing the children and feeling guilty about the divorce and is therefore overdoing his weekends with them. Weekends with Dad are such fun, and home is just ordinary.

The most common complaint I hear from divorced parents is that the absent parent indulges the children and makes it difficult for the other parent to raise them properly. I think that since you originally worked out the visitation agreement in an amicable way, you should now go to your former husband and say, "I'm not blaming you for this because I know it's a normal thing that tends to happen, but here is my problem and I need your help with it. The children feel that our house is just too routine. They think that visiting you is just a ball, but I have to get them to brush their teeth, pick up their socks, quit hitting each other, and all that. Is there any way you can reinforce the routine while they are with you? Can you back off on some of the candy and amusement parks and whatever else is making the rest of their life seem dull?"

I think that a man who was concerned enough to work out this first agreement with you will be able to understand what you are saying. Whether he will act on it or not is something else. You cannot control the behavior of another person. You can only control your own behavior. If he ignores your request and buys them more things and does more with them, you will have to fight the desire to act in a non-Christian manner, to seek vengeance, because that will hurt the children too. Two wrongs don't make a right.

EX-HUSBAND'S ALL PLAY ●

I am divorced and have two children. My ex-husband lives in another state and sees the children for one month every summer. When they are with him, all they do is play and stay up late. But when they are with me the rest of the year, they have to go to school and go to bed early. I'm afraid they think I'm the big, bad wolf. And I'm afraid they enjoy being with their father more than being with me. How can I deal with this?

First of all, you need to ask yourself, "Is this really true, or is this only a feeling I have?" It sounds to me like you may be unnecessarily insecure about this. Your husband, in one month, can't undo your eleven months with the children even if he wanted to, and he probably doesn't.

We face a similar situation with our Youth for Christ staff. We do "stress camps" where we take kids canoeing and mountain climbing and things like that. I say to my staff, "Never forget that the parents of these kids are the ones running the real stress camp. They put in 168 hours a week saying, "Brush your teeth," "Pick up your socks," "Get in on time." Now that's real stress. Your couple of weeks are not quite the same stuff."

So you face the grind of day-in, day-out discipline, and he has the fun of vacation. No wonder you are concerned. But it would be dangerous to say, "I'm going to get even with him; I'm going to be more 'fun and games' than he is." That would only lead to a competition to see which parent could make the kids more irresponsible. Some parents do this. They see who can buy the most stuff for the kids, take them to the most places, do the most playing around. Such behavior does not help the kids at all.

Other parents take the opposite approach. They say, "I've got to balance this out. Because he gives them all play, I'm going to give them all work." And suddenly they become, as you say, the big, bad wolf. I would encourage you instead to try to keep a good balance between discipline and fun. You need some fun too. You need to stay up late sometimes. You need to do some things the kids enjoy. But most of all, do your duty.

I like the phrase, "Right makes might." Do right and then trust God, who will come and help you and lead you to right conclusions. Many people falter in this task. They get the idea that compromises will make things turn out right. They won't. Do what you know is your duty, and then believe that twenty years from now the kids will come back and say, "Mother, I know it was tough for you to raise us kids by yourself, but you did a good job. We understood Dad and we understand you too, and we appreciate your contribution." That's the thing to aim for.

BROKEN AUTHORITY ●

My sixteen-year-old son refused to register for eleventh grade. In fact, he skipped a lot of school last year and failed half his classes. His father, from whom I am divorced, has a summer cottage in another part of the state that he is letting my son live in. The boy is working now, and his father is sending him money for gas. At this point, I don't know if I should give him additional help, or if I should just let him find out for himself how hard life can be. Won't it be a bad influence on my son if his father, who isn't a Christian, helps him while I, a believer, withhold help?

I think you're working off your own guilt and your own set of problems. Life has been hard for you, and you think it will be hard for your son. Since he doesn't know it will be hard, you're going to help him find out. Yet life may not be as hard for him as it has been for you.

One unfortunate effect of divorce is that it tends to break down the parents' authority in the eyes of the children. "If my folks were so smart," the children think, "how come they have so many problems? If they tell me to do something, maybe the same process that led them into their problems is leading me astray. Therefore I'll be independent and do my own thinking." Both you and your husband have less authority over your son than you would have had if you had remained married. That's just one of the unfortunate by-products of divorce that you have to live with.

The boy quite naturally will be selective. He'll take the advice of the parent he wants to listen to. He doesn't want to finish school; he wants to live in a cabin and to be on his own. Dad's letting him do this, so Mom must not know what she's doing. You're in a position of having no leverage.

Rather than worrying about whether or not to send financial aid, you need to think more about your relationship with your son. Invite him home. When he comes, don't pry into his affairs. He wants to be independent, so let him be independent. Let him volunteer how things are going. If he needs help, let him ask for it.

I would suggest that you say to him, "Why don't you come home for Sunday dinner every week? That would give us a chance to see each other." You might even say, "If you don't have laundry facilities there at the cabin, feel free to bring your laundry home and do it here." Don't do his laundry for him—he wants to be independent, remember—and don't cook up a bunch of food to send back with him. Let him be independent, but leave your door open.

You may find that after he's had his Smokey the Bear experience for a while, he will want to come back and live at home again. Reestablishing a good relationship with your son will tell him far more about the Christian faith than any amount of money could ever do.

BICKERING BROTHERS ●

I'm the father of two boys, aged nine and fifteen, who are constantly fighting with each other. Their mother and I are divorced, and I have custody of them. The older boy is the strong, silent type and the least thing sets him off. The younger one knows just what makes him angry. I need some real answers on how to stop this constant arguing.

Fighting brothers are like rainy Aprils. There's not much we can do to stop them. Rivalry seems to come with being siblings and with growing up. Because you are divorced, you may think that all your problems somehow relate to that fact. "My sons are arguing; it must be because I'm divorced." Such a focus on divorce may rob you of clear thinking. To have sons, whether you are divorced or married, is to have sons who argue.

If you could be a mouse in a corner of your home and watch your boys without their realizing you were there, you'd probably find that the younger boy almost always says to the older boy, "You're not my dad and you aren't responsible for me." The older boy then tries to show how big he is either by cuffing him around or by ordering him to do something. The problem is that the older boy feels responsible for his younger brother, but he does not have the authority that he needs to back up this responsibility.

I think you need to do one of two things. On the one hand, you could say to the older boy, "I want you to remember that I'm the father in this family. You are not in charge. You are not responsible for what your little

281

brother does. He will have to answer to me when I get home. Whatever his behavior is, I will handle it." This will relieve your older son of the responsibility, so he will not feel the need to order his brother around so much.

Or, on the other hand, you could say to the younger boy, "Now, we don't have a mama around to take care of us, so we have to make some adjustments. Your brother is six years older than you, and he has learned some things during that time. He's a little more mature, so I'm going to put him in charge when I'm gone. Here are the areas he is in charge of. So when he tells you to do something in one of those areas, even though he's not your father, you are to do them." This will give your older son the authority to go with his responsibility. You may find that he handles it very well. But if you choose this approach, be sure to tell him what authority means. It does not give him license to hit his little brother, for example.

If you establish the authority patterns in your home, your sons will not need to argue about who's in charge. But don't be surprised if they keep on arguing about other matters. That's what brothers do.

DEPENDENT ON PARENTS •

I'm divorced, and my sons live with their father while my daughter lives with me. For months I have prayed for guidance in raising her. The problem is that she is able to talk her grandfather (my father) into almost anything. It seems as if she is the boss of the entire family. Lately I've been trying to limit our visits with my parents, but moving to another town is out of the question because I can't drive. What do you suggest?

You can't have it both ways. You can't be independent and run your own family while still depending on your parents in various ways. You have to make a decision about which is more important to you, your independence or your dependence.

You may feel incapable of managing your own affairs by yourself. That's not a terrible admission; most of us need help in some areas. But if you need your parents' help—whether financially or for transportation or in some other ways—then you have to realize that to some extent they will interfere with your life. On the other hand, if you choose to be independent of them, you will have to make fewer requests. You will have to begin to run your own life, learn to drive, manage your own affairs. This may or may not be possible for you.

Often when a woman returns to her parents after a divorce, she has a great sense of failure. Because her marriage has failed, she feels as if she doesn't have the authority or self-esteem to make decisions for her children. Children usually pick this up. They know Mother feels guilty and incompetent and so they often use her feelings to get what they want. In reaction, some parents go to the opposite extreme and become unreasonably strict with their children. Then, if Grandpa is close by, the children know where to turn.

Let me encourage you to sit down with your parents and try to state your frustration. Sometimes people can write a letter to me and explain their problem beautifully, but they don't talk about it to the people involved. Your parents may have no idea of how you feel. After you have told them, let them give you their side. Perhaps they will observe that you have been too strict with your daughter and they are only trying to balance the situation. If you can analyze the situation and work this through together, your daughter will soon lose her position as family boss. You and your parents can begin implementing a strategy that will guide her instead. She needs the change and so do you.

A HOLLOW CHRISTMAS ●

I was recently divorced after seven years of marriage and now face the prospect of spending Christmas alone. I know I have a lot of adjusting to do, but right now the loneliness seems especially hard. All my friends are married and have children. I have nobody. I know Christmas is supposed to be a joyful family time, but here I am by myself. What do you suggest?

You can't undo what is true. The fact is that you don't have access to wife and children, and this is one of the tragedies of divorce. Interestingly, people don't often think about times like these when they enter into divorce. They want to get away from the problem so badly that they don't consider the new problems divorce will cause.

Let me suggest that your church can help you at this time of year. Attend the special Christmas activities—concerts, plays, worship services. There is a danger that, feeling lonely and rejected, you will stay away from people and thus feel even more lonely and rejected. Force yourself out the door, or you may find yourself in such a self-defeating spiral.

Make yourself join groups. When they say, "After the program we are going to have pie and coffee in the church fellowship hall," you may think, "I don't know who I'd eat with. I think I'll sneak out the back door and head for home." Instead of doing that, go downstairs to the fellowship hall, drink the coffee, talk to people, and give them a chance to befriend you. This can help you a great deal, and it can also help the many others like you who are also feeling lonely at Christmas.

I wonder if there is a need in your group for some person to take the initiative and organize the people who are spending Christmas alone. Try calling four or five of them and saying, "Hey, I'll bet you feel like I do this Christmas. I'm tired of staring at the wall. Shall we plan a party or something?" Get a group together—age and sex don't matter—and have a good time of Christmas fellowship together. Care for each other as human beings. The combination of the Christmas season and your partic-ular spirit will make some wonderful relationships.

Another suggestion is to get involved with volunteer service. There are a great many people whom no one is thinking about right now—people in nursing homes who never have visitors, for example. Go to one of these places and say to the administrator, "Is there anything special I could do for the people here this Christmas?" My wife and I did this a couple of years ago. We found a nursing home where they were going to serve the people right off the Formica tables, without any tablecloth or candles or anything special for Christmas. So we made table decorations. We thought it was fun, and the people in the nursing home did too.

You don't have to sit home and stare into your own loneliness. Why don't you get up now and do something to add some Christmas joy to your heart and to someone else's?

Living in a Broken World

We would not have it be so, and neither would God, but there is a great deal of brokenness in our world. Some people hastily blame God for the pain and suffering they experience, but a look at Jesus Christ shows that God is not the villain. Jesus Himself chose to be broken in order to identify with hurting mankind, and Jesus' pain went far beyond what we are ever called to undergo.

Every part of our lives is affected by the brokenness that resulted from the Fall, and Jesus identified with every one of our needs. According to Isaiah 53, He was "despised and rejected of men," "stricken, smitten of God, and afflicted," "wounded for our transgressions," "oppressed," and "cut off out of the land of living." Yet we read the glorious affirmation in verse 5: "With His stripes we are healed."

And so the Christian who lives in a broken world, as Jesus did, has the opportunity to be a healer of the suffering, in the same way that Jesus was. Jesus healed others through His own brokenness. Though He was "in the form of God," He "made Himself of no reputation, and took upon Him the form of a servant." In fact, "He humbled Himself, and became obedient unto death" (Phil. 2:6-8). As we encounter people who have been hurt in our broken world, we often will not be able to share our strength with them. Instead we, like Jesus, can share our weakness. We can tell them how we in our brokenness were made whole in Jesus Christ. This is the message of redemption.

CHAPTER 23

Abuse

Violence is a fact in our culture. Violence within the family is an increasing problem that we are learning to deal with. It's my opinion that there is more abuse today than ever before, but it is also possible that we are just hearing more about it. People are coming out of the closet, as it were, and beginning to tell friends and neighbors what's been happening in many families for a long time.

It is ugly when people turn to violence against their spouses, their parents, or their children as a means of solving their problems. Violence doesn't solve problems; it compounds them. And it's ugly for people to be so bankrupt of options that they can find no other way to deal with their problems than to hurt those they love—and indeed, in most cases of abuse within families, there is love mixed in with resentment, frustration, hate, failure, and so on.

We need to deal with abuse because it's part of our society and because we have to find creative ways before God to deal both with the abused person and the abuser. We know that abuse is a way of life that is passed on from generation to generation. Abused children grow up to be child abusers, and abused children often abuse their parents in return. This is an ugly fact, but within Christ's love is the answer for ending this terrible cycle of hurt.

AFRAID TO ADMIT IT •

One of my son's friends was over the other day and I noticed he had a black eye and a big welt on his chin. Later, the boys were

swimming and I noticed scars on his legs and back. Knowing just a bit about the boy's background, I suspect he may be a victim of child abuse, but he won't talk to me about it. What should I do? Do I have a responsibility to report something like this?

In the case of child abuse, be it physical, sexual, or emotional, every child needs an ally or a friend. We all have a responsibility for one another in a civilized culture, and we surely want to protect those in our society who are helpless. When you see this boy with a black eye or a bruised chin, ask him how this happened. Even if he won't tell you, be gently persistent. In most cases you can get a pretty good idea from the boy's response. If it happened while playing, he won't mind telling you. In fact, if it happened in play, he'll usually brag about it because these marks are "badges of courage" for young kids. But if it happened as a result of abuse, the child will either try to evade your question or just break down and tell you about it and say that he doesn't know what to do—that he's frightened.

If he spills the beans, so to speak, and tells you what happened, share this with someone who has some authority in the situation. Call your pastor or a school counselor and share what the boy said. The reason I suggest using an intermediary in this situation rather than yourself is so that the parent, whom we're assuming is the abuser, doesn't view you as an authority figure—a meddler. If he does, you may not get any results. In addition, it could break a relationship you may later need in order to help the boy or the abusing parent—especially if you know the parents. But if the abusing parent is contacted by an outside person who has authority, like a pastor or school official, he begins to realize that this harmful behavior has to stop or else he's going to get into some kind of trouble. Often the motive for stopping the behavior isn't a good one, but nonetheless, for the child's sake, it is an excellent start. Eventually, the solution will have to go deeper than that. And that is why this should be put into the hands of a competent person who deals with this sort of thing often.

Once the abuse has surfaced, your attitude toward the abusing parent is going to be very important. It is hard for us to imagine someone abusing a child, and therefore we don't want to feel any compassion toward the person. But it's helpful to realize that many abusive parents honestly believe they are doing the right thing because this is what their parents did to them, or this is what somebody taught them. So, if we can try to understand this, we can often be allies in helping these people during their recovery—once they've stopped the behavior.

I SLAPPED MY WIFE ●

The other night I did something I thought I would never do. I slapped my wife in the midst of an argument. I was stunned, and of course she was hurt. I don't think she'll ever forgive me, though I have apologized. I've never done anything like this before. How do I begin to repair the damage I've caused?

Physical violence is the weakest and most primitive of man's responses, though it has been honed to a high level by the Pentagon and its equivalent in other countries. Though violence seems necessary in a fallen world, it surely is something we ought to eliminate from our lives when we're confronting family members, automobile drivers, store clerks, and other individuals. So you need to do more than apologize. You need to ask forgiveness for having done something weak and unworthy of your relationship.

Sometimes people find physical abuse easier to forgive than mental or verbal abuse, because it often appears as an isolated event. Verbal abuse—constantly undercutting someone, finishing their sentences, interrupting them, correcting them—is often harder to forgive, because it seems so constant. And yet I doubt if your one instance of physical abuse is really isolated. I would imagine that you have solved many of your problems by physical responses. You may have hit your car or kicked your garage door or shoved your dog around. You need to find out why you do this. Why do you feel weak and unable to communicate?

Perhaps you would be helped by a marriage encounter or some other group where you and your wife learn how to communicate with each other, how to tell each other your real feelings. Let's face it—even as a Christian man, you cannot avoid becoming angry. Scripture says, "Be ye angry, and sin not"—that is, don't get out of control—"Let not the sun go down upon your wrath," (Eph. 4:26). And so even though anger is a reaction to a sense of helplessness or impotence, it is possible to channel anger and learn to confront things in an adult manner.

I think you need to seek counseling from your pastor or another Christian counselor on this issue of anger. But your specific act, I think, can be forgiven, and your wife should forgive you.

MARRIED TO A TYRANT •

I thought I married a Christian, but now I wonder. My husband ridicules Christians. He says my parents are hypocrites (they are missionaries). He curses me, kicks me, and slaps me. One evening I was reading the newspaper; all of a sudden he wanted it. I asked him to wait until I was finished. The result was another beating. Before we were married, I told him of some mistakes I had made for which I knew God had forgiven me. Now he continually reminds me of those mistakes and calls me bad names. I'm frightened.

Sadly, a great many women are in your situation. One of the first things to do is to seek the protection of your family—your own parents or the parents of your spouse. Often a young man's father or mother will be able to talk with him because most abusive men fear their parents more than they fear anyone else. So in many cases, warm, close-knit families will help.

A second recourse is your pastor. Many times I've been the pastor in such situations. I've talked to the man, letting him know that I was aware of his behavior but trying to be compassionate about why he was acting the way he was.

And then, ultimately, you can seek the protection of the law. There are numbers listed in the phone book and in the classified ads for battered wives to call; you will be put in touch with people who have experienced this kind of problem and who can help you.

A battered wife who is a Christian has an additional consideration because she knows she does not have the right to break up her marriage casually. She does have the right, however, to a separation that will take her out of danger until the man's problem can be dealt with. The abusive husband does not usually hate his wife. Generally he feels impotent, defeated, and trapped by some outside situation, and his wife happens to be the most convenient person at whom to aim his venom.

I encourage you to try your best to be the kind of wife God wants you to be, but that does not mean you should stay and take physical abuse. Seek protection from your family, your church, or the law, and do so as soon as possible. You are not doing your husband a favor by staying around to take more. That only rewards him for being abusive. Far better to find a way to challenge him to deal with his problems and become the kind of man he wants to be.

SCAPEGOAT •

I know a woman who slaps her daughter and beats her with a wooden spoon. This girl cannot even question her mother's opinions without suffering some form of abuse. She is fifteen years old and has a younger brother and sister, but her mother does not do this to them. The father has a drinking problem and is seldom home. Is there anything the girl can do or any way I can help her?

This family obviously needs help, but the beatings with the wooden spoon are not the whole problem. They are only a symptom of something deeper. Back off a little bit and think about what is really happening. Here is a woman whose husband drinks too much. She is trying to raise their three children very much alone. The oldest child is now an adolescent, and Mom is afraid of what her differences of opinion may mean.

Life is coming unglued for that mother. Nothing is holding together, and she is fearful. She wants to get things under control again, but all she can think to do is lash out and beat her child into submission if necessary. She will probably not do serious physical damage with a wooden spoon, but she is in a situation where she needs counseling and understanding. I think the wooden spoon incidents will decrease in proportion to the mother's ability to cope with her life.

The mother seems to be aiming her hostility at the older daughter. I don't know when that child was born, but I've seen situations where, as the family started to break up, the parents turned on the oldest child because he or she was the reason they got married. "If I hadn't had this child, I wouldn't have had to marry this man," the mother thinks. In those cases, the oldest child becomes a symbol of the bad relationship. Of course the child suffers, even though he was an innocent victim and may not have any idea why the parents are rough on him. So there may be much deeper roots to this family's problems than you are aware of right now.

The best way you can help is by offering encouragement and support. Be a friend to this woman and help her deal with her children. You seem to be friends with the daughter; help her become the kind of daughter her mother wants her to be. You may be able to lower the tension level in the family. This woman, however, needs more than the friendship of an individual. She needs counsel and the support of the church. She needs to talk with a clergyman. Without this, I think she will keep on trying to get control through physical means. There's a lot of talk about child

291

abuse today, and we are right to be concerned about it. But I'm also concerned about the deep pain in people who lash out, trying to do good but ending up doing evil.

MOM IS HIS TARGET ●

My son has never said a nice word to me. He physically and mentally abuses me, though he's never left a mark. Many times I have asked him to sit down and talk things over, but he refuses. He lives at home in order to attend a community college, has nice friends, and has never been in any serious trouble. He even gets along well with his father. But he continues to be abusive to me.

I don't think I'm the person to help you. The person to help you is your husband. I can't quite understand how a situation like this can exist. How can your son get along well with his father if he continually abuses you? You need to sit down with your husband and ask for help, and he needs to insist that your son behave in a different manner. A question like yours is not uncommon when a second marriage is involved and the son has not accepted his stepmother. But when the problem is between the son and his natural mother, it surely should be less complicated, and I think your husband owes you help.

There may be some complicating factor in your case that could be unearthed. It's possible that if your son were to open up, he would say, "She's constantly nagging me; she's a perfectionist, and she won't accept anything as good enough." Now I'm not in any way excusing this boy's abusiveness to you; that is wrong, and it needs to stop. But a surly attitude is often the result of parental perfectionism. A neatnik mother may bring out the worst in a relatively sloppy son. In that case, it's important to decide which is more important—neatness or tranquility.

But if you cannot make a difference in your son's behavior, either by your husband's talking with him or your changing your own behavior, I think his privilege of living at home should be taken away. You should then ask him to move out on his own.

292

MOM'S A SAINT, DAD AIN'T •

My mother is very unhappy with my father. She's a saint to have lived with him for over thirty years. He continues to embarrass her, ridicule her, and act rudely toward her. I feel bad about encouraging my mother to leave my father, but I don't like to see her suffer. He refuses to seek professional help, which I'm sure he believes he doesn't need. Our family continues to make excuses for him, like "That's the way he was brought up," or "Maybe he doesn't feel well." How can I help my mother, whom I love very much? Or perhaps I should stay out of it and mind my own business.

That last sentence of yours sounds like good advice. You're not going to change your father's behavior; he will no doubt end his days acting very much like he now does. And if you begin to attack him, you will probably find your mother taking his defense immediately. It's amazing how this works. A woman may criticize her husband herself, but if someone else does, she immediately rallies to his side. If that happens, you'll have two people to fight. Somehow she has been able to accommodate this lifestyle for thirty-plus years. It's become part of her life. As sad as they look to the outsider, marital arrangements like these somehow work, and people manage to live with them. It's highly unlikely that you'll be able to change anything; you're better off staying outside.

There are some other factors to consider here. I wonder if your encouraging your mother to leave your father is a "misery loves company" thing. That is, you have left home. You may be nursing some guilt for deserting your mother and leaving her alone to deal with your father. Now you're saying, "I feel so good being away from him, I think I'd like to get Mother away from him too." Is it possible that you want to do this more for your own sake—so you won't feel like a deserter—than for your mother's? Work on that a while and see if such an attitude may be behind some of your feelings. If it is, you need to realize that you had a perfect right to leave. You didn't marry your father. It was time for you to develop a separate life, and in leaving you did just what you should have done.

In any case, realize that you cannot change your father's behavior. Neither can you undo what your mother decided to do over thirty years ago. What you *can* do is to show love toward both your mother and your father and allow that love to affect their lives. Your mother will enjoy being loved. She needs an ally who will do loving things for her and possibly make up for some of the things your father doesn't do. And your father needs your love too. Remember, the Lord said to "love your enemies" and "pray for them which despitefully use you" (Matt. 5:44). So do your best to love your father. Maybe that will have some effect as well.

CHAPTER 24

Rebellion

When you talk to young people who have run away from home, you usually find that they are running away from something. The problem can be anything from a minor misunderstanding to a life-threatening situation. It can be physical abuse or constant nagging, real neglect or a sense of being misunderstood, intolerable hostility or a kid brother who's a nuisance.

No matter why the young person runs away, of course, he always thinks he will improve his situation if he goes somewhere else. Once in a while he does, but in most cases the problems that develop for a runaway teenager are far greater than the problems he was trying to escape in the first place.

Our society tends to avoid working through problems. Adults run away by drinking alcohol, taking drugs, divorcing, changing jobs. Teenage runaways are simply adolescent versions of this same phenomenon.

The Bible says that God is "not willing that any should perish, but that all should come to repentance" (2 Peter 3:9). That is, in the mind and heart of God is a willingness to receive the prodigal home, to work through whatever problems exist, to find a place of forgiveness, and to rebuild a new life. Running away is the opposite of God's solution for human problems. Jesus Christ provides the way for parents and young people to develop and rebuild lines of communication, to work through problems rather than to run away from them.

STARTING OVER ●

After two months of running, our rebellious daughter has returned home. She says she is sorry, but it's clear the ground rules will have to be different. How do we reestablish our relationship with her and at the same time reestablish discipline? We're treading very tenuous ground.

I wish I knew why your daughter returned home. Was she dragged home by the police, or did she come home of her own free will? That alone makes a lot of difference in how you handle the situation, because if your daughter was dragged home, she will probably try to run away again as no lesson has been learned. On the other hand, if your daughter returned home of her own free will, she's probably learned that it's a cruel, painful world out there, and things aren't as easy as she thought. Sometimes kids come home and actually say, "Mom and Dad, you were right. It is really foolish to be out there; I was actually afraid for my life." After that traumatic experience they begin to really fly right.

As far as new ground rules, realize that your daughter has gone through some rough experiences in the two months she's been away. She is probably a great deal more adult than when she left home. In one sense, she's a lot more than two months older. In fact, she may be a great deal older than you want her to be. So you need to start with some new beginnings. Another thing, I don't know how old your daughter is. I dealt with a family recently who related a story similar to yours, and then I found out that the girl was twenty-four years old.

But let me assume that your daughter is in the sixteen- to seventeen-year-old category and has come home of her own volition. I think you need to sit down and talk about the things that contributed to her leaving. What has she learned through this experience? What have you learned through this experience? What compromises can be made and what things can't be compromised?

We hear many people talking about "tough love," but what does that mean? Let's say you're going to be tough with this daughter. You tell her, "If you are going to live in our home and are going to eat our food, then you're going to live by our rules or you can leave." She will probably leave and move in with a boy down the street, or across town in a back room where they're smoking pot, getting drunk, and all kinds of dangerous things are happening. And you say, "Boy, we really taught our daughter a lesson, didn't we?" You sure did. And you'll probably be sorry for it the rest of your lives. Is that what you really want to do to your daughter? That's not tough love—that's foolishness. Love takes a lot of time and patience to hang in there throughout the situation and find out what's really good for everyone. It often means giving in a little bit in order to win the war, rather than winning the small battles that accomplish nothing but stroking your pride.

HE'S REJECTED THE LORD •

Our child has disclaimed the Lord and rebelled against us. How do we cope with the great pain and sorrow this has caused us?

At the very root, the best coping mechanism is to understand human nature and the way God has ordered creation. God made humankind in His image, which means that human beings have the ability to make choices. We have free will; we can choose right and wrong. In fact, people often do choose wrong, sometimes even to their own hurt.

One reason for our pain is a feeling of failure. We think we have somehow caused this to happen. Realizing that God, the heavenly Parent, has given all of His children freedom of choice will help us understand when others exercise that freedom. And indeed, a great number of His children are in rebellion against Him and against themselves. They are perversely attempting to undo all that God has done for their own good. If the heavenly Parent is having such a struggle with *His* children, then it's not surprising that we're having some problems with our own.

How do we cope? By sticking together as a couple, praying for each other, supporting each other, strengthening each other. We cope by refusing to accept undue guilt and unwarranted responsibility. We cope by crying, by thinking it through, by going over it a thousand times. We do all of these things, but the situation does not go away. It is part of our lives.

I think it's helpful to get together with others who face the same problem and to hear them talk it through. It's also good to try to help others who are in a similar situation. Even in your deepest pain, you will find somebody in deeper pain than your own. Second Corinthians 1:4 speaks of helping others "by the comfort wherewith we ourselves are comforted of God." By helping others cope, we are better able to deal with our own pain.

Another coping mechanism is to understand that we cannot call the score at halftime. The game is not over. Our children have long lives ahead of them. We may die before they repent. They may repent at our gravesides. Sometimes, it takes extreme jolts to get people's attention.

Some people waste most of their lives through alcohol or irresponsible sex or drugs or financial crises. On the surface these look like severe problems, but look at them in the light of eternity. Human beings will live forever. Even if a person wastes all of this life, he may still have a wonderful eternity ahead of him, one that will make this life seem terribly short and insignificant. The point of the Parable of the Prodigal Son is not so much when he came home or how much he wasted, but *that he did come home.* Sometimes, our children have to learn the way he did.

Some people are able to learn by observation, by reading, by listening; others have to try everything to find out for themselves. Some people can read WET PAINT and believe it; others have to touch the wall to find out if it's true. If our children are "touchers," we have to wait for them to work through their problems throughout the long process of life. Some of history's most worthwhile people have worked through their problems slowly. When they did work them through, they had a great contribution to make. Their pain and failures had taught them deep lessons. In fact, this is the stuff of which great literature is made.

Of course, reading about other people who triumph over their failures is far less painful than watching our own children in the midst of their struggles. We can be assured, however, that God will not give up on them, and we must not either.

ARE WE TO BLAME? ●

Why do kids from good Christian homes go bad? Is anyone to blame when this occurs?

It's wrong, I believe, to try to find a casual connection between everything a person does and the way he was raised. People have individual responsibility. If they did not—if we were simply products of our environment, glandular makeup, or genetic structure—then words like *judgment, forgiveness,* and *repentance* would be meaningless.

God constituted the world so that people have individual responsibility, and He holds them responsible for their actions. There is an overemphasis on both environment and heredity that makes us believe we can somehow make things happen. We can cause everything and fix everything.

At base, this is a mechanistic view of man. The fact is that human beings, including our children, have the ability to do wrong—no matter how well they have been brought up. In most situations, they choose to do right. But there are exceptions to this rule; sometimes human beings choose to do very bad things indeed. Fortunately, there are exceptions that go the other way too. Some people raised in unbelievably bad atmospheres turn out to be very good people.

So to spend time in sackcloth over everything our children do wrong is not only to misunderstand the human condition, but also to ruin our own lives. In my opinion, the enemy of our souls takes glee not only in destroying our children, but also in destroying us by making us feel at fault. I am not speaking against trying to do well—this whole book is an encouragement to people to do the best they possibly can. But having done our best, then we must allow our children to be part of the human race, which is deeply fallen and in need of redemption.

WALKING A TROUBLED PATH •

Our fourteen-year-old daughter has stopped going to church. She doesn't like school, has started to smoke, and sneaks out at night with her girlfriend who acts just like she does. She also hangs around a boy who is into drugs. We've talked to her about drugs and smoking and how they can affect her life, but she doesn't seem to care. She continues to lie to us about doing these things. Is there any way we can help her see that this way of life leads to trouble?

I don't know what you can do, really. In fact, it is almost axiomatic that the more parents do during this stage in a young person's life, the more determined the young person is to go off and do the opposite of what his parents want. It is as though teenagers thrive on having something to rebel against. Many parents have no idea that their kids are doing these things, either because the parents aren't close enough to the kids or because the kids are very skillful at hiding their activities. These parents escape much of the worry you are going through now. They may even feel superior to you.

But if you took a poll of all the adults you know and asked them about their teenage years, almost all of them would tell you that for a time they went off to the "far country" and began to experiment with things their parents disapproved of. Some would laugh about how silly they were, and some would look back and say, "That was when I really got messed up." But almost all young people *will* go through a period of rebellion. It comes with the territory.

In a way, this rebellion is a compliment to the parents. The kids have learned the lessons you've taught; now they want to test them. You have told them that "the wages of sin is death" (Rom. 6:23) and that people who live non-Christian lives are basically sad. But when they go out into the world, they find that some sinners are having a lot of fun. So some young people conclude, "This way of life is better than what my folks taught me."

It usually takes time for young people to mature to the point of discovering that the sinful way of life is not better. Sometimes, people have to wait until eternity to find out how bad the wages of sin really are. But a great percentage of kids raised in homes like yours come through this rebellious stage successfully. After they have looked at what the world has to offer, they come back and say with the prodigal son, "My father's house is better than what I experienced in the far country."

THE WRONG CROWD •

My seventeen-year-old sister has been giving Mom and Dad some pretty rough treatment. Since school started this year, she has gotten increasingly involved with the wrong kids. So far she has tried smoking and drinking beer, and recently we found some pot in one of her travel cases. She's developing a bad attitude toward her teachers. She distrusts everyone and rebels at anything we say.

You should do the strongest possible thing you can do for your sister—pray for her. The Scriptures say we are to pray for the people who despitefully use us (Matt. 5:44). This is not how people usually pray. Instead, they pray about the person's bad habits or attitudes. They focus on the badness rather than trying to love and pray *for the person.*

You see, your sister is smoking and drinking and taking drugs because she has needs in her life. These activities are never going to fill her needs, but she doesn't know that yet. She wants to grow up. Some kids grow up by taking on more and more responsibility. Others—especially if they have no job and if their parents are making all their decisions for them—

grow up irresponsibly. It seems grown-up to drink, to smoke, and to take drugs, because that is what many older people do.

How can you help your sister? By praying that God will begin to work in her life, then by doing things to affirm her and build her up so she doesn't feel the need to act "grown-up" in a destructive way. Your sister needs to be given more and more meaningful responsibilities. A job, for instance, would help her a great deal, because she would soon learn that you can't function on the job and do irresponsible things on the side. But in the meantime, you need to pray for her, support her, affirm her, and build up that side of her that has become weak and is causing her to move toward destructive things.

Don't focus on the bad things she does; focus on her. You can't keep her from doing what she wants to do, but you can help her in other ways. When she starts feeling your support, your love, and your trust, she will try to live up to the trust level she is given. Most adolescents will break their backs to prove they are trustworthy.

OUR DAUGHTER THE RUNAWAY •

In the past two years our daughter has run away four times. She does what she wants when she wants and we just can't stop her. We're getting some counseling, and I know that God is working in her life, but I also know that Satan is working even harder. I pray for her every day, and I'm trusting the Lord, but saying this is different from living it. If she's out late, I get upset and imagine the worst. There has been little communication between us except in the counseling sessions. How do parents love their children without condoning the bad things they do?

One thing to do is assess your real options. That is, what can you realistically do, and what can't you do? A lot of parents spend a lot of time on "I wish we had" and "Why didn't we?" thinking. Most of that is unproductive. Your counselor is probably a real asset to you. She has, no doubt, had a lot of experience with girls like your daughter. Let me suggest that you search together for the reasons that your daughter ran away.

It's possible that her reasons are totally unreasonable, that she wants to do things that you simply cannot put up with. If this is the case, there's not much you can do. You have reached the end of your tether, and you are just going to have to allow your daughter to learn about life's realities on her own. This will probably cost her—and you—a lot. In fact, your worst imaginings may be well-founded. On the other hand, perhaps you and your daughter can make some compromises. This would be ideal, if it is indeed possible. Your counselor will help you see what your options are.

One of your comments bothers me. You say that God is at work in your daughter's life, but that Satan is working even harder. Well, that's not true. Satan is not working harder than God. God loves her very much, and He loves you too. He certainly is working in her life. Though Satan's power seems strong, God's is stronger still.

You also mention not wanting to condone your daughter's behavior. Sometimes parents get the idea that by allowing a child to live at home even though she is doing bad things, they are condoning the child's behavior. Not so. Just because God doesn't hit us all with lightning bolts does not mean He condones our behavior. He allows a great many things to go on that He does not condone. "[He] sendeth rain on the just and on the unjust" (Matt. 5:45). If God can act that way, so can parents. I hope your counselor will be able to help you and your daughter work out a compromise that will enable you to live together. This is a very difficult time in her life and she needs your support.

SHE WON'T LISTEN TO REASON •

My granddaughter, who lives in another state, won't help her parents in any way around the house, and she won't do her school-work either. She wants to be a model. She says that models don't work and don't need an education. When her parents exert authority, she becomes very angry and once kicked a hole through the wall. She's run away from home several times. Our son and daughter-in-law aren't very active in their church, so spiritual training in their home isn't what it ought to be. We try to counsel them without coming on too strong, but we really don't know what advice to give. We're afraid something serious may happen to our pretty runaway granddaughter who knows nothing about the real world.

It sounds like your granddaughter has a movie magazine approach to the world. Many of today's youth think that what they read about models and movie stars, what they see on TV shows and at the movies, is the way life is. These young people have trouble accepting the real world, which is so different from the world of their fantasies. The world we live in is not nearly so attractive as this make-believe world, and your granddaughter has become a victim of her illusions.

As grandparents living at some distance from your son's family, there is precious little you can do to help the girl. I doubt if you can help much by offering advice. Though you are giving counsel in a spirit of tenderness, care, and prayerfulness, you cannot force your insights on your children.

It appears that they have chosen some ways of living that are contrary to yours, and all you can do is stand back and pray. Yet prayer is a very powerful thing. Pray that your son and his wife will wake up to their problem and ask for help. If that happens, you may be able to offer counsel. Pray also that your granddaughter will come to her senses. When she finds out what the world is like, she will have loving grandparents standing behind her ready to help her, maybe even able to take her into their home and help her adjust to the shock. Beyond praying for your family, however, there is little you can do. You musn't think you should be doing something more or feel guilty because you are not.

CHAPTER 25

Suffering

The *why* question has always caused people to struggle. It's at the root of the Book of Job, the oldest book in the Bible. Why do people suffer? What can they do in the midst of suffering?

I don't believe that God picks up one car and crashes it into another in order to create an opportunity for people to grow and to become long-suffering and patient. I believe instead that we live in a world with conflicting autonomies: individuals and systems, separately independent, often collide.

This is true in the physical world. Two objects cannot occupy the same space at the same time. When they try to do it, there is a problem, especially if one of them is a car and the other is a pedestrian. When a particular storm system comes in contact with a flimsily built trailer park, conflict results. When certain microorganisms attach themselves to a host that encourages them to reproduce, disease develops.

Christ suffered more than any other man on earth. He doesn't promise that we won't experience suffering. But He does promise that we'll never suffer alone.

WHY GOD? •

My mother is dying of cancer. She is in great pain, but the doctors have determined there is nothing more they can do for her. I'm very close to my mother and just can't bear to see her in this kind of pain. I'm angry and confused. If God is all-powerful, why does He allow one of His own to suffer to this extent?

Your question is not easily answered. There are whole libraries full of reasonings about God's ways, and they haven't solved the problem. I struggle with it myself, and I haven't solved it in my life either. I have a working hypothesis that helps me, but other people who are equally sincere and who impress me with their credentials have other opinions.

I get some help by asking, "Why did Jesus suffer?" I believe that Jesus' suffering was God's way of identifying with mankind's suffering. He suffered so that we would know, in our suffering, that we do not suffer alone. Some people think that the Christian suffers because the rest of the world suffers, and God does not make differences for Christians. If He did, they would become useless in the world. If a Christian's non-Christian neighbor was suffering, and he went to the Christian for help, the Christian could not identify with him and could not relieve his suffering. So I believe Christians suffer for the same reason Jesus did—in order to help a suffering world. As 2 Corinthians 1:4 says, "We may be able to comfort them which are in any trouble, by the comfort wherewith we ourselves are comforted of God."

But why does anyone suffer? Why doesn't God just wipe out suffering altogether? When we see Him, we will be able to ask Him about this, and at that time I think His answer will make sense to us. In the meantime, here is my partial answer. I believe God has limited Himself in direct proportion to how much freedom He has given to man. He has given man a great deal of running room on this earth, and man uses his freedom in a way that causes a great deal of pain. Of course, there is still a great deal of pain that I don't understand at all.

Two books have been very helpful to me on this: *Where Is God When It Hurts?* by Philip Yancey, and *Affliction,* by Edith Schaeffer. Neither book solves the problem, but both have given me helpful flashes of insight. Ultimately, though, I have to rest on my understanding of God's nature. Our God wants us to call Him Father. Though the world often appears cruel to me, God has allowed it to be as it is, and someday He will explain to me why that was so.

IS DEPRESSION "CHRISTIAN"? ●

My sixty-seven-year-old aunt has become deeply worried and depressed over the last few years. She can no longer carry on her normal activities. Other family members must pay her bills and tell her what needs to be done around the house. She appears

forever worried. Sometimes she vents her frustration by tragically uttering pleas for God's help or forcibly hitting things. She refuses to consult doctors of any kind, and it seems that all we can do is pray for her. Is there anything else we could do to help?

There is a fallacy being perpetuated among some Christians that depression is always a spiritual problem. Often it is. That is, all of us mildly neurotic people occasionally need advice to put old sunnyside atop, give old man gloom the shake, and that kind of thing. The power-of-positive-thinking Christian preaching that is so popular today has been very helpful to some people. But there are other people who are in desperate need of professional medical attention. Their problems are emotional and chemical at base, and no amount of positive thinking is going to help these people without the medical help to back it up. It sounds to me as if your aunt is struggling with a real medical problem.

At certain times in our lives, our bodily secretions may get out of balance. This throws us into various kinds of mental states that are difficult or impossible to overcome on our own. Fortunately, these imbalances can be straightened out medically, and yet some people will insist on saying to someone like your aunt, "Well, what is your spiritual problem? You need to pray more, you need to find your guilt"—and so on.

In addition, some Christians are intent on depreciating psychiatry, the branch of the medical profession that deals with mental illness. They seem to think that to need a psychiatrist is to have failed spiritually. These people aren't consistent—they don't generally think that putting a splint on a broken arm is an admission of failure. Do not be influenced by their prejudices when you think of how best to care for your aunt.

Your aunt needs professional medical attention. Getting her to accept it will, apparently, not be easy. For many people who resist treatment, a two- or three-step process is best. Someone—a pastor, your parents, or you—has to develop a high level of trust with your aunt. When this person has her confidence, he can say, "I think Doctor So-and-so could help you feel better." You probably won't get her to a psychiatrist right away. Your next stop will likely be the family doctor, who, after he has won her trust, can say, "Let's go to this other doctor, who deals with the kinds of depression you face. He's been able to help a lot of people who have experienced the same feelings you have."

A person in your aunt's situation, who is afraid of doctors in general, needs a great deal of support and help. You can best help her by getting her the medical help she needs.

OUR BABY IS HANDICAPPED •

Eight months ago we had our first child, a little girl. We've recently discovered that she has a mental handicap and will never be normal like other kids. We are both Christians and cannot understand why God would allow our child to be like this. We are hurt and angry with God just when we really need to rely on Him to guide us through this situation. We love our little daughter and are grieved that she must go through life handicapped. Is there any way to put this in the proper perspective?

It isn't easy for an outsider to help you with this. I read a lot of advice given to people with children like your own, and I always wonder if the advice-giver, who thinks this situation is such an enriching experience, has ever raised a handicapped child. If it's such a great thing for the family, perhaps the advice-giver should go out and adopt a handicapped child—there are plenty who need homes—rather than talking about it so much.

Books like Edith Schaeffer's *Affliction* and Philip Yancey's *Where Is God When It Hurts?* give theological and biblical perspective on the issue of suffering. Generally, though, I think that people who have gone through this experience can help you more than people who have not. Many people have found Dale Evans' book, *Angel Unaware,* about her family's experience with a Downs Syndrome child, very helpful. I think you will find that the people you run into as you treat your child, as you are in contact with doctors and hospitals and those who care for handicapped children, will be your greatest help. I remember when one of our children had eye surgery. At first I felt like our child was the only child in the world who ever had eye surgery. When we arrived at the hospital, we discovered that everybody's child was having eye surgery. I think you will develop friendships with some people who also have handicapped children. You will find that they are some of the finest, most mature people you have ever met, people who understand life more deeply than they ever would have if they had not had problems to work through. From these people God will give you the help and sustenance and strength you need.

God is at work in your lives, and as you yield yourselves to His revealed will for you, which right now is caring for this child, He will strengthen you in a miraculous way. I know something of this from personal experience, and I assure you that at some point you will find that God has given you a greater gift than you now realize.

HOW TO HANDLE HANDICAPS •

A few months ago my grandson was paralyzed in a tragic accident. The doctors give him little hope of walking again. My daughter and her husband are having a difficult time handling this problem. She shows a great deal of sympathy and waits on her son hand and foot, but her husband takes the opposite approach. He's been pushing him to go back to school, to use his wheelchair, and to get involved in school activities again. My grandson is getting confused by these opposite approaches and my daughter and her husband are having conflicts about what to do. Is there a right way to approach this problem?

A few years ago I read an article describing a family that adopted handicapped children. They had just agreed to take a little boy on crutches who was barely able to walk. When the father picked him up and brought him home, the rest of the family waited on the porch. The father lifted him out of the car and set him down on the sidewalk, then walked to the porch and joined the others. The whole family stood there and waited for the little fellow to struggle up the walk. As soon as he got up the steps, they all surrounded him and loved him and affirmed him. The idea in that home was that everyone had to put forth effort in spite of handicaps.

Obviously, this wouldn't work in all situations; no amount of cheering would motivate a person in an iron lung to wriggle up any steps. But the family's spirit is correct. I think that is the spirit your grandson's father is trying to encourage, and I think he is right. The boy's mother, of course, is concerned. She's no doubt seen some of his weakest moments. But to continue to wait on him hand and foot could thwart his need for independence, and it could also have a bad effect on her. Some people get all their meaning from having other people depend on them. If they are caring for an invalid who stops being an invalid, these people themselves become invalids—their lives seem to lose their validity.

Your daughter isn't doing this in the extreme form. She's simply adjusting after the terrible accident and trying to be as kind as possible to her injured son. But you need to help her and the boy understand that he desperately needs to learn to be as independent as possible, as soon as possible.

HOW MUCH MORE CAN I TAKE? •

About a year and a half ago I had a nervous breakdown. I still have thoughts that make me wonder if I'm going to lose my sanity. I'm so often at the desperation point, feeling like I'm going to break. I'm seeking counseling and have joined a prayer group. I thought if I had a full-time job and a boyfriend I would be able to recover. But sometimes I really hate God and my life and everything else. I've given myself to God, yet I feel that there is no solution or end to what I am going through. I don't know how much more I can take.

You're doing the right thing by going to a counselor and being involved in a prayer group. I would also strongly urge you to go to a medical doctor who deals in spiritual, emotional, and physical problems—preferably a Christian psychiatrist.

"My goodness," you may say, "I don't need a psychiatrist." Well, why not? If I had diabetes I would go to a doctor who would diagnose me and give me insulin. I wouldn't think it was wrong to take insulin. If I didn't take it, in fact, I would die of diabetic shock. It's important to take the medication I need to control whatever disease I have. There may well be a physiological reason for your depression. If so, you are not likely to get well without medical help. You should seek it as soon as possible.

Your prayer group may be a big support to you. On the other hand, some prayer groups seem to be distrustful of the medical profession. They lay hands on the person and pray for him and say, "Now you just stiffen your upper lip, trust in the Lord, and get strong." I call that approach the "Help, help, swim, swim" method. A drowning person is yelling, "Help! Help!" and someone on shore is calling back, "Swim! Swim!" The people in the prayer group may know how to swim, but the troubled person who comes to them for help may not. Be sure to look for an answer that fits *your* needs, not somebody else's.

So I would beg you, in addition to your counseling and prayer group, to go to a medical doctor and find out if there is a physiological base to your depression. If there is and you get help for it, you will be amazed at the difference it will make in your life.

CHAPTER 26

Death

Death without Christ is always a tragedy. Life without the perspective of eternity is only a terrible dreading of its inevitable end. For the Christian, however, death takes on an entirely different perspective. Death, the great enemy, has been brought into captivity by the resurrection of Jesus Christ. Thus, Christians can look at both life and death in a different way than can people who have never known the Saviour.

Christians are not terrified by death, but we still have many questions about it. Why do people die violently, or after much suffering, or when they are young? Our all-wise and all-knowing God will tell us the answers when we see not "through a glass, darkly; but . . . face to face" (1 Cor. 13:12). In the meantime, we know that a loving and caring God is watching over us. He has given us a glimpse of the ultimate victory over death by Christ's triumph over death and the grave. As the Apostle Paul said, "Death is swallowed up in victory. . . . Thanks be to God, which gives us the victory through our Lord Jesus Christ" (1 Cor. 15:54, 57).

GOD AND EVIL ●

Does God always have a reason when someone dies? Thirty years ago my husband died, leaving me to raise three children. I never remarried, and I believe the kids were adversely affected by growing up without a father. I'm not blaming God, but I wonder if my husband was simply a victim of this sinful world. The Bible itself says it rains on both the just and the unjust.

I feel much the way you do: we do not have to make a causal connection between every experience in this world and the will of God. I do not believe that God sits up in heaven and says, "I think I'll come down and take this woman's husband away for some great cosmic purpose." Everything ultimately fits into God's larger purposes, of course, but to say that God brings good out of evil does not mean that God sends the evil in the first place. Though God is always in charge, always sovereign, and not limited in any way, He has decided to limit Himself in order to give freedom to the human race.

We live in a world filled with conflicting autonomies. That is, the laws of physics work for Christians as well as non-Christians. A falling object does not ask if the person it is about to strike is a Christian or an unbeliever; it will kill one as readily as the other. A car that hits a patch of ice will react precisely the same way for a Christian driver as for a non-Christian driver. Even microbes and viruses and other things that cause our health to fail seem to affect Christians in the same way that they affect non-Christians.

It's possible that your children have been adversely affected by not having a father. On the other hand, some very healthy people have been raised in one-parent families. I'm always grateful for 1 Corinthians 13:12— "Now we see through a glass, darkly; but then face to face." I believe that sometime in the future, both of us will understand these situations much better than we do now. In fact, I have a sneaking feeling that when we hear the answer from God, we'll say, "Of course. Why didn't I see that? I understand now."

I also believe that eternity is one answer God provides for many absolutely baffling questions. After we've spent a thousand years with the Lord and all of our loved ones, these experiences that seem so huge right now may seem like a momentary blip on the screen of our experience.

One thing I know: God is a God of love; He is a God of justice; He is a personal God who cares about me and you. When I do have the answers to my questions, they will be totally consistent with His nature. He will not have done arbitrary things with my emotions and my sensitivities. God is consistent with His own nature, and His nature is love.

PREOCCUPIED WITH DEATH ●

My friend has a preoccupation with death. He asked me if I ever thought about death, and he said he has thought about committing suicide. I have noticed a scar on his wrist, and I wonder if he has tried to take his life already. On the outside this person seems normal. What can I say or do to help?

I've learned to take all people who talk about suicide seriously, because if you don't take a person seriously, he may follow through with his threat. I've known it to happen a few times. On the other hand, you are limited as to what you can actually do unless you are with the person every moment of every day.

Usually, suicidal people are depressed. Because depression can take various forms, each requiring a different approach to treatment, I think you need to involve a professional—a pastor, a counselor, a psychologist, or psychiatrist—who can help you with your situation. It would be best, of course, if you could get your friend to talk with a professional. But even the best professional help is not a guarantee. People who are under professional care have been known to commit suicide also.

Depressed people have different needs. An outgoing person who likes drama, acting out emotions, and getting attention can be helped by encouragement and positive affirmation. A withdrawn and self-preoccupied person needs to focus outside himself, to get involved in a worthwhile activity that will bring meaning to his life. Some forms of depression require biochemical help. People whose depression is physiologically based need medication to restore the normal balance in their systems. If you would like to learn more about helping depressed and suicidal people, you might wish to read *The Masks of Melancholy* by John White, a Christian psychiatrist.

Your friend needs an expert diagnosis to find out why he talks about death all the time. If you have enough leverage with him to make a difference, encourage him to get a medical diagnosis and then to take action on that basis.

HE WAS SO YOUNG ●

Recently my son's best friend was killed in a car accident. He was hit by a drunk driver. I can't understand why God would allow

this to happen. He was a Christian, very active in church, and one of the most thoughtful boys I've met. Why would God take someone who had so much potential?

This is one of the largest questions faced by mankind. Job, one of the oldest books in the Bible, is about this very subject: Why does evil exist, and how can these things happen if God loves and cares for mankind?

After you've spent a lot of time thinking about the problem, you'll discover three basic approaches. The first is that there is no God. Many people believe this, because they have seen tragedy so often. The second possibility is that God causes these things to happen. That is, God reaches down into the world, picks up two cars, and crashes them into each other. We would call that *bad,* but because He's God, He can call it *good.* He has reasons for acting that way that are beyond our powers of comprehension.

The third possibility is that God allows these things to happen, but He does not cause them. There is a physical law that two things cannot occupy the same space at the same time. When two cars try, they crash, even if a nice Christian boy happens to be in one and a drunk driver in the other. God created the laws of physics, but He did not cause the cars to crash. In God's mind, allowing physical laws to operate so that airplanes don't fall out of the sky, for instance, is a great good, even though those same physical laws sometimes lead to terrible tragedies like the death of your son's friend.

I get more help from believing that God allowed this to happen for reasons far beyond my ability to understand, than from asking, "Why did God take this boy?" I think God is as sad about this boy's death as you and your son are.

A STILLBORN BABY •

My sister recently delivered a stillborn baby and is still trying to recover emotionally from the shock. I am five months pregnant and full of anticipation about the birth of my own child. I want to share these joys with my family, but after my sister's experience, I don't know if this will make it worse for her or help her get over her sorrow. How can I be sensitive to her needs?

Every time she sees you pregnant, she will be reminded of what she has gone through. Nevertheless, I think you will probably help her more by sharing your excitement—it's the natural way to feel about being pregnant, and she surely won't be comfortable if people start to tiptoe around her. Of course, you will want to be aware of her feelings. If you sense that a discussion is bothering her, back off a little. You might ask her how she feels. Stay tuned to her feelings, but be as natural as you can.

You may find it hard to be natural, because deep down you may feel a sense of guilt. It's a totally unwarranted kind of guilt, but almost everyone has it to some degree in situations like this. If we know someone who experiences a tragedy, we tend to ask ourselves, "Why did it happen to her and not to me?" Our own happiness makes us feel guilty by comparison, or else we fear that we may be next.

The Old Testament account of Solomon and the two women who both claimed to be the mother of a particular baby shows how this kind of guilt operates. When Solomon said, "Cut the baby in two," it was the real mother who agreed to give the child up. There were two reasons for that: she loved the child dearly and did not want it to die, and she felt guilty for having a child when the other woman did not.

But this kind of guilt is unreasonable. You have to realize that you have done nothing to bring about the death of your sister's child. It is totally beyond you. For you to have a healthy child is not a slap in the face to your sister. It is an affirmation to you that God is good. In most cases, babies are born in fine shape. Your child is a child of hope, not a child of despair.

I'M AFRAID TO DIE •

I am eight years old and I'm afraid of dying. My grandma died a little while ago, and I went to the funeral. It was real sad; a lot of people cried. My mom says not to be worried because I know Jesus. But it still seems scary. How can I not be scared to die?

The way adults act sometimes can be very confusing. I remember when I was your age going to a wedding and seeing a lady crying. I asked my mother why, and she said, "Because she is so happy." I thought, "That's funny. I only cry when I'm sad."

Then I discovered that adults cry at other times too—sometimes when they're worried or mad or discouraged or lonesome. Some people cry at funerals because they think they will never again see the person who died. But that's not why Christians cry. They know that, if the person knew the Lord, Jesus is taking care of her just like He will take care of them when they die.

Then why do they cry? Because they miss her. They know they will not see her for a long time, and they are sad to think of life without her. When someone gets on an airplane and goes away for a long trip, we are sad because we won't be seeing him for a year, or a month, or all summer. We may be so sad that we cry—and that's the kind of crying people do at Christian funerals.

You say you are afraid of dying. None of us knows what dying is like, but Jesus, who really does know, said this: "There are many homes up there where My Father lives, and I am going to prepare them for your coming" (John 14:2, TLB). In other words, He went to make a comfortable place for your grandmother and all of us. Jesus went on to say, "If this weren't so, I would tell you plainly" (v. 3, TLB). Maybe you know somebody you can really trust, someone who never breaks promises, someone who always does what he says he will do for you. Jesus is like that. If He says something, He really does it. So when He says He is preparing homes for all of us who love Him, we can know He's really doing it. He is taking care of your grandma, and He will take care of you.

CAN I COPE WITH THE PAIN? •

Eight months ago my husband and I had our first child, a beautiful daughter. But she was born with many handicaps and unable to breathe without a respirator. Surgery did not help and she died soon afterward. Following her death God gave me a great peace and a greater understanding of His love than I have ever had. My problem now is that, though I can accept her death, my heart-aches are still very strong. Sometimes my arms feel so empty that I want to scream. I feel that my faith must be weaker than I had thought because I miss her so much. How can God lead me through this period?

I'd like to encourage you to separate your feelings right now from your faith. The two are not directly related in this situation. You are feeling tremendous pain, because you are capable of great love. Shallow people don't feel anything—love, fear, hate, anticipation—as deeply as you do, but you wouldn't want to be emotionally flat. It is a great gift to be able to love deeply.

Your tragic experience has hurled you to the bottom of your emotional range. You are feeling the depths of grief. You anticipated the birth of your child; she was born handicapped; medical science was unable to help; and she died. Those are all major traumas, and they happened only eight months ago. That's a relatively short period in your life; it is no wonder that you still feel pain. Time is required to heal wounds like these, sometimes a great deal of it. You must be patient with yourself.

These deep feelings of yours certainly do not mean that you lack faith. There are people who go around saying, "Your faith is directly proportional to your ability to act happy about bad things." Frankly, I think they are foolish and shallow—and usually quite unable to handle trauma in their own lives. Your faith will help you in two ways. First, it will help you understand God's nature. He is loving, caring, and just. Somehow, in a way beyond our understanding, He will work this child's death into His great eternal plan and will bring good out of it. Today, "We see through a glass, darkly; but then face to face" (1 Cor. 13:12). Second, your faith will give you courage to love again. It truly is better to have loved and lost than never to have loved at all. You have a great capacity for love and your faith will enable you to use it.

THE PERIOD OF ADJUSTMENT ●

My best friend's mother died a couple of weeks ago. I don't know what to say to help her through this hard time. She has two younger brothers and I know it's going to be hard adjusting to their new life. Should I treat her any differently now than before her mother died? Should I talk with her about it, or would it be best not to mention it and keep on going like nothing happened? We are both thirteen years old.

We all feel uncomfortable in these situations. At thirteen, you are beginning to be aware of other people's feelings. This is important, because there really isn't any official thing to say. What is important is being sensitive to your friend.

I think it would be wrong to ignore her mother's death. In fact, a little pressure from you to talk about her mother might help your friend sort out her feelings. Bring up nice things you remember about her mother. Mention pleasant things that happened when you visited her home. These little reminders will help your friend be grateful for the time she had with her mother.

We need to keep in mind that God loves us even more than we love ourselves. God loves your friend's mother even more than she does. This can be hard to believe. We say, "I wouldn't wish death on my mother." Well, neither would God. He loves her, and He is grieving too. This can be very helpful for your friend to understand.

By all means, continue your friendship with this girl. Try to keep things as usual as much as possible, but help her work through her sorrow by being willing to talk about her mother. Fortunately, God has made human beings so that they heal. He will help you be your friend's helper in this time of need.

Living in a Permissive World

As you drive along the Capital Beltway around Washington, D.C. you pass the Federal Bureau of Standards. In this building is a standard for the real meter, the real liter, the real kilogram. Because these standards exist, we are able to make accurate measurements and judge whether we are getting the right treatment out in the world. A pound of meat or a pound of butter should weigh the same in Minnesota as in Missouri.

We are living in a world in which many standards have broken down. People have substituted the will of the majority for the will of God. Since human beings are fallen, we are operating by fallen standards.

A generation or two ago, most Americans still gave at least lip service to Christian standards. Now the Christian memory is being lost. Sex has been perverted into nothing but recreation and selfish stimulation. Large numbers of people abuse alcohol and other substances. People are afraid of the commitment that marriage implies, so they experiment with other lifestyles. These abuses are surely not God's intention. Yet even people who know they are wrong are so surrounded by them that they are getting used to them. It's one thing that evils exist, but it's quite another when Christians shrug their shoulders.

We must always deal compassionately with people who have fallen, for, after all, "all have sinned, and come short of the glory of God" (Rom. 3:23). None of us dare point at other people. But we must still never allow ourselves to become lax or permissive about the evils themselves. When the standard is lost, then all is lost.

I remember as a boy listening to my father tell a story about a neighbor whose barn had burned down. The entire community gathered to help him rebuild it. My father and some other young men were told to saw the rafters. They first cut a rafter, then traced around it with a pencil and cut another one. They based the third rafter on the second, the fourth on the third, and so on.

What they didn't take into account, of course, was the width of the pencil mark. Each rafter was one pencil mark wider than the one before. This can add up to quite a difference after a whlle. By lunchtime, they looked at the barn and discovered it was going up at a very strange angle. Only then did they discover they had left the standard.

We live in a world that left the standard long ago. We must constantly come back to Scripture to find God's standards, or we will soon find ourselves getting used to things we have no business getting used to.

CHAPTER 27

Sex as It Was Not Meant to Be

Sex was God's idea. When we see the perversions of it in our modern world, we may think it was created by the enemy. Not so. Satan cannot create anything; he can only twist and bend and pervert that which is already created. God made us with bodies, and maleness and femaleness are part of His great plan.

In every great gift lies the possibility of great hurt. Mashed potatoes don't have much capacity for either a great deal of good or a great deal of evil. Atomic energy, however, has both possibilities. Either it can provide light and power for a whole city, or it can blow up an entire civilization. Sex, God's great gift, also has tremendous potential for both good and evil. Sex is meant to provide the deepest communication between human beings, the greatest expression of intimacy and love. But when sex is perverted and twisted, it can cause unimaginable grief, illness, and even death.

Because of the many obvious violations of God's intention, some Christians think they should avoid sexuality altogether. But for most of us, this is neither necessary nor good. We can safely and joyfully celebrate our sexuality within the context of marriage. Through the gift of sex, we can gain deep understanding of God, others, and ourselves—perhaps more so than through any other of our physical capacities.

SEXUALITY OUT OF CONTROL •

I grew up without God and led a promiscuous life. Eleven years ago, when I was twenty-four, I began having affairs with married

men. I soon found myself trapped in a lifestyle I did not like and I lost all my self-respect. Eventually, I cried out to God for help because I knew I could not change myself. Then the Lord brought a wonderful person into my life who helped me change my lifestyle. But after a few years of Christian growth, I found my old desires creeping back. One thing led to another and I am once again involved with a married man. Was I ever saved? How could I have overcome so many problems and now be back where I started? How can I get back to my growing life in Christ? And how do I control my sexual desires?

The only thing for you to do is start where you are and work your way back, as if you were untying a knot. First, you need to confess this new involvement. Accept the Lord's promise that "if we confess our sins, He is faithful and just to forgive us our sins, and to cleanse us from all unrighteousness" (1 John 1:9).

Then realize that, just as nobody is saved by good deeds, nobody is unsaved by sinning. A great many people seem to think they are saved by something other than the blood of Christ. The truth is that He forgives us only when we understand how helpless and wretched we are. Only then are we willing to allow His death on the cross to be a substitution for us. The Lord has forgiven you and it's through His grace that you are saved. Your performance is not involved. That's fortunate for you and for all of us. Nobody is righteous before God; all of us depend totally on His grace.

Basically, your problem is not your sexual desire. Probably you are closer to understanding your behavior when you talk about your lack of self-respect. You need to see a Christian counselor who understands both the Bible and human behavior. You are a creation of the living God. That is what gives you value—not your looks, your bank account, or your ability to change yourself. Until you are sure of your worth in God's eyes, you will continue to reach out in false ways for love. A good counselor can help you learn to love yourself.

HIDDEN PASSIONS ●

How do I handle the feelings that come over me when I look at women? I'm married to a dear wife and we have a good relationship. But every now and then I'll go on a lusting binge and look at every woman in sight. It only lasts a short while, but the guilt I feel afterward is devastating. Is there an effective way to resist these feelings of lust?

Martin Luther once said that you can't keep birds from flying over your head, but you can keep them from nesting in your hair. To look at a woman and recognize that she is physically attractive is not, in itself, sinful. But acting on that information is. You are not acting on your lustful thoughts in an overt, physical way, but you may be sinning in your heart by taking these attractive women into some warm, moist corner of your mind and devouring them mentally.

When a very young man lusts in his heart, it's usually because he wants to experiment and test his powers. When an older, married man lusts, it's generally for a different reason. It has little to do with the sex drive. It has a lot more to do with fear of impotence. "Would I attract that woman?" the man wonders. "I'd better live my life quickly before it's all over for me." Examine your own situation. When you're on a "lusting binge," are you feeling competent at work? Do you fear that younger men are taking over your position? Do you feel yourself slipping? The fears that drive you to lust cause some men to buy sports cars or to grow moustaches. You do these things to restore your sense of vitality.

The best answer to a lusting problem is first to recognize that sex is not what you're really after, and then to think about other things. Try the Apostle Paul's formula in Philippians 4:8—"Whatsoever things are true, whatsoever things are honest, whatsoever things are just, whatsoever things are pure, whatsoever things are lovely, whatsoever things are of good report; if there be any virtue, and if there be any praise, think on these things."

HE HAD AN AFFAIR ●

Two years ago my husband was unfaithful to me. He told me about the affair and I forgave him. He took his second chance seriously and has been a loving and devoted husband ever since. But I still have a great deal of emotional pain—sometimes so much that it keeps me from functioning as a mother, wife, or employee. I want to put this behind me and grow as a Christian, but I don't seem to be able to forgive and forget.

I think the words *forgive* and *forget* go together in the Christian life. A person who does not forget has not really forgiven. The whole message of the New Testament is that God's grace is greater than all our sins. By not forgetting, you rob yourself and your husband of what God wants to give Christians—reconciliation.

Please understand that when I say *forget,* I'm not talking about amnesia. Even though "time heals all wounds," this event will always be part of your memory. By *forget,* I mean that you shouldn't hold your husband's sin against him any more. You shouldn't let it come between you and him. What often happens in situations like this is that the woman feels her self-esteem and personal worth have been attacked. Her husband's unfaithfulness makes her think, "I've failed somehow as a wife." You need to find your self-esteem, not in your husband's behavior, but in the fact that God created you and loves you. If you accept the fact that God made you the woman you are, you will be able to forgive and forget much better.

Scripture says, "As far as the east is from the west, so far hath He removed our transgressions from us" (Ps. 103:12), and, "Thou wilt cast all their sins into the depths of the sea" (Micah 7:19). God forgets our sins—isn't that beautiful? Now *we* need to learn to forgive and forget too.

SIS IS ON "THE PILL" ●

I was devastated to find a package of birth-control pills with my sister's name on them. She was home from college one weekend and accidently left them out where I could see them. I knew she had been leading a different kind of life this past year, but I have not had the chance to talk with her alone for many months. I've considered writing to her and confronting her with my knowledge of the pills. I know I'm not her parent, and she owes me no explanation for her behavior, but I care. What should I do?

I would strongly urge you not to write to her. Often when a person receives a letter of confrontation, she responds in anger and then deepens her resolve to do whatever offended the letter-writer. This kind of situation demands a face-to-face conversation so that you can respond to each other. Anything else comes across as a sermon.

I think you *do* need to confront her about this, however. First, you need to do so because of your own feelings. You feel betrayed. You are both Christians, yet she may be acting in a non-Christian way. "How could she do that to me? How could she do that to Christ?" you wonder, and you feel angry. So you need to deal with your anger.

Second, you need to help her understand something about which many people are mistaken. She needs to know that God's prohibitions against irresponsible behavior are not made for God's protection, but for ours. People get the idea that God's rules are imposed on us for His benefit. But sin is not sin because of what it does to God. Your sister's promiscuity does not affect God; it affects her. It may break her heart, make her feel rejected, burden her with guilt, or even lead to a child to raise by herself. That is why God speaks against fornication.

Now that I have said this, there may be a perfectly legitimate reason your sister is taking these pills. It is entirely possible her doctor has prescribed the pills to correct menstrual irregularity or even something like severe acne. With this in mind, don't immediately assume that your sister has done something wrong.

You are right—it is her life, and she owes you no explanation. When you approach her, be sure she knows you understand this. Be sure also to let her know that you are meddling and taking the chance of damaging your relationship only because you love her. Don't take the attitude of, "You have done something wrong; I'm going to straighten you out and make you agree with me." When confrontation comes across like that, it just hardens the person's resolve to do things her own way. Only confrontation nourished in love is likely to have any effect.

PREGNANT AND UNMARRIED ●

I'm seventeen, very lonely, and pregnant. I know it was dumb of me to get into this situation, but now I'm miserable. My parents and I decided I should go through with the pregnancy and give the baby up for adoption, but ever since we made this decision, there has been no more talk about it. In fact, my family seems to be avoiding any discussions. Sometimes I can see my baby move and it's awesome to think there's a new life being created inside me, but I can't share these feelings with anyone. Everyone seems so cold and indifferent. I suppose they are trying their best to keep me from getting emotionally attached to this child, but I'm starved for someone to talk to.

I commend you first of all for not having taken this society's casual way out—abortion. More and more girls are doing what you are doing, and I think it is the Christian thing to do. I commend you for that, but don't expect it to be easy.

You must understand that being pregnant and living in your parents' home is not a typical situation. Your parents don't have a lot of examples to help them know how to act. You can't expect them to say, "Oh well, we're going to adjust and our feelings will all be ordinary and normal." They sense a certain amount of personal shame and failure. They are blaming themselves, perhaps, feeling they could have done something to prevent your pregnancy. Or perhaps they think their neighbors and friends are criticizing them, holding them responsible for you.

So you must accept at the outset that your situation will carry with it a certain amount of pain, estrangement, and loneliness. Fortunately, pregnancy ends. It lasts nine months and then you begin to get on with life. In the meantime, try expressing your feelings to your mom or your pastor's wife or one of your friends. Tell them what you've told me. Confront the situation and see if you can get help. This will not take your loneliness away, but it may help to have someone share your burden.

I'd like to add a word to parents on this subject. I just read a book that I think is very helpful, a little novel by Lissa Halls Johnson called *Just Like Ice Cream*. This is a Christian book that deals with all sides of teenage pregnancy in a very responsible manner. Both you and your kids will benefit from reading it.

NO LONGER A VIRGIN ●

You wouldn't know my fifteen-year-old daughter is a Christian by the way she acts. She grew up attending a good church and we have tried to teach her biblical morals, but she is rebellious. Many boys call on her all the time and I had an idea that she might have been intimate with them. So I read her diary and sure enough, she has been intimate with all of them and has gone all the way with one. She wrote that it was the happiest day of her life. I am shocked at what she has done. I feel bad about reading her diary, but I thought that was the only way to find out what was happening. Should I tell her what I know and have her hate me for snooping? What do I do about her way of life? I'm desperate.

Most parents would be desperate in your situation. In fact, it is often much better to only suspect things about our children. When we know for sure, we can become very frightened. You fear that your daughter is evil, because she is doing things that are clearly forbidden in Scripture. You must keep in mind that our society has begun to accept many things that are not biblically correct and that we older people know are harmful. It is entirely possible that your daughter, though knowingly violating *your* moral standards, may not be violating *her own.* She may even feel that, within the standards of the group she moves with, she is a good person.

In her mind, she is probably not so much doing something evil as responding to deep needs within herself. Why are people promiscuous? Almost never because of glands, almost always to get affirmation and assurance that they are loved. Insecure people have to go from one person to another to fish for affirmation. Each new conquest means that somebody else has found them attractive. How many does it take until these people feel good about themselves? Always just one more.

I would suggest you go to your daughter and confess that you feel guilty for snooping. Ask her forgiveness for having violated her privacy. Then say, "Honey, this is overdue—let's talk about human sexuality." Tell her that casual sex will not make her feel affirmed and accepted in the long run. Warn her that if she continues acting this way, she will begin to feel cheap and used. Instead of feeling good about herself, she will feel like bargain basement leftovers. Then you and her father need to start giving her more affirmation. If she feels secure in your love, she may feel less compelled to look for affirmation elsewhere.

Helping your daughter turn her behavior around is not an overnight job. It will take time and you may need to seek professional counseling. But even if you do not see changes right away, don't withhold your love. If she ever changes, it will be because you've affirmed her and believed in her.

HER SECRET ABORTION ●

Our daughter is a senior in college and has been dating a young man for some time. After her last weekend visit with us I was tidying up her room when I came across evidence clearly indicating she had an abortion a few months ago. She's a sensitive young woman, so I know she has been devastated by this. I imagine she

has feelings of guilt and shame, because we have expressed our strong opinions against abortion in the past. During her last visit home she told us she is very interested in working with young girls who are pregnant and I'm sure this came about after her sad experience. So what should I do with the information I accidently discovered?

A college senior is a mature adult, so you will have to approach her differently than you would if she were fifteen years old. I do think, since she left the room for you to tidy up and left this evidence in it, that you should discuss the matter with her. Perhaps she wants to talk with you about it—she surely could have hidden the evidence, whatever it is.

Approach your daughter and say just what you said to me. "Honey, I was tidying up your room and I ran across this evidence, and these were my conclusions." Now you may find that you don't know as much about this as you think. If the evidence is a receipt or an appointment slip, it may be for someone else's abortion. Your daughter may have been helping a friend, or perhaps she's already trying to help young girls who are pregnant. So take the approach that your daughter is innocent until proven guilty. If you discover that the abortion was indeed for someone else, you will be tempted to breathe a sigh of relief and go on to other things. But perhaps you need to talk with her about the ethics of helping someone do something you wouldn't do yourself.

If it turns out that she was the one who had the abortion, you will need to discuss your feelings with her. You can't reverse your beliefs because she's your daughter. If abortion was wrong before she had one, then it's still wrong. Let your daughter know your feelings and help her understand that God will forgive her if she asks. Be sure she knows that you will forgive her also. This will keep the door open for future discussions about morals and behavior.

MOM DOESN'T KNOW ●

While home from college for the summer I accidently discovered that my father is having an affair. Mother doesn't know anything about this as far as I can tell, and Dad doesn't know that I know. I'm angry at Dad and very hurt that he would do a thing like this. I sure don't want my parents to break up after twenty-four years of marriage, but I don't know how the matter should be handled.

Is it right to hurt Mom by telling her what's going on? Should I confront my father?

What you are going through right now is probably one of the most shattering experiences a son or a daughter can have. We put our parents on pedestals, and when we discover their feet of clay, we are confused and angry. All children have to discover at some point that their parents are not perfect and then move on to trusting God rather than their parents. But in your case, the realization hit you abruptly, through extreme circumstances.

I would encourage you to go to your pastor with this problem. I'm a great believer in helping people save face. Suppose you confronted your dad. For the rest of your life, he would know you know something of which he is deeply ashamed. He might or might not be able to handle that. He might avoid you, feel hostile toward you, or resent you because your very presence would remind him of his failure.

So go to your pastor and explain what has happened. The pastor may well be aware of the situation. Ask him to confront your father without revealing you as the source. Your pastor and your parents can keep this information between themselves, working it through in a closed group. As far as your parents would know, you would be none the wiser. If you do this, it will help you for the rest of your life, especially at family occasions like Christmas and Thanksgiving.

Sometimes, this is impossible. The affair breaks open and everybody finds out. Then we have to allow the grace of God to work. We have to understand and forgive. We have to humbly tell ourselves, "My dad is part of the human race, just like I am. Both of us are capable of sinning. I ask God to forgive me, so why shouldn't I forgive Dad?" I hope your pastor will be able to handle the situation before this happens, because otherwise the process of healing will be longer and more difficult. And you aren't looking for revenge—you want healing and oneness to come back into your family.

SHOULD I TELL MY DAUGHTER? •

I got pregnant four months before I was married. That was fourteen years ago. My husband and I are both Christians, but we got carried away. I'm afraid if my daughter learns the truth it will destroy my credibility with her as I try to counsel her regarding

premarital sex. Yet, sooner or later, she is bound to put two and two together and figure out what happened. Should I tell her before then? I have found, as King David did, that though our sins are forgiven we sometimes have to bear the consequences of them for years to come.

It probably is not wise for you to talk to your daughter about it now. Personal sins should be confessed between the parties involved and the Lord. Public sins must be confessed to the public. But to make a confession to someone who is unable to handle it can be cruel, and a thirteen-year-old is not likely to be objective about the circumstances of her own conception.

For fourteen years you have lived responsibly. You repented, you married, and the two of you have raised your daughter together. Your sin is covered. Now the devil, I think, specializes in dragging skeletons out of the past and hanging them up in front of us, trying to turn them into the most important things in our lives. If this is happening to you, you may be tempted to confess to your daughter as a means of clearing your own conscience. But this is unnecessary, because the Lord has already freed you of this sin.

Wait until she is older, at least. The time may come in her later teen years when you are talking to her about premarital sex, and you say, "Honey, I do understand this; let me tell you why." Then you should be totally vulnerable and share your heartache and your burden, not just the act. The act that you committed was small compared to its consequences for you and everyone else involved. If you talk to your daughter openly, you do not need to fear losing your credibility. If anything, you will enhance it.

IS MY SON GAY? •

I'm afraid my son is becoming a homosexual. He's a senior in high school and doesn't seem at all interested in dating or going to parties. When he was little, he wasn't particularly interested in sports like the other boys his age. Now he has gotten active in drama at school and wants to go to college to study theater. I know what kind of crowd he would be associating with there. Do you think his actions indicate that he's turning to a homosexual lifestyle?

I sympathize with your concern, because I think the publicity the homosexual community is getting these days arouses fears within many parents. We look at our children and get frightened at things we never would have noticed before—our daughter touching another girl, for example, or our son preferring to spend time with other boys. Yet I think it is unfortunate to stereotype people on the basis of external things. In fact, it seems tragic that we have associated sensitivity, tenderness, and concern with being feminine and cruelty, crassness, and crudeness with being masculine.

From your letter, I would not conclude at all that your son is toying with a homosexual lifestyle. There are many young people who go into the theater without being homosexual. In fact, the overwhelming majority are heterosexual. Likewise, your son's lack of interest in sports and dating doesn't say a thing about his sexual preference.

But let's assume for a moment that your worst fears are true. If your son were a homosexual, what would be the best thing you could do for him? I think in that case you would need to separate his person from his sexuality. You would need to love him, support him, and encourage him as a person. The best way to help him straighten out his sex life would be to accept the rest of him as a whole person. But don't worry prematurely. I don't think you have that problem and there's no point in losing sleep over a normal son just because his interests are not exactly like everyone else's.

HOMOSEXUAL MOTHER-IN-LAW ●

I married my husband knowing his mother is gay. He was raised by her and another woman. Since our marriage, they have figured more prominently in our lives than I had imagined. I don't ever wish to break up my husband's relationship with his mother, but what will I do when children come? What should I tell my children about their grandmother and this woman, and at what age? I would be afraid to leave them with their grandmother for any length of time, yet I know this thought would hurt my husband's mother deeply. How would you handle this delicate situation?

Many heterosexual people have trouble dealing with homosexual people and it is probably good that our society is not completely comfortable with the idea of homosexuality. However, it is important to feel comfortable enough about one's own sexuality not to be threatened by someone else's. A lot of people are paranoid about homosexuality because they don't understand much about it.

In your worries about your future children, you may be asking for trouble. Matthew 6:34 is a good text for you to think about: "Take therefore no thought for the morrow. . . . Sufficient unto the day is the evil thereof." In other words, wait until the situation happens before panicking. The problem may never come up.

You know, kids have great difficulty thinking of their parents (and grandparents) in sexual terms. They know there is something called sex, but they don't think they came into the world that way. Other people might participate in sex, but not their parents. I don't think your kids will think their grandmother is any different from other kids' grandmothers. Grandmothers, as far as kids are concerned, are asexual. So don't ask for trouble where none exists.

If the idea of leaving your child or children with their grandmother worries you, I think you should first discuss your fears with your husband. After all, she raised him, so he probably has a fair idea of how she acts around children. If your concerns persist, have a frank conversation with her. Don't condemn her; simply share your feelings. Let her share with you who she is, what sort of behavior she countenances, what she would and wouldn't do, and so on. The better you get to know your mother-in-law, the more you may appreciate her good points. You should not approve of her homosexuality—after all, Scripture clearly says that such behavior is wrong—but you will be much better off if you do not have irrational fears about it either.

CHAPTER 28

Unhealthy Relationships

If there are such things as healthy relationships, then it follows that there can also be unhealthy ones. Rebellion against God inevitably results in unhealthy relationships. In fact, it may well be that all evil is nothing but a mirror reflection of good.

Human beings created in the image of God have been given the capacity of free will. In order for free will to mean anything, they must have alternatives. When we choose the anti-God alternatives that have resulted from the Fall, we inevitably run into social problems and difficulties. When people decide to live separate from God, deep problems develop in their lives. "I want to do it myself," if it means living outside the Father's house, leads to disaster rather than to freedom.

LIVING TOGETHER ●

Our twenty-year-old daughter told us she wanted to share an apartment next year with her friend, Jean. We thought that would be a great idea until we found out that Jean is a man. We were devastated. She was brought up in a good Christian home and we tried to teach her to live by Christian standards. But now she does this to us. We are paying for her education and wonder whether we should withdraw our support.

Most parents would like to help young people see the bigger picture. We know that uncommitted relationships like your daughter's lead to rejection and heartbreak. We know that God opposes sin because He knows it hurts people. We are frightened, but when kids start wanting to play house without commitment, they don't listen to our fears.

You'd like to force your daughter to do what is right, but you know you can't do that to a twenty-year-old. It's important to consider the results of any actions you might take. If you withdraw your financial support, will she meekly say, "Well, Mother and Dad, if you are not going to support me unless I move back into the dormitory, then I will move back tomorrow"? That's possible, and *if* that's her reaction, withdrawing your support might be a good thing. On the other hand, living in a dorm with a female roommate doesn't insure that she won't be sexually active with her boyfriend. You can't control that by controlling where she lives.

Therefore, I think the best way to approach her is to express disapproval of her behavior and to try to show her the compelling logic of why you are against it. Tell her you are opposed to it, not because of some standard she is breaking, but because people who live together usually get hurt and you are afraid she is in for a lot of sorrow. Help her see that your concern is not for your reputation or God's (God takes care of His own pretty well), but for her well-being. Then, whatever she decides, try to do one of the most difficult things anyone can do—love and accept her even if you must reject some of her behavior.

DATING A DIVORCEE •

We desperately want to help our son. He's a Christian, but about six months ago he started dating a divorced woman whose Christianity is questionable. Very early in their relationship they started sharing everything: personal mail, paychecks, and even bank books. Our son changed almost immediately after starting to date this woman. He became rebellious, resentful, and disrespectful. We invited them both to our home for dinner on Mother's Day, but they never even responded. He has never forgotten Mother's Day before. Later, his girlfriend admitted that she convinced him not to make contact. Our son doesn't appear to be happy with this aggressive woman and sometimes he even seems trapped, but he doesn't have the courage to break off the relationship. We simply don't know how to help him.

I can surely empathize with your concern. We parents feel threatened when our children get involved with someone who seems more experienced than they are, and we think we have perhaps failed. But in your son's situation, the more you try to pull him away from this woman, the more likely you will be to push him toward her.

It sounds to me as if your son has "traded mothers." This woman is probably older than he is; she's experienced; she likes to tell him what to do. Most important to him, she is encouraging him to be independent of you, his parents. To him, this sounds like freedom. He hasn't quite realized that, in this woman's book, the price of his independence from you is submission to her. And you are not the ones to tell him this, because he's probably incapable of hearing it at this point.

You say his girlfriend "admitted" she convinced him not to contact you on Mother's Day. Your use of the word *admitted* makes me think you may have accused her of doing this. You pushed her into a corner, and she reluctantly admitted it. Keep in mind that when you do this, you put yourself in an adversary position with respect not only to her but also to your son. By attacking her, you are probably driving him into her arms.

It would be better to allow your son the freedom to learn on his own what is happening. Some morning he will wake up and say, "My goodness, I'm being controlled by this woman. I don't feel comfortable here." Believe me, very few young men want to be dominated on a long-term basis, whether by their girlfriends, their wives, or their mothers. When he begins to feel uncomfortable about his relationship with her, he will begin to come back to you. He will realize that your love is based on honest concern for his well-being. In the meantime, back off and give him growing room.

ABANDONED UPBRINGING •

I have two daughters who are pregnant and living with their boyfriends. They were both brought up in the church, but have now completely abandoned their upbringing. I love my girls dearly and I know my teaching hasn't been entirely in vain, but I feel defeated. I'd always looked forward to having grandchildren, but I wonder how I will feel about the babies they are expecting. I plan to talk to my pastor, but I'm waiting until I can talk about it without falling apart.

You do need prayer and support, and one way of getting this is to take the risk of sharing your anguish with some people around you. You may find other people in your church who have gone through experiences like yours; they too may be afraid and lonely. Go to your pastor and begin talking to him. If he's the kind of person I think he is, he will be able to understand your anguish, despair, concern, tears, and sense of defeat. Don't be afraid of falling apart. If he's had any experience at all, he's used to that, and he's probably fallen apart a few times himself. I once heard a story about someone who washed up so he could take a bath. Don't be like him; don't wait until you've solved your problem before you look for help.

Your daughters' situations are extreme by some terms, but in the context of our society they aren't extreme at all. A great many young people get into this kind of situation because they fear commitment. Then they end up with children, who are about as big a symbol of commitment as anything in the world. Unfortunately, the children are sometimes seen as extra baggage.

At this point, there is nothing you can do about your daughters' situations except make the best of them. Certainly, you should not penalize your grandchildren. These kids are going to need all the support, love, and stability they can get. It will be very important to them to have a stable, loving grandmother who is not harping on their mothers or tearing them down, who is not moralizing and saying how bad they are, but who is supporting them. And I think you will need to be there when your daughters learn the real danger of live-in arrangements. They usually end up being temporary, and when your daughters come home they will need you to be ready to receive them with love.

MARRIED TO ANOTHER FAITH ●

Do you have any advice for a Christian husband married to a woman of another faith? We have two children and I want to have a peaceful home, but my wife and I disagree far more than we agree.

You are taking the right path by trying to avoid arguments. Try your best to practice your faith without arguing, because in your situation the way it goes is like this—you say what you think; she says what she thinks. You say what you think more loudly; she says what she thinks more loudly. You say it more loudly still . . . and so on. It isn't as if you had faith and she didn't. You each have a position and this can only lead to arguments.

Some people misunderstand how to win people to their side. They think arguing, building a good case, forcing them to agree, will do it. Not so. Argument often only hardens the other people in their opposition. There is a way to win people, though, that goes beyond words and arguments. It is the way of love. It is to imitate the Lord Jesus Christ, who took a towel and basin and washed the disciples' feet. Jesus became a servant, and you can follow Him by serving your wife. Live for her. Give yourself to her. Become a caring and loving husband.

Don't by any means give up your Christian faith or compromise it. But don't talk about it, either. Demonstrate it instead. Show her how it works. I will guarantee you that the Holy Spirit will give content to your actions. At some point, if you do this sincerely and maintain your own close relationship with the Lord, the Holy Spirit will get through to your wife. She will become curious, just like the people in the New Testament who noted that the disciples had been with Jesus. If we Christians could just replace a lot of the argumentation with action, the whole world would sit up and take notice.

MIXED MARRIAGE ●

I'm a Christian, but I've backslidden and am now living with a non-Christian. We've had a baby, yet my boyfriend is afraid to marry. He feels that if we were to divorce I might take half of everything he's worked so hard for. He complains that I waste time, can't keep the house clean, and don't have meals ready on time. I realize I am dealing with a non-Christian and can't expect as much from him. Trying to talk things over doesn't work; we just end up in an argument. I don't want to walk away, yet I'm not sure what to do. Do I leave because I'm a Christian and living together is wrong, or do I stay because I'm a Christian and don't believe in a broken home?

Your dilemma demonstrates some things we try to tell people before marriage. Marriage is commitment; marrying unbelievers causes problems. But it doesn't do you much good for me to lecture you on things you've been told a thousand times. The fact is, you are living together as if you were married, and you have a child.

Your boyfriend may not realize this, but he may already be responsible for you and your child financially. He may be unwilling to make an emotional commitment to you, but in many states, the very fact that you are living as husband and wife makes him legally committed. So his economic reason for fearing marriage may not hold water. Likewise, his objections about your housekeeping are probably just a smokescreen. He's trying to think of something to justify his unwillingness to commit himself.

I think you and your boyfriend need counseling. He needs to understand why he is so afraid. He has to see his unwillingness to commit himself as a problem, something that needs to be changed. Until he is willing to commit himself to you and, I would hope, to God, you are unequally yoked together and you can anticipate that the tensions you are experiencing now will continue. If it turns out that he cannot or will not commit himself to you, then it is probably worse to remain with him than to raise your child as a single parent.

But if the two of you can agree together that you both have problems—you for going outside the Lord's will, getting involved premaritally, and having a baby out of wedlock; he for being unwilling to commit himself to you or to Christ—and if both of you want to work on your problems, then you can stay with him and work toward a solution.

FLAUNTING HER SIN? ●

My daughter, who is twenty-six, is living with a forty-three-year-old man who has long hair, a long beard, and stands a head shorter than she does. I believe he smokes marijuana. She knows I'm opposed to this relationship, but she doesn't know how heartbreaking it is for me. Whenever I invite her to dinner, she brings this man along. She should understand that the invitations are for her only, but it almost seems as if she is flaunting her sin. I do not try to talk to her about spiritual things, because she is not open to them. Considering the circumstances, we have a good relationship. She often calls me long distance just to talk. I don't want to hinder my relationship with her, but I don't know what to do about this man.

Obviously, a battle is going on inside you, and you need to share your concerns with your daughter face to face, in private, with no one else around. Here are the things that concern me and probably concern you about her relationship with this man. First, there is a big age difference between them. He is closer to your age than to hers. Some situations like that can be very happy and successful, but they can create potential problems. Second, you are concerned about his lifestyle and habits that are contrary to your values. Third, you are worried that she seems to have turned her back on her Christian faith. Fourth, it is possible that later on he will reject her. Their kind of live-in relationship, though it is common today, is never a good situation. We must keep in mind, however, that some people drop spouses just as quickly as others drop roommates; marriage today is no guarantee of permanence unless both people believe in commitment.

Once you have clarified to your daughter why you are concerned and why you are uncomfortable, then drop it. You will have made your point. You are free to proceed with her on friendly terms. She's an adult; you have no responsibility to force her to change her ways. You should begin to adjust to the fact that she thinks an invitation to her includes him too. If you start insisting that she come alone, she'll probably stop coming and you'll have deeper heartaches than you have now. Winston Churchill once said about the United Nations, "Better jaw, jaw, than war, war." I think that if you keep the door open so you can communicate with your daughter, you will be better off than if you break it down and start a cold war.

WHAT DOES SHE SEE IN HIM? ●

Our seventeen-year-old daughter has a boyfriend of the same age who uses a fake ID to get liquor. When he was twelve, his parents threw him out of their house, and now he lives with a forty-year-old man in a neighboring city. It doesn't sound like a reputable situation to us. We've talked to our daughter about this, but she continues to write, call, and see him. We can't understand what she sees in this boy. She is an intelligent girl. We are afraid she is getting into something that could bring her a lot of hurt in the future.

Relationships between people are very complex and hard to analyze. It could be that she is legitimately attracted to this boy. He may have virtues of which you are unaware. A boy who has been on his own this long is usually pretty worldly-wise. He's a survivor; he lives by his wits; he's resourceful. He probably appears much more mature than boys in her class who are struggling to earn a letter jacket. He no doubt seems like a man to her.

In addition, she probably feels sorry for him. She sees him as a wounded cocker spaniel, and she is going to help him. Everyone else picks on him and gives him a bad time; no one understands him but her. So she will be his little Florence Nightingale.

Now, what is the best strategy for you? Realize that she has an adolescent sense of fairness—a wonderful thing, by the way. If you start putting him down, she will try to balance the teeter-totter. You will be critical because you don't know all the facts, and she will counter with her understanding of the situation. Trying to separate them will almost assuredly drive them closer together.

Here is what I think will work best. Have a little confidence in what you are doing in your own family. Don't push this boy farther away; draw him closer. Bring him into your home and make him welcome. Become substitute parents for him—he needs someone like you. You won't lose a daughter this way, but you may gain a son. Remember, to reject someone who doesn't meet our standards is to show a lack of faith in Christ and in our own Christian homes. We don't have to let others' problems rub off on us. We can let our happiness rub off on them.

CHAPTER 29

Alcohol, Smoking, and Gambling

All of God's creation was given to us to enjoy, yet mankind has persisted throughout history to misuse what God has given us. Alcohol, tobacco, and gambling can be addictive. People who are caught in their clutches would sooner destroy their health, their families, or their financial solvency than give up their use.

Alcohol has become a national embarrassment. Drunk drivers kill hundreds of innocent people every day; teenage alcoholism is epidemic; businesses lose millions of dollars from Monday-morning absenteeism. The surgeon general regularly adds new diseases to the list of problems caused by cigarette smoking, yet the same government that bans certain nonnutritive sweeteners actually supports the tobacco industry. And Gamblers Anonymous testifies to what people will do when they let supposedly harmless games get out of control.

Virtually half the money spent on health in America could be saved if people stopped using alcohol and tobacco altogether. Yet we live in a world that insists on their use and even people who don't use them suffer from the results. God loves the people who have been crippled by alcohol, tobacco, and gambling, but He grieves to see the losses they suffer in relationships and in health. When we see what these crutches have done to people made in the image of God, we are encouraged to lay them aside. Maybe we can live more effectively for God without them.

CHAINED TO THE BOTTLE •

My husband is an alcoholic. He is not a violent drinker; he has never abused me or the children, but he drinks steadily every evening from the time he gets home until bedtime. He doesn't really get drunk, but he consumes a great deal of liquor. I know he must seek help soon before this problem destroys his health. I've been praying about this and I've come a long way in understanding him. I don't nag him anymore and I can love him where he is, but how can I help him with his problem?

One person who has given me insight into alcoholism is Harold Hughes, former governor of Iowa and a United States senator. Hughes has written an autobiographical book called *The Man from Ida Grove* in which he describes his own struggle with alcoholism. I would encourage you to read this book and perhaps share it with your husband. It provides a description of various drinking patterns as well as help in finding solutions to this problem.

Generally, people with a drinking problem fall into one of three categories. Some are heavy drinkers. Your husband may be one of those. He drinks a great deal, but he functions. Some are problem drinkers. They may drink less than your husband, but they don't function normally. Their drinking interferes with their work and their family life. And some are alcoholics. They have a physiological dependence on alcohol. Any of these patterns can cause tremendous problems for the drinker and for his family.

I don't know the style of your marriage. Perhaps your husband is dominant and you are afraid to discuss things with him, or perhaps he resents any advice. But if you can, say something to him like, "Honey, I love you and I care about you. I see your drinking becoming more and more of a problem to you, and I want to help you." Don't try to get him to meet some standard. Don't preach him a sermon on the evils of drinking. Those would not be effective ways to approach him. But you may get through to him by expressing your genuine concern.

You might consider calling Al-Anon, a support group for families of alcoholics, and asking for advice. These are very wise people, I've found, and they know how to deal with drinking problems. They might help you figure out what your first step should be. But remember that, ultimately, you can't do anything about your husband's problem. He has to do something about it himself. If he does take action, it will come as a result of your love, your tenderness, your compassion, and your prayers.

A PROBLEM DRINKER? ●

My son is twenty-three, doesn't have a job, and does nothing but sit at home and drink. He's been drinking since he was about sixteen. I give him a good home and I love him, and it would be hard to put him out. We've gone through some tough times with fighting and accusations, and sometimes even the police have been involved. I can see him slowly changing as I love him, but my husband only sees him wasting his life. He gets on his back, and then my son shuts himself in his room and drinks more. It seems like our family is in a cold war and no one talks.

Your problem is not at all unusual. Many young people find it difficult to enter the adult world. Economic struggles prolong adolescence for many of them and many are withdrawing and staying home longer. They fear the world; they lack the skills required to enter it; and besides, there isn't much opportunity in the job market right now.

Your problem is made even more difficult because of your son's drinking. I don't know if he is a problem drinker or an alcoholic; you need to establish what his situation is and find a solution for it. I suggest you bring someone in from outside the family. Your pastor might be able to help you assess the situation. If your son is indeed an alcoholic—and he very well may be, since he has been drinking for several years and drinks in private—he needs to get into a rehabilitation program and begin to learn how to face life. Look for a program connected with a church-related hospital, where they will look at your son's spiritual side as well as his alcohol dependency. Ultimately, of course, his problem is spiritual. Your son needs the inner strength and purpose that only Jesus can bring.

You also need to help your son develop independence. Once he has conquered his alcohol problem, I would encourage you to help him find a place to live separate from your home. He needs to begin to face the real world and learn from the greatest teacher, cause and effect. There's nothing like being responsible for oneself to help a young person change his behavior in a positive direction. This would not be putting him out. It would be helping him become an adult, which is certainly a good thing for parents to do for their son.

WHEN ALCOHOL DIVIDES •

My granddaughter is fifteen years old. Recently, her best friend has started drinking. My granddaughter wants no part of it, but is afraid of losing her friend if she tries to tell her she shouldn't drink. How should she approach this situation?

It is beautiful to see grandmothers and granddaughters talking about things that even mothers and daughters don't talk about. Parents should not feel threatened by this—young people sometimes just feel more at ease with someone not quite as close as a parent.

As you know, teenage drinking has reached epidemic proportions. I can think of no redeeming value whatever to America's liquor traffic. I despise it and I despise the fact that the church is becoming comfortable with it. I feel so strongly because of what I have seen alcohol do in the lives of young people. Tragically, there's a chance that your granddaughter's friend will become an alcoholic. She doesn't intend to, of course—no one starts drinking with the idea, "Someday I'll be an alcoholic." But people become what they become by starting somewhere. So by all means continue to affirm your granddaughter's distaste for drinking.

At the same time, help her to do something that is really quite difficult. Help her to accept her friend as a person without accepting her behavior. It is a cop-out if we retreat from our friends when we don't like what they do. We then lose all influence over them. Instead, we need to love them as persons while finding some way to demonstrate—not say, but demonstrate—that the Christian way of life is superior to theirs.

A person does not need the social crutch of drinking. You can feel at home in a social situation carrying a ginger ale around. Your granddaughter should show her friend that she can be happy and well-adjusted without alcohol. If your granddaughter accepts her friend, loves her, and lives a Christian life in front of her, eventually this girl will ask, "Tell me, how do you get along without drinking?" Then she can tell her about how Jesus wants to live in our hearts and satisfy all our needs.

PARTY SPIRITS •

The alcohol problem is quite severe in my children's high school. I've heard that kids won't come to a party unless there is liquor. A few Christian parents have forbidden their children to attend

344

any parties because of this problem, but these children are few in number and walk a lonely road through their high school years. It seems a shame to have only the extreme choices of staying home or getting drunk.

―――――――――――

We need to understand how serious this problem is. Teenage drinking is a major problem being faced by educators and others who work with young people today. Teenage alcoholism has reached epidemic proportions. You mention parties. When you went to school, *party* was a noun. It stood for an event that you went to. Today *party* is a verb. It describes a way of life. Your young people are in an atmosphere where partying goes on constantly. Some teachers say that they've had kids in class who have never come to class straight—they've been on something all through high school.

One purpose of Youth for Christ, Campus Crusade, and Young Life is to provide positive peer pressure, to provide a place for kids to go and have fun without doing destructive things. Even though drinking is a major problem, it's not true that everybody's doing it. There are a great many kids like yours who would love to find a group where they can have a good time without partying. In Youth for Christ we've found that it takes a lot of innovation, hard work, dedication, training, and money to combat the party scene. It isn't very resourceful, really, to turn out the lights, turn on the stereo, open some liquor bottles, and call it a party. It takes a lot more effort to put together something that will be really exciting. Christian parents need to put forth that kind of effort. Then their kids won't have to face the depressing choice of staying home or drinking.

SHE JUST CAN'T QUIT ●

―――――――――――

My friend drinks too much. A few months ago she said she'd given it up and turned her life over to God. But the other night I saw her drinking again. It tore me apart. Is there any way I can help her? I've witnessed to her, but it seems she just doesn't care anymore.

―――――――――――

We all see people who make commitments to Christ and don't follow through. Jesus, in His Parable of the Sower, said that "some [of the seed] fell among thorns, and the thorns sprung up, and choked them" (Matt. 13:7). In other words, various influences came in and choked out the seed of the Gospel. If an individual has propensities toward alcohol, or toward escapism, these old problems tend to rise up again as the intensity of the conversion experience wears down and his newfound faith begins to seem ordinary. Your friend may have this kind of problem. It is good that you love her and are concerned about her.

There are two kinds of people with alcohol-related problems. One kind is undisciplined, looking for an escape, wanting to dull the sharpness of life's assaults. They use alcohol as a narcotic to desensitize themselves. The other kind is physically dependent on alcohol. They are alcoholics. If you think your friend may be an alcoholic, try to plant in her mind the idea of visiting Al-Anon and getting involved in their program. I wish I could say that we Christians have been helpful to people with alcohol-related problems, but so often we tend to reject them. We give them the feeling that they're bad and we're good because they have this problem and we don't. People in AA have had the problem themselves and they know how to provide support. In addition to AA, problem drinkers need Christ. But the first step for alcoholics is to want help from a group like AA.

SMOKING—JUST A BAD HABIT? ●

A couple in our church has been involved with our outreach ministry as bus captains. Their names are never mentioned on our church progress report, however. They were told they would not be included until they quit smoking. (They have never smoked on the bus or near the children.) The bus children have grown to love this wonderful couple and I think they deserve credit for what they are doing. In fact, they have grown quite discouraged over the church's lack of acceptance. I know smoking isn't good for our bodies, but do we have the right to exclude these people from the fellowship and love they need? Why are some Christians so opposed to smoking? Is it really worse than any other bad habit?

I once saw a sign on the soft drink machine in a church basement that said, "Please do not buy pop on Sunday." One of the children had written underneath, "For by not buying pop on Sunday are ye saved." I suppose smoking is in a similar category. There is no place in the Bible that says, "For by not smoking are ye saved," even though it is not good to smoke.

I think Christians object to smoking because it is bad for the health. It is tied to lung and liver cancer, various respiratory problems, and heart

346

disease. In fact, if we could do away with smoking in this country, we could do more for the nation's health than we could do any other way. But if we are opposed to smoking because it hurts people, then we have to realize that rejection hurts people too. Casting people out hurts them, not in their lungs but in their souls. While we are saving their souls, we had better be careful that we are not destroying their lives.

Some years ago cartoonist Al Capp had a fellow named Fearless Fosdick in his comic strip. Fearless Fosdick always carried his gun on crime-solving missions. Often, in order to save a person from "harm," Fosdick would shoot him. The church does not need Fearless Fosdicks. Even though smoking is a habit that does only harm, we can do equal or greater harm by piously rejecting the person who smokes.

CHOKING HIS TESTIMONY? •

I watched as a man gave a moving Christian testimony while smoking a cigarette. This seems inconsistent with his new life in Christ. It's true we don't get to heaven by good works, but if we know something is bad for us and continue it, will the Holy Spirit still work through us?

I've tried to establish why many Christians feel they shouldn't smoke. Historically, there have been two arguments. The older argument is that the ethos surrounding smoking is bad—one thinks of smoke-filled rooms and bars and that sort of thing. More current is the argument that smoking is bad for the health. Why should a Christian not do something that is unhealthy? Because Scripture teaches that the body is a creation of God and the temple of the Holy Spirit. To hurt what God has given us is bad. Sin is sin, not because of what it does to God but because of what it does to us. God loves us and does not want us to be hurt by smoking or by anything else.

Sometimes, though, the choice seems to be between two bad things. It is bad for a person to smoke, but it is also bad to reject a person because he has a bad habit. Driving a person out of a family or away from the church can be a very damning thing. It may help to think about your own approach to health. Lack of sleep, lack of exercise, drinking coffee, and eating sugar are all bad for the body, yet almost everyone does some of these things. Do we reject Christians who abuse their bodies through overwork? Or do we reserve our harsh words for smokers?

Of course, it would be better for Christians if they did not smoke. That's beyond question. But to love and accept them is an even greater value, in my opinion. God has always had to use flawed instruments. If He waited to use perfect people, He couldn't use any of us at all.

GRANDDAD'S BAD INFLUENCE ●

I'm single and recently had a baby. Having no other option, I moved in with my father's family. A few weeks ago I rededicated my life to God and am now trying to live for Him. The problem is that no one in my father's family is a Christian and now I'm faced with our differences such as drinking, smoking, and swearing. I feel I can't witness to them because of my carnal past. I'm also afraid they will influence my baby even at her young age. Am I lacking in faith because of my fears? How can I handle these differences?

You have a very difficult situation on your hands, one that will require a great deal of attention. Start by counting your blessings. Give thanks that the Lord is able to forgive us thoroughly and to restore us to fellowship with Himself. You are His child and He loves you dearly. He is on your side, helping you to solve this problem and to be the kind of mother and woman you really want to be. He's also interested in your child's welfare.

Second, give thanks that your father is willing to open his home to you and provide a place for you to live. I can tell you that there are many Christian families where the parents don't drink, smoke, or swear, but they reject their children when they get into trouble. Then these children have to go out on the streets to find another home. So be grateful, not only for God's forgiveness, but also for your father's generosity.

Third, relax about the effect your family's behavior is having on your newborn child. Fortunately, for the first few years this kind of behavior won't affect her very much. It is important that she not be physically abused, of course, but I'm assuming your father's family loves your child and wants to hold her. Physical love is very important even if it comes from people who are not committed to the Lord.

Then, relieve yourself of your sense of obligation to witness to your family, if by "witness" you mean talking to them and convincing them that you are on the right path and they are on the wrong. Witness rather by being with them and showing the quality of your life as you walk with the Lord. You are doing that now and I'm sure you are doing very well.

You need to find Christian fellowship in the right kind of church with a wise pastor, so you can be surrounded by a group of caring Christian people who will be an extended family to you. These people can help you get established and make the many decisions you will face. You can't just join the first church you see, however, and hope it will be the right one. It probably won't be. You'll need to put some work into this. For the moment, put your emphasis into finding a good church rather than on trying to solve your other problems. You'll be ahead in the long run.

THE SUCCESSFUL GAMBLER •

My father, after becoming a Christian, has fallen back into his old habits. Once again he has started gambling. I get nowhere when I try to talk with him, so instead I pray. He has won a lot of money gambling and this only encourages him. Once I shared this with my pastor. He and my father talked, but nothing came of that either. Is there anything else I should be doing?

I can't think of anything else you can do. It is more difficult to work with successful gamblers than with unsuccessful ones. The stereotype of the gambler is a person who gambles away his paycheck, goes to loan sharks, loses his house, lets his children go hungry, and so on. That syndrome is obviously negative, and when a man is caught in it, he wants help. But when a man is a successful gambler, everything seems to be going great. He buys new boats, a swimming pool, and big cars. He can't see why his hobby is wrong—it seems to be doing well by him. He is further encouraged by the fact that some municipalities and states run lotteries to help support school systems and other public projects. He doesn't realize the problems associated with gambling.

I believe your father probably will not learn his lesson until he goes full circle. No one can be a successful gambler long-term. Gambling doesn't work that way. The house always wins in the end. Your father may win short-term, but if he stays at it long enough, he will eventually fail. Many people can't look up until they hit bottom. Your father may be one of them.

Hitting bottom will be a painful process for your father and for your whole family. I would encourage you to stick with him and to keep on praying for him. Advising him will probably do no good as long as he is winning. But when he hits bottom, be there waiting for him. Don't say, "I told you so," but love him and point him again toward the better way.

LOSING BY WINNING •

My husband is heavily involved in gambling, and I am concerned about his influence on my son, who is a Christian and recently joined a church youth group. Now my son is beginning to seem worldly concerning money and is actually condoning my husband's winnings. How should I deal with this?

Preserving a relationship between a parent and a child is more important to a young person than virtually anything else. Very few things are worth driving a wedge between a father and his son. True, gambling is a vice that society would be better off without. It is sometimes not an obvious evil like drunkenness or drug abuse. Many states encourage gambling through state lotteries, so many young people conclude that there's nothing wrong with it. Besides, your husband is apparently a winner, so he is not causing his family to suffer. It is not surprising that your son is less than horrified by his gambling.

Of course, what your son doesn't see is the other side of gambling. For many people, it's addictive. They take out loans at exorbitant interest rates and get deeper and deeper in debt; they can't seem to stop, even when their family's security and happiness is endangered. This is why Christians are opposed to gambling, but your son may be too inexperienced to have figured that out.

Certainly you can share your views on gambling with your husband and your son—you probably already have. It's fine to let them know why you're opposed to it. But then, let the subject drop. Your son is a Christian. Trust that the Holy Spirit, through the influence of your son's church and his Christian friends, will begin to speak to him. Trust that the Lord is at least as concerned about your son as you are, and let Him work on him in His own way.

Understand that nobody grows from a babe in Christ into a full-grown Christian overnight. If you look at a baby every day to check his growth, you can't tell much. But if you check him on a yearly basis, you are amazed at how much he's grown. That's the way it is with newborn Christians. Sometimes a lot more cell division and growth and calcium development is going on in a Christian's backbone than we think. It can be happening to your son even while on the surface he is agreeing with his dad.

CHAPTER 30

Drugs and Problems with the Law

Who would have dreamed that in the last quarter of the twentieth century virtually every American would have some experience with drugs through a family member or loved one? Drug abuse has become part of many people's lives. The attempt to avoid all pain and to live outside reality has become commonplace. Rather than enjoying God's creation and dealing with it sensibly and responsibly, many of us are tempted to avoid the natural system of cause and effect by escaping when the going gets rough.

Even religion has turned to this type of wishful thinking. To many people, God has become a utility. We have a washer to wash dirty clothes, a dryer to dry wet ones, a range to heat our food, and God to take away our sins. Books and articles tell us how to use God so that we do not have to feel pain. Promises are made that the Christian can live without struggle, without the usual unpleasantness of life.

People who wish to escape daily reality through religion have the same problem as people who wish to escape through drugs. Both are unwilling to live in God's world within the confines of natural law. Both wish to remain children rather than becoming loving, cooperative adult members of God's family.

DO I TELL THE POLICE? •

I am heartbroken. I've discovered that my teenage son is taking drugs and stealing to support his habit. At this point, I'm the only one who knows about this. Should I turn in my own son? Isn't there a better way?

You haven't mentioned your husband so I am going to assume that you're a single parent. If you're not, the first person you need to turn your son over to is your husband, and the three of you should deal with this together. This sounds obvious to many, but it's amazing how many husbands and wives don't really trust each other with this kind of information. Either the husband feels the wife will be shattered and fall apart, or the wife feels the husband will be too harsh on the kid and he won't be able to handle it. So each of them tries to handle it alone.

If you're trying to raise this son alone, find someone who has a good relationship with him—a favorite teacher, a school counselor, a pastor, or a youth leader. Unlike parents who usually have limited experience with this sort of thing, and who have a difficult time remaining objective, youth directors and other people in these kinds of positions most likely have dealt with this type of problem before and will have some good suggestions.

Personally, I feel that the business of your son's stealing should wait for a while. When Scripture uses the phrase, "Let him who steals steal no longer" (Eph. 4:28, NASB), it doesn't say anything about the process of restitution or how quickly it should take place. It would probably be most helpful to first get the boy past the drug problem because this is the real reason he's stealing. Then once the drug problem is under control, have your son begin giving back to the people from whom he's stolen to make amends.

But how do you cure the drug problem? There is no perfect answer, of course, but first find out why he's involved and how deeply he's involved. For instance, many kids who are involved in drugs aren't in it so much for the drugs but rather as a way to gain friends, make a quick dollar, or find adventure. If there's a Youth for Christ, Young Life, or Campus Crusade for Christ office in your town, let me encourage you to call that office and speak to the staff there, explaining the situation. They would be happy to talk with you and your son. I've done it many times, and that is what staff members of Christian youth organizations are trained to do. Your pastor or youth director can be of great help as well. But I don't think you will solve anything by turning your son over to the police. I think there is a better way, and I would encourage you to try the way I have suggested before doing anything more drastic.

DRUGS AND PEERS •

What do you say to a teenager if you suspect he is smoking pot? My son has become friends with a new neighbor who comes from a broken home (he lives with his grandmother because he doesn't like his stepfather). I've been watching this friendship closely because I've been told this boy smokes pot. I'm not sure what I'd do if I found out my son was doing this.

There is no way to put your son in an atmosphere where he can't come in contact with kids who smoke pot. It's just too pervasive in our society. That in no way belittles your concern. I would be just as concerned as you are. Even if pot is common, it is still dangerous and, of course, you don't want your son to use it.

Let me suggest to you that drug use is not a person's primary problem; it is a symptom of other needs that have not been met. Usually high school kids use drugs for acceptance or to fill some emptiness in their lives. This neighbor boy obviously has problems. He is new in town. His parents are divorced. He doesn't like his stepfather. He needs friends. Why not take him on as a project?

Invite him to your home. Make him comfortable around your table. Don't try to drive a wedge between him and his parents, but be surrogate parents to him since they're not around. Be a model for him. You will find that this kind of kid is like a sponge. This boy will start soaking up your family—even more than you want him to. You may think you have an extra son on your hands. But think of what a blessing that will be—to help a kid who has been hurt by society.

Why should your son be the passive absorber of this boy's bad habits? Why not enlist him as an active participant instead? Take the offensive with this boy instead of trying to defend your son against the bad influence he might have. Then both your son and his friend will come out on top.

WHEN EVERYONE DOES POT •

The other day I found some marijuana joints in my daughter's coat pocket. I confronted her with this and she said it's no big deal—"Everyone's doing it." Why is it so easy to get drugs? How can I get my daughter to see the seriousness of her offense?

Your daughter is almost right. Not everyone is doing it, of course, but a large percentage of young people use marijuana, and many glamorous people in the media make marijuana use look sophisticated. Though marijuana is against the law, society often smiles at the problem. Penalties for using it are usually light, and some people charged with enforcing the law either use it themselves or have friends who do. And yet marijuana use is not a harmless pastime, particularly for teenagers.

Tell your daughter you are concerned because you love her very much. You don't want her doing anything that could harm her health or her mind. Tell her what you have read or heard that has alarmed you. (An excellent book on the subject is *For Parents Only: What You Need to Know about Marijuana,* published by the U.S. Department of Health, Education, and Welfare [National Institute on Drug Abuse, 5600 Fishers Lane, Rockville, Maryland 20857].)

She doubtless will counter with other information she has picked up from her friends. She may say that marijuana is less harmful than tobacco and alcohol. I think we have to concede some of these points and say, "Yes, it's possible that these other things are more harmful. They cause cancer, automobile accidents, heart disease, broken homes, and so on. But two wrongs don't make a right. I want to protect you from *anything* that would harm you."

Once parents have done this, there's not much more they can do. Teenagers feel so casual about marijuana. To them, pot in the park is roughly equivalent to corn silk behind the barn in grandfather's generation. When we show concern, they feel we're overreacting, making mountains out of molehills. Only when they are exposed to certain kinds of information do they begin to think twice about it, and that's usually after they're past adolescence.

We parents need to bear in mind that drug use is more than a physical problem. It is symptomatic of underlying problems of rebellion, desire to escape, willingness to take shortcuts, an inordinate need to fit in and be accepted by peers, and so on. Drug problems reflect deeper problems of purposelessness and emptiness. This is why we in the Youth for Christ ministry are committed to presenting the Gospel. We believe that when a person's life is truly in tune with God, he or she will find meaning and purpose in Christ. Then the young person will no longer feel the need for life-changing, behavior-modifying, consciousness-altering drugs.

A TROUBLED TEENAGER •

My teenager is a very troubled young man. He is confused about many things and he even questions why he is alive. Quite often he gets in trouble with the law. Is there anything we can do? Where could we have gone so wrong?

I've spent my life talking to teenagers and listening to their problems, and I've learned that virtually every young person at some time or another asks why he is alive. However, when normal teenage questioning goes over the boundary into destructive behavior, as your son's has, then it is in a different category. It has left the range of normality and has become a problem that needs professional help.

I would suggest that you make every effort to get your son to sit down with a qualified counselor—a pastor, a youth pastor, or a parachurch youth worker from Youth for Christ, Young Life, or Campus Crusade— and let him attempt to get to the bottom of his problem. It's true that you can lead a horse to water, but you can't make him drink. Nevertheless, a skillful counselor can often make it possible for a young man like this to open up and get to the root of his problems.

I have sat with many troubled teenagers and simply said, "John, I know this is difficult for you and it's difficult for me as well. Your parents are troubled about you. They're troubled because they love you and they are baffled. They somehow have the idea that I can help you. I'm not sure I can, but I'll do my best. What I can do is this: I've had friendships with many young men who have faced some of the things you are facing. I'd like to help you. Let's talk." Often a teenager will be able to talk more easily with a friendly stranger than with his own parents.

By the way, don't discount a good counselor in the school, court system, or in social work just because he is not a Christian. Sometimes these people are able to help a great deal. In fact, the good ones practice the same kinds of procedures that Christian counselors use. Of course, Christian counselors have the added motivation of the Gospel of Christ and they also have the insights provided by God's Word. Nevertheless, if your son already has a trusting relationship with a non-Christian counselor, consider the possibility that the Lord will work through him.

I do not believe it is wise for you to spend much energy asking yourself what you have done wrong until the counselor is able to help you with this. There are a thousand possibilities, including the possibility that you have not done anything wrong. Your son's counselor will want to look at your individual situation and help you where you are. There are many people who are committed to helping young people like your son, and then you can go to work on changing whatever needs changing.

For your encouragement, let me assure you that many great people went through dark periods during adolescence or early adulthood when they were finding themselves. In fact, confusion and despair are almost a way of life among many young people, especially in major cities and intellectual centers. Thousands are searching for meaning, and this is why people in youth work make so much effort to provide ways to meet young people and talk with them about their deepest concerns. And it always helps us to know that their parents are praying for them, even if they are thousands of miles away.

THIEF GONE STRAIGHT ●

Some time ago I stole some clothing from a store. Since then I have become a Christian. I know I am forgiven for past wrongs, but this is something I feel I should right in some way. I don't have the money to pay the store back, even if I knew what I owed. And I don't have the clothes anymore. What can I do?

Let me commend you for your honesty and encourage you to follow through in making this right. A great many people seem to forget that in cases like this, other people are hurt. You have already been forgiven, so the relationship between God and yourself is clear. But what about the people who owned the clothing? After all, they bought the clothing and planned to make a profit on it, and by taking it, you spent their money. You are right in wanting to make it up to them.

I would encourage you to write them a letter in which you do not identify yourself. Simply tell them that you have shoplifted, that you owe them some money, that you intend to pay it back—over the course of a long period of time, if necessary. Enclose the first payment with your letter. They will then realize that you are going to make it up. Go ahead and tell them you are doing this because of what Christ has done in your life. Say you wish to follow Him by doing what is right.

Then, even if the weekly or monthly amount is very small, you will know that you are straightening out a wrong and doing the Lord's work. You will find that as you do this, your sense of guilt will go away. Be grateful for your guilt feelings. The Apostle Paul spoke of people whose consciences are "seared with a hot iron" (1 Tim. 4:2). These people don't feel guilty when they do wrong. It's dangerous not to feel responsibility for one's own actions, so be grateful for your sense of conviction.

JUVENILE DELINQUENT? ●

My fourteen-year-old daughter is a thief and a liar. She steals things, even if they have little or no value. Then she has the nerve to say she didn't do it. I don't know how to handle this. My other five children have given me no problems in this area.

Undoubtedly you love your daughter, so let me encourage you to begin thinking of her not as a "thief and a liar," but as a person. Just as a doughnut is not all hole, your daughter is not all stealing and lying. Don't bundle up her whole little life and call it "liar" or "thief." She is not that; she is a person who has some problems.

Usually, people who steal things have a problem understanding person-hood in others. If you took something of your daughter's, she would cry out vehemently. "That's mine!" she would say, meaning that you had taken something attached to her. She probably doesn't extend that concept to other people's property. She doesn't understand that that apple turnover belongs to the 7-Eleven store owner, or that those earrings belong to the discount store owner. She just thinks of them as things. So she needs help in understanding the relationship between persons and property.

At fourteen, she also no doubt has a problem with postponing gratification. She wants something now and she doesn't want to wait until she earns the money for it. So she takes it. Your daughter's problems—understanding personhood and delaying gratification—are matters of maturity. Most fourteen-year-olds are more mature than your daughter in these areas, but that does not mean that your girl is hopeless. She may need wise counseling from someone outside your family, or you may be able to help her gain a mature perspective on life that will make stealing and lying unnecessary. Start doing this by affirming her own personhood and helping her see the connection between her things and her person. Then perhaps she will begin to see the connection between another person's things and his person.

SECTION 8

Living in a Spiritual World

In the life of Jesus Christ, there was no distinction between the sacred and the secular. The Apostle Paul tells Christians to commit every part of their lives to the Lord: "Whatsoever ye do in word or deed, do all in the name of the Lord Jesus, giving thinks to God and the Father by Him" (Col. 3:17).

There's a hymn entitled, "This Is My Father's World." This is true in the sense that God has created the world and owns everything in it. But in another sense, this world is no friend to grace. The Christian is a citizen of God's kingdom temporarily living in a worldly kingdom. It's easy to be like a chameleon—to pick up the color of whatever we sit down on, to become part of the world. That's why Paul urges us, "Be not conformed to this world: but be ye transformed by the renewing of your mind" (Rom. 12:2). Fortunately, we have institutions and activities especially designed to help us with our spiritual activity. Chief among these is the church.

I believe that every Christian should be part of a local congregation. There is no such thing as true growth apart from the church. You can do many things by yourself, but you can't have fellowship alone. The fellowship of the body of Christ is one of the most important features of the Christian life.

The church does not exist to keep Christians away from the world, but to give them strength to go into the world. It challenges us and gives us the opportunity to witness. It helps us deal with our problems and maintain our Christian character in a wicked and perverse generation. It helps us live Christian lives in the midst of a world that has forgotten all about Christianity, if it ever knew it at all.

CHAPTER 31

Becoming a Christian

Both witnessing and becoming a Christian have this in common—both speak of something you are, not something you do. Often people confuse witnessing with the techniques involved in sharing the Gospel message. But we witness to the validity of our Christian faith by the quality of our lives and relationships, as well as by the words we speak. Lifestyle witnessing is the natural way for a person to witness. In fact, the Great Commission itself is really saying, "As you are going, therefore, into all the world, preach the Gospel to every creature." So the emphasis of witnessing is on what we are, not what we do.

By the same token, people have often confused becoming a Christian with adhering to a set of do's and don'ts. My father lived a great portion of his life believing that to be a Christian meant not to smoke or drink or go to movies. Later in life, he learned that we become Christians by faith, by putting our confidence and trust in Jesus Christ, by putting our whole weight on Christ as Saviour. Then the Holy Spirit can guide us into the do's and don'ts that fit our situation.

We become Christians when we allow Jesus Christ to become the center of our lives. He will take over the steering wheel when we put faith and trust and confidence in Him to be our sole salvation. Then Christ becomes our strength and our Redeemer. "For by grace are ye saved through faith; and that not of yourselves: it is the gift of God: not of works, lest any man should boast" (Eph. 2:8-9).

AM I REALLY SAVED? ●

I became a Christian recently, but now I'm wondering if I'm really saved. When I asked the Lord into my life, I was at a church meeting. Everyone's eyes were closed as the speaker asked those who wanted to accept Christ to raise their hands. Shouldn't a person stand before a group of Christians and publicly proclaim his faith when accepting Christ?

You don't have to make a speech in order to be a Christian. Paul was on the road to Damascus when the Lord spoke to him and he was converted as soon as he rose to his feet. It was later that he went about telling others what had happened.

In the church we have a service that makes it easier to proclaim our faith publicly. In New Testament times, people went down to the river to be baptized. This baptism was a public act that no doubt looked rather absurd to society, but it symbolized the death, burial, and resurrection of the Lord Jesus. When the newly baptized people came out of the water, people knew they were Christians. Your church probably makes provision for baptism also. Most churches allow the person at baptism to say a few words about what his faith means to him. They may even help him put his words together.

One good thing about sharing your experience verbally is that other Christians will be happy to know you have come to the Lord. They in turn will be glad to help you as you grow in the faith. Christian fellowship is an important and wonderful feature of the Christian life. But don't think that a Christian witness always means saying something. It also involves changed behavior, a loving spirit, charitable acts, and caring for other human beings. Most people are terrified of public speaking, but they may be gifted at doing the works of the Lord. So work out your Christian experience in the way that best expresses your own personality and gifts, whether by words or by actions.

NO CHRISTIAN JOY ●

I'm a Christian, but I don't feel the love and joy of the Lord. I am deeply committed to God, but I rarely get those enthusiastic feelings. At times it's easier to show love and joy when I'm with my Christian friends, but it's the non-Christians who need it!

People come in an assortment of personality types. Some people find it easier to be up and happy and positive than do other people. I know many people who feel exactly like you do. They find it much easier to be joyful and happy with other Christians, especially in worship, than they do in the workaday world. So their worship experiences become a kind of group therapy as they "hype" each other up. They feel that by singing together and holding hands and talking about the Lord, they can raise their spirits.

I don't think there's anything wrong with that behavior. In fact, it may help these people to get out of themselves for a while. After they've stretched their spirits in that kind of setting, they're able to be more stretched when they're in the world. Unfortunately, though, it doesn't always work that way. I find that in many cases people find such happiness in worshiping together that they begin to equate the Christian life with this emotion. They then build their lives around this emotion rather than around Jesus Christ. They get so involved in a continual round of worship services that they don't have time for their non-Christian friends.

I have a friend who earns his living in the "positive living" circuit. He hypes people up with his enthusiasm and exuberance, but when he comes home he's a basket case. When he walks through the front door, he goes from one end of the continuum to the other. As far as his family knows, he's a totally depressed human being. His Christian "joy" disappears in the real world.

It's important to keep in mind that feelings follow actions. True joy is the result of worthwhile activity. That activity can be something as simple as expressing gratitude. Counting our blessings is a great way to raise our spirits. There are other actions that lead to joy too. Do something useful. Make a contribution. Help somebody. Too many people try to work up the emotion, so that they will feel like doing something useful. The truth is, it works the opposite way. Get involved in some loving activity and joy will follow.

HOW DO I BELIEVE? •

I'm sixteen and want to become a Christian, but I don't know how. I want to know God better and learn more about Him, but I'm not sure how to do that either. I've been praying and reading the Bible. But I need to talk with other Christians and begin going to

church again. How do I decide where? My friends are not Christians, so they can't help me.

Let me assure you that you don't have to go to church to become a Christian. Christ is present with you now and He is very interested in your life. And, though the church could help you receive Christ, you could open your heart right now and invite Christ in. All you have to do is hear Him knock at your heart's door and open it to Him. He has promised to come in and He will keep His promise.

It is still important for you to become part of a church. You need to have fellowship with other believers, including those your own age. Go to your phone book and look up Youth for Christ, Young Life, or Campus Crusade—these are all organizations that have high-school ministries. Call and explain your situation to them. Tell them where you live and they will help you find a Christ-centered church near your home where there's an active youth program and an understanding pastor.

You need to be with other Christians so you can grow as a Christian. Scripture speaks of the Christian church as Christ's body. Each Christian is a member in that body—an arm, a leg, a hand. None of us comes complete with all the equipment we need to function. We need others to help us. I've often said that the last individual act a person ever does is to receive Jesus Christ as Saviour. From the moment you invite Him into your heart, you are part of His body, and you're never alone again. You always have others who can come to your side and support you.

Besides the fellowship of other believers, you need a pastor. *Pastor* means "shepherd." A shepherd guides his flock to places where the sheep can find food, water, and protection. Similarly, there are many pastors who would be willing to be your friend and help you with your day-to-day problems. Don't try to go it alone any longer—make that phone call and start looking for your church.

WAYS TO WITNESS •

How do you witness to someone? What are the basic tools and guidelines? Are there any good resources to help me lead others to Christ?

Some people witness out of a sense of guilt or duty. They go out and buttonhole people to tell them about Christ. The witnesser may feel like he is fulfilling God's command or at least satisfying the pastor, but in reality this kind of witnessing doesn't accomplish very much. It is mechanical and it comes across as an attack.

True witnessing is built on relationships that say, "I care." When we really care for an individual, we get to know him and find out his needs. Then, on the basis of our friendship, we can quite naturally introduce him to Christ. If witnessing were just a matter of telling, God grossly overcomplicated the Incarnation. He could have done skywriting, for instance, or He could wake up the world every morning with an announcement on some great loudspeaker. But God doesn't do that. Instead He tells us to go into the world just as Jesus did, as a servant.

There are several fine books on witnessing. I recommend these five: *Evangelism and the Sovereignty of God,* by J.I. Packer; *Good News Is for Sharing,* by Leighton Ford; *Life-Style Evangelism,* by Joseph C. Aldrich; *Out of the Salt Shaker,* by Rebecca Manley Pippert; and *How to Give Away Your Faith,* by Paul Little. All these books put the emphasis where it ought to be—on a God-centered approach that gives the Holy Spirit room to work, rather than on a man-centered, manipulative approach.

A FOOL FOR CHRIST? ●

How do you overcome the fear of rejection? I want to share Christ with others, but I'm afraid they will ridicule me or make me look foolish.

I think the fear of rejection comes from a misunderstanding of the nature of witnessing. It is important for us always to realize that we're not presenting ourselves, but Christ. We're not telling people that we have it all together and they should be like us. Instead, we're like one beggar telling another beggar where to find bread. Both the person who is witnessing and the person he is witnessing to are sinners. The one who has been redeemed tells the one who hasn't yet heard the Good News that he too can be redeemed. Witnessing is simply sharing.

Then too, the motivation for witnessing should be joy and love rather than guilt and obligation. If a person's motivation is wrong, I think he should stop witnessing and spend time refining his personal relationship with the Lord until he's glad he's a Christian. Then let the witness be a spillover of God's goodness.

Most people do most of their witnessing in their first year of being a

Christian. This is because when they first come to Christ, they have non-Christian friends with whom they have real relationships. They are forced, then, to share with these friends what has happened in their lives, and many of their friends come to know Christ too. But eventually, they get into the Christian hothouse and no longer have close friends among non-Christians. Any time you try to witness to someone you don't know really well, you feel threatened. The natural conclusion is that we need to develop relationships with non-Christians before we can witness to them. If you witness to a friend, the fear of rejection is much less.

MY TESTIMONY IS DULL ●

My testimony is not very exciting. I grew up in a Christian home and have been a Christian for as long as I can remember. At times, members of our church will stand up and share their testimonies. I'm afraid to, because I don't have any wonderful stories of rising from some dark hole of sin and seeing the light. I think people would be bored to tears with my testimony. I almost want to make something up to give it some excitement. Can a person be a witness for Jesus without a good story to tell?

There are a lot more people like you than like the others, so people can probably identify more with the person who has lived a relatively level life than with those who have gone to extremes. In fact, the kind of testimony meeting you describe can easily become a "Can-you-top-this?" kind of thing. When that happens, people are no longer glorifying the Lord. The listeners are getting vicarious enjoyment from hearing about sins that they haven't experienced, while the speakers are enjoying talking about themselves rather than about Christ.

Generally speaking, people who have been caught in the depths of sin and have felt its true agony don't want to talk about it. It's sort of like war stories—people who were in the thick of battle are not the ones who tell the stories. You almost have to pry information out of them, because the experience was so unpleasant that they want to put it behind them.

This urge to embellish a testimony can be a real trap. I have a friend who, when he was a young Christian, spread the word that he had been a professional baseball player. I think he had actually had a tryout someplace, and they sent him home. Yet most of the kids in his town hadn't even had a tryout, so eventually it got into his testimony that he had played for one of the major league teams. The story got more and more elaborate, until one day he decided he had to put an end to it. It was very difficult, but he felt very relieved to finally be able to say he was just an ordinary guy who wanted to serve the Lord. I think we were all relieved, in fact, because that's what people suspected all along.

Stick to the truth. The Lord will bless your testimony if it is true, not if it is embellished.

SHARING WITH THE FAMILY ●

I am the only Christian in my family. When we get together, everyone seems uncomfortable because of my faith. They keep asking why I'm not like the rest of them. I don't want to cause family dissension, but I would like to share Christ with them. They refuse to discuss anything connected with my faith, however.

When you are the only Christian in your family, it is easy to feel like a marked person. You tend to think that people are always writing you off because you are a Christian, whereas, in reality they may not give your religion much thought at all. I had a problem like yours when I first became a Christian. Unfortunately, I didn't handle it well. I went through our family and systematically alienated everyone.

This happened because I thought of the Christian faith in terms of two things: judgment and martyrdom. I was so convinced that I was right and they were wrong that they thought I was judging them all the time. Maybe they were right. And then I went around emphasizing what I had given up. When offered a drink, I couldn't just ask for a Coke; I had to discuss the evils of alcohol. My emphasis was on lifestyle rather than on the reality of the hope and peace and confidence found in the Gospel of Jesus Christ. I became argumentative and tried to work every situation around to a discussion of the Gospel. Before long I had nobody left to talk to.

Since then I have discovered something important about communication. People talk about things in a kind of ascending hierarchy. It is easiest to talk about impersonal things like the weather, events, automobiles, and ball scores. Next, we talk about people; then ideas, and finally, our feelings. Only a few people can handle talking about ideas and almost nobody is comfortable talking about personal feelings. In fact, you can go to group meetings or neighborhood parties and find that no one ever gets above the people level. Yet, new Christians often jump in to conversations at the idea or feeling level. This is very threatening to most people.

If we jump in like a bull in a china shop, we are likely to do damage. Far better to show by our changed attitudes and lives that Jesus has made a difference to us. Then we can wait until the Holy Spirit opens up opportunities for us to speak to individuals privately.

DISCUSSING GOD WITH KIDS •

How do we make God relevant to a teenager's daily life? Sometimes, it's difficult to discuss spiritual matters with my children, and yet as a Christian parent, this is supposedly one of my greatest responsibilities and privileges.

To understand how we can apply spiritual things to a teenager's daily life, it helps to first take a broader look at youth in general. In other words, we communicate much differently with small children than with high schoolers. When children are quite young, we try to develop an open and accepting attitude toward God. God is good; God is loving and caring. This is where Bible stories come in. Children are interested in knowing how God dealt with people in the past, and though their attention spans are relatively short, children are eager and open to learn about spiritual things.

When you communicate with kids who are junior high age, you'll discover they have an incredible appetite for facts. They know all the names of all the dinosaurs and the names of all the ships in the British navy. They also like to correct adults; if you give a list of items and leave anything out, they'll be the first to remind you. Because they like facts, lists, and memorization, this is a good age to encourage memorization of Bible verses.

High school kids are primarily into the business of applied information—assimilating truths into real-life situations. So when trying to talk to a high schooler about God, understand that the kid is really not interested so much in data as he is in knowing how this verse or truth affects his life. Apply the Christian faith to situations that come up around the home or to situations at school. Don't force your teens to sit and listen to long portions of Scripture every evening. You need to be a little more creative than that. Once you've established the attitude that God is relevant to a teenager, he will develop a hearty appetite for God's Word.

OPENING DOORS •

I think it's impossible in today's world to hold a family together without Christ, but a friend of mine is trying. She doesn't know Jesus personally, but does know that her home and family are worth saving. I would like to lead her to Christ but feel that the time is not right. She lives far away, so it's difficult. But she is receptive to talking about the Lord. How can I open the door of salvation for her?

It is probably wrong to think that your friend's marriage will be saved if she comes to Christ. Sometimes, if one partner is a Christian and the other is not, this even makes the marriage more difficult. In fact, I would not go so far as to say that it is impossible to hold a family together without Christ. We simply have a better chance of doing so with Christ, because then we agree on a set of values that are centered on one Person and we are going in the same direction. Of course, you want your friend to come to Christ, but don't get the idea that this will solve all her problems.

Let me suggest that you write her a careful letter describing how you yourself came to Christ. It would be a good idea to take your letter to your pastor to let him read it and make suggestions. Then pray about the letter before you send it off. Encourage her to read good books, particularly *How to Be Born Again,* by Billy Graham, or *Born Again,* by Charles Colson. Both books are by respected people who present the Gospel in an attractive way. You might want to send her one of the books along with your letter.

Pray that your friend will receive your letter well. Call her up after she has had time to read it and ask how she feels about it. Suggest that she talk the ideas over with her husband. Then give the Holy Spirit time to work. If your friend knows that you are not meddling, but that you have a genuine love and concern for her family, this can be a powerful witnessing tool. Perhaps you will indeed be able to "open the door of salvation for her."

REACHING EAST •

My friend's family is Buddhist. Her parents won't allow her to go to church with me until she is eighteen (she's fifteen now). She

doesn't want to follow her family's beliefs, but at the moment she has no choice. I pray for her all the time, asking the Holy Spirit to work in her and in her family. Is there anything else I can do for her?

We evangelicals believe that in obedience to Jesus Christ, we must go into all the world and preach the Gospel to every creature. We believe that because Christ has done so much for us, it would be unfair not to tell others about the best thing that has ever happened to us. It would be like discovering penicillin and keeping it a secret. Christ has made such a difference in our lives that we want everybody to have the Good News.

Our attitudes may create problems among people whose religion teaches, above all, tolerance for all faiths. Buddhists feel that it is very bad to try to convert them from their faith, which they think embraces all of reality, to another one, which by definition could embrace only part. They see Christian evangelism as a sign of arrogance and intolerance. So if we are trying to share our faith with Buddhists, we must be very perceptive. We must never be combative, argumentative, or judgmental.

The first step in winning your friend is to show her its validity by the quality of your life, your own personal happiness, your ability to cope with challenges, and your compassion for her and for others. In other words, show her by your lifestyle rather than by words that your faith is adequate or perhaps superior. Then begin to share the source of your lifestyle. Christ is the center of your life. When you're sharing, keep in mind a person and not a system. You might invite her to Campus Life or some other Christian group at school; such meetings might not threaten her family like church would.

Whatever you do, don't drive a wedge between her and her mother. Family is extremely important to Buddhists, and by doing that you would lose all the way around. Embrace the whole family in your love. Let them know that it is because you love them that you want to share the Good News about Jesus Christ.

I'M A HYPOCRITE ●

Recently I dated a non-Christian, and one evening we had sex. I feel sick about the situation because I've never compromised in this area before and have always tried to demonstrate Christian values to this person. I feel especially bad because he told me he was attracted to me because my life was different. Will I be held responsible if he doesn't become a Christian? I apologized for being a hypocrite, but since then he has moved away.

Christians often feel that they are in a control position, that they are in some way responsible for other people's actions. We seem to think we have the power to change their lives. I think we need to realize that, though we do affect other people's lives, we're not responsible for them. After we've done everything right, our friends can do wrong. And conversely, after we've done everything wrong, they can choose to do right. Each person stands on his own two feet before God.

Your sexual encounter was a two-way street. You were both involved in it, and you are equally responsible for it. There's a side of it that you, as a woman, need to understand. Males respond to brief sexual encounters quite differently from females. A woman is affected much more deeply by a one-time sexual experience than is a man. That is, the man does not feel nearly the sense of guilt and involvement that the woman feels. My guess is that it's not nearly as important to him as it seems to you, and that you are reading your feelings into his.

You've done the right thing. You've asked his forgiveness and the Lord's. That's all you can do. You have to move on now, realizing that you've learned a valuable lesson. Sex, contrary to what people tell us today, is not a mere physical amusement. It's not like eating chocolate. It involves your emotions and your spiritual life. Forget this incident, but plan in the future to express yourself sexually only within the confines of marriage, where your deep emotions can be used for growth rather than for guilt.

COMMITTED OR NOT? •

A year ago our twenty-six-year-old son moved out of the house and into an apartment with his girlfriend. He says he believes in God and he thinks he made a commitment at the age of ten at a revival meeting in our church. But after that, the pastor and the church members didn't give him the teaching and support he needed and now he says he isn't really sure if he made that commitment. I feel like I've failed him in this matter and the church should have followed up better too. Is it too late to begin discipling him now?

It is legitimate for parents to want their children to be in the kingdom. But sometimes, to assure ourselves, we reach back to some very weak events. The commitment a ten-year-old may have made in a revival meeting may have been based on a real desire at the moment, but if in the intervening sixteen years there has been little indication that the person has received Christ, we would have to conclude that the seed fell on stony ground. Jesus said, "Ye shall know them by their fruits" (Matt. 7:16).

This does not mean that your son is beyond salvation. The important thing to consider is not what happened when he was ten, but where he is right now. His behavior would indicate that he's a considerable distance from the Christian church and from Christ's teachings. He has apparently become enamored with the prevailing societal norms. Society sees no problem with his lifestyle; in fact, many respected people who run banks and businesses live this way. But just because society accepts it doesn't make it right. Jesus has set up the norm for Christian relationships.

I would encourage you to pray for your son. Think of him as a person who definitely needs to come to know Christ. Emphasize his experience today rather than sixteen years ago. Pray that somehow, as he tries to fill his soul with the husks that society provides, he will become hungry and find that leftovers won't meet his needs. Pray he will then turn to the living Christ. Don't spend your time blaming others or trying to fan the spark of a ten-year-old's commitment. It is as a twenty-six-year-old that he needs to face up to his real needs and make a commitment to Christ. Pray that he will obey the voice of the Holy Spirit as He faithfully speaks to him.

UNBELIEVING ROOMMATE •

I'm attending a secular college and I feel this is where the Lord wants me to be. But I'm having problems with my non-Christian roommate. We live in a coed dorm with almost no restrictions on having women on the floor. Often I will come back to the room after studying, and my roommate will have his girlfriend there. I feel impolite for walking into my own room. They've never asked me to leave, but I sure get the impression that that is what they want me to do. I want to be a witness to my roommate, but I don't want to put him off either.

One answer would be to apply for another roommate at the end of the quarter. Find a Christian to room with and uncomplicate your life. But I'm not sure we ought to be looking for uncomplicated lives. You may be able to have a real effect on your roommate.

I've lived in non-Christian fraternity houses, and over the years my fraternity brothers have, almost to a man, contacted me at stress points in their lives. They have asked for help and spiritual counsel, and some have become Christians. But people like this are impressed by consistent Christian living, not by verbal witnesses. They aren't interested in listening to sermons.

My specific suggestion to you is this: you paid for your half of the room; live in it. If your roommate were to write me, he'd probably say, "I have this roommate, sort of a religious fellow, who comes in and sits in his chair and studies at his desk and sleeps in his bed right when I want to bring my girlfriend into the room. What do I do?" I'd let him deal with that. Go about your life in an orderly and thoughtful fashion, and let him figure out how to solve his problem. To make arrangements so he could have his hour of freedom would be bad for both of you.

Don't be judgmental about this; just live your Christian life in front of him. *Witness* isn't something you say or do; it's something you are. At some point he is likely to say, "You seem to be a normal person. How do you live without the things that make my life interesting?" You can then say, "Well, I don't have as many headaches; I don't have as much struggle; I don't have as much guilt. I live this way not because God forces me to, but because He loves me and shows me a better way."

BABE IN CHRIST ●

I recently led a younger friend to the Lord and have been trying hard to get her involved in a good church. I want to get her life in Christ off to a good start. But she has resisted my efforts and continues to wallow in her old ways. She has a promiscuous past and is trying to get her act together. I really believe she is saved, but I don't know how to encourage her without sounding like a parent. I don't want her to get angry with me.

First, I would like to deal with the possibility that your friend is not a Christian. You mention that she is younger than you. It is sometimes possible for a respected older person to dominate a younger person and force him to agree with certain principles. But the Christian life is not agreement with principles; it is a work of the Spirit. In fact, unless the Holy Spirit draws a person, that person cannot come to God.

But in our day we often reduce Christianity to a set of precepts. If you get these ideas across and the other person agrees with them, then suddenly, he is a Christian. It is usually a losing battle to take a person who has given mental assent to certain precepts and expect that person to give evidence of the transforming, miraculous power of conversion. I would leave the possibility open that your friend is not yet a Christian. Continue to pray that the Holy Spirit will speak to her and that she will respond and truly become a new creature in Christ Jesus.

On the other hand, many people who are genuinely converted (and you say you believe she is) struggle their whole lives with their besetting sin. I always think of the nobleman in Charles Dickens' *A Tale of Two Cities,* who for many years worked as a shoemaker in prison. Later in life, whenever he ran into problems, he went up to the attic and made shoes. When a person has been enslaved by sin and then suddenly becomes a Christian, often he reverts to his sin whenever stress comes.

You need to help your friend replace her besetting sin with a new lifestyle. This is best done by surrounding the newly converted person with caring friends who live for Christ. Get her in a church where she can be supported by the body of Christ. A new environment will help her grow and move along. You know all this, of course, yet she resists your efforts in this direction. But ask yourself, "How patient has God been with me? How often have I had to claim 1 John 1:9 and confess my sins?" If God is so patient with us, then we should be equally patient with new babes in Christ.

DEAD TO THE GOSPEL •

Recently I came to know Christ at a church retreat. My parents are not Christians, but they encourage us kids to go to church if we want. I'm concerned about my parents' salvation. Every time I try to share Christ with them, they seem to have a "Don't-start-preaching-at-me" attitude. Is there a way I can witness to them without turning them off?

It's very hard to witness to parents by talking. They always see you "bottoms up"—they remember putting a diaper on you; all your life you will be their "child." This is especially true during your adolescent years. Most parents simply aren't willing to admit that a child of theirs knows a secret of the universe that they don't know. If you lock horns with them, they will feel threatened.

You can witness without words, however, through living the Christian life in a manner that is winsome, attractive, and convincing to your parents. If you've been a grump, a smartmouth, or a scatterbrain; and then suddenly after you become a Christian you become caring, consistent, and helpful, your parents will notice. They may wonder what you're up to, but if your good behavior continues, they will be impressed.

Most parents, no matter what they think about Christ, want their children to be happy and joyful, to lead meaningful lives and to have a sense of purpose. If your parents sense that your Christian faith has given you these things, they are likely to be interested in it. Now, families vary a great deal. Some, at this point, will want to sit down and have a long discussion with you about why you've changed. Others won't want to talk about it at all. You'll have to figure out your family's style and build on that. Just remember that the most powerful witness you can give them is a consistently Christian life.

EXCUSES, EXCUSES ●

My mother is not a Christian. I've tried to talk with her about the Lord, but immediately she gets defensive. "I can't go to church," she says, or, "I have too much to do." I suggested she watch a minister on TV, but she still makes excuses. I've suggested she read and study the Bible, but she won't do that either. I'm afraid she will die without being saved. She is eighty-four years old. What more can I do?

You need to pray for her, of course, and love her and support her. But realize that very few parents are ever led to Christ by their children, especially when the parent is eighty-four years old. People get very defensive about their experience at that age. They don't like the fact that no one takes their advice anymore and everyone is trying to lead them around like a child. Therefore, they say, "I have a little bit of me left and I'm going to be stubborn about it. I know what I believe and you're not going to tell me to change it."

Nevertheless, a great spiritual battle may be taking place inside such a person's mind. One old gentleman told me once, "I have long days and weary hours and much time to pray." Many old people may do a great deal more praying than we think. Separate the idea of going to church from being a Christian. Your mother can become a Christian without ever setting foot out of her house or listening to a TV preacher.

I have found that there are people who make bargains with God. They say something like, "At least I'm not a hypocrite. God and I know where I stand. I've talked to God and I'm willing to face Him on my conditions and my terms." Sometimes, those terms are very biblical. The person is not rebelling against Christ, but against a kind of "churchianity" or imposed phony Christianity that he encountered in the past. So don't believe that what you see on the surface is all that's happening. God works in us "both to will and to do of His good pleasure".(Phil. 2:13), and He is working in your mother too.

CHAPTER 32

Growing As a Christian

Devotions, prayer, and the study of Scripture are all means to the Christian life, not the Christian life itself. The devotional life allows us to meet with God; it becomes a time of communicating with Him and hearing His Word to us. Prayer is more than asking and receiving: in its deeper sense, it too is relational communication. In prayer, we enjoy God's loving presence, and we learn to listen for His voice. The Scriptures are a trustworthy written record of God's revelation to man. Scripture, for the Christian, is like a plumb line. It provides a reference point, a way to compare our experiences with God's truth. It becomes a guide to faith that keeps us away from the ups and downs of a life based on experience alone.

A Christian who has no devotional life, spends no time in prayer, and does not read the Scriptures is like a lover who never spends time with his or her loved one. Absence does not make the heart grow fonder. "Out of sight, out of mind" is the more applicable phrase. Brother Lawrence had the right idea when he wrote his classic handbook on the devotional life, *The Practice of the Presence of God.* If we remember that we are always in God's presence, our devotions, prayer, and Scripture reading will take on new meaning.

FAMILY DEVOTIONS A FLOP? ●

Family devotions are a flop. How can we make devotion time an interesting and rewarding experience?

We must understand at the outset that family devotions are a modern invention of the church, encouraged by pastors and youth workers to help our children. They are not, however, a fetish, something we must do a certain way or risk failure as parents.

Our lives are divided into chapters, and certain things will work at one time that don't work at all at another. It is virtually impossible to have a spiritual discussion at the breakfast table with a ten-year-old while a two-year-old is eating his cereal. A devotional approach that appeals to a kindergartner would bring tears of boredom to the eyes of a high school student. The time, the method, and the content of family devotions must all be adapted to your own family's ages and stages.

Rather than making the whole family sit around the table while the baby plays with his food or tries to climb out of the high chair, put the baby down for a nap and then gather the older children around you to listen to Bible stories. We've found that the family Bible story series by Gilbert Beers is very appropriate for children with a fifteen- to twenty-minute attention span. The children enjoy the stories and are usually quite willing to discuss them.

As children become teenagers, devotions are usually more effective if carried on informally. Many teenagers don't particularly enjoy being forced to listen to Dad read for a while. But parents can bring up a topic and say, "What do you think of this?" I try to ask the question from the youngest to the oldest, so the little ones get a shot at it before all the good information is used up.

Probably the most damaging approach is the one that seems to be advocated by some Sunday School literature. Dad is at one end of the table; Mother is at the other; the children are looking with rapt attention while Dad reads some long text. In my thirty years of ministry, I've never run into anyone who has made this method work. All teachers know that the lecture method is the least effective way to get ideas across, so let's quit wishing we could more consistently use this ineffective method with our families.

Instead, let's be creative about devotions. We don't have to be reading proof texts to be talking about God or His creation. When we talk with our children about respect, authority, values, habits, society; when we watch television, question the world's values, and discuss what God's Word says about these things; when we talk over a problem from school concerning unfairness, unkindness, or insensitivity—we are indeed having devotions and instilling Christian values.

We should ever be aware that we live in our Father's world; He created it and all the beauty and goodness in it are His. We see the glory of the Lord in His love for us. God loved us so much that He sent His Son to the world, and He came among us and identified in every way with the human condition. As a human being, He understood our failures and offered Himself as the substitute for our sins and the Saviour of our souls. This scheme of things is beautiful. It is not stilted and wooden and "religious," but living and full of song, joy, common sense, and goodness. We are trying to convey this beauty to our children. We do it with a smile, with discipline, with laughter, with prayer—by our lifestyles as well as our words. This is what family devotions are all about.

QUIET TIME IS TOO ROUTINE ●

Daily devotions seem so routine and mechanized to me. Quite frankly, they are boring. I've tried everything from devotional guides to group study, but my heart just isn't in it. Others can't wait to dive into their daily quite time. How do I catch this enthusiasm and make devotions an interesting and exciting time?

When I don't have my devotional time, I don't necessarily feel guilty, but my day doesn't seem to go as well. Yet I know what you are talking about, because I have also experienced occasional boredom with the devotions routine. People love to set up standards and say, "This is the way the Christian life is supposed to be lived." You hear slogans like "No Bible, no breakfast," or "No prayer, no pillow." These are intended to help us. But if the helps to Christian living become confused with the Christian life itself, and if we feel guilty for not practicing the helps, we may be confusing the means and the end.

Prayer, Bible study, and having a devotional life are not the Christian life; they are means to it. The Christian life is based on discipleship and obedience to Christ. It involves living in accordance with His will, being His representative in the world, doing practical works of charity, and doing the work of the Lord. If the devotional life is a help to that, that's great—but devotions should never replace discipleship in our minds.

To have a successful devotional life, it's important to establish what your best time is. We tend to be either morning people or night people. Some people consider it a great accomplishment just to get vertical in the morning without running into walls and sharp objects. Other people jump out of bed singing. A morning person should no doubt have his devotions in the morning, but morning would be a dreadful time for a night person.

Whatever time you choose for your devotions, first pray for the Holy Spirit's guidance. Commit this time to God and say, "Dear God, through the power of Your Holy Spirit, help this to be a valuable and important time to me." Then open your Bible and read until God gives you something. When He does, stop and apply it to your life. Make it part of yourself. Then go into your prayertime. Let me encourage you not to make prayertime a "gimme" time. I've found an acrostic that helps. It's based on the word *ACTS:* Adoration, Confession, Thanksgiving, Supplication. Paying attention to all sides of prayer helps make my devotional life more meaningful. I hope these ideas will help you too.

DOES PRAYING HELP? ●

At times I struggle in my Christian walk with doubts and unanswered questions. When I search for guidance, I am always told to pray. I do pray, but sometimes it seems as if God doesn't hear my prayers or doesn't answer them. I wonder if it really helps to pray.

We can be sure God hears our prayers. Scripture says, "The Lord's hand is not shortened, that it cannot save; neither His ear heavy, that it cannot hear" (Isa. 59:1). The problem in communication is obviously not with God. However, I think there are a lot of misconceptions about prayer. A lot of the current books on prayer ought to have titles like, *How to Get Something You Want from God,* or, *How to Push God's Hot Button.* In the secular world there are terrible books about manipulation and taking care of "Number One." Some Christian books on prayer seem to be trying to keep up with them.

The prayer of asking is only the kindergarten of prayer. The graduate school of prayer is attempting to align oneself with God's will. Prayer is spending enough time in God's presence to know His will and to be ready to move within its confines.

Over the last few years, perhaps because of some of the stresses that come with my work, I have become a real believer in prayer. I don't understand completely how it works, but I know it does work in my life. As I pray about things, I get poise; I get confidence; I feel direction; I sense

God's presence and partnership; and God helps me. Therefore, I pray about everything. I give God the right to say no if He wants to; I can accept that. The important thing is that I'm talking to God about it.

After they tell me their problems, people often say, "Jay, don't tell me to pray about it. Tell me something real." Well, to a Christian, the most real thing we can do is communicate with God. What better could a child do, for instance, than tell his parents about his problem? The child may not know what the parents are going to do, but he knows they will put some forces in action that will somehow help him. That is the way I look at prayer. I bring my concerns before God, knowing that He will work in ways I don't understand to bring about what I really need, though not necessarily what I want.

UNANSWERED PRAYERS ●

All my life I prayed that my children would grow up to love the Lord. Two did and two didn't. I'm disappointed that God didn't work in their lives to a greater extent. Did all my years of praying go to waste?

First of all, understand that God has worked and continues to work in their lives as well as in yours and mine. Our prayers for one another are not to make God work harder. They are not to talk an unwilling God into doing something He'd rather not do, or an unloving God into being kind, or an insensitive God into caring, or a casual God into getting serious, or an ineffectual God into using more powerful methods on people. To think this way is to distort the very meaning of prayer.

God is at work in all of our lives, at all times. By His Holy Spirit, He speaks to us through every human experience as well as through His Word. Your children do not prove God's lack of interest, but rather the fact that God has given us the right to choose good or evil. And sadly, many choose evil.

You are at a time in your life when you are undoubtedly becoming a bit anxious about the future. You know you will not be around forever, and you would love to see your effort bear fruit in your children's lives. But it may well be that your children will not respond during your lifetime. Indeed, they may never respond to God's grace. But given human experience, given the history of young people who have been raised as your children have, it is likely that they will eventually commit themselves to the Lord and begin to live for Him.

Your prayers and effort have not gone to waste. They are at work this very moment—but perhaps not in the way you have imagined. You are not like a person at a carnival who has to squeeze a machine at a certain level in order to get results. God is not in heaven waiting for us to squeeze harder before He answers our prayers. In fact, His answers are not related to our efforts.

When we pray, we align ourselves with the primary will of God. We agree with Him about what is good. Then we allow Him to work in our lives as well as through independent circumstances in order to bring about His will in the life of the person we are praying for. Prayer is not magic or hocus-pocus. It is talking to a Person who loves our children infinitely more than we do. When we pray, then, we are siding with God against evil and for the good of our children.

HOW TO KNOW THE BIBLE ●

There must be a way to understand the Bible better. I'm not always sure what it's trying to say. I also find it difficult to concentrate when I'm reading the Bible. How do I get started?

To get to know the Bible is more than a lifetime task. The secrets of God and mankind are hidden within Scripture. Therefore, the greatest scholar can spend his entire life in deep study of God's Word and never plumb its depths. On the other hand, the simplest of us can expect the Holy Spirit to help us understand and interpret what we read in Scripture. The Apostle Paul did not write his letters so that people could subdivide them, comparing one against another. He wrote so that simple people could hear, understand, and apply his counsel to their lives. So the first and most basic step in understanding Scripture is to pray that the Holy Spirit will open it and enlighten you as you read.

Nowadays, there are many helps available to you. First and foremost is the church. Join a local congregation where the Gospel is preached and the Bible taught in a serious manner from the pulpit. Find a Sunday School class where you can get to know God's Word. The church is a great resource. It is free, and there you can be with people who will understand you and share your concerns.

At many churches, you will find small-group Bible studies available. The people who attend these are like you—wanting to learn more, hungry and thirsty for the Word of God. Through group study and good guidebooks, you can learn more together. You can also go to your local Christian bookstore and find many books, including modern Bible translations, that will help you understand Scripture, book by book or topic by topic. And Christian radio brings you Bible classes and quality preaching. Find a radio speaker whom you especially like and make a habit of tuning in regularly to hear that person. This will give you continuity, not bits and pieces. You can even take correspondence courses from Bible colleges or institutes that will help you understand the Word.

So you are in much better shape than a person would have been in Corinth or Galatia in Paul's day. There are so many places and people who are ready to help you study Scripture. I encourage you to begin to take advantage of these resources, beginning this Sunday, by getting into a church and Sunday School class.

LOST MEMORY? ●

We have a son who is eighteen and a daughter who is sixteen, and we love them dearly. They are both intelligent children, but for the life of me, I can't get them to memorize Bible verses or to try their best in school. I know my working forty-five hours a week doesn't help, but with what little energy I have left I have tried to make learning interesting to them. But they won't listen. Where have I gone wrong?

Probably in your understanding of human nature. We read the verse, "Thy word have I hid in my heart, that I might not sin against Thee" (Ps. 119:11), and we would like to think of our young people like the shepherd David, sitting on the hillside thinking great eternal thoughts. But stop a minute to think about David. He's a young boy sent out all alone into the wilderness to watch his father's flocks. He wrestles with a bear and kills it with some primitive tool. He kills a lion by grabbing it by the beard and slaying it.

Now think of our own protected young people. You call your son and daughter "children," even though they are eighteen and sixteen years old. You work forty-five hours a week so you can buy them everything they need. They don't sense that they need God; their parents stand between them and God to cushion life's shocks.

People memorize Bible verses and gain knowledge in order to cope with difficult situations. A person who is allowed to struggle with his own problems eventually says, "I need help." And then he begins to look to the Lord. Most of our children in America are not going to turn to God until they get out on their own and begin to struggle. This may happen in their mid-twenties rather than in their teens, because young people in our society are kept dependent so long.

There's nothing wrong with you or your son or daughter. You'll be amazed, when they start raising their own children, how much they will do it just as you have done. By the time they're thirty, you'll realize you taught them far more than you thought.

WHY GROW? ●

My husband only recently began to read the Word. Just when he was beginning to learn about the Lord, a fellow at our church told him that he should ask Christ into his heart and he would be saved. He did this, but then he stopped reading the Bible. He doesn't think it's necessary anymore because he is already saved. I know a commitment must take place, but doesn't a person have to continue in prayer and Bible study?

Prayer and Bible study don't save people. Christ saves people when they put their faith and trust in Him. As Ephesians 2:8-9 says, "For by grace are ye saved through faith; and that not of yourselves: it is the gift of God: not of works, lest any man should boast."

And yet there is great danger in seeing the Christian faith as a transaction with God rather than a relationship. In the Bible, becoming a Christian is likened to being born, to marriage, and to adoption. All these are ongoing human relationships, not one-time transactions. No one ever becomes a person without being born, but we wouldn't say that birth is all there is to life. Life just starts there; then it continues for another seventy or eighty years. The Christian life also has a very important starting point, but it continues far beyond that.

Your husband is probably a victim of an emphasis you hear in certain churches where the story of salvation is made more important than anything else. People who have been Christians for forty years go over it again and again every Sunday morning. Repeatedly, they reaffirm what has taken place in their lives. But Hebrews 5:12—6:2 talks about laying aside these initial things and moving on, going from milk to meat.

Personally, I find that while my *becoming* a Christian is entirely Christ's work, the implications of *being* a Christian are so very involving that they take up my whole energy. Prayer and Bible study don't save people, but they certainly help people as they walk with Christ in their new lives in Him.

PROBLEMS IN THE PARSONAGE ●

My husband is a minister and counsels people about the necessity of having devotional time with God, but we don't have family devotions ourselves or even devotions as a couple. We had family devotions for a while, and I complained; I'm afraid I discouraged my husband. Now I really see the need for them. I apologized, but we still don't have them. How can I encourage my husband to begin devotions again?

From thousands of letters I have received, I have concluded that family devotions is an idea whose time has not come. People talk about them, but they don't do them. They can't seem to have devotions together because of schedule problems, personality differences, physical differences (some are morning people, some are night people), unresolved conflicts in their relationships, and a host of other barriers. Now, of course, having devotions together would help to break down those barriers. It would help to bring about forgiveness, understanding, and unanimity. But it seems to be a vicious circle. By the time a couple has reached the place of being capable of having devotions together regularly, they have probably solved most of the problems that keep people from having them.

Maybe for many of us the problem is with the methodology of devotions, not the idea itself. Most people don't think they are having devotions unless someone sits down and opens the Bible and says, "Now we are going to have devotions; let's communicate about God." That's a frightening thing to do. The fact is, you probably already communicate with each other about God, but it becomes almost impossible to do in this kind of artificial situation.

Family devotions don't have to be based on some picture you may have seen in Sunday School literature. Try instead emphasizing unity, commitment, and communication in Christ in all your family's interactions. Let your husband join the human race; he's human just like you are, and it's just as hard for him as for you. Start breaking down the barriers that may be keeping you apart—you may even get to the point of being able to have devotions together regularly. Until that day comes, don't enjoy your guilt too much. You are working on something more basic than a family ritual—you are trying to build family understanding and unity.

BETWEEN THE COVERS ●

The market today seems amply supplied with books that talk about Christianity and the Bible. Are there any guidelines for determining what is a biblically sound book?

Simply put, a biblically sound book is one that is consistent with Scripture—it teaches what Scripture teaches. The problem is that all too often the Bible is quoted out of context. Someone pulls a particular verse out of the Bible and writes an entire book on it, yet contradicts the Bible as a whole. Biblically sound books first discover the context of where the Scripture verse fits into the Bible and, second, what the Bible teaches on a particular issue in general. In the broadest sense, a biblically sound book is consistent with the Bible, teaches the scriptural message in a consistent manner, and doesn't use some portions of Scripture while throwing out others that should be included as relevant to the topic being explored.

When looking for good Christian books, you are probably safest beginning with a well-known publisher rather than an obscure one. It is also helpful to read reviews in trusted magazines. Many Christian magazines have book review columns. I read these constantly because there are so many books out there I couldn't begin to read them all. So I have to trust endorsements and recommendations. You might also talk to your pastor or to other people you trust. Ask them about a particular book. Frankly, I'm most worried about picking up a book that will waste my time. I have read many books, biblically sound and not, that have not contributed anything to my life because they were shallow, uncreative, or poorly written. Finally, the best book is the one that meets your personal preferences and needs. At different times in our lives, different things are important. At one time a particular book may have a great meaning; at other times it doesn't. I can remember as a boy reading a book called *In the Twinkling of an Eye*. It was a book about the Rapture and it so fascinated me that I must have read it a dozen times. But today, I think that book wouldn't speak to me in quite the same way. So as you look through the growing pile of Christian books, these are some guidelines that might help. And trust your Christian bookseller. Talk to the manager at the bookstore; he or she can help you a great deal.

CHAPTER 33

Living As a Christian

Henry David Thoreau spoke of marching to the beat of a different drummer. By and large, this is what it means to be Spirit-filled rather than worldly. It's the process of learning to listen for the quiet cadences of the kingdom instead of the loud, harsh drumbeats of this world's demands. We learn to listen for God's voice in every part of life, every part of the day's activity.

This process of marching to God's cadence separates us from the world. We become different creatures, witnesses of the power of God to a fallen world. We learn to trust in Him, to seek "first the kingdom of God, and His righteousness" (Matt. 6:33); and we discover that God embarrasses us with His goodness and His care and concern for our lives. He knows what we need before we even ask.

BUILDING A CHRISTIAN HOME ●

My wife and I recently became Christians and have had the joy of leading our two children to the Lord. How do we begin to create a Christian home? Just where do we start in developing an atmosphere of love and worship?

Without a doubt, this atmosphere starts with your relationship to one another. Few things are more powerful to young people than the knowledge that their parents truly love one another and have a commitment to God that means something in their relationship. As we live our lives in front of our kids, our example probably makes some of the strongest statements we'll ever make about God and His nature. God has chosen to reveal Himself to mankind through the vehicle of the family. God is a Father, we are His children; He is the Bridegroom, we are the bride; we are brothers and sisters in Christ; all these are family illustrations. I believe that most young people develop their ideas of God from a composite of their parents. So first of all, develop a godly, loving, caring, and consistent relationship to each other as husband and wife.

The second step has to do with your lifestyle and your relationship to others. Does the Christian faith you profess on Sunday relate to all people at all times? Do your children see you treating people fairly and carefully? And how do you relate to things? Are you more interested in material things than you are in people? Do you use God to get what you want, or do you see things to be used to the glory of God? However you respond to these questions will send a message to your children as to what you really think about your new Christian faith. It is your response that creates the atmosphere, not your words. Words are simply the vehicles to convey ideas. Living a consistent life in front of your children shows them that your Christianity is valid, real, and has meaning. The old saying, "Actions speak louder than words," has never been more relevant.

ARE OUR KIDS SPIRITUAL? •

How do we know where our kids are spiritually? They seem to be growing up fine and we don't really have any problems with them, but they don't talk about God and spiritual things too much.

In some ways what you're describing may be very healthy, because our Christian faith should not be something tacked on, a nonfunctional appendage at the outer edge of our lives. It's intended to work through the warp and woof of our daily lives. As Scripture says, "Whatsoever ye do in word or deed, do all in the name of the Lord Jesus, giving thanks to God and the Father by Him" (Col. 3:17). So in one sense, a person with a well-integrated Christian personality is not one who is religious but one who is Christian. That is, he worships God through all he is and does. He builds his whole life on the foundation of the Gospel, within the confines of the Christian world view.

In this sense, the best Christian is the least religious person. Religious activity can even militate against true spirituality. However, young people do not come equipped with Christian understanding. It's important to make connections for them, to help them understand why we act and believe the way we do. Why do Mom and Dad believe in fidelity, trust, and honesty with each other? Why are they committed to each other "till death us do part"? Why do we go to church every week and support the Lord's work financially? Why do we give our time to serve others and help the poor? We need to help our children see how these things are connected to the Lord who told us that the world is not our own, that nothing we have belongs to us. We are simply stewards of God's vineyard. As our children understand the motivation for what we do, they will understand spiritual values.

WHAT IS GOD'S WILL? •

How do I know when I'm doing God's will? How do I know that what I'm doing now is part of His plan?

A lot of people would like to open up the book of their lives and read the last chapter in order to find out if they're heading in the right direction. But our lives are much more like scrolls than like books. That is, the past is rolled up on one roll, and the future is rolled up on the other, and we can read only the part that is open in front of us.

What we have to do is make sure, first of all, that we want to follow the Lord. Then we have to obey Him specifically and consistently in every aspect of our lives. If we do the small things He asks us to do, we can be confident that the larger picture will turn out to be God's will for our lives. We read in Proverbs 3:5-6, "Trust in the Lord with all thine heart; and lean not unto thine own understanding. In all thy ways acknowledge Him, and He shall direct thy paths." So as we acknowledge Him in smaller things, He will direct us so that our lives will fulfill His purposes.

In my own life I have been blessed by seeing God's will in retrospect. As I do God's will daily, trying to obey Him in every decision, I cannot always be sure I am making the best choices. But as I look back at the past I can say, "I see how God worked in my life there. At the time all those things seemed confusing, but now they fit together to make a picture that glorifies God."

SPIRITUAL UPS AND DOWNS ●

Why do I have so many spiritual ups and downs? I look around at my friends and see how strong their faith is and what good Christians they are. I wish I could be like them, but I have such a long way to go. Is this a normal feeling? Maybe if I could get past these spiritual highs and lows, I would grow.

I don't think you are describing your spiritual life at all. What you are describing is your emotional nature. You apparently are the kind of person who has a broad range of highs and lows. I don't think you'll find anything in Scripture or human experience to indicate that becoming a Christian changes our emotional nature. Paul, before he became a Christian, was a single-minded, goal-oriented, driven kind of person. After he became a Christian he stayed that way, only he was driven for God. Peter, before he was a Christian, was impetuous. Afterward he was still impetuous, but God used his impetuosity for the kingdom.

It is important to remember that even though your emotional nature alternates between highs and lows, God's is stable. His promises are sure and true. He never fails. When people ask you, "How are you doing spiritually?" you can say, "Fine. God's in His heaven. All's right with the world. Christ died on the cross for my sins. He has promised that His Holy Spirit will never leave me nor forsake me. He is a friend that sticks closer than a brother. He has guaranteed my eternal life."

All these statements are stable and permanent. We may flop around like fish in a skillet, but God will not. We have to learn to rest in Him and His nature rather than in our own. Our faith needs to be in God rather than in our own emotional stability. The New Testament speaks about our being in Christ about ten times as often as it speaks of Christ's being in us. The secret to spiritual success is not changing our own natures and then relying on them; it is putting our natures in Christ's and allowing Him to take us to His destination.

I've often thought that the spiritual life is like a 747 jet. You could get in a 747 and *drive* it from Chicago to Dallas if you wanted to. It would be a little clumsy, but you could do it. Or you could *fly* the plane to Dallas. It would get to Dallas either on the ground or in the air, though the inventor's way is obviously best. Similarly it is far better for me to allow God to control my life rather than me try to control Him with my own nature. When I compare bumping along on the ground with flying through the air, I choose flying.

IS RELYING ON GOD ENOUGH? •

Whenever I have a problem and want to share it with someone, I hear a little voice inside me saying, "You should trust the Lord. He'll answer you." I feel guilty if I want to talk to someone because I think I'm not being as faithful to Christ as I should be. Am I really lacking in faith if I ask advice from others?

The Apostle Paul says in Galatians 6:2, "Bear ye one another's burdens, and so fulfill the law of Christ." I'm sure it's possible for a person to lean too much on other people. But it's also a danger to think, "I should never ask anybody for help." In fact, it's more dangerous than relying on others too much. We read in Proverbs 11:14, "In the multitude of counselors there is safety." When a person is surrounded by friends and family, he is very rich indeed.

But there is an idea afoot among some Christians today that I think is a dangerous heresy—that one is supposed to get all help from God alone, without any other agencies or intermediaries. But God created everything. He created the human mind and is behind the development of counseling, surgery, and medicine. In fact, it is God who makes people want to help each other, so to refuse all help is to refuse gifts that God has lovingly provided.

Of course God *can* help us directly, without any human intervention. But He seems to have ordered the world so that Good Samaritans, if not totally necessary, are at least desirable. He seems to want to work within the social order, so that people help people in cooperation with Him. The spirituality that says, "I'm spiritual only if I cut out everything else and deal with God alone," is a perversion of God's intentions for this world. God has given us one another and we should be thankful.

ANGRY AT GOD •

At times I get angry at God. For instance, it makes me mad when I think that He put a curse on *all* women for something *Eve* did. I know that if I ever have a baby I'm the one who must stay home and stop doing most of the things that mean so much to me. I'm single and terrified to get married for that very reason. Is it possible for someone who has been a Christian for years to still have these pockets of anger and resentment toward God?

It's very possible; in fact, many people's problems are tied to anger against God. A young man came up to me after I had spoken at his church and said, "I can't be a Christian because I don't believe in God." I responded, "Tell me what kind of God you don't believe in." By the things he told me, I knew he believed God to be cruel, arbitrary, untrustworthy, and unloving. I said to him, "If I believed God were as you describe Him, I wouldn't be a Christian either."

People labor under a great many misconceptions about God. I think you have one of them. To think that womanhood is connected to the curse is to misunderstand Scripture. If you look carefully at Genesis 3, you will see that the serpent and the ground were cursed, but the man and the woman were not. God told Eve that her lot would be difficult, but no more difficult than Adam's. Your problem is not so much with God as with society. You feel that the distribution of labor in families is unfair, and in many cases you are absolutely right.

But I wonder why your feelings about fairness make you afraid to get married. Married women can have careers today, and they don't have to have children. If they do have children, there are families where both parents work and share equally in taking care of the children. I get the feeling that your strong reaction against marriage and motherhood may be based on specific things you have seen that have frightened or angered you. Perhaps you have seen some particularly unloving marriages where the wife/mother's life did indeed seem cursed. Or maybe friends and relatives have put down your interests by telling you that God made women to produce babies and nothing else.

For whatever reason, your view of God and your view of marriage and motherhood are both out of touch with reality. I think your misperceptions are making you miserable now and quite possibly will keep you from the happiness that should be yours in the future. I think you need to find a counselor, perhaps a pastor, to help you understand your reactions and to help you destroy your pockets of anger and resentment before they destroy you.

TRUE CONFESSIONS ●

I was always taught in church that God would send sinners to hell unless they repented. So at an early age I asked Jesus Christ to forgive my sins. But every time I sin I have this awful feeling that

if I die before confessing or if I forget to confess something, God will reject me. I try to keep from sinning, but I find it's impossible. Would God really send me to hell for just one unconfessed sin?

Your experience is typical of the way many people understand Christianity. But in fact, this idea that God is waiting to throw out sinners is based on a wrong interpretation of Scripture. In Ephesians 2:8-9 we read, "By grace are ye saved through faith; and that not of yourselves: it is the gift of God: not of works, lest any man should boast." That is, we are not saved by our works, by our ability to overcome sin, or even by the work of faith. Faith itself is a gift of God.

In Sunday School or catechism class you may have learned a definition of grace—the unmerited favor of God toward man. Nothing you can do merits God's favor at all. As the hymn writer put it, "Nothing in my hands I bring, simply to Thy cross I cling." We are all sinners, but we are condemned only if we reject God's grace.

Now repentance is not simply a transaction with God that we have to repeat every time we sin. It is a relationship with God that is initiated when we accept Jesus as Saviour. A repentant Christian continually says, "Christ, I have no merit and no hope without You. I put myself at Your disposal; do with me as You wish." And Christ continually offers forgiveness. A repentant Christian lives in a position of forgiveness.

Christ is not a heavenly bookkeeper waiting to trap one of His people on a technicality. He is instead the One who wanted to forgive us so badly that He died to do so. He says, "Come unto me, all ye that labor and are heavy laden, and I will give you rest" (Matt. 11:28). He does not want you to be tormented with fears that you won't measure up. He knows you won't—and He has made provision for that because He loves you. He has given you salvation, and He wants to give your spirit rest.

I'M A CHRISTIAN, HE'S NOT •

My husband says he feels uncomfortable that I'm a Christian. We were separated for a year and during that time I accepted Christ. Now we are back together but, though he respects my Bible study and prayer times, we don't do anything together like we used to. Instead he drinks, smokes, and stays out late. When I talk to him about this, he says he doesn't know how to act around religious people. I'm trying to improve our marriage, but it takes two to

**make progress. Neither of us wants a divorce, but staying togeth-
er like this seems so empty to me. I'm frustrated and feel rejected.**

It looks to me like you're on the right track, painful as it is, in that you are trying to reconcile with your husband. You are doing what Peter and Paul encouraged women to do who were caught in similar situations: being the best wife possible and letting your life be your testimony to the power of the Gospel.

However, sometimes people in your position have a misunderstanding that leads to problems—they confuse being religious with being Chris-tian. They hear in church that they ought to be studying the Bible and praying, so they turn their homes into miniature churches. They hang religious pictures on the walls, constantly play sentimental religious music on the stereo, leave their Bibles conspicuously open, and walk around as if they had a deep burden on their hearts. To look at them, you'd think the lost were tumbling into the abyss of hell right before their eyes. The spouses of these super-religious men and women begin to think, "It isn't any fun to live with him/her anymore." Such "religion" tends to build walls rather than bridges.

There is a vast difference between religion and Christianity. Being in Christ, belonging to Christ, ought to give a lift to our souls. Christians ought to be happier and more fun to live with than non-Christians. Chris-tians should show the attributes of the Holy Spirit: love, joy, peace, long-suffering, gentleness, goodness, faith, meekness, and temperance. These characteristics attract, while sentimental religiosity drives peo-ple—especially husbands—away. Let me encourage you to take the side of your life that you share with your husband and make it the best you possibly can. Make your homemaking, your cooking, and your personal life together so inviting that instead of saying, "This wedge has been driven between us unnecessarily," he'll see your life as being positively affected by the Gospel.

NINE-YEAR-OLD BACKSLIDER? •

Our nine-year-old son doesn't seem very interested in the Lord. He did ask Jesus into his life when he was six, but I'm not sure he has really grasped what that means. He reads one chapter a day in the Bible mainly because he has to. Sometimes he jokes about spiritu-al things and this frustrates me. Do you think I'm taking this too

seriously? How can we raise him in the faith and help him grab hold of prayer and Bible reading? How do we help him live the way Jesus wants without turning him off? Are we expecting too much?

You are expecting far too much from a boy this age, even though your motives—to help him follow the Lord—are fine. I have a friend whose parents were on welfare during the Depression. When he was six years old, someone gave him some wool pants to wear to church on Sunday. He wore those pants to church every week and scratched all during the service. Though he gave up wool pants long ago, he still can't sit through a church service without scratching his legs. A lot of kids are forced into religion when they are growing up. When they get big, they say, "I can hardly wait to get away from that." As soon as they hear anything religious, they turn it off. You don't want to condition your son that way.

A nine-year-old is unlikely to understand many parts of the Bible. Asking him to read a chapter a day is just inviting him to avoid Scripture later, when he would be able to understand it. But you can teach him Bible stories that he will enjoy. Look into the *Muffin Family* series by Gilbert Beers. It's one of my favorites because it understands kids and the books are available in just about any Christian bookstore.

Nine-year-olds usually can't understand the abstract truths in Scripture, the real meaning of love and commitment, Christ's atonement, and that sort of thing. But they enjoy learning information, such as how long the ark was, or how many smooth stones David put in his sling, or how many wise men are mentioned in the Bible. They can also understand security, love, understanding, and authority as demonstrated by caring Christian parents. Then, when they are old enough to understand the abstract truths, they will have a framework in which to place them. What your nine-year-old really needs most is living in a family that teaches him trust and confidence on a practical level.

MY CHURCH OR MY CHEVY? ●

This past year my dad gave me a 1955 Chevy to fix up. I've worked hard restoring it and now it's the talk of the high school. I love that car and too often I'm tempted to stay home and work on it instead of going to church or youth fellowship. It's as if the car means more to me than God does. Why isn't God as interesting as my car? How do I get my priorities straight?

I think the idea that your car is replacing God in your life is a little heavy. I know that well-meaning religious people will tell you everything is a god if you get your priorities out of place. But I doubt if you plan to worship this car or try to get out of it what only God can give. Instead, you have made a priority choice based on your normal adolescent need for attention, affirmation, and approval. In fact, you probably don't even like the Chevy all that much; what you really like is being noticed, having something special, accomplishing something, and being somebody. Everybody wants those things. That's why people amass fortunes, become generals, and go to college. So don't blame yourself too harshly for having normal needs and desires.

Fortunately, you have discovered an important truth early in your life. You know that it is possible to make poor priority choices that will eventually rob you of what you really want. The most helpful verse to me on this topic is Matthew 6:33: "Seek ye first the kingdom of God, and His righteousness; and all these things shall be added unto you." The verse starts by telling us to put God first. But it goes on to say that the other things you need will be given to you as well. God is not saying, "Choose Me and starve to death," or "Choose Me and never enjoy art," or "Choose Me and give up your car." He is saying, "You have to learn where the real values are and start there." A 1955 Chevy is obviously a pretty weak starting point: God wants your life to have Christ at the center. I have found that as I put Him first, I am overwhelmed by His goodness in taking care of my needs.

A MAN OF THE WORLD •

I am married to a man who serves the world. I'm a Christian and have had continual problems with him. We have been separated and close to divorce, but we got back together when he served the Lord for six months. Now he is back to smoking pot and using other drugs. He sure makes life hard on me, but I'm trusting in the Lord. Can you give me any encouragement?

The great encouragement is that many thousands of women since the beginning of the Christian church have lived for Christ in such a way that their husbands have come to know Him too. They have raised Christian families in spite of their husbands' lack of support. Both Peter and Paul wrote to women in situations much like yours (1 Cor. 7:12-16; 1 Peter 3:1-2), telling them that their Christian lives might be the means of their husbands' conversion. These women's husbands may not have been using drugs, but they were part of Roman society which means they were probably involved in violence, alcohol, and adultery.

One reason Jesus died was to teach us that some of the world's problems cannot be solved apart from suffering. Someone has to pay the price to show how terrible sin is in what it does to human beings. You may endure some suffering as you follow the biblical model of living with your husband for Christ, not nagging or preaching, but patiently loving him. The process may seem slow, but it is the only process with any hope of reaching him for Christ. If your husband is indeed drug-dependent, I would also advise you to look into various treatment and counseling programs that are now available.

DOES SHE REALLY HATE MOM? •

Can you hate your family and still be a Christian? My friend claims to be a Christian, yet says she hates her family, especially her mother. She says her mother favors her brother and is not nice to her. My friend wants to run away. We are both fourteen.

People between the ages of twelve and fourteen often do what your friend is doing. They get frustrated at everybody and lash out, trying to get attention by saying things that will shock people. This is why she tells you she hates her family. She doesn't hate her mother. She's just jealous because her brother seems to be getting more attention than she does. She has a problem, all right, but it isn't that she hates her family. It's that she doesn't think she's getting enough response from her family. She loves them so much that she wants more of them. So she says shocking things as a way of trying to get her family's attention.

As this girl's friend, you need to stick with her and respond to her only when she makes sense. When she makes off-the-wall comments, just ignore them. Don't say, "Oh, my goodness, how awful! You shouldn't hate your mother. You shouldn't run away." That would give her the kind of attention she's looking for, and she'll start saying more off-the-wall things to get you to respond. She'll grow out of this phase in a year or two. Then she'll wonder how she ever could have said such things.

CAUGHT IN THE VALUE GAP •

My daughter has a close friend named Jenny. Jenny's divorced father often leaves her and his other children in the care of an aunt who lets them wander in the park alone or play in the cold without coats. I told my daughter that Jenny could play at our house, but that she could not play at Jenny's house. We told Jenny's father, as kindly as we could, that we wanted our child to have more supervision and that our values were different from his. Now our daughter tells us that Jenny's father and aunt say obscenities about us. I want to honor Christ and be friendly with this family, but I don't know how to relate to them.

You're right—you do need to set the standards for your family and not allow other families to decide them for you. Still, as Christians we have to be careful not to pull ourselves away from others and live in our own comfortable little subculture. Jesus told us to be the salt of the earth and the light of the world (Matt. 5:13-16). It isn't easy, however, to protect our values while living in a world that doesn't share them. Probably what happened is this: When you told Jenny's father that you wanted your child to have more supervision, that was fine; but when you went on to say that your values were different from his, he felt that you were condemning him. Not knowing how to respond, he lashed out.

I would encourage you to see Jenny as separate from her father and her aunt. She is in no way responsible for what has happened in her family, and she provides a marvelous opportunity for you. She is at an impressionable stage of life, and you can show her by example what a normal family is like and what caring is all about. It may be that when Jenny's father sees what you are doing for her, he will feel better about you; or he may always feel antagonistic toward you. Even if you cannot avoid some unpleasantness with Jenny's father, keep in mind that your pain is probably worth it for her sake.

MOM'S CALL VS. GOD'S CALL •

My mother doesn't want me to go to the mission field. She is a Christian, but she can't accept the idea of her daughter going to Africa for two years. This makes it hard on me. I don't want her to be unhappy, but I want to do what God has called me to do. How can I help my mother adjust?

It's helpful to look at the situation from your mother's point of view. Her concerns probably fall into three categories that are not hard to understand. First, she knows she will miss you. I talk to many parents who are deeply hurt because their grown children don't seem to want to be with them anymore. It's hard for parents to let their children go, especially if the children seem indifferent to them. Second, she is afraid that something will happen while you're in Africa—perhaps she will die, or your plane will crash—and she'll never see you again. That makes the thought of missing you even more painful. Third, she may have a mental image of *darkest* Africa—scary pictures of caldrons with missionaries in them, for instance, or more up-to-date fears about anticolonial riots.

It's good that you're concerned, that you love your mother and want to dispel her fears. It would be un-Christian to leave a worried mother in a cavalier or unfeeling manner. At the same time, as we've told thousands of Youth for Christ missionaries, God's calling comes first, and parents need to adjust themselves to their children's leaving because leaving is a part of growing up. You can put many of your mother's fears to rest by keeping her well informed about your plans, the situation in the country to which you are going, and your own feelings. Once you are overseas, write to her regularly and in detail. I've talked to parents in your mother's situation who have said, "I never really knew my daughter until she went away and began to write to me." It was not "Things are fine, wish you were here" letters that comforted these parents, but letters in which the young missionary shared her own heart with them. I hope you will do this for your mother, and I hope she will come to accept your plans and even rejoice in having a dedicated daughter.

MUSIC OR MISSIONS? ●

I just graduated from college with a music degree and my parents have high expectations that I will make a name for myself as a concert pianist. I won several competitions in college and played with the school orchestra. But now I feel led to be a missionary. My parents, who are not Christians, won't hear of it. They say I am wasting my education and my talent. I know that the things I've learned in music would be a great benefit to me in whatever I do, but my parents have let me know in no uncertain terms that they are against anything that interferes with my musical career. How do I know what God wants me to do?

Parents often try to direct their children in directions the young people do not wish to take, but your case is more extreme than many. There is a world of difference between the concert stage and the mission field. Certainly you must follow God's will for you. You can't follow someone else's will and then try to adjust it to fit God's will.

Basically your parents want you to be happy and fulfilled. They think you would best do this by becoming a concert artist. But parents are not notorious for their objectivity. The concert circuit is a very difficult life, and only the best survive. You were good at home and at college, but is your talent equal to the challenges of being a professional musician? If it isn't, and you try to become a concert pianist anyway, your parents will be supporting you for many years to come. It would be only fair to have someone they respect warn them now. If you do have what it takes to be a professional—and if knowledgeable people in the music world have affirmed this—then you have a choice to make.

A lot of Christian college students have a romantic idea of what mission service is all about. Since you think God is calling you to the mission field, talk to as many returned missionaries as you can to get firsthand information about what mission service is really like. Read about missions—not just thrilling biographies of heroes of the faith, but also books that get down to brass tacks about what it takes to be a missionary. Attend Urbana, the missions convention sponsored by Inter-Varsity Christian Fellowship. Make sure you know what mission service is and where you would fit in, and then give your parents the facts. They'll be impressed by your knowledgeability, if nothing else.

It crosses my mind that you may be very tired of the pressure your parents are putting on you—so tired that a mission appointment to a remote place 10,000 miles away couldn't look better. Be sure you are truly responding to God's call and not to a need to escape. Problems also exist 10,000 miles away; sometimes they even get worse. It is possible that God doesn't want you to be either a concert pianist or a missionary.

If, after you have looked carefully into all aspects of your decision, you are fully persuaded that God wants you to be a missionary, then go in confidence. Be as gentle as possible with your parents and give them time to adjust to your plans. Even if you could be the greatest concert pianist in the world, if God calls you to something else, you should do it. Charles Spurgeon put it this way: "If God has called you to preach the Gospel, don't stoop to be a king."

IS IT A SIN TO CONFRONT? •

My boyfriend and I are both Christians, but I have been struggling over breaking off the relationship. I feel that some of his actions just aren't right. I know the Bible says we aren't to judge one another (Matt. 7:1-2), but I also know it says that if someone is caught in a sin, the spiritually minded people should gently restore him (Gal. 6:1). Would I be judging him if I talked to him about what he does wrong?

I think you are misunderstanding Jesus' words in Matthew. He tells us not to judge, lest we be judged by the same judgment. In other words, don't talk to somebody about his sins if you have the same sins in your own life. But this surely doesn't mean that Christians can't tell right from wrong, or that they can't tell when someone else is doing wrong.

You do not have the right to condemn your boyfriend for what he is doing, but you do have the right to point out to him that his behavior goes against your understanding of Christian principles. If you plan to break off your relationship because of what he is doing, you owe him an explanation. Just breaking up without saying anything gives him no opportunity to change his behavior. People can change their behavior— but not unless they know what they are doing wrong.

Perhaps you can help your boyfriend by explaining your convictions to him. He may not know that you feel as you do or that his behavior is contrary to your beliefs. If he decides to change his behavior, perhaps you will find him more attractive. But beware of short-term changes. Don't say, "Well, if he stops doing this for a week or two I'll marry him." I've seen many girls do that, and then six months later he is back to the same old habit pattern. The only difference is that this time they are caught.

So yes, I think you are right to confront him, and no, I don't think you are judging him by pointing out the sin.

OUR NEIGHBORS ARE DIFFERENT •

My husband works for the military. We live in a government housing compound, and our teenage children find that the peer pressure in school and in the neighborhood is heavy. It is difficult to enforce family rules and guidelines when so many other parents don't. Consequently, we have trouble with our children smok-

ing behind our backs, skipping school, and who knows what else. These certainly are not behaviors we are demonstrating to our children. How can we set a good example for them when those around us do just the opposite?

————————————

You could look at this situation as an opportunity. Light always shines best in darkness, because you can see the contrast. All Christians are strangers and pilgrims, kingdom citizens surrounded by citizens of the world. Because of where you live, you, unlike many Christians, are very much aware of the differences between your family and others.

Start by sitting down with your family and explaining, "We are a Christian family. We follow Jesus Christ. We attempt to obey Him, and that makes us unique." Then begin demonstrating your Christian faith. If your neighbors are living by secular values, then your home will be unique because you will love your children enough to discipline them, and care for them enough to teach them. You will spend time with them, communicate with them, and live lives that are consistent with Scripture. You will be special parents, and young people will be able to see that. Think of yourselves as a missionary family, called to work in a totally different value structure. I think your concern means you will come out ahead. It's people who think they are living in Christian America with no enemy around who are in real trouble.

| CHAPTER 34 |

Living with Other Christians in the Church

The church is the only institution that Jesus Christ set up while He was on earth, and He has promised to bless it. The church is universal. It is the body of Jesus Christ spread across the world. It contains all the gifts needed to serve the world in which we live and glorify God. The church is also local. It is the group that meets in the little frame building on the corner. It involves real people, fallen people who have been saved by grace, people who function together to the glory of God.

The church has been responsible for nearly all the humane attributes and institutions of Western culture, from the abolition of slavery to the valuing of women, from humane penal systems to great institutions of higher learning. The church is far from perfect, because it is not com- posed of perfect people. But it obeys—sometimes more, sometimes less—a perfect and loving Lord, and to the extent that it follows Him, the world is a better place for everyone.

TOO INVOLVED AT CHURCH? ●

I think our family is too involved with our church. Almost every night at least one member of our family is there. We love the church and enjoy helping others, but our family life is suffering. We don't want to neglect our church, but we don't want to neglect

our family life either. Can you give us some guidelines on establishing priorities?

What is the definition of the church? There is the church on the street corner, the brick and mortar building. And there's the church of Jesus Christ, the body of Christ, the church universal. There's also the church expressed through the local congregation in the sense of programs and activities.

I believe that worshiping God in the church of our choice is one of the most important things we can do. Hebrews 10:25 talks about not forsaking the assembling of ourselves together. The worship service should be somewhere near the top of our priority list, but to define church worship in terms of a program every night of the week can become oppressive. One has to realize that these activities, though they take place within the walls of the church, are really parachurch (alongside of church). Sunday School is parachurch; clubs, Bible studies, small groups, and prayer meetings are also parachurch. It's possible to create a church with so much program, so much obligation, and so much guilt connected with attendance, that in reality it becomes as destructive of family life as the country club or an excessive interest in golf or social groups or anything else. It keeps the family on a merry-go-round.

The church exists for the family; the family doesn't exist for the church. The family is not the fuel that provides the grist for the church's activities; the church's activities should be designed to support family life. So at times, parents have to make some hard decisions. Is this particular activity helping or hindering our family? Is it bringing us together or pulling us apart? It's better to pick up the child than to pick up a book about the child; it's better to play with one's family than to go to church every night of the week to be challenged to play with one's family. All of us who are clergymen have to deal with the fact that there are times when people must make decisions that go against our programs. Our success as pastors shouldn't be rooted in the attendance figures of our weeknight programs, but in the health and spiritual integrity of our families. So it helps to make a distinction between what the church *is* and the kinds of tasks a church can offer to be helpful.

WANTED: CHURCH HOME •

My wife and I feel the need to get involved in a church body, but we can't find a church we really like. Neither of us had a positive church experience while growing up. We have found fellowship in a small Bible-study group, but we fail to find this kind of warmth and sincerity within a church. We both want to belong to a church family where our gifts can be used to minister, but we feel like outsiders at the churches we've attended. What are we doing wrong in looking for a church home?

It takes more time to get acquainted in an established church, I think, than in a small-group Bible study. Usually, small groups are made up of people of similar ages and interests, while a church covers a wider range of people. So, whereas you might feel well-accepted after the first night in a small-group Bible study, it will take longer to feel part of a church family. But the effort is worth it, because in a larger, more diverse group you have more opportunity to accomplish a great deal.

Getting accepted in a church may be easier for you if you realize that all churches are made up of small groups. Most churches have several Sunday School classes as well as Bible-study groups, men's and women's fellowship groups, service groups, and other special-interest groups. Find a small group where you are comfortable and use it as your point of entry.

All churches need people who are willing to get involved. Some pastors are wary, however, of people who come in with an agenda, a set of teachings they have learned in a small-group Bible study or from a TV preacher or wherever. They have been burned by people who came in with an arrogant spirit and tried to straighten out the church, so they may want to look you over before giving you something to do. Once they find out that you really want to be part of the church, your problem won't be finding something to do; it will be learning to say no.

Go to the pastor of a church you like. Tell him how you feel. Describe your backgrounds. Answer his questions and get to know him. As you build relationships and earn the church members' trust, you will find ample places to serve. But, as in most cases, you can't start at the top. You usually have to start in lower positions and work your way up.

WHAT ABOUT TOGETHERNESS? •

Our thirteen-year-old son goes to a different church than we do. He loves it and never misses a service. He thinks his Sunday School teacher is wonderful and he seems to be growing in the Lord. Our son wasn't excited about going to church until he started attending this one with his best friend. I want him to be excited about church, but shouldn't we be attending the same church as a family? Should we let him continue attending the church he enjoys or make him go with us?

I think a lot of parents would be happy with the arrangement you have— that is, to have a teenager who is interested in going to church at all. When kids reach their teens, a great percentage of them fall away from church. The attendance curve doesn't start up again until they get into their twenties and have children of their own.

It may help you to back off and look at the church from God's perspective. The Apostle Paul wrote, "There is one body, and one Spirit . . . one Lord, one faith, one baptism, one God and Father of all" (Eph. 4:4-6). This means that God's church includes all churches that exalt the name of the Lord Jesus and preach the Word of God, no matter what their denomination. Your son's real motivation for going to this other church probably has little to do with things that lead to denominational differences anyway. It has much more to do with the fact that the people are friendly; he likes the youth group; the kids do fun things together. Most people, in fact, choose their church more for sociological than theological reasons.

I think you have a good situation here, even if it isn't the best. If your son stays interested in Christianity during his teen years, you will have more family togetherness than if you attended the same church but he went unwillingly. Encourage your son to attend the church he likes. Ask him questions about what he is learning. Show an interest in his religious life. Perhaps you and your husband could attend some services at his church from time to time. This would help you get acquainted with people who are important to you son, and it also may make him willing to attend your church occasionally.

WHY WON'T HUBBY LEAD? ●

I can't get my husband enthusiastic about attending church. How can I motivate him to want to go to church and take the responsibility of being the Christian leader of our home?

One way that won't work is to nag him and tell him that he ought to be the spiritual leader of the home. "Ought to" statements are wonderful exercises for those who are making them. It feels so good to say things like "Husbands ought to lead their families." But "ought to" statements tend not to change people.

You have probably heard that particular "ought to" statement, and that puts you in an interesting position. You quite naturally think, "Then I ought to lead my husband into being a leader." The contradiction there is obvious. You can't make him lead if he doesn't want to lead.

What you will have to do is begin to take responsibility for your own Christian life and for the lives of your children. The New Testament gives us a lot of examples of female spiritual leadership. Apparently, when the church first began, it attracted a large number of women whose husbands were not interested in the Christian faith. Peter encouraged these women to be good wives, faithful in carrying out their duties. Eventually, their godly lives—not their words—might win over their ungodly husbands to Christ (see 1 Peter 3:1-2).

A husband can lead in many areas in the family, but if the wife has more light than he does spiritually, she should walk in that light and not stumble around in his darkness. Minding her own walk is far more effective than trying to coerce him into leading in an area he doesn't understand or care about. When men like your husband talk about religious things, they often say something like, "Well, I'm not too involved in church, but if I ever do get involved, I want to be the kind of Christian my wife is." They say this because their wives have convinced them through their daily lives. This, I think, is the most winsome way to solve the problem.

SEX EDUCATION AT CHURCH? ●

The Christian Education Board at church has been planning a sex education class for the young people's Sunday School. They feel the church has a responsibility to present sex education from a

Christian perspective. I'm having trouble accepting this. Isn't sex education something we should be teaching at home, not at church? Young people are too preoccupied with sex anyway.

I think the two very best places to have sex education are the home and the church. In fact, they are the only "institutions" I would really trust with it. Unfortunately, often neither one does it, and then caring school teachers, realizing how abysmally ignorant the kids are on the subject, try to do it themselves. But they have their hands tied, because sex education has to include so much more than the physical or even emotional aspects of sex. Sex involves the whole person, and therefore it has spiritual aspects as well. But because church and state are separate in this country, public school teachers cannot talk about the Christian approach to sex.

You are right that sex education should be taught at home. But many parents don't do it. If you took a poll of your church children and asked them how many had learned about the sanctity of sexuality from their parents, you would no doubt find that not one in twenty have had any kind of conversation on this subject other than an embarrassed, "Don't talk about that." A group of Sunday School teachers, guided by concerned parents, could do a great service for everybody by presenting a serious curriculum in Christian sex education.

Keep in mind that sex was God's idea. Unfortunately, sex has often been separated from the rest of life. Some people want to make sex all of life and others want to treat it like a momentary pleasure unrelated to other parts of their lives. When anything gets out of context, there's trouble ahead. But sex, in its God-ordained context of Christian marriage, contributes to the most beautiful and intimate relationship that two human beings can have. And so I think that when sex education is done tastefully and reverently, respecting the sanctity of this part of God's creation, children can grow up with a healthy understanding of sex. Instead of sneaking around, talking behind people's backs and acting as if sex were bad and taboo, kids can understand that sex in context is a way to glorify God.

KIDS BORED AT CHURCH ●

Why don't our kids like church? It seems they don't get anything out of it. Is there any way to make church interesting and relevant to young people?

It's very possible that your children don't like church because it is not meeting their needs at this time in their lives. Many young people, self-centered and caught up in their own activities, say things like, "I don't get anything out of it."

Even to say this is to misunderstand the nature of church. You'd be hard pressed to find any Bible verse that says we're supposed to get something out of church. Instead, church is a place where we worship and adore God. God has done a marvelous thing in creating the world and giving us life. We come together to thank Him for this. We also thank Him for forgiving us when we've rebelled against Him and for offering us His grace through Jesus Christ.

People who are unappreciative, who do not understand the scope of God's Creation, who aren't really thankful for what has happened to them, who feel the world owes them something—these people find it hard to worship. Young people almost by definition are like this, not because they are bad, but because they are immature. So, it is not surprising that they often find church boring.

That's why we've added many functions—extracurricular activities, if you please—to make church more attractive to young people. We organize young people's groups, hiking, camps, and all sorts of Sunday School activities geared to young people's somewhat self-centered interests. I believe that when our kids are growing up, it is wise to find a church—even one of a different denomination from the one we're used to, as long as it takes Scripture seriously, preaches the Word of God, and exalts Jesus Christ as Saviour and Lord—that provides some of these activities for kids. Let's face it—few seventeen-year-olds really enjoy being in a group of a few fourteen-year-olds. Kids need to be in an atmosphere where there are many young people about their own age.

If necessary, I'd drive a few extra miles to put my kids in a church with a strong program for young people. Then, after they know I'm committed to helping them find a church that meets their needs, I'd sit down with them and explain what church is supposed to be about and why we go through the experience of worship. If they expect the church to be some kind of pop psych clinic or entertainment equal to a TV variety show, then they will have a hard time identifying with it. It's up to the parents to help their kids understand the meaning of worship. Some kids have never thought about worship, and when they are told about it, they say, "Now I see what they are doing. That's pretty good; I understand now."

Of course, if the parents don't understand the meaning of church either; if they always have roast preacher for Sunday dinner; if they have no tolerance for things that are not specifically aimed at them on a particular Sunday morning, then they create a climate that encourages kids to rebel against church. Conversely, parents can create a climate that encourages their children to appreciate church. They can do this through tolerance, love, understanding, and careful explanation that helps the kids recognize God's greatness and the importance of praising and worshiping Him. Ultimately, children will catch their parents" attitude. More is caught than taught.

I CAN'T RELATE ●

I'm bored with my church. Being single and twenty-one, I can relate to few people in this small congregation. I don't expect a church to be perfect, but I desire the fellowship of a more active church and what it might provide. Would it be wrong to visit other churches and let the Lord lead me to join one of them? I don't want to walk out on my church if the Lord wants to use me there.

This may be a good opportunity for you to develop independence from your parents. Perhaps this is the time for you to look around at various churches, find out what they believe, and join one that suits your needs. Joining a church, however, is not something to do casually. It is making a serious commitment to a body of people, their goals and directions, and methods of achieving them. Your need for more fellowship must not be your only consideration in looking for another church.

It may be, however, that you have strong family ties in your present church. Perhaps you like your denomination's approach to Scripture, its worship style, its theology. Maybe your family would think you were repudiating them and their values if you joined a different church. And as you suggest, it is possible that the Lord wants to use you in your own little church. In any of these cases, it would pay to look for intermediate ways of solving your problem.

Consider looking for a large church that supports an active singles' program. Attend that program evenings or weekdays or whenever they get together socially. Then worship in your own church on Sundays and continue to be active in it. There would be nothing wrong with doing this, though I think you should let your pastor and your parents know why you are attending events at another church so they won't feel insulted or abandoned. We have different needs at different times in our lives, and no one church can provide for all of them. Whether you decide to join another church or simply to attend some of its functions, I think you will find your own Christian life growing as a result of your deeper involvement.

CHURCH BAZAARS •

Recently, our church has been having some financial needs, and some of the newer members suggested holding bazaars to raise money. The first one went so well that we are going to continue having them in the gymnasium part of the church building. We never did anything like this before; the previous pastors wouldn't allow it. Some of us feel this is wrong because it makes the Lord's house a marketplace. Are we too narrow-minded?

By *bazaar* I'm assuming you mean something like a flea market or a rummage sale, perhaps with a car wash going on in the parking lot. Some people oppose such activities on the basis of Jesus driving the money-changers out of the temple. What these people don't realize is that Jesus was not objecting to the buying and selling as such. In fact, the merchants and moneychangers performed a valuable service. People coming from foreign countries had to make change in order to pay the temple tax, and people coming from afar to sacrifice needed to buy the sacrificial animals. But the priests had cornered the market. They offered a ridiculous rate of exchange, and they charged exorbitant prices for the necessary animals. Worshipers were trapped. Either they paid the price or they went home without worshiping. Poor people were out of luck. So Jesus was not opposing selling things on church property; He was opposing price-fixing, extortion, and indifference to the poor.

Even though there is no scriptural command against church bazaars, your church may have a problem. Any church that begins seriously depending on bazaars to finance its work is in trouble. If you are at this stage, it will soon be all over for you. The work of the church has to be carried by people who are committed to Christ and who give their tithes and offerings to support His work locally and worldwide. Jesus said, "Where your treasure is, there will your heart be also" (Matt. 6:21). Our giving is a good thermometer of our spiritual temperature. So if a church is really having financial problems, it probably indicates a spiritual problem.

But perhaps you are using the money from bazaars to finance worthwhile activities that are not part of the regular church budget—a camping trip for the teenagers, for instance. Why not wash cars or sell junk to each other? The kids and adults will have fun doing it together; community people will be encouraged to come onto church property; and the kids will get their trip. It certainly sounds innocent to me.

THE REVEREND FIBS ●

Our pastor doesn't always tell the truth. For years I've been aware of minor distorted facts, but I put them toward the back of my mind. Then my children picked up on these little lies and came to me with some tough questions. I had no choice but to privately confront the pastor about this. He says I'm not making enough room for human error. What do you say?

You do need to deal with this in a compassionate manner and allow for human error. First Corinthians 13 clearly says that in love we ought always to give the other person the benefit of the doubt. But when the situation gets to the place where even the children are noticing it, then it may be quite serious.

There is a scriptural pattern for handling this sort of thing (see Matt. 18:15-17). You have already taken the first step, talking to the individual personally. The second step is to go to the person with two or three witnesses. Now, don't do that in the church foyer. Do it in the pastor's study or another private place where he can save face. Choose responsible leaders to go with you, a couple of people who have also noticed this problem. Find people who have already said something to you about this, so you won't be responsible for spreading gossip. If the problem is indeed noticeable, others will have spotted it too.

The third step, if the first two do not bring results, is to bring the problem before the appointed body in your church—the board of deacons, the church board, or a pastoral committee. Bring it to the attention of whoever is in charge and let them deal with it. This is the time for you to back off and believe that the structure God has ordained in your church will handle this in a responsible manner.

Whenever children bring this kind of thing to parents, parents have to ask, "Is my child really giving me an independent analysis, or is he picking up on something I have transmitted to him? Am I telegraphing my own distrust of the pastor?" As a general rule, one should not break down authority structures. You lose trust by correcting small errors, and trust is more important than straightening out the minutiae. But in this case, it appears that the problem is more than a few minor errors. As you deal with it, try always to think of your pastor as a human being who needs your love and support, not just as a servant of the church who has lost your confidence.

UNWELCOME IN THE BODY •

I feel very unwelcome returning to my home church after four years at college. It seems as though I've been away so long everyone's forgotten me. I don't understand why I'm never invited to church activities. I asked my youth minister if I could sing with the youth choir, but she never answered or got back in touch with me. I am really being hurt by this.

As the old saying goes, "You can't go home again." When you go home after an extended absence, you are a different person. You are older; you've grown and changed; your life is much different. Things have also changed in your church. We live in a mobile society, and many people have come and gone. I remember how I felt when I returned to my college after many years. I went to my old haunts, the places I once felt I owned. Suddenly, I found I knew no one there and nothing was familiar about them anymore. I felt a deep sense of loss.

Your experience with your church shows you can't pick up right where you left off. You have to pay attention to how you make your reentry. An effective reentry is much like going to a strange place. You can't just jump into the middle of things and expect to be accepted by everybody. You have to start at the edges and work your way in. I think you will need to do this, even though this was once your home church. As you have discovered, it is no longer yours or "home."

First, don't be hurt by the youth minister's response to your request. This was just a careless oversight. She doubtless has several other things to do and simply hasn't been able to respond to your request yet. Next, come regularly to the public meetings that are open to everyone so that your face will become familiar and people will consider you part of the group. When they plan activities, they will think of you and remember to invite you. Then, find two or three people—old friends or new—who are active in church activities and will help *you* get involved *too*. Finally, consider the possibility that the youth group is no longer the best place for you. You are now a college graduate, an adult. Perhaps people of your age and with your interests are involved in a different group in your church. Check it out.

It's an old cliché, but it's true—if you want a friend, you must be a friend. If you conclude that everyone you meet wants to meet a friend, you will be right ninety percent of the time. Be a friend to the people you meet at church and they will respond to you. Soon you will be in a group, one you have created through your friendship.

CULT LEFT BAD TASTE ●

When our daughter and her husband were in college, they joined a church that developed into a cult and then later dissolved. Now they have stopped attending church altogether and won't let their children attend either. They say we worship a false Christ because the real Christ hasn't revealed Himself to us yet. Even the mention of religion makes them angry. Is their anything we can do or say to change their minds?

Probably *doing* and *saying* are the least effective approaches. The strongest weapon you have is prayer, because this is a spiritual battle. Pray for their protection from the evil one; pray that the Holy Spirit will continue to work in their lives. The other strong weapon you have is simply to live your Christian life in their presence so they begin to see the validity of your faith.

Young people of college age are very idealistic. They want to see the world in a simpler way. They want it explained and quantified. A cult leader comes along with well-formed, black-and-white ideas. He persuades them that it is their duty to break with their families (a task that is important in late-adolescent development anyway). He gets their full allegiance, and then the thing falls apart. It always does sooner or later, as Gamaliel wisely pointed out. He said of the New Testament church, "If this counsel or this work be of men, it will come to nought: but if it be of God, ye cannot overthrow it" (Acts 5:38-39).

When a cult fails, your problem is no longer theological. It is psychological. Its members must now rebuild bridges they have burned; they must admit they were wrong. This is very embarrassing and it may take some time for them to put the whole experience behind them. They usually do not jump immediately from the cult into the Christian faith. More likely they will be gradually led back toward the Gospel by someone who has had an experience similar to theirs and who therefore understands where they are coming from.

The time of rebuilding may seem long. You can be grateful that your daughter and son-in-law are out of the cult, but it doesn't feel good to see them away from the church too. Still, they have taken the first step by escaping the cult's influence. You need to pray much for your children during this time. Love them and care for them. Wait for their embarrassment to subside. Try to avoid discussing religion with them, and allow the Holy Spirit to heal their wounds.

SECTION 9

Living in a Real World

Being a Christian is not living in never-never land. The Christian faith was never intended as an escape from anything. In fact, rather than being a way out, the Christian faith is a way in. It's a way into the real world because it touches everything we are and do.

Someone has said that hermeneutics—biblical interpretation—is the business of learning to think like a Jew rather than a Greek. As heirs of Greek culture, we tend to think about religion as if it were separate from material things. We may think that everything spiritual is good, whereas everything physical or material is bad. But the Christian faith has nothing to do with Greek philosophy. It lives instead on Jewish roots. The faith of the New Testament, like that of the Old, is tied to a real world of things and events. It acknowledges, affirms, and gives guidelines for sex, education, food, money—in short, the full range of human experience.

God touches us where we are, in a world that is physical and material as well as spiritual. True spirituality is concerned with living in our real world.

CHAPTER 35

Money and Things

A wise person once said, "God is to be loved, and things are to be used." We get in real trouble when we reverse this order, when we begin to love things and to use God.

There is nothing intrinsically wrong with money or things. Things cannot sin; money cannot sin—people sin by misusing them. The Christian must learn to make things and money his servants and God's servants, or he risks becoming a servant to things and money.

A biblical word for the proper way to handle money is *stewardship*. People often think this simply means giving money away; they probably get this idea from the stewardship departments of some colleges and churches! But true stewardship has a larger scope. It has to do with the fact that all of our lives, resources, and energies belong to God. God has made us stewards over a portion of His creation, and He expects us to use that with which He has entrusted us to His glory. If we constantly realize that our possessions are not really our own, that they are lent to us on trust by the Creator Himself, then we will not be tempted to hoard them or use them selfishly. We will want to use everything we are and have and do to build Christ's kingdom.

Matthew 6:33 states the stewardship principle this way: "Seek ye first the kingdom of God, and His righteousness; and all these things shall be added unto you." Notice that Matthew doesn't say things are bad. He simply points out that they must be put in their proper place.

MORE IS NEVER ENOUGH •

I'm never satisfied. The more I get, the more I want. God has blessed me with wonderful kids, a wonderful husband, a fine home, and a good job. But I still want more. For example, the home we just bought wasn't what I really wanted, even though it was much better than what we had. If the least little thing goes wrong on the job, I'll leave. The same thing is true in the church choir—I don't like pressures and confusion. I want to be satisfied; I'm just not happy like this.

If happiness is your goal, in my opinion you're on the wrong track. Besides, I think the pleasure principle is highly overrated compared to the much more worthy goal of fulfilling one's duty and responsibility. Nonetheless, most of us want to be happy, and most of us try to get happiness by following the world's method.

The principle of the world is this: "If I keep getting more and more, at some point I will be filled. If I fulfill my wants and desires, someday I'll be happy." But in fact, as you've experienced, the more we seek, the more we want. We never seem to get full. The whole Book of Ecclesiastes is about the futility of trying to make ourselves happy. Solomon observes, "I was great, and increased more than all that were before me . . . and whatsoever mine eyes desired I kept not from them. . . . Then I looked on all the works that my hands had wrought . . . and, behold, all was vanity and vexation of spirit" (Ecc. 2:9-11).

This brings me to the upside-down teachings of Jesus. Jesus said a lot of things that are backward as far as the world's system is concerned. They seem backward because the world has fallen—in reality, it's the world that's backward. Jesus said that in the Christian life, you get happiness not by seeking it for yourself, but by giving. To gain yourself, you have to lose your life. So instead of spending your life trying to get more for yourself, if you're a Christian you go the opposite way. You give away and you serve. And then one morning you wake up and say, "I'm happy—how did that happen?"

So I would encourage you to turn your back totally on your philosophy of more, more, more. Begin serving others, and suddenly you'll discover that by getting outside your own wants, you will have allowed happiness to come in through the back door.

MAKING ENDS MEET •

My husband and I both work. His salary is low compared to others in his field and we're barely keeping ahead of the monthly stack of bills. It bothers him that we need my salary to make ends meet and he feels he isn't being fair to me. It bothers me to have to face a pile of bills every month. When I get discouraged about the bills, he gets even more discouraged about his salary. I want to be supportive and encourage him, but this is not easy for me.

Start by counting your blessings—especially that you are employed. You are better off than a lot of people nowadays, even if your income is small. Then consider the principle that for most people, expenses rise to meet income. Whether they make $100,000 a year or only $10,000, people talk about all the bills they have.

There are only two ways to solve a cash-flow problem: make more or spend less. You do not mention any chance that your husband might transfer to another company at a higher salary or earn a promotion where he is, so perhaps making more is not an option for you. In that case, you need to set a budget and cut your expenses below your income so that you can stay afloat. Then you need to have the discipline to stick to your budget.

Don't be unrealistic about debt. It is good to be out of debt, but almost everyone below retirement age owes money for big-ticket items like a house or a car. If you owe someone money and are able to meet your obligation, you do not have a problem. Don't be so worried about debt that your worry hurts your home more than the debt itself.

But money isn't your only problem. You also mention your husband's feeling that it isn't fair that you have to work. Perhaps he was raised by a father who said, "A real man can support his family all by himself." But that idea comes from different economic times with different expectations. Today most American families have working wives and most working women say that they work primarily because they need the money. This should no longer be a matter for embarrassment. In fact, most working women enjoy their jobs and would not want to give them up even if they could afford to. If you can let your husband know that you enjoy your job, he will probably feel far less guilty about your having to work.

MRS. BREADWINNER ●

My wife makes twice as much money as I do. At first I thought it was great that she was offered a job that she really enjoys. But it's hard for me to accept that she is the main breadwinner in our home, not I. I think the problem is with my ego, but how do I keep this from bothering me?

If understanding the problem is nine-tenths of the solution, then you're well on your way. But this will not be an easy problem to solve. We're raised to think the man should be the hunter, the one to bring home the slain mastodon for the wife to cook. If we're not doing that, it's easy to feel depreciated and emasculated, even if we rationally understand and accept the situation.

The two of you need to sit down together and talk about this. Why are you earning half of what she's earning? Perhaps this is a choice you made with your eyes open. A person who wants to be in the arts or a people-helping profession—the ministry, teaching, social work—is never going to earn a big income. Maybe the two of you rationally decided that in order to fulfill a dream or make a contribution to society, you would take a lesser-paying job and she would supplement the family income. This is a perfectly good decision to make.

On the other hand, maybe your wife thinks you are earning less because you are lazy or unaggressive. If she feels compelled to go out and give you a boost, that could create a real problem. In that case, you would need to deal with your problem and get a better job, or lower your standard of living and refuse to be intimidated.

But you say that in your case, the problem is with your ego. Then the important thing is to watch your actions, not your feelings. Sometimes a man in your situation begins to do things to bring his wife down a peg or two. He refuses to help her around the house and then complains about her housekeeping. He lets her work all day and all night and then says she isn't meeting his sexual needs anymore. You may find yourself trying to dominate your wife. Actions like these will be far more damaging to your marriage than these little feelings you have. Make sure the feelings don't become unloving actions, and eventually you will work the problem out.

MY KIDS WANT AN ALLOWANCE •

My kids are starting to bug me about receiving allowances. I'm not sure how to handle this. I never had an allowance when I was a kid. I had to earn any money that came my way by cutting lawns or shoveling sidewalks. I was expected to work around the house because I was part of the family. It seems as if kids would be more responsible if they had to earn their money. Do you think kids should receive allowances?

I think we adults have selective memories. We remember the times we did things right and acted responsibly; we remember the hardships we overcame by our hard work. I suspect if we talked to our parents, though, we would find their view quite different from our own. That is, they probably gave us a great deal more than we remember.

In theory, the idea of earning money through paid work outside the home is excellent. In practice, it isn't quite so easy. Labor laws keep kids under sixteen from getting almost any kind of job, which is no doubt why at our door we have a steady stream of younger kids wanting to sell us something or do odd jobs for us. As good neighbors, we hire some of these kids, even though we don't usually need their help. We certainly don't need to buy the things they are selling. But it's our contribution to their allowances.

Even when a young person is sixteen and can legally work, it's not easy to find a job. When I was a kid, I could work in the basement of the grocery store, putting potatoes in sacks. Nowadays potatoes are put in sacks by huge machines that put in hundreds of them each minute. Grocery stores don't need kids to help them anymore and couldn't afford them if they did, because they would have to pay minimum wage.

So I firmly believe that an allowance is a good thing. Even though paying children for working around the house is a bit artificial, it teaches children how to manage money, how to make it last until the next installment is due, how to work until the job is done, and so on. When kids don't have their own money to manage and they constantly come to their parents asking for a dollar here and fifty cents there, nothing is taught except that Dad is a money tree and if you just keep coming to him, you'll get what you want. It is a much better alternative to give a kid a set amount of money for a set list of chores well done, with no additional money until the regular time. An allowance is a good way to teach them what zero means—a valuable lesson for them to learn before they go out into the world.

TEENAGE SPENDTHRIFT •

Our teenager earns his own money, but he wants to spend it all on junk. How should we guide his spending?

Parents need to start teaching their children to handle money when the children are very young. Children do not learn proper money management by being told how to spend every cent they have. This actually prevents their learning how to do it on their own. Children—and teenagers—learn best when they have money to spend as they choose, and when no misguided parent comes along to replace that money when it's gone. If a young person wants to spend his money on the wrong things, let him. Just be sure you don't give him more money to make up for what he wasted. Left to himself, he'll learn soon enough that money spent in one place can't be spent again somewhere else. A few mistakes can provide a good foundation for later ability to manage money well.

Parents should provide their children with the basics. Sometimes, however, a child gets label conscious. He may want a little alligator on everything he wears, even though another store sells similar items at a much lower cost with little foxes on them. If the difference between the alligator and the fox is important to him, let him pay for it.

Part of being an adolescent is making bad choices, so don't give your son choices if you strongly value one outcome over another. For example, if he has to choose between a video-cassette recorder and piano lessons, he may well choose the recorder. If you want him to take the lessons, be prepared to pay for them yourself. That's not money management—that's just good psychology.

KIDS AND CASH •

Do parents have a say in their teenagers' finances? Our sixteen-year-old daughter recently got an after-school job and says that since she earns her own money, she can spend it any way she pleases. We'd like to see her save some for college, but she says she'll do what she wants. Do we have any say in this matter?

The area of finances is a very important part of raising a family. Personally, I believe in allowances. I believe in kids being on salary as opposed to being on an hourly rate. I don't think it's good to attach a monetary value to every little thing someone does. But, in general, if you're a cooperative member of the family and you meet the basic requirements of the family, then you receive an allowance. The allowance should be firm, and the young person should learn how to handle it. When it runs out, it shouldn't be replenished until the proper time. The worst thing a young person can learn in the area of finances is that there is no such thing as zero. For example, your child splurges his allowance the first day of the week and the next morning he comes to you for some extra lunch money. Feeling sorry for the little guy, you bail him out. But what you are teaching him is that when he wants something badly enough, someone will always get it for him. The real world doesn't work that way.

In the specific case of your daughter—she is a sixteen-year-old adolescent and is acting her age. Maturity is the ability to postpone gratification, and a person is immature to the degree that he or she cannot do that. A sixteen-year-old has a lot of trouble with postponing gratification as your daughter is demonstrating. So initially, until your daughter becomes a little more mature, it might help to try a little different approach. If you are still purchasing extras for her—like special kinds of makeup or certain kinds of clothes—stop buying these. Say to her, "Since you're earning your own money, if you want these extras, you can buy them yourself." Then take the money you were formerly doling out and begin to put that aside for her college education. Let her know that you're doing this. Now you have given her a choice; either you can keep buying these little goodies and she can set something aside for college, or she can buy these little goodies and you can set something aside for her college. That is one suggestion. Often kids that age prefer to buy their own things anyway because they are so label-conscious and feel they've got to look a certain way at school. Since your daughter has a good job, let her buy her own things. This will teach her how much things actually cost and she will eventually develop a deeper appreciation for the sacrifices and effort you've made for her throughout her earlier years.

You've also got to ask yourself, "What are we trying to achieve with this whole business of finances? Why do we want her to go to college?" Obviously, it's for her own benefit so that as an adult she can look back on her childhood and the lessons that prepared her for adulthood. It's important to develop creative methods of handling family finances so children learn how to handle money responsibly.

COLLEGE EXPENSES—WHO PAYS? •

We could probably scrape up enough money to send our children to college, but wouldn't it be wise to make them earn part of their way?

You're on the right track. Kids tend to appreciate something they have earned themselves. I've noticed sometimes that when kids go straight from high school to college, they don't get as much out of it as do those who spend a couple of years working before they go to college. The older kids understand why they're there and what they're trying to do.

I'm very impressed with the Mormon young people who start saving their money when they're in junior high school so they can use it—not money they've raised from church members, but money they've earned themselves by their own hard work—for two-year missionary activities around the world. This makes sense for people who are sharing their faith, and it also makes sense for people who want an education. If a young person earns money himself, then he values what he spends it on.

But I must sound a note of caution here, especially for parents who worked their own way through college and assume that their kids ought to do it like they did. I had to earn all of my college expenses, and I did it by holding a variety of jobs and by spending six years getting through my undergraduate work. But times are different today. Economics are different. Students' ability to earn their own way is considerably hampered by a tightening job market, increasing specialization, and rising college costs.

Parents need to stop and think about all the factors entering into a teenager's ability to finance his own education. What kind of school has he chosen? How expensive is it? How heavy an academic load will he need to carry? What kind of study habits does he have? How important is social life to him? What kinds of skills does he have to compete in the job market? Will he be financially ahead by completing his education quickly and going directly to work, or by working at low-paying jobs while spreading his education over a longer period of time? Does his college restrict the number of hours he may work on a work-study program?

Parents who are facing college bills have to consider all these factors. How much aid they give is an individualized decision, one that may vary from child to child according to each child's needs, abilities, and school. But as a general rule, I agree with you that it is good for students to take at least some responsibility for financing their educations.

CAN A CHRISTIAN BE RICH? •

Is it wrong for a Christian to be rich when so many people in the world are starving? I've worked hard for years to build my business and just now I'm beginning to reap the rewards of that work. I don't feel guilty about my money because I know I made it honestly, yet many Christians warn against having too much of it. I don't think I've made a god out of my money, but I'm wondering how to justify having so much when others have so little.

In one sense, there is nothing wrong with being rich or having a great deal of money. In fact, we know there were rich people among Jesus' early followers. For example, someone let Him use an upper room for group meals. On the Day of Pentecost, that room held 120 people. That's a good deal larger than my living room; I assume the house's owner was not poor. Jesus went to a marriage where apparently the whole town was fed; that's not a poor person's wedding reception. A number of wealthy women traveled with the apostles and supported them financially; and when Jesus died, He was laid in a rich man's tomb.

The fact that Jesus had some rich followers, however, does not solve the problem of the "haves" and the "have-nots," a problem which may be more extreme today than ever before. Scripture says, "If a brother or sister be naked, and destitute of daily food, and one of you say unto them, 'Depart in peace, be ye warmed and filled'; notwithstanding ye give them not those things which are needful to the body; what does it profit?" (James 2:15-16) In other words, compassion is more than a tear in the eye. We need to put our money where our mouths are.

But, as someone asked Jesus, "Who is my neighbor?" If I found a starving child on my doorstep, I would feed him. If he were fifty feet away, I might still feed him, or I might think my next-door-neighbor should do it. Move him to the next block, and I would think someone should do something about him. Move him to the next town, and I might no longer know he was hungry. Multiply him by 500 million, and I would say, "But what can I do?"

Yet if there are millions of starving people in the world, there are also millions of Christians who might be able to help them. So many Christians, though, do not understand the one principle that might free their possessions to do some good in the world—the principle of stewardship. Let me start with you. You say you own a business; it is yours. Many people, when they say "mine," do not stop to think that the earth is the

Lord's. In reality, they do not own anything. They are simply God's stewards, entrusted with a lot or a little to be used for Him.

Some of these people try to appear to be stewards by using Christian buzz words. "You know," they will tell you, "this is the Lord's house and the Lord's business." That sounds good, but if they really mean it they will be asking, "How can I make this business as productive as possible so that I can be the greatest possible help to the kingdom of God?" That is what stewardship boils down to—not whether you are rich or poor, but whether you have committed whatever you have to the Lord Jesus.

WHY ARE WE POOR? •

My husband and I have always struggled to make ends meet. I can't imagine why God would allow a believing family such as mine to remain poor while so many of our Christian brothers and sisters are rich. God promises to help those who call on Him, but I don't see it happening in my family.

Your question, like many others that come my way, is prompted by a kind of preaching that takes God's promises and turns them into formulas. "God is a wealthy King," these preachers say, "and I am His child. Therefore if I obey Him, I will be wealthy too." They seem to think that God is a giant vending machine who will automatically give out whatever we need if only we push the right buttons. I suppose this thinking is inevitable in our mechanistic age, but it is not the kind of thinking that lies behind the biblical promises.

God's promises, especially in the Proverbs, are made in this way: "If all the people on earth follow these behavior patterns, more of them will end up on this side of the equation than on the other." Furthermore, in the Bible, *riches* may not mean money. The term may just as likely refer to happiness, personal security, or family. You say that you have a family; there are millionaires who would trade places with you. In that regard, you are rich and they are poor.

Some people manipulate others by making promises about riches. They are really appealing to greed, one of the baser human characteristics. The most unfortunate part of their teaching is that the flip side is so cruel. If you really believe that people who love God end up rich, then you have to say that the world's poor people are bad, immoral, or faithless. That, of course, is simply not true. The Bible is full of compassion

428

for the poor and warnings to the rich. Hebrews 11 points out that many people who have served God have suffered deeply, while others have had things turn out beautifully for them.

God says that true faith is believing in Him and trusting Him regardless of circumstances. Habbakuk had the right idea about faith and riches: "Although the fig tree shall not blossom, neither shall fruit be in the vines; the labor of the olive shall fail, and the fields shall yield no meat; the flock shall be cut off from the fold, and there shall be no herd in the stalls: yet I will rejoice in the Lord, I will joy in the God of my salvation" (Hab. 3:17-18).

ALWAYS PASSING THE PLATE •

We have so many bills to pay that by the time Sunday comes, there is not much left to give to our church. I know we are not giving anywhere near ten percent of our income to the Lord and this bothers me. I wonder if we are letting God down and I feel guilty because of all the blessings He is giving us. But that doesn't change the situation—there really isn't enough money to go around. Is it really necessary to tithe? Am I wrong for feeling guilty?

The Apostle Paul spoke to the spirit of this issue in 2 Corinthians 9:7. He said, "Every man according as he purposes in his heart, so let him give; not grudgingly, or of necessity: for God loves a cheerful giver." In Old Testament times, the tithe was a kind of tax. In the Jewish theocracy, the tithe supported the entire culture, including its welfare system. Not all Christians agree about the significance of the tithe in the New Testament. It has been my experience, however, that the tithe is a good minimum standard.

When Janie and I were first married, we had the kind of approach you have. We wanted to tithe, but we spent our money and then at the end of the week looked to see if any was left. Sure enough, most of the time, there wasn't. We were a living demonstration of the principle that "expenses rise to meet income."

Being under great conviction about it, and with the help of some Christian friends, we decided to begin laying aside ten percent at the beginning of every week and see what would happen. A miracle began to take place in our lives—we found that the nine-tenths went farther than the ten-tenths had gone. I know that anybody with an adding machine can show you that that is impossible, but it happened. In our family, when we put the tithe first in a spirit of giving and helping, everything else seems to fall into line beautifully.

This gives me the feeling that God is actively involved in our concerns. It also makes me a productive unit, a giving unit, in society, and I like that. My task is not just to take care of myself. God put me here to do as well as I can in order to help His redemptive process with my time and energies, my know-how, and my money. Tithing has turned into a terrific blessing for us. I think it can do the same for you.

COULD TITHING CAUSE TROUBLE? ●

If your spouse is not a believer, how do you handle tithing? My husband is a member of a cult. I do not work, so I have no income of my own. And yet I want to give something to the Lord. I haven't discussed this with him because I'm afraid he will then want to give equally to his religious group, and I certainly don't want any of our money going to help a false religion. What do you suggest I do?

I wish all ethical choices were black and white, but very often we run up against conflicting values that make it difficult to discern right and wrong. I would encourage you to give what you can of your own money and abilities. Perhaps you have a household allowance that would allow you to make small contributions. You certainly have talents that you could contribute to your church. These may well be more valuable than money. But once you have done this, don't feel guilty because you aren't paying a full tithe. It is more important for you to live peaceably with your husband.

Apparently a lot of women came to Christ through the Apostle Paul's preaching, and you can be sure their unbelieving Roman husbands did not pay a tithe to the church. Paul never talks to these women about financial giving. Instead, he tells them that they may be able to win their husbands through their winsome Christian lives. Your husband, of course, is worth more than the whole church budget—there is absolutely no way to compare a person and a dollar.

God says, "Every beast of the forest is Mine, and the cattle upon a thousand hills" (Ps. 50:10). Everything we see already belongs to God.

His efforts on earth are not tied to our giving. But God graciously chooses to use our gifts and our abilities to give us a sense of participation in His kingdom work. Giving does not help a poor, struggling God get His work done. Instead it gives meaning to our own lives.

But we cannot be legalistic about exactly how much every Christian should give; your situation proves how dangerous that would be. It's the spirit of the thing that counts. People who live pinched, selfish lives end up with a tight-lipped, ugly spirit. People who live open-hearted, loving lives have hearts that are open to be flooded with God's blessings. You can have a generous spirit with a little giving as well as with a lot.

TIGHTWAD HUSBAND ●

When I was growing up, I noticed the problems my parents got into because of their mismanagement of money. In fact, that was the real cause of their divorce. They overspent, got into debt, and then took it out on each other. With my own family I have tried to avoid these problems. I feel I should put as much into savings as I possibly can and spend only what is absolutely necessary. But my wife complains that I am too tight and never let her spend money on things she says we need. Have I gone too much the other way?

It sounds to me like you have gone too much the other way. You have overreacted against the excesses you saw in your early life. There is a law of physics that says, "To every action there is an equal and opposite reaction." This is often true in human affairs as well as in the natural world. People whose parents were alcoholics may have severe views about alcohol, for example.

It may be that we react against our upbringings because we are afraid of repeating our parents' mistakes. We build walls around ourselves to keep this from happening. But our overreactions can cause problems just as bad as the original problems we are trying to avoid. It sounds as if you are a materialist in that you spend much of your time thinking about money and things or putting an inordinate trust in them. You don't have to have a lot of money to be a materialist. My father struggled with this for many years and eventually overcame it very well. The Depression was the climactic experience in his life, and he thought about it constantly. He knew it was going to happen again, and every day he warned me about it. His obsession with providing against disaster cost him a lot of joy.

Let's face it, money is to be used, not worshiped. If a person can trust in God and allow God to give him a generous spirit, at the same time that he keeps good accounts and is prudent in his spending, he has a good combination. Money is a dangerous thing to trust. Some decision at the world bank could wipe out all your savings in a minute. Money should be only a springboard to taking care of our basic needs.

I can say all this, and you may agree, but actually putting it into practice will not be easy because your present behavior is based on real fear. Consider trying this as a first step toward changing your attitude and making peace with your wife: Divide your income so that you are responsible for some areas and she is responsible for others. Keep separate checkbooks if this helps keep the areas separate. Be sure she has a regular sum of money to cover her responsibilities, and then back off and let her do it her way. She will feel a great sense of freedom, and you may be surprised to see how well she handles money. As you see that her more relaxed approach is not leading the family to financial ruin, you may be able to relax more yourself.

CHAPTER 36

Work and Out of Work

If someone were to ask me what I see as the most difficult problem facing twentieth-century man, I would say that it is the prevalent conception of man as a means rather than an end. In an industrialized society, man becomes a mere cog in the great industrial wheel. He sees his life as merely a means to some form of production. He describes himself in terms of his occupation and accomplishments.

In reality, all of man's value is given him by God. God made us unique creations, valuable persons. Our work is not our person; it is simply an extension of it. But in our society, we undergo tremendous difficulties because we misunderstand the source of our value. We mistakenly attach life's deepest meanings to our function, and then we rightly complain that we have been stripped of our personhood.

Man is not a function. Man, by himself, is dignified and has value before God. Even when he's not functioning, he is valuable, because he is created in the image of God Himself.

THE DEMANDS OF THE JOB •

I'm in a very competitive job situation. I work long hours and my family is beginning to suffer. I obviously need the job to support them and take care of their needs, but I feel guilty and confused about my priorities. Do I have a right to ask them to hang in there with me?

The husband's time away from the home is one of the most potentially explosive issues in the family. There are some men who find themselves in tremendously difficult job situations and it is very hard, if not impossible, to just walk away from it all when you have little mouths to feed, a large mortgage payment, and a pile of other bills. So yes, I think you do have the right to ask your family to hang in there with you at this particular time. And yet, you do have to carefully assess your situation.

I think it helps to go beyond just talking about your job strains and its problems. You need to get a little more specific and tell them what exactly is required of you on the job. Many times family members don't really know what's involved. Maybe your family has gotten the impression that you sit around all day and drink coffee or putt golf balls across your office floor.

The second thing you need to do is look at some of your own family desires. Many times our suffering is self-inflicted because of the complexity of our lifestyles. It's very important for all of us to strive toward simplifying our lives rather than making them more complex—especially in the area of material things. A boy is far better off raised by his father on linoleum than raised without his father on carpeting. Can we resist the great pull we feel to "keep up with the Joneses?"

Third, there are some priority choices you need to make. When a person becomes a parent, he chooses to take on a great responsibility and he has to make certain choices about old habits. For example, some family men try to maintain their relationships with their old bowling partners or fishing pals or golfing buddies. But if you've got a family, you've got to decide at some point that instead of being one of the boys, you're going to devote yourself to the family and find things you enjoy doing with your wife and children. This is especially true when your job situation is tough and you don't have much time to spend with your children as it is. So cut out the extracurricular activities and let your family know you *want* to be with them, even though you can't be all the time.

CAN'T FIND A JOB •

My mother wants me to help her with the bills, and I would really like to help, but I don't have a job. I've been looking everywhere but can't seem to find anything. She keeps nagging me about it

and makes me feel so guilty. But it is really not my fault. Sometimes the pressure is so much I feel like leaving. I've tried to explain the situation to her, but she continues to nag. I'm nineteen years old.

———————————

This is a time of great difficulty for young people like you. Your parents may not know anyone who is unemployed and may believe that anyone can find a job who really wants one. That's because they haven't been out there looking for work lately.

But agreeing with you that the situation is tough does not make the pressure go away. I can't suggest anything that will directly affect your mother's nagging, but here are some ideas that may help you find work. If you're out of the house all day looking for a job, at least you won't be around to listen to her.

Jobs do open up, and people are there to find them. You're going to have to begin to be a little more persistent than other people who are looking for work. It isn't enough just to go around and put your application in. You have to be there when the job opens up. Things open up more often in some places than in others. One high turnover area is fast food. Fast-food chains often change an employee a day. Somebody gets discouraged, someone quits, something doesn't work out. If you happen to be there when they come up short, perhaps you can land something.

Another thing you could do is odd jobs. An enterprising young man of nineteen could photocopy a sheet saying, "I'm willing to shovel snow, trim bushes, put up storm windows"—whatever is appropriate for the time of year. Hand these out to a couple hundred people in your neighborhood, saying, "Call me if you need something done. I'll do odd jobs or day work." Even if work isn't regular, it will help to tide you over, and often the people you meet while doing one job lead to opportunities for another one.

It is not easy to be unemployed. In fact, it probably takes more energy to be unemployed than to work full-time. It can be very discouraging. But each day is a new day. Get up, commit the day to the Lord, and begin a round of activity. Sooner or later if you keep knocking on doors, one will open.

MOTIVATION'S GONE •

My husband has been laid off work for almost a year now. At first he halfheartedly looked for a job, but the last few months he has done almost nothing. He stays home, sleeps, and watches TV all day. He doesn't even help with the housework. I've tried to be encouraging and have even suggested moving to another state where job opportunities seem better. Maybe it's been so long since he had to look for a job that he doesn't know how anymore. In the meantime, I'm at the end of my rope.

I've come to the conclusion that most of us have been living under an illusion for the last thirty years or so. We've assumed that life rewards hard workers, that competent people earn more and more money throughout their careers, that there is opportunity enough for everyone, that people who don't work are lazy, and that it is disgraceful to lose a job. That's the way it's been throughout most of my working life, but that isn't the way it is anymore. In fact, if you look at history, you'll find that the prosperity we've enjoyed in America since World War II is far from usual. But those of us who are working now aren't old enough to have experienced any other kind of world, so when we ourselves become victims of a changing economy, we don't know how to think about what's happening to us.

It's easy for a man who's been laid off to feel guilty. Even though he knows he's hard-working and competent, he still judges himself as he has judged unemployed people in the past. He has lost his job and has not found another one. Therefore he must be lazy or inadequate. If he stopped and thought about it, he would realize that he has not done anything wrong. The economy changed, and some man in New York sent out a memo that led to the firing of 1,000 men in Chicago. He is a victim, not a culprit.

But for years he has lived by the idea that if you do everything right, everything is going to turn out right. This idea is simply a myth. We like to believe it when we are doing well, but when the bottom falls out we have to deal with the other side. When a man who has lived by this myth loses his job, the sense of rejection, disappointment, and failure is overpowering. Such men, especially if they have put in many years at the same job, quite predictably will go into a state of shock. They have to spend time in the valley before they can pull themselves together.

What your husband needs now is affirmation about himself. He needs to restore his sense of self-worth. He needs to believe in himself again. It is important for him to let others help him bear his burden. It would be good if he would open up about it at church. I encourage you to keep affirming him. I think he will recover on his own, but it may take even more time for him to work this through.

A CURE FOR LOAFING? ●

How do you motivate a son to get out of the house and find a job? Since graduating from high school a couple of years ago, our teen has held two jobs. He quit one and was laid off the other. Since then he has done nothing. He is not belligerent or sassy and seems agreeable and content. We have gently tried to persuade him that it is time to look for another job, but he would rather lie around the house, watch TV, and eat. He has lost all motivation. We have contemplated kicking him out of the house, but don't have the heart to do so.

Your son has several problems: the job market is tough, he doesn't have a college degree, and there are a limited number of jobs for people with only a high-school education. But his biggest problem is that he's too comfortable. Watching TV and eating can be very pleasant. So I think you need to make him a little less comfortable.

Once when I was camping in Colorado, I noticed some sticks falling down past my window. I went out the door and looked up, and high on a crag above my cabin I saw a huge eagles' nest. The mother eagle was up there throwing sticks every which way. A conservationist at the camp later told me that if young eagles get to a certain age and refuse to fly, the mother eagle tears the nest apart until there's nothing left to sit on. The young eagles have to get out because there's no comfort in the nest.

How can you make your son less comfortable? One way is to establish a value for the room and board he is receiving. If he does not have the money to pay in dollars and cents, let him work off his obligation by doing tasks around the house. Don't let him watch daytime TV—watching that stuff all day is sure to lead to despondency and despair. Insist that he get out and look for work. And don't feel bad if you decide you must push him out of the nest. This isn't "kicking him out." It's gently but firmly telling him that he is a grown-up, responsible man.

437

ETHICS ON THE JOB •

How do you deal with an unethical employer? At times I am asked to lie or cheat in order to save the company a buck. If I refuse, I might as well start looking for another job. The problem is that jobs are scarce and I have a family and a mortgage to think about.

This kind of situation is very difficult. I believe it can only be dealt with one way, by a straightforward and carefully thought-through confrontation with your employer.

You need to sit down with your supervisor or employer and simply tell him you cannot do this sort of thing. Tell him too that you are convinced that if you were to do your work honestly, in the long run the company would be ahead. Be sure he knows that you're willing to put forth every possible effort and all kinds of hard work to make the company succeed without shaving edges.

Sometimes this approach persuades the employer that he is dealing with a valuable, trustworthy employee. Sometimes it does not. Instead, he gets angry, and the employee either is fired or feels he has to quit. Because this situation is so difficult, I think it's wise to gather a group of Christian friends to talk about it and pray with you before you approach your employer. Let the pastor help you discuss it. If the bottom drops out and you end up unemployed, you have your friends' support. They are praying for you and they also can provide practical help.

It's in situations like these that we can most justifiably call on God and ask Him for His help and strength. He will never leave us nor forsake us; He will not abandon us. Hebrews 10:36 has been helpful to me: "For ye have need of patience, that, after ye have done the will of God, ye might receive the promise."

That verse doesn't mean that things will start coming up roses immediately. Virtue is not always appreciated; there is often pain and a great price connected with doing right. Jesus Himself "endured the cross, despising the shame" (Heb. 12:2). But when we're pushed into a corner we can, with total and absolute faith, believe that God will honor and bless us for doing right, even if not in ways that are immediately evident. We may find ourselves financially penalized, but some rewards are larger than money, and the knowledge that we have honestly served the Lord and not compromised our character and honor is itself a reward from God.

Incidentally, your honesty is also an example to other people. It could even be the means by which your employer might eventually come to salvation. If he has never been confronted by honest behavior, he may really think the world runs on trickery and cheating. Never challenged, he never changes. But perhaps through you he will catch a glimpse of the God who honors His own commitments, a God who is completely trustworthy.

A CAREER DRIFTER ●

Where do you draw the line between God's purpose for your life and your own shortcomings? My brother-in-law has lost twelve jobs in the last nine years because of poor interpersonal skills. He always blames other people or circumstances for the problem, or sometimes he says it's just bad luck. His wife accepts whatever he says, because that's her concept of Christian wifely submission. What really bothers me is the way they keep spiritualizing everything, saying, "God must have a purpose in my getting fired," or "God has led us to this situation for a reason—we just don't know what it is." Is there anything we can do to help them see reality?

I doubt it—it's very difficult for in-laws to give this kind of advice. God *is* speaking to him, incidentally, through these circumstances. He could have learned a lot about relating to employers by now. The trouble is that he isn't listening.

The amazing thing is that happiness isn't necessarily related to job stability. I've met people like your brother-in-law who go on through life this way, and their wives are dutifully loyal to them, and they make excuses and bring God into it. "Everybody else is wrong, and we're right," they say, and their wives add, "My honey is always getting picked on." But somehow the two of them stick together and operate as a unit—and this, it seems to me, is more important than whether they keep a job.

Your brother-in-law has spent over thirty years becoming what he is, and you're not going to be able to undo that just because your sister married him. I'd encourage you, rather than trying to solve this problem for them, to affirm them and help them however you can when they get themselves into tight spots. Most people like your brother-in-law are helped more by affirmation than by confrontation—they've been confronted many times already, and they seem to be unable to hear. Almost everybody fits in someplace, and someday your brother-in-law will land on his feet. Maybe he will find an employer who doesn't care about interpersonal skills, or whose skills are even worse than your brother-in-law's, and things will begin to work out. In the meantime, the worst thing you can do is look down your nose at him and have him feel you have become part of the enemy.

SECOND-CLASS CHRISTIAN? ●

My family treats me like a second-class Christian because every member of my family and my wife's family is in Christian work except me. It's as though they think my work isn't as important or as meaningful as theirs. I feel I can be just as effective a witness for the Lord in the job I have and resent the attitudes of the other family members.

There seems to be a tendency for people in vocational Christian service to marry other people in vocational Christian service. There are whole clans of people like this, and they can be insensitive to people like you. However, the Bible is on your side. Paul must have given the illustration about the various members of Christ's body—the church—to help someone who was feeling rejected and unimportant. That is why he said that each member is vital, including the ones we don't see (1 Cor. 12).

Many people feel the same sense of rejection that you do. Unfortunately, too many churches are set up on the Boy Scout model. The foreign missionaries are the Eagle Scouts, the pastors are the Life Scouts, the Christian educators are the Star Scouts, and so on down the line, until a person with a secular occupation feels like a Tenderfoot. This is a perversion of scriptural truth. All of us are in full-time Christian service, whether we are preaching or making tents, because we represent the Lord every minute that we breathe. I'd like to see us change our terminology: *vocational Christian service* would be a far more accurate way to describe what your family members do. Try to see their slights as insensitivity rather than persecution, but don't let them make you feel second-rate inside. Your work and your life are just as important as theirs.

NOT GOOD ENOUGH? •

I'm one of those people called "just-a." I'm "just-a" worker in a factory. When my wife and I spend an evening out with friends, we feel embarrassed because so many of them are office managers or self-employed business people. How can we overcome these feelings of not being good enough?

Every Sunday morning I listen to people in the church foyer. I hear them say, "I'm just-a teacher," or, "I'm just-a homemaker," or, "I'm just-a plumber," or, "I'm just-a brain surgeon." It's amazing that they can say that about any occupational level. What they're really saying is that they have felt depreciated by the fact that they are identified with their occupations. This opens up an important truth for all of us. One of the definitions of being worldly is to accept worldly identifications for our lives, to let the world set the standard rather than Christ. But Romans 12:2 tells us not to let the world squeeze us into its mold. We think our self-worth is tied to what we do—our function. This is a false identification, yet almost everyone accepts it. "I'm not that important because all I really do is teach, or run a forklift, or do surgery." That mindset is wrong. One does not have worth based on function, but on who he is as a person.

Sometimes in the church we make this same mistake. Let's say there is a godly milkman and a godly executive. Immediately, we set up the church like a Boy Scout troop, and the man who has the white-collar job gets the position of elder or deacon, and the milkman gets to teach junior high boys. This misconception also seeps over into women's lives. Women have decided that they have value only if they can perform a function, such as running an office, typing, or selling real estate.

The whole thing is a terrible lie. Human beings do not have value based on what they do for a living. People have value because God has created them in His own image for the purpose of relating to Him and to one another. The Christian message says that man has intrinsic value—he has value because he is created of God. When you grab that message, you can be a godly person and do any task, however menial, to the glory of God.

VOCATIONAL CONFLICT •

For years I have earned my living as a secular singer. About a year ago I came to know the Lord. Almost immediately people began asking me when I was going to get out of the business and into sacred music. They seemed to assume that no Christian should be involved full-time in secular music. I have never thought the Lord disapproved of my vocation. In fact, I can see many ways in which it can be a real ministry, especially to the people I work with. But I'm having a hard time feeling accepted by the Christian community around me. In one way, I don't care what people think, because I know God has placed me here. But in another way, I care very much. I don't want to be a stumbling block to anyone.

Most importantly, you say you are convinced God has placed you in your work situation. If that is true, then the question stops there. You must do what God asks you to do. On the other hand, I wonder if you are seeking my advice because you are feeling ambivalent about your situation. Many Christians are suspicious of the entertainment industry, not because it is secular, but because its environment is not always conducive to Christian living. A Christian entertainer has to think of the work he does—the roles he plays, the songs he sings—and also of the whole atmosphere he has to do it in. How will he have to dress? What kind of value system is he projecting? How will he handle money?

These questions should be asked by all entertainers, not just those catering to a secular market. It's possible for the Christian music industry to be very commercial and materialistic. So the real issue is this: Can you do your work so that you glorify God and bring people closer to Christ's kingdom? If you can, then you may be just where God wants you. And if you are, don't move for the sake of some Christians who don't understand. Instead, try to educate them, if possible.

I'M TOO YOUNG TO RETIRE •

I'm fifty-nine and was recently laid off from a job I've held for many years. After numerous interviews with different firms the bad news is always the same—my educational background is not good enough. I grew up on a farm, and after I finished the eighth grade my parents felt it was more important for me to work on the

farm than to go to high school. Now I'm too old to go back to school and too young to retire. I've learned a lot over the years and feel I'm better educated than many younger people who have all kinds of degrees. It just doesn't seem fair.

Your education is undoubtedly an issue with these employers, but an even larger issue is your age. Because of various rules involving insurance and retirement plans, larger companies are often unwilling to accommodate people your age. In fact, you could face the same problem if you were fifteen years younger. What you will probably have to do is look for a job with a privately owned firm or small business where your experience will be honored and your age will not be a problem.

Obviously there are other ways to learn than in a degree-granting institution. The school of hard knocks is tougher and takes longer, but its lessons are deeper. Unfortunately, job applications don't have a place to indicate the knowledge you have gained from experience, so you have to persuade someone face-to-face that your experience will be valuable to his company. I would encourage you to do two things. First, check with your local community college and arrange to take a high-school equivalency examination. If you pass such a test, a potential employer will consider you a high-school graduate. Second, look for work in places where the person you talk to is the person you will be working for. You won't stand much chance with an employee who has to go by the book, but the boss himself has the freedom to go beyond written job requirements. Again, a small company will be your best bet.

This time of job hunting will be tough, so invite your Christian friends to pray for you. Then keep plugging away and someday someone will recognize your value.

CHAPTER 37

Love and Sexuality

Sex, after all, is God's idea. Therefore sexual relationships are important. God has given our sexuality to us for two purposes—to propagate the human race and to teach us about intimacy with other human beings.

Our world has twisted and perverted things God has made beautiful. We must be careful not to reject the things themselves just because they have been twisted. Instead, we need to find a way to properly recommit these things to God for His use. We glorify Him by living out our sexuality in the context He originally intended.

FINDING OUT THE FACTS •

I'm seventeen and my mother has never talked with me about the facts of life. Everything I know I've learned from my friends and from reading books. My mother thinks she doesn't need to tell me anything because I'll learn it all in health class. What little instruction we had in health class was only enough to giggle over. It did not tell us anything important. I want to ask my mother about these things, but she either gets embarrassed or acts as if it's unimportant. Is there any way I can get her to open up and talk to me, or should I just stick to my books and friends?

Ideally, of course, parents will be secure enough, informed enough, and articulate enough to tell their children about sex, but very few of them are. Most people, like you, got their sex education from friends and books; and for most people, that's adequate.

444

The physical side of sex is relatively simple. This may surprise you, but they probably gave you the whole story in health class. The larger part of human sexuality, though, has nothing to do with the physical body. Ninety-nine percent has to do with human relationships, fidelity, trust, love, caring, sharing, giving, forgetting about yourself. These things, not physical techniques, are what make sexuality work. Your mother is probably quite willing to talk with you about this larger side of sexuality.

Don't feel your mother is letting you down because she is not drawing pictures of human organs for you. That probably doesn't feel right to her. She has a strong sense of privacy about the relationship that belongs to her and your father, and there's no need for you to ask her to violate it. If you need to discuss questions relating to sex, you're probably better off going to a caring friend, your pastor, a trusted teacher, or your youth group.

INFORMED BUT ... ●

I am beginning to think that our children know more about the facts of life than my husband and I do. I'm afraid this knowledge may lead them into compromising situations because they think they can handle them. Are our fears unfounded, and what can we do to help our kids?

Young people today, even young children, have a lot of information about sex. Unfortunately, most of them have been exposed to some very irresponsible, suggestive, and ugly literature they've found on the playground or some other place. Once a mother showed me some things she found in her boy's bedroom. The best word I can think of for them is disgusting. Children are not only exposed to the physical side of sex and anatomy (which in itself is not a great problem), but they're also exposed to the twisted, perverted side of sexual expression and exploitation. This can be dangerous.

To say, however, that your kids know more about the facts of life than you do is probably a misnomer. I doubt if they really do. They might know more about some particular perverted act, or they might come home and use some word you know is dirty but don't know what it means, but you know the *real* facts of life, that is, you understand the context in which these things are *supposed* to take place. The greatest need in sex education is not so much physiological as it is moral and contextual. We as parents have to help our children understand how sex fits into the context of a marriage relationship without making them afraid of the physical side of sex, or giving them the impression that this part of nature is dirty and ugly. We must acquaint them with God's purpose in all of this. The entire business of human sexuality was God's idea, after all, and God gave us our sexuality for two purposes. One purpose has to do with procreation. Man has to reproduce in order to survive. The second purpose has to do with intimacy and teaching us how to know one another and be closer to one another as human beings. When people understand these purposes within the context of Christian marriage, they can begin to see the importance of fidelity, responsibility, true love, and concern for one another. These things cannot possibly take place in a moment of passion in the backseat of a car. That is not the right context. To help our kids see this, we have to demonstrate before them the beauty and depth of our relationship with each other.

TEENAGE KNOCKOUT ●

Our fourteen-year-old daughter is very attractive. The boys flock around her and she loves it. I'm sure we're going to have trouble with her and her boyfriends. Can you help us combat this problem before it starts?

I can remember how I felt when boys started hanging around our two daughters. But I think a lot of times there's more going on in our minds than the kids would ever dream of. Usually all a fourteen-year-old girl wants is to be popular and all a fourteen-year-old boy wants is to be accepted. If the girl is popular and the boys flock around, she is delighted. And if a boy is liked by a popular girl, he feels wonderful about himself. Of course, fourteen-year-olds are discovering their sexuality and have within them the various urges and responses that come with adolescence, but they don't really understand how these things relate to their social lives. They just know it feels good to pay attention to members of the opposite sex.

A concerned mother tends to see more in this than the kids do. You are saying, "I can see what's happening here," and in a sense you are right. But it would be very wrong to attribute bad motives to your daughter or to get suspicious and begin to put on the thumbscrews. If you do this, you will find that she will start living up to your suspicions. Instead, revel with her in her newfound popularity. Then help her get a better idea of what teenage dating is all about by giving her good Christian literature to read. Get her a subscription to *Campus Life* magazine, or buy her Tim Stafford's book, *A Love Story*. It helps young people understand what's happening with their changing bodies and how to relate to teenage sexuality. My own book, *Too Big to Spank,* deals with some of the same topics. Reading these books might also help you know what to expect during your daughter's teen years.

PUPPY LOVE OR TRUE LOVE? ●

My boyfriend and I are both seventeen and have known each other for two years. Our parents haven't allowed us to date yet, so we just enjoy spending time together at church activities. Even so, we feel strongly for each other. We are planning to attend the same Bible college next year. I am not sure if our feelings are true love or infatuation. Can two teenagers really be in love? Does our relationship have any chance of succeeding over the years?

Certainly two teenagers can be in love. Some of the great love stories of all time are based on relationships that started during adolescence. The capacity to love doesn't have much to do with age. There are people incapable of love at fifty, and there are people capable of love at fourteen.

And yes, teenage love can survive. Some of my best friends were married when they were very young and their marriages have held together beautifully. On the other hand, one's feelings are usually more trustworthy when one is more mature. It is unusual for people to really know their hearts when they are young, especially if they have had little experience with people of the opposite sex.

Most kids by the age of seventeen have had dates. For whatever reason, your parents have not allowed you to do so. I applaud you for not breaking over the barriers and going against your parents' wishes. I will warn you, however, that when you go away to college, even Bible college, you will face dangers. You may be full of pent-up emotions. Like a stream that has been dammed up, your emotions have been held back. When the two of you are on your own at college, even though the college will have some rules, the dam may break. If it breaks all at once, the flood of your emotions may damage your relationship by causing you to do things you will later regret. Be careful not to get in over your heads.

But don't give up on your relationship just because you are young and this is your first love. Often first loves are great loves. One thing I know about love is that real love will stand the test of time. It doesn't have to be in a hurry; it doesn't have to sneak around. It can wait while the Lord is working in your lives. I believe that since God is a partner in your relationship, Bible college will be one of the best places in the world to find out if you are really in love and made for each other.

WHAT'S WRONG WITH ROMANCE? ●

My sister reads romance novels all the time. I took a look at one and found that they can be pretty graphic in their description of romantic encounters. I'm wondering if it's harmful for her to be reading this kind of book.

It depends on the kind of book you're talking about. The well-established romance books produced by the major publishers are not harmful, but they are time-consuming and should be put in the same category as all time-consuming, nonproductive activity. Let's face it—we humans can't always have our noses to the grindstone. We all need relaxation, and romance novels are probably a legitimate outlet.

There are several things that make romance novels attractive. True love always wins out, and that's actually rather beautiful. The stories take place in fantasy settings where glamorous, larger-than-life people carry out their lives in wonderful, dramatic ways. We enjoy this—as we enjoy all literature—because it allows us to go places and have experiences vicariously. As for the graphic passages, unless she's reading books that are far worse than the standard romance novel, she's not likely to learn anything from them that she doesn't already know.

I'm going to guess that you're an older sister. You sound like someone whose mother has said, "I want you to take care of your little sister and keep her out of trouble." Now she's grown-up, but you're still trying to do that, this time by protecting her from possibly harmful reading. It's time to face reality—this taking care of little sister is going to be an oppressive burden as you grow older. In fact, you won't be able to do it. Realize that that part of your life is over; you no longer take her by the hand when you cross a street together. But if you want to direct your sister to better reading, begin to acquaint her with good novels. When someone has read a truly great book, formula plots start to look boring.

In a good book, the characters are developed so much more deeply; the struggles and the victories are so much greater; the lessons are more important and true to life—everything is better in really good literature. Give her some good novels that you have read and enjoyed.

BRIDLING A FRESH KID ●

For three years my eight-year-old grandson has been using bad language involving parts of the body. He uses the proper names for everything, but he keeps repeating them to the other children and laughing. Many times we've heard him tell off-color jokes. This is really starting to worry me, but I haven't discussed it with his parents. I know all children are interested in sexual matters, but I'm not sure that his pattern is normal, and I hate to think what it could develop into.

It sounds like his parents have a different philosophy of sex education than you do. I think you need to discuss what you have observed with them; they may not realize the effect their form of teaching is having on the boy. On the other hand, they may say, "In our home, we are all open and honest about the body. We think it's much healthier for our son to call things by their proper names rather than thinking sex is taboo and dirty." If you respond by pointing out that apparently the little fellow is treating the proper names as if they were dirty, his parents will no doubt say, "He'll grow out of it. He'll lose his fascination when he gets a little bigger." And they may be right. In any case, if they object to your viewpoint, you need to back down and let them raise their son as they wish.

Of course, if you spend a lot of time with the child or if he comes to visit you, you may not want him to give an anatomy lesson to all your friends. Don't put a moral judgment on his behavior—at this stage, it's no more than an attention-getting device (notice how effective it is). Don't tell him he's talking dirty. Just say to him, "It's fine that you know these words for the way God made us. God gave us all the parts of our body. They are His creation and they are very good. But all of us need a sense of privacy about ourselves, so we don't talk about some things to each other. Most people don't think it's appropriate."

People who speak openly about sexual matters think we more reserved people are trying to put moral judgments on them. That's not our point. We are simply trying to act civilized.

HIS LORD, HIS JOB, OR ME? •

I've been dating a man whose work causes him to miss a lot of church. He puts in twelve hours a day on the job and is on call seven days a week. He loves the Lord and has a daily quiet time, but I get tired of going to church by myself. I question whether his commitment is the same as mine, or if we just show it differently. Is it necessary for us to have the same level of commitment for our relationship to work? And why do I get so upset when he doesn't attend church with me?

I don't know how serious your relationship is. If you are just dating, I think you're making more of a problem for yourself than you need to. Why not just date some other people who will go to church with you? But if you are thinking about marriage, then I think you do have an incompatibility. It may be a different incompatibility from what you think, however.

Often young lovers do not understand the realities of life. Most love we see on TV doesn't talk about the lovers going away to work and drudging away for eight to ten hours a day. Instead we see pictures of people in canoes and on beaches all the time. So sometimes we romantics say, "I want him with me all the time." We haven't faced up to the demands of adult life.

Then you have to consider that it is not easy to find employment nowadays. Your boyfriend may be afraid that if he gives any less on the job, he will find himself on the outside looking in. If that happened, your problem would become much more difficult than it is now.

I'm very much impressed by the fact that he has daily quiet times with God. That puts him in the top five percent of all Christians; a lot of people are talking about quiet times, but very few actually have them. So I think your real concern is not his level of commitment, which seems high enough, but the amount of time he is spending on the job.

A person usually works long hours for one of three reasons. He may be a poor manager of time, and therefore has to spend twelve hours doing what other people can do in eight. He may have an unfair employer who is demanding more than he should. If that is the case, eventually something will have to give. You can't work twelve hours a day, seven days a week, forever. Or he may like being indispensable. Most workaholics enjoy thinking that "they can't get along without me." The sense of worth this gives them keeps them going back for more.

If you and your boyfriend have a serious relationship, you will have to deal with this area of incompatibility. You will want to find out why he works such long hours and if this is the way he is likely to continue living. Your potential differences are not in the area of your commitment to Christ, but in the area of how you spend your time. If you find that you cannot come to an understanding in this area, you are unlikely to be happy together for long.

CHAPTER 38

Education and Its Challenges

Education is the process that prepares us to live adequately in the world. It helps us cope with the challenges that are before us.

One can approach education from a worldly orientation, or one can build one's education on biblical presuppositions. There is a big difference between Christian education and secular education. It's true that a frog dissected in a Christian college will be just like a frog dissected at a secular university, but the conclusions drawn from that dissected frog can be very different.

We believe that the world was created by God; we see science as thinking God's thoughts after Him. We believe that to know God is to know truth. Truth and God are synonyms; the more you know about one, the more you'll know about the other. Christians should not be afraid of education, because God is at the root of all truth.

UNMOTIVATED IN SCHOOL •

How do I motivate my children to take an interest in school? It just doesn't seem important to them.

Nothing will motivate children so much as parents' showing interest in their work, looking at their papers, asking questions about what they're doing, complimenting them on assignments well done, pointing out their good points, and so on.

Nothing will demotivate children so much as parents who treat the school as if it's just kids' stuff that's not really important. "After all, you're just in elementary school and this doesn't matter; I'm the important person doing my adult things and your little work isn't worth much."

Parents can also demotivate children by perfectionism, always seeing the hole rather than the doughnut. Many parents think they're helping their children by constantly pointing out their flaws. When their son or daughter shows them a test score, they immediately say, "Oh, I see you got one wrong," instead of, "My goodness, you got almost all the questions right. That's terrific!"

Children are helped much more by positive reinforcement than by negatives. To motivate them, notice their skills. Point out what they do well; compliment them and affirm them. Never make fun of your children in front of others. Say good things about them instead. Many parents are afraid of doing this for fear it will look as if they are bragging. That is not the point. The point is that our children need to know they can count on us. They need to know that of all the people on earth, we at least are allies who will never, ever, turn our backs on them. If, after all this positive reinforcement, your children still are not motivated, then you need to look into other possibilities. Do they perhaps have problems with seeing or hearing? Do they have a learning difficulty such as dyslexia? Fortunately, in today's school systems most teachers are aware of these possibilities and usually are able to point them out to us. It is the parents' job to cooperate with the school in getting whatever help is needed, and to provide an atmosphere of encouragement for the child at home so that the teacher has a moldable, motivated, excited young person to teach.

PUBLIC OR PRIVATE? ●

Our son will be starting high school next year and we are struggling to decide where he should attend school. The public school and the Christian school are the same distance from our home, so transportation is not a factor. I'm afraid that if he goes to a Christian school he may be too sheltered from the world, but if he goes to the public school he may make friends with the wrong kids and be steered in the wrong direction.

I was faced with precisely this problem when our children were growing up. It was probably even more complicated for me than for you, because of my work with Youth for Christ. Each year YFC works with about

50,000 kids, almost all of them from public schools. YFC's basic thesis is that young people *can* stand with Christ in the high school, have integrity, and not absorb the environment like a chameleon. They *can* be salt and light and, if necessary, sheep among wolves. They *can* make a difference for Christ. Because I've dedicated my life to the ninety-seven percent of American schoolchildren who attend public schools, I tend to be a little prejudiced in their favor. My children went to public school because I found it impossible to say to other parents, "Your kids can make it in public school, but mine can't."

On the other hand, I'm not at all opposed to Christian schools. I think they have a lot of value. I like to think of them as "preparatory" schools— they prepare young people for entering into life as a Christian; they equip them to enter the world. And our goal as Christians is to enter the world. If we spend our lives encapsulated, going from Christian home to Christian school to Christian college to Christian church work, then the world misses out on the Gospel.

I think Christian school is a fine option for those who can afford it, who live nearby, and whose children need the additional stiffening of the spine so that they will be able to make a difference in the world. But if you are thinking of using the Christian school as an escape hatch, then I would encourage you to think again about what you're doing. There is no escape. We live in this world, and it is no friend of grace. But "greater is He that is in you, than he that is in the world" (1 John 4:4).

BLACKBOARD BIAS ●

Every day my kids go to school and listen to teachers who teach things we don't believe in, such as evolution. I know my children are struggling with this because the teacher is always supposed to be right. But what they're learning at school is often in conflict with what we've taught them from the Bible. In addition, they face the pressure of having to answer a certain way on tests to get good grades. Do you have some suggestions as to how we can support our kids and keep them on an even keel while they're learning?

Some parents have felt so strongly about this situation that they've pulled their kids out of the public schools and sent them to private schools. In our experience, it wasn't this way. Our children grew up in the public school system, and for the most part, their teachers and school officials were positive and responsible people whom we felt were very supportive of family life. When our kids did get into a class where the teacher seemed to be teaching things contrary to the Scripture, or was downright antagonistic, we would discuss what the teacher said and why he said it. I remember one afternoon our daughter came home with a survey about children's relationships with parents. It asked whether the child agreed with his or her parents on twenty value items. Our daughter ended up agreeing with us on every one of them. The teacher used her paper as an example of what *not* to do. "Here's a kid who has no opinions of her own and doesn't think for herself," the teacher told the class. After class some of the kids made fun of our daughter because she agreed with us on so many things. When she came home crying about it, I asked, "Well, why do you suppose your teacher said that?"

And she said, "Well, I think she probably fought a lot with her own parents and felt that everybody ought to."

"Why did she think that was normal? Do you think her way was normal? Do you have a bad family?"

"No, I like my family."

"OK, then we understand that she's coming off a one-person sample, which isn't a very big one, so we won't take her reply too seriously. When she tells you the location of Cheyenne, Wyoming, should you believe her?"

"Sure, she understands geography. She just doesn't know a lot about the family."

So help your kids question and test the things they learn at school. Let them use their Christian values as guides from which to measure the validity of what they are taught. Frankly, one of our greatest deficiencies as Christian parents is that we don't get into the compelling logic behind what we believe. We say we disagree with this and that, but we don't tell our kids *why* we disagree.

THE HOMEWORK DILEMMA ●

We just can't get our twelve-year-old daughter to do her homework. She is the queen of procrastination. After school she plays until supper. When we ask about her homework, she says she doesn't have much. After dinner she fools around with it all evening and then pleads to stay up past her bedtime in order to get it done. How can we convince her either to start her schoolwork earlier or concentrate on it so it doesn't take so long?

Rejoice that you have a normal daughter and the usual kinds of problems parents face raising children. Then realize that it's past time for your daughter to begin learning about the law of cause and effect. She needs to understand that if she doesn't do her homework, she has her teachers to deal with. It's not up to us parents to see that every bit of it is finished. We don't really know what the teacher is demanding anyway. Homework is an obligation between teacher and student, and the student needs to be responsible for it herself.

It is your responsibility, however, to see that your daughter gets enough sleep so she can function at school the next day. It may be that if you insist on her being in bed at a certain time whether or not her homework is finished, after a few days she will see the advantages of finishing it earlier in the evening. Or you may wish to approach this from the other end. Let her stay up as long as she likes. The next day when she's so sleepy she can hardly eat her breakfast, say, "I wonder why you're so tired?" After a few days of this tactic, she may decide she ought to be in bed earlier. Our children, after a couple of years, figured out that they had to be in bed by a certain time or they couldn't function the next day. We let this dawn on them through cause and effect, so the decision would be theirs and we wouldn't have to nag.

Generally speaking, kids who live in cold climates have problems in the wintertime. They sit in a warm classroom all day without moving their bodies much, and their circulation is slow. They come home and eat a cookie and take a nap and watch TV. By dinnertime they don't have any energy at all. I think it's good to get them to put forth some physical energy when they get home from school. Keep them active until dinner-time, reward them with a TV program after dinner, and then send them to do their homework.

You may improve the situation with your daughter, but don't expect perfection. Parents always have this kind of tension with children. Let's face it—a lot is demanded of them. Try taking a group of adults on a weekend retreat, putting them at desks from eight until three, and then telling them to work all afternoon and evening. They'll say this is the worst way they've ever spent a day. And that's how the kids have to spend every day. So we have to be patient, understanding that they are in the midst of a learning process and will eventually figure out how to manage their time. But we need to make cause and effect the teacher.

VALUE CLASH ON CAMPUS •

I'm a Christian college student at a secular university. I've become very discouraged because so many of my friends are involved with drugs, alcohol, and promiscuity. How can I keep my faith and values? And how can I help my friends?

A lot of Christians would like to delay entry into the world forever. They go to Christian elementary school, Christian high school, Christian college, and Christian graduate school. Then they buy a house in Wheaton, Illinois! But Christians should find themselves in the same kind of situation you're in now, surrounded by people whose lives are focused on something other than Christ.

It is very difficult to be in your position all alone. That is why the Lord has encouraged us not to forsake the assembling of ourselves together (Heb. 10:25). It's important to get together with other Christians at church, and on campus you can find additional support through organizations like Campus Crusade and Inter-Varsity Christian Fellowship. If you meet with other Christians, you can support one another; you can "bear . . . one another's burdens, and so fulfill the law of Christ" (Gal. 6:2). You can also strategize as to how to begin to knock the gates of hell off their hinges.

God is greater than the powers of this world, and worldly people should be threatened by Christian principles more than Christians are threatened by the world's values. Kids ought to be writing me letters saying, "I'm trying desperately to hang onto my drugs and alcohol and promiscuity, but these Christian people keep challenging my value system by showing me how self-defeating it is. I can hardly hang onto my irresponsibility in light of the fact that I'm a creation of God." That's the effect Jesus expected salt and light to have in the world. So don't be afraid to declare your faith. I have lived in fraternity houses and secular dormitories, and I know how it can work. The first step is to declare your position; the second is to begin to propagate the faith. Suddenly, it isn't "How can I hang on?", but how can *they* hang on?

MAKING THE GRADE •

I'm attending a Christian boarding school that is very expensive. My father told me I must make straight A's or he won't send me again. I do my best, but I can't make all A's. Dad says I'm not

really trying if I make B's. I like this school, but I'm worried about my grades. I want my dad to know I study hard and do my best in school.

Have you ever sent your father a letter that might help him understand how you feel? Another strategy might be to ask your school counselor to write your dad and tell him about this apprehension you have about your grades. Your counselor will understand; he has probably dealt with this problem every year he has been in education. Perhaps the next time your dad comes to campus, your counselor can sit down with him, go over your grades and other achievements, and talk with him about who you are. Maybe your dad will return home, thinking, "I can be really proud of my child. He's doing the best he can in class and being a good citizen as well."

Keep in mind that we parents face a difficult challenge. If we don't act concerned about grades, then lots of times our kids think we aren't interested in their achievements. On the other hand, if we talk too much about grades, then the kids feel pressured. It's a fine line to walk. With our own kids, I often asked, "Are you trying? Are you doing your best?" instead of "Did you get an A?" It's important to offer your best, not just to please your parents, but because as a Christian you want to please the Lord. But your best reasonable effort in some classes may lead to a B, or even a C or a D in some cases, and your dad needs help in understanding this. The pressure he is putting on you to succeed may backfire; you may get so tense wanting to make A's that you can make only B's. Your counselor can help you live with your dad's expectations and he can also probably help your dad understand your situation. Talk to him.

SICK OF THE CLASSROOM ●

My son doesn't want to go to college. I have sacrificed a lot so that I would be able to send him to a good Christian school, but he says that when high school graduation comes, he will go no further. He is sick of school. I'm worried, because this city is full of drugs and alcohol. Should I try to persuade him to pursue an education? He is a good student.

What parent hasn't felt as you do—wanting to do the very best for your children, but sensing that you are losing control? The difficulty for you is that your son, by the time he graduates from high school, is becoming a young adult. He needs to find his own way in life and to move out from underneath your parental guidance.

You seem to think that by going away to college he will solve any problems he might have. Recognize that going to college sometimes leads young people into more problems than they would have had if they had stayed home. And, though I hesitate to say this, the fact that a college is Christian is no guarantee that it is problem-free. Somehow or another, in every atmosphere and at every college, there is a negative peer group dragging people down. They don't post signs at registration saying, "All the kids that want to experiment with drugs come over here," but they find each other somehow.

Still, going to a Christian college would probably help your son. In most cases, Christian schools are good influences. On the other hand, perhaps he shouldn't go to college. He may not be college material, or if he is college material, he may not yet have his goals very well set. A boy who is confused and defeated by classes he doesn't understand or like will tend to look for ways of escape, and drugs and alcohol are popular ways to get away from reality.

If the boy has a goal he can fulfill at home, even if it is only to buy a new automobile, he is much less likely to look for escapes than if he is frustrated. Proverbs 22:6 advises parents to train up each of their children in the way he should go. As I understand it, this text means to train the child according to his own gifts and inclinations. Let him follow his own bent. Usually when we lose our kids, it is because we have tried to bend them in the wrong direction. So follow your son with prayer, but don't assume that the Christian college experience is the best answer for him.

RACING THROUGH COLLEGE •

My daughter is trying to get through college in three years instead of four, so she's taking extra-heavy class loads. She stays up late to study and then has to get up early to make it to her first class. Lately she looks tired and complains of headaches. She's been taking aspirin once or twice a day for the headaches and now has started taking sleeping pills before she goes to bed. I'm concerned about all the pills she's taking.

With the exception of the sleeping pills, you've pretty much described the typical college student—stays up too late, gets up too early, wanders around bleary-eyed. College students and men on sentry duty look about the same. Sometimes you see kids in the morning on a college campus, and you think, "Who kept them up all night?" Generally, it's a combination of messing around, putting things off, and frantic last-minute studying.

I imagine you've already expressed your concerns to your daughter. You might try this tactic: ask yourself what makes your daughter run. Why is she insisting on getting through college in three years? Why is she working so hard to get good grades? Whom is she trying to please? Is it possible that you've unwittingly put too much emphasis on how much it's costing to go to school? She may think, "If I can just finish in three years, I'll save my folks some money." Or is she trying to earn good grades because she needs affirmation and acceptance? Maybe she's not getting good grades. In that case, she may feel that if she works hard and is obviously exhausted, that will let her off the hook. Someone will say to her, "Honey, you ought to slow down."

Whatever the reason, it's likely that her behavior is a bid for someone's attention, and very likely the attention she wants is from you and your husband. Sit down with your daughter and review what she is trying to achieve by going to school. Let her know that her happiness is more important to you than her achievement or the possibility of saving a few dollars. Tell her that you want to see her succeed, but not at the expense of her health. If she continues to take sleeping pills and doesn't seem to be able to sleep without them, encourage her to go to the doctor and find out what's wrong. Perhaps the doctor can help her see the physical dangers of her lifestyle. It sounds to me as if your daughter just needs the pressure taken off, and you're probably the person to do it.

SECTION 10

Living in a Changing World—the Second Forty Years

We can't really prepare for many things in life. No one gives us a little rubber baby or a wind-up teenager to work with before we get the real one. No one gives us a trial run through old age either. We have to do it right the first time.

I'm finding old age at least as exciting and baffling and frightening and awesome as anything I've ever done. There's no point in sitting around and dreading it—it comes to everyone lucky enough not to die young. I am determined not to be bitter about it or defeated by it. I'm not going to spend any time looking in the rearview mirror. I want to look through the windshield of life.

I believe that God has put this life together so that old age is the blossoming time. Earlier we burst from the seed, get our roots, begin to grow, and eventually bud. Finally we blossom into old age and then into eternal life. Of course, we must deal with all the changes and adjustments that old age brings. But the human life cycle was God's idea, so it must have been a good one. Part of our love and reverence for God is discovering what old age is all about. I am determined to do that and to make the most of it.

CHAPTER 39

Dealing with Life's Dramatic Changes

Many people feel that old age is a disease, something to avoid. Retirement is a kind of punishment, something one is forced to do. The Christian sees it differently.

Old age is the blossom of life. It prepares for the shedding of the invalid physical life, a life limited to this world, a life that has meaning only within the temporal sphere. It prepares for eternal life with Christ. Old age is not the beginning of the end, it's the end of the beginning.

Yet even though this is true, old age still brings us major challenges, things we have never faced before. Retirement. Menopause. Loss of friends and family. A sense of being obsolete. These are physical and cultural problems that demand our attention. Fortunately, they have nothing to do with the inner man that God is preparing to live with Him for ever and ever.

MID-LIFE CRISIS •

I have a fine wife and three outstanding teenagers. We live in a comfortable home, and I've been a vice-president in my company for four years. Suddenly, for no apparent reason, I find myself fighting depression. It seems like there are no challenges left, and if there were, I'd be too tired to face them. I think of what life holds in the next twenty years, and sometimes I break out in a cold sweat. I wonder if I've thrown my life away in a job that isn't really doing anybody any good, and I've given some thought to leaving it and going into the ministry. Sometimes I

get so down that I think I'm losing my mind. I'm forty-three years old.

Mid-life crisis is the realization that we are no longer young, and that there are some things we just can't do anymore though we'd really like to. This often brings a great deal of depression and discouragement to men and women alike. How can people help themselves and others through this time?

Mid-life problems fall into three main categories: achievement and identity problems, fear and insecurity problems, and problems of impotence and helplessness. Christ is the answer to all three kinds of problems.

First, at mid-life, people often wonder who they are and what their worth is in the world. Society values people because of their function—their achievement or position, title or occupation. The day comes when we realize that we may never accomplish all our occupational goals or, if we have accomplished them, that we will never climb any higher. If we have adopted society's values, we may feel our lives have lost their purpose. But Christ tells us we get our worth from being created by God; that God Himself accepts us and tells us we are valuable to Him.

Second, we may begin to wonder what the future holds. "Can I take care of my family? Will I be able to deal with old age? Will people take away from me what I have earned?" But Christ says, "I will never leave thee, nor forsake thee" (Heb. 13:5). A Christian can have the assurance of the Gospel song that says: "Many things about tomorrow, I don't seem to understand; but I know who holds tomorrow, and I know He holds my hand."

Third, we may fear the helplessness that often comes with old age. But God is Alpha and Omega, the beginning and the end. Old age was His idea. It's the blossom of life, the preparation of the soul for eternity. Jesus said, "Fear not, little flock; for it is your Father's good pleasure to give you the kingdom" (Luke 12:32).

And so as Christians, we have less to fear from the mid-life crisis than other people do. We can allow Christ to handle our specific concerns. Several excellent books have been written dealing with mid-life. I'd recommend *Stages,* by John Claypool, as well as the books on this topic by Jim and Sally Conway: *Men in Mid-Life Crisis, You and Your Husband's Mid-Life Crisis,* and *Women in Mid-Life Crisis.*

FEAR OF THE FUTURE •

My husband is in his mid-fifties and says he probably won't live to retirement. Yet he gets upset with me because I have taken a part-time job, attend evening classes, and do some volunteer work. The kids are all grown, but he says I keep myself too busy. If he won't live to retirement, why shouldn't I be prepared to support myself?

It is true that women tend to outlive their husbands, and I'm sure you've seen on TV or read about women who are helpless when their husbands die. It is understandable that you want to prepare for this possibility ahead of time. Still, let's look at the situation from your husband's point of view.

He is of a generation that believes it's a man's duty to support his family. His sense of self-worth is tied to fulfilling this duty. For many men of his age, a working wife means that he is failing at the most important duty. He has also been taught that a woman's place is in the home and he has come to expect certain services. He does his part by supporting you and he wants you to do your part by making home pleasant.

Probably most important, he's fearful of the future. He's afraid to retire, and he may be afraid of death as well. So he reaches out to you and says, "I don't think I'll live to retirement." He's hoping you'll say, "Oh, Honey, of course you will. You're healthy. We're going to have a wonderful old age together." But instead of allaying his fears, you get a job and go back to school. "My goodness," he says to himself, "she thinks I'm not going to make it either."

You have good reasons for wanting more education and work experience. You are facing the future responsibly. But at the same time, in doing this you have affirmed your husband's deepest fears. Is it possible for you to put less stress on him, while continuing your preparation? Perhaps you could arrange to be gone only when he is out of the house, so your absence does not remind him of what you are doing. Pay special attention to the housework and cooking that he has come to expect from you. When you talk about your work or studies, emphasize that you are doing these things because you enjoy them so much—not because he may not be around much longer. If you just go out and assert yourself, as the media seems to be telling women to do, you will continue to have tension with your husband, because he doesn't know any other way to react.

RETIREMENT—A DISEASE? •

My husband is a workaholic. For forty years I've looked forward to the day he'd turn sixty-five. But now that that day has come and gone—he says he has no intention of retiring—and I feel crushed. I had visions of traveling to distant lands, candlelight dinners lasting into the wee hours, and days on end of just getting to know again the man I married. But now it looks like I'll be sitting at home keeping the furniture dusted for another ten years. Is there anything I can do to change his mind, or am I just being selfish?

Many men are afraid to retire for a number of reasons. Over the years they have risen to positions of authority and importance in their companies or fields. It's difficult to give all that up because they think that retirement will mean obsolescence.

Some people make a connection in their minds between retirement and death. They notice that death often follows soon after retirement. Part of the reason for this trend, of course, is that retirees are growing older, and death is more common to their age-bracket. But in their minds they may think, "I've got to keep functioning or I'll just die." When a man is caught in this trap, we must realize that he's afraid and insecure. He's trying to hang on to some meaning in life and he's trying to hang on to life itself.

The fact is that many men look on retirement as a punishment rather than a reward received for a life well lived. There's an ad on television where a man says that his company makes money the old-fashioned way—they earn it. That really bothers me because it implies that no one else is earning it. That commercial is an example of the great myth of our culture and society which says that in order to have value you've got to be constantly working—you've got to be a workaholic if you want to be successful in life. Your husband is probably a victim of that thinking. The only way you're going to help release him is by showing him that retirement is not a punishment but a reward. And he's earned the reward. It's time to relax and enjoy life a little bit. After forty years in the saddle, your husband may not know how to do this. Don't put your foot down, but lead him gently. Let him see how much fun you can have together. You may have to wean him away from work until he gets used to leisure, but hopefully one day he'll wake up and say, "Hey, this is a lot better than going to work. I can finally do some of the things I've always wanted to do!"

RETIRED AND BORED ●

My husband recently retired and he's driving me nuts! He is bored to tears and can't stand just sitting around. He looked forward to his retirement for years, but now I think he really misses his job. What can I help him get involved with that will blow off some of his steam?

You haven't told me how long he has been retired and for how long he has been driving you up the wall. If it's a relatively short time, then he may just be in the adjustment stage where he's finding out what interests him. If it's been a longer time—a year or so—then together you need to begin to get interested in some activity outside yourselves. This could be travel, community service, working at the church, visiting the sick, helping other people with their family needs, or even remodeling your house.

It's also possible to do volunteer work with many agencies. We have an eighty-four-year-old man working in the Youth for Christ office. He comes to work every single day, and he's worth as much as any employee in the entire building. He does this as a service to God. As a young man, he was trained as an accountant, and throughout his career he worked for many companies around the country. Now that he's older, he enjoys coming to work and being around younger people. We dearly love him. He's the least neurotic, happiest, best-adjusted, most smiling person that I've met in a long time.

Perhaps you could sit down with your husband and say, "Honey, we've been looking forward so much to your retirement. Let's talk about what we can do that will really make our lives exciting." If you and your husband are Christians, you will have a solid base for this discussion, because you both know that we are not our own; we "are bought with a price" (1 Cor. 6:20). We are not to spend our lives heaping up enjoyments for our own selves; instead we are committed to the Lord's service.

But if your husband has just retired, let him rest awhile first. Wait until he begins to sense a need for more activity before you talk with him about it.

MENOPAUSE ●

My wife is going through menopause, and I have never seen her so discouraged. It's as though she suddenly realized the full effects

of what's happening. How can I help her come to grips with this stage of her life and bring some encouragement to her?

———————————

To both you and your wife at this stage in your lives, I'd recommend Charles Swindoll's book, *Growing Strong in the Seasons of Life,* or Paul Tournier's, *Learn to Grow Old,* both of which deal with major life adjustments.

Your wife may need some medical help and you should encourage her to discuss this with her doctor. Some of her moods, fears, highs, and lows may be evened out with medication. Often people ask, "Is it godly to do this? People have told me I should just pray about the problem and it will go away. I shouldn't take medication." Let me ask you this: If you knew someone who had diabetes, would you think it was wrong for him to take insulin? Of course not; a person with diabetes has to have insulin in order to live. Other disorders—emotional and psychological as well as physical—also can be greatly helped with the careful and responsible use of medication. Don't be afraid of this; God has provided medical help to make our lives more fruitful.

On the spiritual and psychological side of this issue, it's important that we spend time when we're younger thinking about what kind of older people we want to be. I know some people in my church who are handling old age very well. I want to learn to be like them. They are positive, happy-to-be-older adults; they are making a contribution, are a blessing to their children, and are a delight to have around. Perhaps you and your wife need to sit down and talk together about what you have learned from middle-aged and older people, then determine what kind of contribution you can make.

These days we face a lot of pressure to remain young. People worship health. On TV they see people strapped in strange machines, huffing and puffing in order to be slim and beautiful. Actually these people were slim and beautiful before they ever saw the machine, but we don't think of that. Instead we are intimidated by the cult of youth. But there are deeper values than these. Being young is not everything.

I think of the time we performed a wedding with a young couple. As we left, my wife began to giggle, and I asked her what she was giggling about. She said, "I wouldn't be that young and that ignorant again for anything in the world." We hugged each other and thanked God right then that we have a few miles on us. That mileage has taught us something, and every experience has enriched us. A conversation along this vein might be of great help to your wife.

WE WISH WE'D HAD CHILDREN ●

My wife and I never had children and now we are beginning to regret our decision. As we pass the mid-life point, life is becoming very lonely. Sure, we have each other and love each other very much. But we miss the fellowship of a family. How do we bring some spark of joy and enthusiasm back into our stale lives?

There's no sense spending time looking back, saying, "I wish we had," "Why didn't we?" and so on. I would suggest a marvelous answer to this kind of dilemma—adopt a family in your church.

Industry demands mobility; the average American father under the age of forty moves every three years. Look around your church for some family that has, because of economic necessity, moved away from their own extended family, a family that is now trying to make it on their own. I can think of half a dozen such families in our church without straining. These are young couples who come from good families, have several small children, and are now a thousand miles away from both sets of grandparents, aunts and uncles, and cousins. Or look for a widow or a divorced woman who is trying to raise children alone.

Offer yourselves to such a family. Don't talk about the issue straight out; just begin to love them and care for them. Begin to love the children and become surrogate grandparents for them. Begin to invite them over, to notice their birthdays, to pay attention to what happens to them in school. Send them a letter or word of encouragement.

Adopting a family will do something for you, but more than this— many young families desperately need your attention. Children need to grow up around adults who are loving and caring. Young people are looking for parental figures as much as older people are looking for someone to bring meaning to their lives. You will suddenly find that God has specially prepared you for one of the most needed ministries on the face of the earth, to fill in the holes made by some of our society's deep problems. It will be enriching to you. In fact, down the road you may feel as if you have actually added members to your family.

CHAPTER 40

The Empty Nest

For people who have spent their entire lives living for their children, the idea of an empty nest is indeed very frightening. And they aren't the only ones to be afraid—recent studies indicate that people who buried themselves in work and never got to know their children are even more terrified at the prospect of their kids leaving home. We feel totally unprepared because it seems to happen so quickly. All parents shed a private tear when they hear the song from *Fiddler on the Roof,* "Sunrise, sunset—where is that little girl?"

And yet if we deal with it creatively, this time of life can be one of the best for us. Once upon a time we fell in love with a man or a woman and decided to live our lives together. We loved to be together and to have time to devote to each other. We made time for dates, to be alone together, and to share with one another. Then the children came, and we had to devote most of our leisure time and almost all of our working energy to care for them. Now we have time to return to our first love. We can discover each other again. The empty nest can be an environment in which full and loving hearts can be rekindled to levels never before known.

WE DON'T KNOW EACH OTHER •

The kids are gone, the house is empty, and my husband and I don't know each other anymore. If we can't talk about the children, we just don't know what to say. How can we begin again to build a loving relationship?

Many couples have been so child-oriented that when the children leave, they feel a great void. They feel like strangers to each other. They seem to have nothing in common, and they don't even have that affection that drew them together in the first place. A great number of couples divorce or separate at this time. But for some of us, dissolving the marriage is out of the question. Fortunately, it is not the only solution to empty-nest problems.

This is a wonderful time to begin rediscovering each other. Mature romance has a lot going for it that young love can't imitate. You are comfortable with each other. You are not establishing a home, so you have more resources than you once did. You have more time to discover who you and your spouse have become.

It's good to start the rediscovery process by asking yourselves, "Let's see, why did we get married in the first place?" Remember what you liked to talk about, what you enjoyed doing together, how you felt when you were apart. Start doing some of the same things together again, and add new interests you have developed during the intervening years.

In effect, you will be starting your courtship again, and that's one of the most important things you can do. At first you may feel selfish about having so much fun together, especially if you've been denying your-selves for years. But keep on enjoying each other anyway, and your closing chapters can be beautiful.

SCARED OF INDEPENDENCE ●

We don't have any severe problems in our family, but I do find myself very discouraged at times. I'm concerned that my kids are pulling away from me as they reach their late teens. I know this is natural and even healthy for them, but I still get discouraged. I feel I am losing touch with my teenagers, and that frightens me.

You are right—it is normal for kids in their late teens to pull away from their parents. Kids of that age are preoccupied with themselves. They are internalizing their value structures, finding independence from the home, finding a place in their peer groups, and coming to terms with their changing bodies. They are so busy with their own agendas that they forget all the people around them. They really do shut us out, but it is not because they don't care for us anymore.

Actually, this process is what you've been aiming for the whole time you were raising your children. The goal of parenthood is to create independence, not dependence, in our children. Yet when we feel this pulling away, we find it hard to let go. Deparenting can be much tougher than parenting, probably especially so for evangelical parents. I think evangelicals are generally better than other parents at raising small children, but we have more of a problem with our adolescents because we like to run a tight ship and we don't want to let go.

Let me encourage you to continue to be available to your teenagers. At Youth for Christ, we teach our staff a technique we call "creative hanging around." Don't pry, but be there so your kids can bounce ideas off you. Learn to listen to their ideas without jumping in with an immediate value judgment. Kids are often afraid that if they present an idea, we'll shoot it down. Surprise them—wait until they've shared it completely, and then say something like, "Well, you know, I've dealt with that kind of problem and here's the conclusion I've come to. Tell me what you think about it." Learn to relate adult-to-adult rather than adult-to-teen. By all means, accept the reality that your children are becoming independent, but don't let that discourage you. Grown children can be fine friends.

NEGLECTED PARENTS ●

Now that our kids are married and on their own, we hardly hear from them. They never call or drop us a note and don't seem to have enough time to visit. Will they ever appreciate or understand all we've done for them? We raised them to be good kids—I don't think their neglect is intentional. But it does hurt.

I can still see the commercial where the little old mother is sitting in her rocking chair, chewing out her son over the phone, "You never call me; you don't care about your old mother anymore." I think greeting card companies and phone companies have collaborated on this and have tried to put it in a humorous light. But it's not very funny to those who are experiencing the hurt. Many of the tears shed at the funerals of parents are tears shed by children who wish they had said this or had done that.

You're feeling rejected, but when you were your children's ages, did you reject your own parents? How do you respond to your parents even now? If you are not relating to your aging parents, then perhaps you can understand why your own children aren't relating to you. This problem proceeds from generation to generation because it is such a tough lesson to learn. I suppose the answer for all of us is to understand how important family relationships really are. The universal message in the midst of the deepest human trials usually contains this revelation: "I finally found out who my real friends are, who really cares for me—my family." This love of family is worth more than all of the sales ever made or all the cookies ever baked.

Often, however, when kids first get married, they are consumed with their spouses; they're busy having children, setting up house, and getting established in life. They are not consciously neglecting their parents and saying, "I think I will hurt my father and mother today by not calling or visiting." Will they ever understand how you feel? Eventually, they probably will, just as you do now. Somewhere in their thirties or forties this usually dawns on the children; they feel terrible, and begin to do something about it. Of course, some never do, but that is usually a reflection of the parents' failure to establish loving relationships in the early years.

INDEX

475

476

480